Stella Fletcher is an associate fellow of the Centre for the Study of the Renaissance at the University of Warwick.

'*The Popes and Britain* is an ambitious project. Stella Fletcher's book covers the complexities of a changing history both political and religious for Britain and the papacy. From the early tensions between northern and southern Europe, to the significance of the monarchical character of the papacy for post-Reformation relations, through to the gradual development of diplomatic representation, Stella Fletcher's broad canvass tells a fascinating story, encompassing Scottish and Irish as well as English perspectives. This book fills a gap.'

Rt Revd Dr Geoffrey Rowell

'*The Popes in Britain* displays an admirable breadth and depth of research and scholarship on the history of the papacy and its relations with Britain. It provides a comprehensive narrative and justifies the claim to be the "first single-volume of the entire Anglo-papal story to date".'

**Glenn Richardson, Professor of Early Modern History,
St Mary's University, Twickenham**

Stella Fletcher

the
POPES
and
BRITAIN

A History of Rule, Rupture and Reconciliation

I.B. TAURIS
LONDON · NEW YORK

Published in 2017 by
I.B.Tauris & Co. Ltd
London • New York
www.ibtauris.com

ISBN: 978 1 78453 493 6
eISBN: 978 1 78672 156 3
ePDF ISBN: 978 1 78673 156 2

A full CIP record for this book is available from the British Library
A full CIP record is available from the Library of Congress

Library of Congress Catalog Card Number: available

Typeset in Stone Serif by OKS Prepress Services, Chennai, India
Printed and bound by CPI Group (UK) Ltd, Croydon, CR0 4YY

For Dominic

CONTENTS

LIST OF PLATES

Plate 1. St Peter-on-the-Wall, Bradwell-on-Sea (Historic England).

Plate 2. Gregory the Great, *Pastoral Care*, King Alfred's West Saxon version, *c.* 890–97 (Bodleian Library, Oxford).

Plate 3. Detail from the Bayeux Tapestry (Universal History Archive/UIG/ Bridgeman Images).

Plate 4. Sarcophagus of Pope Adrian IV (Alinari/Bridgeman Images).

Plate 5. King John pays homage to the papal legate, 1213 (Private Collection/ Ken Welsh/Bridgeman Images).

Plate 6. Tomb of Cardinal Adam Easton (Julian Gardner).

Plate 7. Pinturicchio, *Enea Silvio Piccolomini as an ambassador to the court of King James I of Scotland* (DeAgostini/Getty Images).

Plate 8. Scottish sword of state (Crown Copyright Historic Scotland reproduced courtesy of Historic Scotland).

Plate 9. Friedrich van Hulsen, *The pope's Bull against the Queen* (Private collection/Bridgeman Images).

Plate 10. Thomas Cockson, *The revells of Christendome, c.* 1609 (Private collection/Bridgeman Images).

Plate 11. John Michael Wright's account of the earl of Castlemaine's Embassy to Innocent XI, 1688 (University of Aberdeen).

Plate 12. Paolo Monaldi(?), *Prince James receiving his son, Prince Henry, in front of the Palazzo del Re* (*c.* 1747–8) (National Galleries of Scotland).

Plate 13. Sir Thomas Lawrence, *Pope Pius VII*, 1819 (Royal Collection Trust/ © Her Majesty Queen Elizabeth II, 2015).

Plate 14. 'HB' (John Doyle), *Absolution, a Retrospective Sketch*, 1835 (© National Portrait Gallery, London)

Plate 15. 'The Guy Fawkes of 1850', *Punch* (Look and Learn).

Plate 16. 'The Pope', *Vanity Fair*, 1878 (Private collection).

Plate 17. Pius XI opening the Holy Door at St Peter's Basilica, 24 December 1924 (Private collection).

Plate 18. Visit by Princess Elizabeth and the Duke of Edinburgh to the Vatican, 13 April 1951 (Popperfoto/Getty Images).

Plate 19. Sir Mark Heath presenting his credentials to John Paul II, 1 April 1982 (*L'Osservatore Romano* ©, all rights reserved).

Plate 20. Benedict XVI at the Birmingham Oratory, 19 September 2010 (*L'Osservatore Romano* ©, all rights reserved).

ACKNOWLEDGEMENTS

We are constantly reminded that we live in an ageing society, one consequence of which is that increasing numbers of middle-aged people feel obliged to devote themselves to caring for their elderly parents. Carers are advised not to neglect their own health and well-being, which is easier said than done. Seeking a distraction from the mundane reality of being a carer, I accepted an invitation from Lester Crook, commissioning editor at I.B.Tauris, to write a history of Britain's relationship with the papacy. At first it was possible to make day trips from home. During that phase I received a bursary from the Catholic Record Society and took the opportunity to interview some of the individuals who have participated in the Anglo-papal story in recent decades: Nigel Baker (British ambassador to the Holy See), Kieran Conry (secretary to the apostolic nuncios Bruno Heim and Luigi Barbarito), Cormac Murphy-O'Connor (elector in the conclave of 2005), Geoffrey Rowell (Anglican bishop of Gibraltar in Europe, who could claim that the pope resided in his diocese) and members of the All-Party Parliamentary Group on the Holy See. As opportunities for travel diminished, I came to rely on the university libraries of Liverpool and Manchester, where the staff were unfailingly helpful, and on access to online resources, which came courtesy of the University of Warwick. When the published record left gaps or provoked queries the brains of the following were picked: Dominic Bellenger, Nick Bent, Sandra Blake, Francis Campbell, Gordon Campbell, Andrew Chandler, Tony Claydon, Julian Gardner, David Hayton, Stephen Holmes, Keith Newton, Peter Nockles, Desmond O'Keeffe, Glenn Richardson, Jane Ridley, John Martin Robinson, Geoffrey Scott, Andrew Starkie, Daniel Szechi, Tony Trowles, John Wolffe, and the staff of the British Embassy to the Holy See, especially Helen Frigieri. Drafts of individual chapters were kindly read – and improved – by Sarah Foot, Brenda Bolton, Margaret Harvey, Joe Bergin, Sheridan Gilley and Michael Walsh. Siân Phillips of Bridgeman Images did much to ease the trauma of sourcing suitable illustrations. Email communications with all of these people helped to offset the isolation of working outside an academic environment and made the entire process rather more enjoyable than would otherwise have been the case, particularly towards the end, when opportunities to work on the text dwindled in time from hours to mere minutes and frequently had to be abandoned altogether. In the light of this experience, I would not discourage carers from doing whatever they can to keep their minds active, but can confirm that it is not necessarily an easy course to navigate.

Stella Fletcher

INTRODUCTION

In 2016 British voters were invited to decide whether their state should remain a member of the European Union or leave that continent-spanning bloc. 'Remain' supporters were more likely to understand the globalised nature of contemporary socio-economic challenges, while populism and xenophobia were channelled into the 'leave' campaign, making it the latest manifestation of an age-old anti-foreigner phenomenon. Buried in the avalanche of claims, counterclaims and statistics about the practical benefits of leaving or remaining in the EU, a handful of commentators noticed a parallel with the sixteenth-century Reformation. In the course of that process the island nations of Western Christendom broke with a supranational authority based on the European mainland. In doing so those nations brought an end to conflicts between competing jurisdictions, and ensured that national wealth was accumulated by a native elite rather than a foreign one. The comparison was not unreasonable, in some measure because one of the most prominent advocates of so-called 'Brexit' was a government minister who had previously celebrated the English vernacular King James Version of the Bible, who knew that his own political tribe had its origins in seventeenth-century anti-Catholicism, and who exploited House of Commons' privilege to taunt a Catholic MP about taking his instructions from Rome.

The generations who lived in Britain between the sixteenth and the mid twentieth century understood theirs to be a Protestant country, which meant that they habitually regarded external religious, political and cultural influences as the marks of Roman Catholicism, which were, in turn, personified by the pope, the bishop of Rome. The characteristics of early modern antipopery could be glimpsed as recently as 1988 when the Ulster Unionist politician Ian Paisley heckled a bemused pope and held up a placard declaring John Paul II to be the Antichrist. Appropriately enough, this incident occurred in the chamber of the European Parliament, an institution to which Paisley was no less hostile than he was to the papacy. Before the Reformation, Western

Christendom was generally, but not invariably, united through communion with the pope, whose authority was exercised by means of bureaucrats and canon lawyers, rather than by force of arms. Lacking a military target, kings regularly and parliaments occasionally expressed opposition to papal policies by whatever legal or financial means happened to be at their disposal. Twenty-first-century Eurosceptics can consequently trace the roots of their political opinions through this tradition of antipapalism.

In 2016 the Holy See was careful not to instruct the British electorate how to vote in the European referendum but, as the hub of a global diplomatic network, it could hardly avoid taking a line on the subject and Archbishop Paul Gallagher, the Vatican's British-born secretary for relations with states, sided with the majority of informed opinion when he declared that Britain was 'better in than out' of the European Union.[1] Some distance behind that statement was an even longer history of co-operation between Britain and the papacy than anything the antipapalists could offer. This began with the Anglo-Saxons' reputation for devotion to and generosity towards the popes, and reappeared in the feudal society of the post-Conquest period, when Celestine III exercised good lordship by declaring the Scottish Church to be immediately subject to himself and his successors, and Innocent III gratefully accepted King John of England as his vassal. From 1213 onwards England was a papal fief: at least in theory it was under papal rule. This relationship went the way of other feudal bonds and fizzled out, both sides adapting to the post-feudal emphasis on less formalised patronage and clientage, which meant that popes were the ultimate ecclesiastical patrons, the kings of England and Scotland reaching a mutually beneficial accommodation with them by the end of the fifteenth century. Even after both kingdoms broke with Rome, popes made regular attempts to bring them back into the fold, an objective made easier in the seventeenth century when Scotland and England shared a ruling dynasty and their kings married Catholic princesses. Thereafter the path of reconciliation can be traced in the shared heritage of ancient Rome, which Britain's wealthy socio-political elite could afford to indulge during and after their 'grand' tours of Italy. The French Revolution and Napoleon's military campaigns halted habitual travellers in their tracks, after which the nineteenth-century popes renewed their focus on Britain's royalty and aristocracy as the group most likely to influence wider attitudes towards the Holy See. From the First World War onwards career diplomats – lay or, like Gallagher, clerical – have been at the forefront of the Anglo-papal relationship, effectively completing the process of reconciliation.

Exactly how these two contrasting narratives meshed together in reality will be seen in the following chapters, after a survey of some of the sources on which the Anglo-papal story is based and a selection of the scholarly studies it has inspired.

Drawing on the pope's title of 'pontifex maximus' (greatest bridge-builder), the *Liber pontificalis* was first compiled in the sixth century and updated periodically through to the fifteenth.[2] It divides papal history pontificate by pontificate and, for the earlier centuries, relates its material in a formulaic manner: each pope is introduced by his geographical and family origins, and his contribution to the life of the Church is measured in terms of the numbers of bishops, priests and deacons he ordained. This chronicle format could easily be applied to bishops, abbots or kings, and developed to create more ambitious histories, as the prolific twelfth-century English monk William of Malmesbury demonstrated by trying his hand at a version of the *Liber pontificalis* before concentrating on histories of the English kings and bishops.[3] Later in the same century the lives of the most recent pontiffs, Eugenius III, Anastasius IV, the English pope Adrian IV, and Alexander III, were added to the *Liber pontificalis* by Boso, one of Adrian's cardinals, and greatly benefit from the author's first-hand experience of the events he describes. For more specific material on the Anglo-papal relationship in that period one should look instead to John of Salisbury, bishop of Chartres, whose *Historia pontificalis* and *Policraticus* ('The statesman') reflect his experiences of the papal court during the pontificates of Eugenius and Adrian respectively.[4] The sheer oddity of a single English pontiff among a majority of Italian popes and a minority of French ones may have inspired a thirteenth-century Silesian, Martin of Opava, to make a curious insertion in his *Chronicon pontificum et imperatorum*. After the ninth-century pope Leo IV he states that 'John, English of nation, born in Mainz' allegedly reigned for over two years and was only exposed as a woman when she gave birth in a Roman street. The legend of Pope Joan then remained popular through to the sixteenth century, though more in Germany than in England.

Still inspired by the *Liber pontificalis*, the earliest papal biographies written in English appeared in William Thomas's 1549 *Historie of Italie*.[5] By the time Thomas's work appeared Londoners had embraced Protestant religious reform and his coverage of recent history was designed to appeal to their prejudices. Beginning with John Bale's *Acta Romanorum pontificum* and its English translation, that was the level at which papal history continued to be pitched for well over a century, simply because there was a London-centred market for it.[6] None fed that demand quite like the seventeenth-century Milanese adventurer Gregorio Leti, whose life of Pope Innocent X's sister-in-law Olimpia Maidalchini Pamphili included the suggestive assurance that Oliver Cromwell watched a comedy entitled 'The marriage of the pope'.[7] On the other side of the confessional divide, Dom Wilfrid Selby was not exactly overworked as the English Benedictines' procurator in Rome and chose to devote his time to compiling a defence of Pope Boniface VIII, which he published under a pseudonym.[8] Thus there was a distinct cultural divide between a scholarly cleric who had access to the source materials of papal history and his fellow-countrymen in their homeland, who were positively encouraged to wallow in ignorance. Antipapal histories and polemics reveal more about their authors and intended readers than they do about the pontificates under review. In this category can be found the embittered ex-Jesuit Archibald Bower and his *History of the Popes*, which was written to reinforce the prejudices of a predominantly Protestant eighteenth-century readership.[9]

Serious British interest in the popes developed in proportion to the book-buying public's ability to travel to Italy and appreciate its culture. In 1729 the prime minister, Sir Robert Walpole, subscribed to the first sizeable English-language biography of a pope, that of Alexander VI by the Aberdonian antiquarian Alexander Gordon.[10] Walpole did not travel to Italy, but his son Edward toured the peninsula in 1730–1, soon after Gordon's work appeared in print. The next such biography was of Leo X, another of the popes whose cultural patronage could be seen by visitors to the Vatican. Its author was William Roscoe, who never left England but relied instead on the goodwill of an international network of scholars.[11] More significantly, Roscoe was a Unitarian, so free from the confessional bias of a Catholic or that of the Anglicans who had broken with Rome and distinguished their national Church from the pope's supranational empire. The Lutheran Leopold von Ranke went further, combining objectivity with a higher standard of scholarship than Roscoe could manage; his papal history was available in English translation from 1840.[12]

Papal Rome was still a political backwater in the early nineteenth century. All that changed with the Risorgimento – the process by which the Italian peninsula became unified under the rule of a secular monarch – which left Pope Pius IX as a stateless, politically impotent prisoner in the Vatican. Here was history in the making and British authors rose to the challenge. While many intellectuals favoured the new Italian state, Pius VII's Catholic biographer Mary Allies linked the vulnerability of previous popes with post-1870 reality by pointing out that 'a royal locksmith has again taken possession of the Quirinal', which had been the pope's principal Roman residence and became that of the Italian kings.[13] Allies' monograph was a rare achievement, for the nature of papal history generally lent itself to multi-period chronicles.[14] Her father, the former Anglican Thomas Allies, devoted himself to a history of Christianity in which the papacy looms appropriately large.[15] In the 1870s another needy convert, Joseph Stevenson, was engaged by the British government to copy documents in the Vatican archives and briefly enjoyed the unique distinction of roaming at will among its fragile treasures, until the authorities from the pope downwards put such constraints on his work that there was little to show for it.

For Pope Leo's XIII's golden jubilee of priestly ordination in 1887 the archbishop of Westminster, Cardinal Henry Edward Manning, assembled a large consignment of books by more than 400 Catholic authors who had lived in England since 1837.[16] Manning doubled up as one of the most prolific contributors to the collection, alongside his predecessor at Westminster Nicholas Wiseman, the influential Oratorian John Henry Newman, the theologian W.G. Ward and the Jesuit H.J. Coleridge. Reflecting Manning's personal priorities, papal power and infallibility loomed suitably large as a subject, though there were also traditional multi-period 'lives of the popes' (by John Charles Earle and Thomas Meyrick) and studies of individual pontiffs (Mary Allies on Pius VII, J.F. Maguire, M.J. Rhodes and George M. White on Pius IX, and Wilfrid Meynell, writing as 'John Oldcastle', on Leo himself). It was an impressive tally, designed to demonstrate loyalty to the Holy See on the part of Britain's increasingly significant Catholic minority. British Catholicism had experienced this productive 'second spring' by the time James Paton published a decidedly partial account of what he termed the 'greatest problem in British history', by which he meant the struggle for power, authority and, by implication, sovereignty between the pope, on one side, and the Crown and Parliament, on the other.[17] Paton sensed that matters were coming to a head when he wrote in the 1890s. As far as Anglicans were concerned they did, because 1896 brought the papacy's decisive condemnation of Anglican orders as 'absolutely null and utterly void'.[18]

Books were an appropriate gift for Leo XIII, the pope who opened the Vatican archives to scholars, regardless of their confessional allegiance. As a consequence of this decision, William Henry Bliss succeeded where Joseph Stevenson had failed: his calendar of medieval documents relating to Britain and Ireland was published from 1893 onwards.[19] The wider reading public remained fascinated by the period that Roscoe had made popular, which they could now identify as the 'Renaissance'. Even more remote than Roscoe's Liverpool was the Northumbrian parish of Embleton. There the Anglican cleric Mandell Creighton began to write his history of the papacy in the fifteenth and sixteenth centuries.[20] The resources of the Vatican archives were well beyond his reach, which is one reason why Creighton's six-volume work fell out of favour once Ludwig von Pastor's archivally-based *Geschichte des Päpste* was translated into English.[21] Pastor's account opens with the election of Clement V in 1305, so Horace K. Mann complemented it with another multi-volume papal history, covering the era from Gregory the Great in the sixth century to Clement's immediate predecessor, Benedict XI.[22]

Mann was vice-rector of the recently-founded Pontifical Beda College for mature vocations to the priesthood, particularly those of ex-Anglicans. Elsewhere in Rome were the English, Scots and Irish Colleges, all of which dated from the early modern period. Term-time studies for seminarians were not compatible with historical research but, especially for those individuals who did not come from moneyed backgrounds and would not otherwise have been able to travel, their priestly formation in Rome could be the origin of an interest in papal history that yielded literary fruit some years later. Thus William Barry, a humbly-born product of the Venerable English College, asserted himself with nothing less than thirteen centuries of papal history, published in two separate volumes.[23] Similarly, the temperamentally awkward Scots College reject Frederick William Rolfe extended his time in Rome by accepting the patronage of Caroline Shirley, the widowed Duchess Sforza-Cesarini. She lived the palace built by Cardinal Rodrigo Borgia, the future Pope Alexander VI. This connection helped to focus Rolfe's mind on the Borgia popes, with the initial results published as *Chronicles of the House of Borgia*.[24] All the while, Britain's wealthier classes were able to travel to Italy as a matter of course. Some were content to rely on their Baedekers to guide them round the peninsula, but for those who required more extensive background reading the Renaissance papacy remained a popular subject, and various authors obliged by meeting that demand.[25]

Twentieth-century Britain produced a wealth of specialised scholarship on the medieval papacy, which could be regarded as the common heritage of both Catholics and Protestants. When popes and prelates made news headlines at the Second Vatican Council (Vatican II), it was surely no coincidence that accessible English-language histories of the papacy appeared from 1964 onwards.[26] Later still, J.N.D. Kelly and Eamon Duffy published complementary and highly successful works on the entirety of papal history, and that from opposite sides of what had previously been the Anglican/Catholic divide.[27] Kelly and Duffy came from different generations, each of which produced a number of specialists in modern papal history. Owen Chadwick and Anthony Rhodes were direct contemporaries. The former generally focused on nineteenth-century subjects, while the latter's trilogy relates the story of the papacy from 1870 onwards.[28] From the younger generation John F. Pollard kept his focus almost exclusively on early twentieth-century papal and Italian topics, thereby contrasting with John Cornwell who, like Rhodes, has been prolific across a range of genres, papal history forming but one strand of his literary career.[29]

With more specific regard to Anglo-papal relations, canon law texts inspired Zachary Brooke's pioneering study of the period between the reigns of William the Conqueror and John, a work originally published in 1931, and the financial dimension of the relationship was traced by the American William E. Lunt over a longer span of time.[30] As with more general histories, the period of Vatican II witnessed the publication of a useful collection of essays on the medieval papacy and its connections with the English Church, a work that has since been expanded.[31] In subsequent decades scholarly attention became increasingly focused on individual pontificates,[32] on delegated papal jurisdiction in England and Scotland,[33] and on the three-way contest between popes, kings and cathedral chapters over the appointment, nomination or election of bishops.[34]

All aspects of the relationship feature in a regional study of Scotland and northern England in the mid-fourteenth century.[35]

For Anglo-papal diplomacy – and here the term does not extend to Scottish examples – there are detailed studies for the fourteenth, fifteenth and early sixteenth centuries.[36] In that diplomatic relations were then broken, it should not be surprising that the secondary literature becomes relatively sparse and not particularly recent.[37] Only in the nineteenth century did the possibility of diplomatic relations with the Holy See become a live political issue in Britain, and that because of the reconfiguration of the Italian states in the Risorgimento, though a number of recent historians have also been attracted to this period of Anglo-papal history because of its pronounced Irish dimension.[38] Although diplomatic relations were not normalised until 1982, Britain was such a significant global player in the earlier twentieth century that the Vatican was determined to maintain the best relationship it could, which it did by means of senior clerics in London and British ministers accredited to the Holy See. The scholarly literature reflects this significance.[39] Since 1982 the British mission has been a fully-fledged embassy, which sponsored a colloquium on the Anglo-papal relationship in 2012 and subsequently published the proceedings.[40]

Arguably the most distinctively British contribution to papal history can be found not in academic history, popular history or any 'crossover' between the two, but in other literary genres altogether. The fourteenth-century poet John Gower looked back eight or nine decades for a moralising tale from papal history, incorporating the life of Pope Boniface VIII into book 2 of his *Confessio amantis*. In 238 octosyllabic lines, envy drives Boniface to trick and 'supplant' the virtuous Celestine V, after which pride undoes him and he dies of hunger in a French prison.[41] The emergence of English drama as a cultural force coincided with Henry VIII's break with Rome and his successors' maintenance of that schism, resulting in negative portrayals of Pope Innocent III in Bale's *Kynge Johan* and Alexander VI in *The Devil's Charter* by Barnabe Barnes.[42] Alexander went on to feature in the myriad Borgia fictions of more recent times, but British novelists refused to limit themselves to the popes of history and created their own pontiffs, among whom Paschal IV, Hadrian VII, Silvester III, John XXIV and others happened to be as British as their creators. Only by this means can Britain claim to have produced its fair share of popes.

Hitherto, there has been no single-volume survey of the Anglo-papal story in the wider sense of the term, though such an exercise has been undertaken for Scotland.[43] Given the limitations of the format, the present work can be no more than a pale reflection of the available scholarship, much of which derives from the archives of various departments of the papal curia and leads to the creation of more thematic histories. In contrast to such works and in the spirit of the *Liber pontificalis*, this volume emphasises the popes themselves: from *c.* 1100 coverage of each pontificate can be read more or less in isolation.

The result is as much a compendium of information as it is a narrative of events. A certain level of familiarity with British history is assumed, so that the reader is encouraged to map existing knowledge onto the corresponding continental and papal chronologies. The emphasis is predominantly political, which means that the cast of characters changes constantly, often at breakneck speed. With the exception of popes, emperors and the Philip who was king of England and Ireland before he was king of Spain, anglicisation is deliberately kept to a minimum, though any such rule can prove awkward to maintain across so many centuries. A multi-period work also serves to highlight inconsistencies in published practice with regard to the capitalising of titles, offices and corporate bodies. Any attempts to iron out those inconsistencies are likely to end up satisfying no-one. Finally, the available space means that references are restricted to a select range of primary sources, though the story itself is told in ever-increasing detail. It begins in the mists – perhaps more specifically, the coastal mist – of time.

CHAPTER 1

I FOLLOW PETER

Othona, the Roman fort near the mouth of the river Blackwater in south-east England, was not built on the firmest of foundations, for much of its site has given way to salt marsh, through which thread so many vein-like watercourses, connecting the land to the wide expanse of the sea. The fort was presumably in military use throughout the fourth century, and its subsequent history is a matter of even greater conjecture, relieved only by Bede's reference to a 'city called *Ythancæstir* in the Saxon tongue'.[1] His sources were Northumbrian and his subject is the life of Cedd (Cedda), a monk of Lindisfarne, who was chosen in 654 to be bishop of the East Saxons. At Ythancæstir and Tilaburg (Tilbury) Cedd established Christian communities and introduced as much of the monastic life as his followers were able to appreciate. Bede mentions only one other location in connection with this sphere of Cedd's ministry: Rendlesham, where he baptised Swithhelm, king of the East Saxons (d. 663). Otherwise, he associates Cedd with the foundation of a monastery at Lastingham, in the kingdom of Northumbria, and with the Synod of Whitby in 664. At the synod Cedd's contribution was to mediate between the 'Ionan' minority, led by Bishop Colmán of Lindisfarne, and the 'Roman' majority, whose position was articulated by Wilfrid, then abbot of Ripon. The principal difference between the two parties concerned detailed computations to determine the date of Easter, though they also differed on the cut of clerical tonsures. According to Bede, Colmán traced the practices of Iona and Lindisfarne back to St John the Evangelist, while Wilfrid argued for the superiority of the Roman tradition deriving from St Peter. Cedd had been educated in the Ionan tradition, but sided with the Romans by the end of the synod: when he made his choice, it was for Rome, St Peter and, by implication, the apostle's papal successors. In doing so his purpose was evidently accomplished, for he died later that year.

Bede provides no dedication for Cedd's church at Ythancæstir, but the only one by which it has been known is that of St Peter-on-the-Wall, from its position on the western wall of the Roman fort. With the fort all but lost, the restored church now stands in serene isolation near the village of Bradwell-on-Sea in Essex. At Rendlesham in Suffolk there are no visible signs of the palace where Cedd baptised Swithhelm, though the parish church, a later building, is dedicated to St Gregory the Great (590–604), the pope who was recognised as the apostle of the English. The Thames estuary at Tilbury may have been the closest that Cedd ever got to Rome, but Bede proved – and later dedications confirm – that his story encapsulates both the the unifying and the polarising contribution of the papacy to the ecclesiastical history of the British Isles.

From the time of St Peter to that of Sylvester I (314–35) Christianity remained a 'hidden' religion, so much so that it is not possible to make any firm connections between Christians in the Roman province of Britannia and St Peter's successors in the Eternal City. In this otherwise undocumented void the *Liber pontificalis* appears to shed a remarkable light by stating that a British king called Lucius wrote to Pope Eleutherius (*c.* 175–89) requesting acceptance as a Christian.[2] This statement seemingly gives Britain an exceptionally venerable relationship with the Roman see. The absence of any corroborating evidence of Lucius's very existence was no bar to the story being accepted as fact; it was repeated in numerous subsequent histories and in a wealth of legends. More critical minds may seek satisfaction in the argument that 'Britium', a fortress in the kingdom of Edessa, was mistaken for 'Britannia', with the unintended consequence that a near-eastern ruler was transformed into one from the far West.[3]

In one sense Britannia – or, more specifically, Eboracum/York – provided Christendom with its first Christian ruler, for it was there that Constantine was proclaimed emperor in 306, even if he was not baptised until shortly before his death in 337. In the city of Rome Constantine's patronage of the Church meant that what had been hidden suddenly became highly visible, with the foundation of basilical churches in honour of Sts John the Baptist and John the Evangelist (S. Giovanni in Laterano), St Peter (S. Pietro in Vaticano) and St Paul (S. Paolo fuori le Mura), and another to house the relics of the True Cross brought from the Holy Land by the emperor's mother Helena (S. Croce in Gerusalemme). While the popes acquired prominence in Rome, Constantine removed the seat of secular power from that city and founded a second Rome, Constantinople, in the eastern half of his empire.

Whether by land or by sea, Britannia was among the most distant provinces from Constantinople, but there is nevertheless evidence of British participation in ecclesiastical assemblies convened by emperors, including the Council of Sardica (modern Sofia, *c.* 343) and the Synod of Ariminum (Rimini, 359).[4] In 314 the bishops of York, London and (possibly) Colchester were among thirty prelates who sent a series of canons from their synod at Arles to Pope Sylvester. The meeting was called to examine an appeal by the Donatist schismatics of Numidia in North Africa. Among the heresies of that era, only Pelagianism was said to have a particular connection with Britain, but it is impossible to confirm the opinion – held by Augustine of Hippo and others – that Pelagius himself was born there. Wealthier Romans appear to have been attracted to this ascetic movement and its teachings about man's potential to contribute to his own salvation, which Augustine countered with a string of works about the unequivocal and unavoidable need for divine grace.

By the time of Celestine I (422–32) the heresy *du jour* was Nestorianism, and the pope was at the forefront of opposition to Nestorius, patriarch of Constantinople. However, in distant Britain, from which the Romans had largely withdrawn, a preacher called Agricola sparked a sudden outbreak of Pelagianism in the 420s. The 'Chronicle' compiled by Prosper of Aquitaine, an ardent Augustinian, relates that Pope Celestine was persuaded by a deacon called Palladius to dispatch a Gaulish prelate, Germanus, bishop of Auxerre, to Britain to counter the Pelagians. In this version of events Germanus was Celestine's 'vicar', the first papal representative ever sent to the British Isles. The year was 429. On the other hand, Celestine makes no appearance in the later fifth-century life of Germanus by Constantius of Lyon, in whose version Germanus is accompanied on his mission by Lupus, bishop of Troyes. Constantius emphasises the miracles performed by his saintly hero during his time in Britain, but demonstrates no interest in its geography, religious organisation or socio-political structures.[5] It seems safe to assume that the Pelagians, whose theological arguments appear to have been easily refuted, lived exclusively in the south-east of Britain and that Germanus did not travel very extensively during his mission. The only British location with which he can definitely be associated is Verulamium, for Constantius relates that Germanus and Lupus visited the shrine of the early fourth-century martyr Alban. From the mid fourth century onwards the southern part of Britain suffered assaults by raiding parties from mainland Europe, with forts such as Othona providing some sort of defence as long as the Romans retained a military presence there. Without the Romans fifth-century Britons were all the more vulnerable. The otherwise hagiographic account by Constantius provides an angle on those assaults when it tells of Germanus's contribution to a British military victory over some invading Saxons and their Pictish allies. First he fortified the Britons spiritually by means of baptism. Then he encouraged them to conceal themselves and frighten the enemy by leaping from their hiding places with a loud cry of 'Hallelujah!' It worked spectacularly well. Germanus may have paid a second visit to Britain in the 440s, but all the essential features of his mission can be traced to 429.

Prosper of Aquitaine also relates that Palladius, the deacon who apparently facilitated the mission of Germanus to Britain, was sent in 431 as bishop to the Christians in Ireland. As with Germanus, Prosper states that Palladius was the envoy of Pope Celestine, making this the earliest formal connection between Ireland and the papacy. The more westerly island had never been part of the

Roman Empire, so there were neither Mediterranean-style settlements to act as episcopal bases nor martyrs celebrated at shrines. On the other hand, there were contacts across the Irish Sea between Roman Britain and Leinster, the eastern part of Ireland, so it seems most likely that Palladius ministered in that region. In the literary tradition initiated by Prosper, his mission was a success. That tradition had no role for St Patrick, the British-born missionary who styled himself 'bishop in Ireland' at some unidentifiable point in the fifth century and whose later biographers argued that Palladius must have failed, so that Patrick could succeed in bringing Christianity to the Irish.

Contact with Britain and Ireland was not a priority for the popes between Celestine I and Gregory I (590–604). The islands' populations appear to have slumped in the sub-Roman era, while the invasions of eastern and southern Britain by Angles, Saxons, Jutes and other continental tribes created a particularly fluid situation. As can be seen in the story of the 'Hallelujah!' victory, the invaders received support from the Picts, who lived to the north and south of the Grampians. To the west of those mountains the kingdom of Dál Riata united the peoples of the western isles and northern Ireland, and never more obviously than in the travels of the missionary Columba (Colum Cille, d. 597), founder of Iona, Durrow and other monasteries. The success or otherwise of Columba's missions into Pictland is impossible to verify. South of the Pictish kingdom was that of Dumbarton. Further south again, the region between the Antonine Wall and that of Hadrian was invaded from the east by Angles in the sixth century. The western side of this region is associated with Ninian, who lived in the fifth or sixth century and is said by Bede to have received instruction in the Christian faith in Rome, before founding his white-painted church (Candida Casa) at Whithorn.[6] Between Hadrian's Wall and the Humber was Deira, an Anglian kingdom by *c.* 600; the sparsely-populated lands further west remained British. South of the Humber, Angles settled in Lindsey, as well as to the west and east of the Fens. East, Middle, South and West Saxons occupied much of southern Britain, while Jutes carved out territories for themselves in Kent, the Isle of Wight and the neighbouring mainland. The south-western peninsula remained British and was known as Dumnonia, while at least half a dozen kingdoms existed in Wales and the Marches by 600, all of them British. At Menevia, in the far west of Wales, St David is said to have established the bishopric which now bears his name. He lived in the sixth century, though the earliest accounts of his life date from a later period.

Demographically, sixth-century Rome was also a shadow of its former self. Politically and militarily, it was at the heart of a peninsula-wide struggle between the Ostrogoths, who had dominated the region for more than a century, and the resurgent power of the Empire under Justinian I (527–65). After Justinian's death imperial authority became limited to the coastal areas of Italy, including the administrative capital at Ravenna, while a new wave of northern invaders, the Lombards, swept through the peninsula and assumed authority from Milan in the north to Benevento in the south. At worst the Lombards were pagans, at best Arian heretics, as the Ostrogothic rulers of Italy had been. In 579/80 Rome was besieged by Lombard forces, causing the pope, Pelagius II (579–90), to seek support from the Frankish king of Gaul, whose dynasty had been keen Catholic Christians since the conversion of Clovis in *c.* 500. By the time Pope Pelagius was succeeded by Gregory I, flooding and plague added to the general woes of Rome's inhabitants.

These multiple disasters were of no concern to Christians in Britain and Ireland, but what did matter to them were the ecclesiastical structures that had developed in Rome before and since the time of Constantine. The popes ostensibly exercised authority over the metropolitans (archbishops) and bishops of Italy, but the bishops most closely associated with them were those of the suburbicarian sees located around the city of Rome: the bishops of Ostia, Albano, Palestrina, Porto and Velletri acquired liturgical functions at S. Giovanni in Laterano, the pope's cathedral church. Similarly, the priests who ministered at Rome's 'parish' churches also had liturgical responsibilities at the city's other major basilicas, but were known by the titles (tituli) of the churches where they were based. Both groups were therefore 'incardinated' – inserted – into the basilicas and became known as cardinal bishops and cardinal priests respectively. Of particular significance during the natural (and unnatural) disasters of the later sixth century were the *diaconiae*, through which charity was dispensed to the poor and needy of Rome. In the 570s one of the city's seven deacons was the future Pope Gregory. As a deacon, his charitable responsibilities drew him from the seclusion of the monastic community he had founded in his family home on Rome's Monte Celio and dedicated to St Peter's brother, Andrew. Other distractions followed, principally service as papal envoy to the imperial court at Constantinople and election to the papal office itself.

Within the Empire Gregory inherited a deteriorating relationship between the Roman popes and the 'ecumenical' patriarchs in Constantinople who claimed to exercise a spiritual authority over Christendom in parallel to that of the emperor's secular authority. Closer to home was the pope's responsibility to provide the people of Rome with physical sustenance, together with the practicalities of dealing with the Lombard rulers to both north and south. The division of Italy into Lombard and imperial spheres was paralleled by a schism which saw the patriarch of Aquileia and archbishop of Milan break off communications with Rome. Peninsular challenges to papal authority did not end there, for Ravenna's status as the imperial capital in Italy gave it ecclesiastical pretensions which Gregory sought to check. Thankfully, Gaul was comparatively quiet, unquestionably loyal to Rome and offered potential as a base for missionary work to the north and east, but Iberia provided the great missionary success story of the era: in 587 its Visigothic king converted from Arianism to Catholicism and his kingdom duly followed his example. Like the earliest Christians, Gregory was sure that he could see signs that the second coming of Christ was imminent. If the world ended and there were still unconverted pagans, people of whose existence he was well aware, how would he answer for that before the throne of judgement? Time was short, so was it necessary to preach to non-Christians in order to secure their conversion.

In 596 Gregory dispatched his party of missionary monks from his own community at Monte Celio with letters of recommendation to the Frankish monarchs who were related by marriage to King Æthelberht of Kent.[7] It was only in the winter of 596/7, when Gregory felt obliged to urge on his somewhat reluctant agents, that Augustine emerged as leader of this group. The pope's next direct involvement in the mission was not until 601, by which time Augustine could report Æthelberht's conversion and Gregory delightedly conveyed news of the mission's apparently miraculous success to his correspondent in Alexandria. A clutch of papal letters was sent northwards in the summer of that year, to King Æthelberht, his consort Bertha, Augustine and others.[8] Bede relates that Augustine had sent Gregory nine questions on organisational and pastoral matters, to each of which the pope made reply.[9] A postscript set out Gregory's blueprint for the episcopal structure of the Church in the Anglo-Saxon lands: the major Roman settlements of London and York were to be the seats of metropolitans, with a dozen suffragan bishops in each province. Augustine's personal authority was confirmed by Gregory's gift of a pallium – a white woollen band worn round the shoulders to signify papal or metropolitical authority – and the mission was augmented by another contingent of monks, including Justus, Mellitus and Paulinus.[10] In 604 Augustine began to enact Gregory's plan by consecrating Justus as bishop of Rochester, also in the kingdom of Kent, and Mellitus as bishop of the East Saxons, with his cathedral in London, but Æthelberht ensured that the metropolitan see remained at Canterbury. By the time of Augustine's death later that year the mission could boast a further set of connections with papal Rome: the dedications of its principal churches. The cathedral in Canterbury was named for Christ, the Church's one true foundation, while Gregory's monks lived in the monastery of Sts Peter and Paul, where the first abbot happened to be called Petrus. Gregory's own monastery was recalled when St Andrew received his first insular dedication, at Rochester, and St Paul was chosen for the church in London.

Among the missionaries known personally to Pope Gregory, seven served as bishops: Augustine, Laurence and Mellitus successively at Canterbury, Romanus at Rochester from 624, when Justus was translated to Canterbury, Paulinus as bishop of the Northumbrians in 625 with his see fixed at York in 627, Honorius at Canterbury in 628/31. The last survivors, Paulinus and Honorius, died in 644 and 653 respectively. Of the seven only Mellitus returned to Rome, to attend a papal synod in 610. When Kent and Essex temporarily reverted to paganism a few years later Justus and Mellitus fled to Gaul, but it was the Roman connection that kept Archbishop Laurence at his post, St Peter chastising him 'with apostolic severity' in a dream.[11] After dedicating his church in York to St Peter and petitioning Pope Honorius I (625–38) to raise his see to metropolitan status, Paulinus suffered a similar reversal when Northumbria reverted to paganism after the death in 633 of its first Christian king. By the time Honorius offered some support by sending a pallium, Paulinus had fled south and been made bishop of Rochester. However, this general reversal was short-lived: before long the rulers of Kent, Essex and Northumbria all returned to the Christian fold.

The fortunes of those various members of the Gregorian mission are vividly related by Bede, whose relatively sketchy information about the south and west of Britain has served to obscure the wider contribution of Pope Honorius to the evangelisation of the Anglo-Saxons. This pontiff sought to develop the mission beyond the Canterbury–York axis by sending another Italian missionary, Birinus, to the Gewisse (West Saxons), though the latter's breakthrough – the baptism of King Cynegils in 635 – was facilitated by King Oswald of Northumbria, who acted as godfather. From his cathedral at Dorchester, in a bend of the Thames, Birinus's mission remained independent from that of the surviving Gregorians. When the faith was introduced into the Mercian heartland in the 650s it was by Northumbrian missionaries from the tradition of Iona and Lindisfarne. The Mercian bishops eventually settled at Lichfield. In the absence of any new influx of missionaries from Rome, it fell to a Burgundian monk, Felix, to serve as bishop of the East Angles from 630/1 to 647/8.

Pope Honorius's interest in this far corner of Christendom extended to Ireland. An Irish delegation travelled to Rome in 631, after which some Irish prelates abandoned their minority position on the calculation of Easter and conformed to the standard 'Roman' practice. Pope-elect John IV (640–2) sought to complete this initiative when he wrote in 640 to a group headed by the abbot/bishop of Armagh urging them to follow suit.[12]

A dynamic new element was introduced into the relationship between the Holy See and the Anglo-Saxon kingdoms when a young Northumbrian nobleman became possessed of a determination to visit the Eternal City. Biscop Baducing had no clerical business to transact; rather, he was the first insular pilgrim to Rome. After his first visit in 653, when he stayed at S. Andrea in Monte Celio, the monastery founded by Pope Gregory, he made four further pilgrimages between 665 and 685. Although he also gained inspiration from the monasteries of Gaul, it was the Rule of St Benedict and that saint's life, as told by Gregory in his 'Dialogues', that gained so great a hold over the Northumbrian that he assumed the name Benedict. After his third pilgrimage Benedict Biscop founded a minster at Wearmouth in 674 and, after the fourth visit,

Wearmouth's sister community at nearby Jarrow, houses dedicated to St Peter and St Paul respectively. With each expedition a little bit of Rome was carried back to Northumbria, be it in the form of books, relics, architectural designs, or the person of John, the precentor of St Peter's Basilica, who taught Benedict Biscop's monks to chant in the Roman style.[13] As a member of the two communities from *c.* 680, Bede was an eye-witness to these developments.

The precentor's mission was not limited to liturgy, for he brought with him the decrees of the Lateran Council of 649. This assembly had been convened by Pope Martin I (649–55) to condemn the monothelite heresy, a movement which caused serious divisions in the Byzantine world. The brief pontificate of Pope Agatho (678–81) brought a revived determination to settle the long-running dispute between Rome and Constantinople over Monothelitism. One man was thought to possess an unrivalled understanding of the issues, in part because he was himself a Greek, but also because he seems to have been a key player in the Lateran Council. This was the distinguished theologian Theodore of Tarsus, a surprise choice for the see of Canterbury after an archbishop-elect, Wigheard, died in Rome in the 660s. Pope Agatho expressed his regard for Theodore's expertise in a letter to the emperor: 'We were hoping [...] that Theodore, our co-servant and co-bishop, the philosopher and archbishop of Great Britain, would join our enterprise, along with certain others who remain there up to the present day'.[14] The 'enterprise' proved to be successful: monothelitism was condemned at a synod in Rome in 680 and also by the ecumenical Council of Constantinople in 681.

Archbishop Theodore was too old to return to either Rome or Constantinople, but the deposed bishop of York was certainly in Rome in 680. This was Wilfrid, spokesman for the 'Roman' party at Whitby in 664, whose career can be traced not only in Bede's more matter-of-fact account but also in the hagiographic life by Stephen of Ripon (Eddius Stephanus).[15] In total Wilfrid paid three visits to Rome. The first was after parting company with his fellow pilgrim Biscop Baducing in 653, though each proved to be as avid as the other in terms of absorbing the ecclesiastical culture of their ultimate destination. Alchfrith, son of King Oswiu of Northumbria, had been prevented from travelling to Rome with Biscop, but played a more active part in the story by ensuring that Wilfrid became abbot of the monastery at Ripon and then, after his decisive contribution at Whitby, bishop of the vast Northumbrian see. In some quarters Wilfrid was thought to have overreached himself by seeking episcopal consecration from unquestionably orthodox Frankish bishops, though it is true that there were precious few British bishops of any description who could have consecrated him before Theodore made a conscious effort to fill the numerous episcopal vacancies. By the time Wilfrid returned to Northumbria, his enemies – essentially the defeated Ionan party – had massed against him and installed Chad (Ceadda), brother of Cedd, as their bishop. Archbishop Theodore effectively resolved this problem in 669 by restoring Wilfrid to his bishopric and appointing Chad as bishop of the Mercians, the latter's subsequent cult at Lichfield underlining the success of this move.

Whether as a bishop or as the founder of monasteries, Wilfrid operated on a scale that went far beyond the borders of Northumbria and involved cultivating various princes, including Wulfhere of Mercia, an enemy of Oswiu's son and successor Ecgfrith of Northumbria. Wilfrid was an overmighty subject and, whatever the more precise motivation, Ecgfrith was determined to destroy both him and his ecclesiastical power base. To that end the king encouraged Archbishop Theodore's tripartite division of the Northumbrian see: new bishoprics were created, based on Wilfrid's monasteries at Ripon and Hexham, and an extraordinarily pliant figure called Bosa was installed at York. This dramatic reversal of fortune coincided with Pope Agatho's campaign against Monothelitism, so the Roman synod of 680 gave Wilfrid an opportunity to present his appeal before a larger audience than would otherwise have been the case. The synod found in his favour. Wilfrid returned to Northumbria not only with papal confirmation of his episcopal status but also with a privilege exempting his monasteries – in Northumbria and elsewhere – from the authority of diocesan bishops. Benedict Biscop obtained a similar privilege from the same pope for his monastery at Wearmouth, and many other monasteries followed these examples.

As Wilfrid's biographer emphasises, Ecgfrith ignored the papal ruling.[16] Wilfrid was forced into exile, first in Mercia, then Sussex, and finally in Wessex. When Ecgfrith died in 685 Archbishop Theodore sought to make amends by encouraging the new king, Aldfrith, to recall Wilfrid from exile. It was the reduced bishopric of York to which he was restored, while Bosa obligingly stood aside. Eager to return to his story of saintliness and suffering, Stephen of Ripon then leaps to the enmity stirred up between Wilfrid and Aldfrith in 691–2 and puts Ripon and its papal privilege at the centre of the dispute.[17] Again Wilfrid headed for Mercia, where his eleven years as bishop at Leicester proved to be longer than any of his three periods in Northumbria; again Bosa was acknowledged as bishop at York. Then the narrative takes another leap, to 702–03, when Wilfrid was invited to a synod at Austerfield ('Aetswinapathe'), on the border of Mercia and Northumbria. Here, Stephen declares, the other bishops – led by Archbishop Berhtwald – appeared in their true colours, their determination to destroy Wilfrid and his ecclesiastical empire motivated by avarice.[18] In turn, Wilfrid denounced their disregard for canon law and disrespect for the decrees of three popes, Agatho, Benedict II (684–5) and Sergius I (687–701). The synod proposed that he be stripped of all his possessions, episcopal and monastic, in both Mercia and Northumbria, but was prepared to settle for a compromise which would see him living an enclosed life at Ripon. In response, Wilfrid recalled his previous service to the Church, not least with regard to the dating of Easter and the cut of tonsures. The meeting dissolved, Wilfrid returned to Mercia and, from there, made his final journey to Rome. This time the pope who greeted him warmly was John VI (701–05). Wilfrid's new petition was based squarely on the previous rulings of 'the holy Agatho, the elect Benedict and the blessed Sergius'.[19] The counter-arguments were presented by representatives of Archbishop Berhtwald. It was several months before a judgement was announced, but the result again vindicated Wilfrid, even if the best that Pope John could propose in practical terms was that the parties should compose their differences at home and only return to Rome if that proved impossible. By the time another synod met, in 706, the king of Northumbria was Aldfrith's young son Osred, who accepted Wilfrid as his adoptive father and acknowledged his rights over the monasteries at Ripon and Hexham. The bishoprics were a different matter, but Wilfrid was over seventy years of age and had suffered a stroke, which may explain why he settled for the see of Hexham and the opportunity to minister from one of his own monasteries, though not the one to which his enemies had sought to confine him. The saintly John of Beverley was translated from Hexham to York. Even then, Northumbria was too narrow a stage for Wilfrid, the inveterate traveller: he died in 709 while visiting his monastery at Oundle and his body was buried at Ripon.

The strength of Wilfrid's character surely accounted for the height to which he rose and the determination of his enemies to destroy him, though his story also sets out some of the fundamental challenges faced by prelates who had little option but to serve two masters. The Church depended on practical support from secular rulers and there was no prelate more assiduous than Wilfrid when it came to cultivating princes. According to Stephen of Ripon, he left a quarter of his worldly wealth to the abbots of Ripon and Hexham for that very purpose.[20] If the cultivation of princes was one of the Church's unwritten rules, as far as Wilfrid was concerned its written ones were those emanating from Rome. Time and again, his appeals to Rome proved that his understanding of canon law was correct, even if they also illustrated the relative weakness of the papacy, which had no means of forcing princes to obey its injunctions. When popes and princes were at variance, Wilfrid's course of action might have been the holier option, the high road to martyrdom, but Archbishop Theodore's was arguably the more sensible one, compromising with the nearer power, even if that was less than ideal.

Aside from the papal privileges for his monasteries, the appeals to Rome, and the building of Roman-inspired churches to house his collection of Roman relics, there was another overtly papal dimension to Wilfrid's story: his devotion to St Peter. His deployment of Peter against John the Evangelist at the Synod of Whitby was part of a larger whole. As bishop of Northumbria he rebuilt Paulinus's church of St Peter at York as his cathedral. His monastery at Ripon was also dedicated to Peter and those he founded at Hexham and Oundle were named for Peter's brother, Andrew. Again we are dependent on Stephen of Ripon, a monk of St Peter's, who emphasises the Petrine connections in his *Vita sancti Wilfrithi*. Thus, when Wilfrid returned from his second visit to Rome, Abbess Æbbe of Coldingham declared that he came with Peter's power to bind and loose, and after he healed an unnamed woman she waited on him in the manner of Peter's mother-in-law.[21] The examples could be multiplied. It would not be consistent with Stephen's argument, and is therefore left to Bede, to inform us that it was Archbishop Theodore, operating well outside the province of Canterbury, who dedicated the church on Lindisfarne to St Peter.[22] Towards the end of the *vita*, Stephen provides an entirely appropriate twist to his story. When Wilfrid fell ill at Meaux, in the course of his return journey from Rome in 705, he had a vision of St Michael, who admonished him: 'You have built churches in honour of the Apostles St Peter and St Andrew; but you have built nothing in honour of St Mary ever Virgin, who is interceding for you. You have to put this right and dedicate a church in honour of her.'[23] In Wilfridian terms, this surely ranks as similar in scale to the prolific thirteenth-century scholar Thomas Aquinas writing no more after a life-changing vision.

There was nothing Gregorian about Wilfrid's devotion to the see of Rome. His Petrine emphasis was utterly deliberate and hints at the nature of the opposition he faced in Northumbria, opposition that had no equal in neighbouring kingdoms. The Christians of seventh-century Northumbria appear to have fallen into the trap identified by St Paul with reference to the earliest Christians of Corinth, who declared themselves to be followers of Paul, Apollos or Cephas, instead of celebrating their unity in Christ. Wilfrid's dedications to Peter and Andrew illustrated conventional practice – these were the two most popular choices for church dedications in Anglo-Saxon England – but they also transcended any local or regional interest and indicated ecclesiastical unity based on Rome. What Wilfrid did not find in Rome was any over-emphasis on the figure of Pope Gregory, but that was precisely what he encountered in Northumbria, and it was devotion to Gregory that united many of Wilfrid's opponents. The line of spiritual descent was tenuous and centred on Hild, a Northumbrian convert of Paulinus, who was abbess of the monastery that has come to be known as Whitby from 657 until her death in 680. When she hosted the synod in 664 she shared neither Cedd's original impartiality nor his eventual preference for Wilfrid's argument. Rather, she championed and remained loyal to the tradition associated with Lindisfarne, and it seems that popes from Agatho to John VI were aware of her subsequent role in harnessing opposition to Wilfrid.[24] Hild was an influential educator who promoted the clerical careers of her pupils, among them Bosa and John of Beverley, the men who replaced Wilfrid in the see of York. They were also the next generation of

Gregorians, for the cult of Gregory had become centred on Whitby in a way that had not occurred in Canterbury or any other insular location. In the early eighth century a 'monk' of Whitby – who may, in fact, have been a woman – presumably drew on an oral tradition that went back to Paulinus when he (or she) composed the earliest life of Gregory. This is the origin of the puns duly publicised by Bede, only one of which has made much impact beyond the Whitby area:

> There is a story told by the faithful that before he became Pope there came to Rome certain people of our nation, fair-skinned and light-haired. When he heard of their arrival he was eager to see them; being prompted by a fortunate intuition, being puzzled by their new and unusual appearance, and, above all, being inspired by God, he received them and asked what race they belonged to [...] They answered, 'The people we belong to are called Angles.' 'Angels of God,' he replied. Then he asked further, 'What is the name of the king of that people?' They said 'Ælli,' whereupon he said, 'Alleluia, God's praise must be heard there.' Then he asked the name of their own tribe, to which they answered 'Deire' and he replied, 'They shall flee from the wrath of God to the faith.'[25]

Stephen of Ripon's life of Wilfrid is surely more or less contemporary with the anonymous life of Gregory. Stephen's direct knowledge of his subject contrasts with the other writer's relative paucity of information about Gregory. Taken together, the two texts are suggestive of a cultural battle waged between monastic houses some thirty-five miles apart, with devotion to two different pontiffs as their weapons of choice.

If the spiritual heirs of Pope Gregory can be traced through Paulinus of York and Hild of Whitby, who were Wilfrid's heirs and was what was his legacy? Among his monks, the most significant proved to be Willibrord, whose monastic life began at Ripon and continued in Ireland, before he followed Wilfrid's example by undertaking missionary work in Frisia, where the energetic Northumbrian had preached before his second journey to Rome. Willibrord paid two visits to Rome, in 693 and 695, securing papal support for his mission and his consecration as 'archbishop of the Frisians', but also echoed the experience of his father in Christ when he was driven from his see by the secular power. It was Willibrord's example that the West Saxon Wynfreth – later known as Boniface – sought to emulate when he went to Frisia in 716. Boniface fared better after Gregory II (715–31) sent him as a missionary to the pagans east of the Rhine, emerging as the 'apostle of Germany', with a posthumous cult and pilgrimage centre at Fulda designed to rival that of St Peter in Rome. Apart from his Frisian mission, Boniface had no particular connection to Wilfrid, though a certain similarity might be traced in his devotion to the papacy and in the opposition he encountered from Irish missionaries in Central Europe.

To the north, Wilfrid's personal empire stretched as far as Abercorn, on the south bank of the Firth of Forth, where he founded a monastery, and his devotion to St Andrew, expressed in the dedication of his monastery at Hexham, may have extended to Kinrymont in Fife, though he is not part of the foundation legend of the ecclesiastical hub that became known as St Andrews. According to Bede, it was shortly after Wilfrid's death that the Pictish king Nechtán mac Der Ilei Romanised the Church in his land, expelling the Ionan clergy, rejecting their calculation of Easter, and seeking assistance from Abbot Ceolfrid of Wearmouth and Jarrow.[26] The abbot sent masons to build a stone church, which the king promised to dedicate to St Peter. This pioneering building may have been at Restenneth, near to the modern town of Forfar.

For a clearer picture of Wilfrid's impact, one should look not only southwards, but also upwards, socially, to the kings whose patronage he courted so assiduously. In 630/1 Sigeberht of the East Angles renounced his throne and entered a monastery. This phenomenon did not recur in the Anglo-Saxon kingdoms for more than half a century, but when it did it became something of a trend, as did renouncing a throne and retiring to Rome. This development coincided with the last twenty-five years of Wilfrid's long life and, thanks to the unsettled nature of his career, involved a number of kings with whom he had direct dealings. In 681, after his first appeal to Rome and Ecgfrith of Northumbria's refusal to comply with Pope Agatho's decree, the exiled Wilfrid spent a short time with King Centwine of the Gewisse. Four years later, in circumstances that remain unknown, Centwine retired to a monastery, though he may have been forced into the cloister by his successor, Cædwalla. This prince first encountered Wilfrid during the next phase of the latter's exile, in Sussex, and made him bishop of the Gewisse when he acquired that throne. In a reign of three intensely bloody years Cædwalla conquered the South Saxons and the hitherto pagan Isle of Wight, together with Kent and Surrey. This left him with many sins for which to atone. Even without Stephen of Ripon's assurance that Cædwalla regarded Wilfrid as a father figure, their relationship surely accounted for the young king's abdication and journey to Rome in 688.[27] The following Easter he was baptised by Pope Sergius, taking the name of Peter. He died ten days later, on 20 April 689, and was buried in the atrium of St Peter's, wearing his baptismal robe.

Wilfrid's most consistent royal patron was Æthelred of Mercia, in whose kingdom he settled throughout the 690s and who positively encouraged the bishop's second appeal to Rome. Like Wilfrid, Æthelred was a founder of monasteries, including St Peter's at Gloucester. In 704, during Wilfrid's absence in Rome, Æthelred abdicated in favour of his nephew Coenred and entered the monastery at Bardney, in the diocese of Lindsey. Wilfrid visited him there the following year and was introduced to Coenred, who promised to maintain the Mercian protection so long enjoyed by the venerable bishop. After a five-year reign Coenred also abdicated. Together with Offa of the East Saxons – himself the kinsman of yet another monk-king, Sæbbi – Coenred travelled to Rome, where they were both tonsured, joined a monastery close to St Peter's and, like Cædwalla, were duly buried in the atrium of the basilica. Their story was remarkable enough to feature in the *Liber pontificalis*, in the section devoted to the Syrian pope Constantine (708–15), and to be perpetuated in later histories of Rome.[28]

Whatever the precise motives behind each abdication, the phenomenon did not long outlive Wilfrid himself. The last Anglo-Saxon king to retire to Rome was Ine of the West Saxons (formerly the Gewisse), who abdicated in 726, though there is no contemporary evidence to support the later assertion that it was he who founded the Schola Saxonum, the Anglo-Saxon pilgrim hospice. The hospice certainly existed by the end of the eighth century, though its precise origins are uncertain. Rome had long been a cosmopolitan city, where the foreign communities of longer standing resided within the third-century Aurelian walls. Those communities of more recent vintage were primarily attracted to the tomb of St Peter and were therefore found on the Vatican side of the Tiber. The Schola Saxonum was the first such settlement. Its location close to the river can be roughly determined by the existing church and hospital of S. Spirito in Sassia (from 'Saxia'), both of which front onto Borgo S. Spirito. By the end of the eighth century, the Anglo-Saxons had acquired Frisian neighbours, so the heirs of Wilfrid were joined by those of his protégé Willibrord. Even closer to the Patrine basilica were the *scholae* of the Franks and the Lombards. For a direct connection between the Schola Saxonum and any of the popes the *Liber pontificalis* offers nothing until the pontificate of Paschal I (817–24). Then, 'through the carelessness of some men of English race', the entire quarter was destroyed by a fire which only abated when the pope himself arrived and prayed for God's mercy. Thereafter, as the residents set about rebuilding their homes and livelihoods, the pope 'supplied everything abundantly'.[29]

An increasing number of clerics from the Anglo-Saxon kingdoms had business to conduct in Rome. In 735 Ecgberht travelled there to receive a pallium from Gregory III (731–41) and thus became the first archbishop of York, a development for which Gregory I had prepared in principle with his vision of a northern province and which Bishop Wilfrid had sought to demonstrate in practice. Ecgberht's enhanced status put pressure on Canterbury, so it is no surprise that Archbishop Nothhelm went to Rome and received his pallium the following year. Nothhelm was already familiar with the city, having been the first person from the British Isles to go there for the purpose of undertaking historical research: his findings were incorporated into Bede's

Ecclesiastical History. Elsewhere on the ecclesiastical spectrum were representatives of monastic houses seeking and obtaining papal privileges designed to maintain the independence of those houses from status-conscious bishops. Aldhelm, the learned abbot of Malmesbury, is known to have journeyed to Rome at an unspecified date, possibly for this purpose.[30]

Visitors to Rome in the second half of the eighth century included the scholar Alcuin of York, who received the pallium of his archbishop, Eanbald (I), and King Offa of Mercia, who answered to no-one. Both of them dealt with Pope Hadrian I (772–95) and Alcuin is thought to have composed the epitaph for Hadrian which was commissioned by the pope's close ally Charlemagne, king of the Franks, and survives in the atrium of St Peter's. More remarkable was a journey made in the opposite direction, when Hadrian sent two legates to Britain in 786. George of Ostia, the more senior of the pair was an experienced diplomat who had undertaken a lengthy mission to the Franks in the 750s and, as the most senior cardinal bishop, had steered the papacy through the attempts of two secular princes to create their own popes – Antipopes Constantine and Philip – in 767–9. This bishop of Ostia was therefore the first cardinal to set foot on British soil. He was accompanied by Theophylact, bishop of Todi. Circumstantial evidence suggests that their mission was prompted by Offa's subjection of the Kentish kingdom before 785, which brought to a head his differences with Archbishop Jænberht of Canterbury. Charlemagne informed Hadrian of a rumour that Offa had proposed to dethrone the pope, reassuring him that it was false.[31] Did the rumour originate in Canterbury? Together the legates visited Jænberht, Offa and the Mercian king's West Saxon counterpart and recent adversary, Cynewulf. As their report relates, they then parted company, George heading for Northumbria and Theophylact apparently for Mercia and Wales.[32] According to a later source, the legates were still in Britain in 787, attended at least one of the ecclesiastical synods held that year, and were present when Offa promised to send to Rome an annual tribute in thanksgiving to St Peter.[33] The development for which Offa felt most thankful certainly occurred in 787 and presumably had papal approval, even if there is no documentary link with the legates. This was the raising of Lichfield to metropolitan status, paralleling the secular dominance of Mercia among the Anglo-Saxon kingdoms. This left the unfortunate Jænberht with a severely reduced province that extended no further north than the dioceses of Sherborne, Winchester and London.

The province of Lichfield was little more than the plaything of the most powerful man in eighth-century Britain and moves to restore the traditional hierarchy began shortly after Offa's death in 796. That the papacy needed to cultivate friends such as Offa was confirmed in 799 when Pope Leo III (795–816) suffered a serious assault by partisans of his long-lived predecessor Hadrian and fled to Charlemagne's court in Saxony. It was in gratitude for that protection and as a warning to potential opponents that Leo apparently surprised the Frankish king by crowning him as emperor on Christmas Day 800, with all that implied for a latter-day Constantine. Meanwhile, Leo rejected a compromise by which the bishopric of London would have taken precedence over both Canterbury and Lichfield, along the lines originally envisaged by Gregory the Great. In 801–02 Archbishop Æthelheard, who was himself a Mercian and therefore awkwardly situated in Kent, travelled to Rome and obtained papal approval for the restoration of Canterbury's previous authority. At his death in 805 the Christ Church community – which was probably composed of secular priests, rather than monks, at this date – elected one of their own number as archbishop: Wulfred emerged as a figurehead for Kentish opposition to the Mercian king Cenwulf. He also led opposition to lay control of 'minsters' – a blanket term that covers various ecclesiastical communities – whether or not they followed a monastic rule. In 814 Wulfred became the last ninth-century archbishop of Canterbury to travel to Rome. The purpose of his mission remains uncertain, but there was presumably a connection with the 816 Synod of Chelsea, which approved Wulfred's views on the rights of bishops to appoint heads of religious houses and, by implication, limited lay power over the Church. Cenwulf responded by asking the pope to suspend Wulfred from office. That the archbishop could be sacrificed was a clear measure of papal weakness. His suspension lasted for five or six years.

By the early ninth century the Anglo-Saxon kingdoms had reverted to their usual lowly position among Rome's priorities, so much so that when papal agents were sent in 808 to Northumbria and in 824 to one of the regular ecclesiastical councils held at *Clofesho*, they were natives of the region. Meanwhile, although the archbishops may have ceased to visit Rome, the flow of lay pilgrims continued throughout the century and included a political refugee, Cyngen of Powys, who appears to have been driven from his kingdom by an invasion of Mercians and West Saxons in 853. He did not survive long in Rome, dying in 854 or 855, but may have lived long enough to witness a pilgrimage by Alfred, son and brother-in-law of the kings who had driven him into exile.

The posthumous cult of King Alfred (d. 899), inspired by Asser's *Life* and the king's own literary endeavours, has tended to invest every period and every aspect of his career with exceptional significance. Asser is the sole source for the story of the child Alfred, youngest son of the West Saxon king Æthelwulf, being sent to Rome in 853 and, as a sign of his future greatness, being accorded every honour by Pope Leo IV (847–55).[34] According to this unverifiable chronology, two years later he returned to Rome, this time accompanying his father.[35] It was not until 871 that Alfred succeeded to the West Saxon throne. By then Northumbria and East Anglia had both been overrun by Viking invaders and the bishoprics of Dunwich, Elmham and Lindsey fell into abeyance. In 873–4 it was the turn of Burgred of Mercia to admit defeat and flee to Rome. Like his former adversary Cyngen, Burgred seems not to have survived long thereafter, and the *Anglo-Saxon Chronicle* relates that his body 'lies in the church of sancta Maria, in the school of the English nation'.[36] Mercia's collapse left Alfred and the West Saxons standing unaided against the Danish forces, which they could no more than contain in the 870s. When another Danish army arrived in the 890s it was a dramatically different story and it could be argued that Alfred's Roman experience contributed to the defensive strategy which he had put into place in the meantime.

The coastal regions of ninth-century Italy were regularly attacked by Saracen raiders from North Africa. In 846 an Arab force got as far as Rome, where they plundered the vulnerable buildings outside the Aurelian walls. Leo IV was the pope who set about defending the area between St Peter's and the Tiber, the walls he built creating the virtually enclosed 'borgo Leonino'. The line of his defences cannot now be traced with absolute certainty, but it is thought that the southern wall ended in the vicinity of the Schola Saxonum, which continued to rely on the waterfront for its defence. The walls were completed and the *borgo* created at the very time when young Alfred made the first of his pilgrimages. Alfred's realm lacked major urban centres, so the *burhs* he constructed were isolated forts which together formed a defensive network across the kingdom of Wessex. The system worked and, in the temporary absence of a Danish army, allowed him to extend his authority over Mercia and emerge as 'king of the Anglo-Saxons' or, more concisely, of the English.

The financial relationship between England and the papacy was well established by Alfred's reign, so much so that it was a cause for comment when the insular levy then known as Romescot was not sent to Italy in 889.[37] Only one late ninth-century pope, Marinus I (882–4), is named in the *Anglo-Saxon Chronicle* and by Asser, and that because he remitted taxes on the Schola Saxonum and sent Alfred a piece of the True Cross.[38] However, there seems little doubt that the pontiff for whom Alfred had the greatest regard was Gregory the Great, who was identified as 'your apostle' by the archbishop of Reims in a letter to the king.[39] Towards the end of his life, Alfred sought to raise the standard of learning among his subjects and to do so by giving them access to 'certain books which are the most necessary for all men to know'.[40] His cultural campaign is explained in the preface to his own translation of Gregory's *Liber regulae pastoralis*, a work which provides guidance for bishops but was evidently no less useful to a man at the apex of the secular hierarchy. At least Alfred was not alone in his mission of enlightenment: the translation of Gregory's 'Dialogues' was allocated to Werferth, bishop of Worcester. Other collaborators included Plegmund, archbishop of Canterbury, and the biographer Asser, who seems to identify himself as bishop of St Davids.[41]

Archbishop Plegmund's only visit to Rome occurred in 908, during the reign of Alfred's son Edward the Elder (899–924) and the pontificate of Sergius III

(904–11), and appears to have been the first by an archbishop of Canterbury since that of Wulfred in 814–15. Given that the visit was followed by the division of the bishoprics of Sherborne and Winchester, the creation of those at Crediton, Ramsbury and Wells, and the appointment of five new bishops, it seems likely that this significant reorganisation was the purpose behind Plegmund's mission. Claims that the archbishop was summoned to Rome either because episcopal vacancies had not been filled or because Gregory's plan for twelve bishoprics in the southern province had never been realised at all have been dismissed as later fictions.[42] By 908 Plegmund's archiepiscopate had overlapped with the pontificate of Formosus (891–6), the pope whose body was later exhumed, put on trial and mutilated, and whose acts were declared invalid, together with a rapid succession of eight further popes and one antipope, so the opportunity for some clarification was presumably appreciated on both sides.

Plegmund was the last of the Mercian archbishops with whom the West Saxon kings had to deal, for the next two primates – Athelm and Wulfhelm – were both translated to Canterbury from the firmly West Saxon see of Wells. Wulfhelm travelled to Rome in 927, presumably to receive his pallium. Whatever he experienced during that visit, it represented a meeting between two otherwise diverging societies. His king, Æthelstan (924–39), completed the unification of the English kingdoms, received tribute from the Welsh princes and launched a military expedition against Scotland, but when he sought marriages for his sisters, it was with the rulers of the Franks, Saxons and Burgundians. The continental churchmen and scholars to whom he gave patronage were from those same regions, and when he augmented his relic collection it was not with items from Italy. While Æthelstan looked to northern Europe, his Welsh contemporary Hywel Dda did make a pilgrimage to Rome in the 920s. Rome itself was then at the centre of a complex struggle for power between the popes and the secular lords of Italy and southern Francia, the flavour of which can be gleaned from noting that the pope with whom Wulfhelm dealt in 927, John X (914–28), was seized by mercenaries the following year and imprisoned in the urban fortress of Castel S. Angelo by Marozia, the so-called *senetrix* of Rome. The chronicles relate that John was either strangled or starved to death. When Marozia was herself deposed and imprisoned in 932 it was by one of her sons, while another was said to be the youth who then wore the papal tiara. The fortunes of the papacy could only rise from such depths of notoriety and relations with Britain could only come back from the brink of non-existence.

CHAPTER 2

PAPAL MONARCHS AND THEIR SUBJECTS

Like the habitual but repentant sinner who again asks for forgiveness, the history of the Church has been punctuated by attempts to start afresh with renewed vigour and commitment. In the tenth century that tendency was most clearly demonstrated in the strict observance of the Rule of St Benedict which began with the foundation of the abbey at Cluny in 910 and spread as far as the original homes of Benedictine monasticism at Subiaco and Monte Cassino. Parallel movements emerged elsewhere, including Lotharingia (Lorraine) and Bavaria. It was not until the eleventh century that this reforming spirit made a significant impact on the papacy, and that thanks to the interventions of Emperor Henry III, not least in the election of his kinsman Bruno of Eguisheim-Dagsburg as Leo IX (1048/9–54). Leo took an uncompromising line on simony and clerical marriage, both of which were thought to tarnish priestly purity, but he also gave the wider reform movement a distinctly Roman dimension by emphasising the unique rights and prerogatives of the papacy. This contributed to the decisive break between the Eastern and Western Churches in 1054. Gregory VII (1073–85) took this emphasis on the authority of the papal office to an unprecedentedly high level, claiming, among other things, the authority to depose emperors, absolve subjects from fealty to wicked lords, and judge others while himself being judged by no-one.[1] Universal jurisdiction brought the popes into conflicts the like of which had hitherto been avoided, especially with princes who traditionally invested the prelates of their region with rings and crosiers, the symbols of their offices, and expected forms of service in return. The assertion of papal authority by popes such as Gregory VII and Urban II (1088–99) meant that the cause of reform became entwined with a reaction against these lay investitures, with awkward consequences for the clerics who found themselves stuck between these two competing sources of authority.

The papacy asserted itself by means of sound administration and a coherent legal system. It was no coincidence that many of the popes of this era were themselves canon lawyers, rather than theologians, who sought to apply legalistic rigour to every aspect of ecclesiastical activity. Contemporary claims for the superiority of canon law over secular law were borne out by the flood of cases into the Roman courts, which were so overwhelmed that a system of judges-delegate was devised, in which particular cases were dealt with close to source by lawyers vested with papal authority for that specific purpose. Cardinals had oiginally occupied liturgical offices, but now acted as a council of advisers to the pope, some of them doubling as heads of the papal Chancery, which issued bulls and other documents, or of the Camera, the finance department. From the early twelfth century a cardinal also headed the Penitentiary, which dealt with serious or disputed cases of conscience and issued dispensations. Together with the judiciary, these bodies collectively formed the papal or Roman curia. The dynamism of reform was steadily quashed by administrative routine and legal wrangling, but not before the twelfth-century popes asserted themselves in one further area: appointments to benefices. In an increasing number of cases, popes declared that they were entitled to 'provide' candidates to vacant – or even yet-to-be-vacant – benefices, over the heads of cathedral chapters or the usual patrons. Again, this brought them into conflict with secular princes. In spite of all these developments, the impulse to reform had not disappeared. It merely existed elsewhere, particularly at Cîteaux – about forty miles from Cluny – where the white-clad Cistercians devised a stricter from of the monastic life, one that spread rapidly from its Burgundian roots.

Irish monks were prominent in the reform of some continental monasteries in the tenth century, but English reform began in relative isolation when King Edmund (939–46) appointed Dunstan as abbot of Glastonbury. From there the monk Æthelwold set out to found his own model monastery at Abingdon in 953. Æthelwold's community benefited from exchanges with continental houses, including Saint-Benoît-sur-Loire at Fleury, while Dunstan's taste of continental monasticism had to wait until his political enemies forced him into exile in 956–7. The cause of monastic reform advanced apace once Edgar, a former pupil of Æthelwold, became king of all England in 959. The death of Archbishop Ælfsige en route to Rome and the swift removal of his successor, Byrhthelm, created the vacancy at Canterbury which was filled by the rehabilitated Dunstan. In turn, Dunstan recommended Oswald, a product of Fleury, for the bishopric of Worcester. The reforming triumvirate was complete when Æthelwold became bishop of Winchester in 963, and achieved even greater prominence when Oswald was translated to York in 971/2. Their reform programme centred on the removal from cathedral churches of secular clergy, who enjoyed incomes from estates beyond the cathedral precincts, and the installation of monks, who had no such worldly interests. No single reforming measure was more notable than Æthelwold's expulsion of the secular canons from Winchester's Old and New Minsters and their replacement by monks from

Abingdon. This was a well-planned operation co-ordinated by the two former monks of Glastonbury and came with a strong papal dimension: Dunstan secured approval for the removal of the secular clergy when he met Pope John XII (955–64) in 960, and Æthelwold probably drafted the pope's letter of authorisation to King Edgar, who in turn ordered his men to evict the seculars in February 964.[2]

The papal connection can also be measured in terms of dedications to St Peter, which were particularly associated with the arch-reformer Æthelwold. Thus Winchester's Old Minster was rededicated to Peter, as was the Fenland monastery at Medhamstede, but whereas Swithun emerged as Winchester's preferred patron, Medhamstede was effectively forgotten and the settlement at the abbey gate became known as Peterborough. Appropriately, the abbey housed relics of St Wilfrid, that champion of all things Petrine. Relatively little is known of Dunstan's brief episcopal career in London, but William of Malmesbury claimed that it was he who installed monks from Glastonbury in the abbey of St Peter at Westminster.[3] What cannot be verified is the popular tradition that a fisherman rowed St Peter to this island site on the Thames and saw the church windows illuminated during its consecration by the apostle himself.

At Canterbury Dunstan pulled in a slightly different direction by giving the abbey of Sts Peter and Paul a new patron: Augustine, the protégé of Pope Gregory the Great. Sigeric, abbot of St Augustine's and another former monk of Glastonbury, was elected as Dunstan's archiepiscopal successor and reformed his nearby cathedral church of Christ Church in what had become the standard fashion, evicting the secular clerks and replacing them with monks. Sigeric obtained permission for this development from Pope John XV (985–96) during an unusually well-documented visit to Rome in 990.[4] He claimed to have visited twenty-three churches in two days, beginning with St Peter's and S. Maria in Sassia, the church of the English community. At the Lateran he shared a meal with the pope and received a pallium. The *Anglo-Saxon Chronicle* relates that Ælfric, Sigeric's successor at Canterbury, also travelled to Rome to receive his pallium, from Pope Gregory V (996–9).[5] Early in the next century Archbishop Ælfheah (Alphege) of Canterbury received his pallium from John XVIII (1003/4–9), but there is no record of the learned Wulfstan, archbishop of York from 1002, doing likewise. Indeed, an undated letter from the 'bishops and priests of the whole island of Britain' to an unidentified pope, written by Wulfstan, stated that the practice of English archbishops making the journey to Rome for their pallia was a recent innovation and one which had become corrupted by simony.[6]

Pilgrimage to Rome was hardly a priority for the rival warlords who faught for control of tenth-century Scotland, though Irish and Welsh sources relate that a king of Strathclyde travelled to Rome in 975 and received the tonsure.[7] From the outside, Scotland's political patchwork was exploited by waves of

Scandinavian raiders, who extended their campaigns southwards from the 980s onwards, attacking the comparatively unified England of Æthelred II (978–1013, 1014–16). Further south again, Richard I, count of Rouen, took advantage of Æthelred's misfortunes by offering assistance to these Vikings. Archbishop Sigeric may have reported as much during his visit to Rome in 990, for a papal legate, the bishop of Trevi, was in Rouen by 1 March 991, when he brokered a deal between Richard and Æthelred in which they agreed not to harbour each other's enemies.[8] By 1000 the county of Rouen had evolved into the duchy of Normandy and attracted hostile attention from the Vikings, causing the Anglo-Norman relationship to be cemented in 1002 by Æthelred's marriage to Emma of Normandy. England was still paralysed by Scandinavian invasions, in the course of which Archbishop Ælfheah was martyred at Greenwich by his drunken captors. In this time of crisis, Wulfstan of York sought to bolster the fighting spirit of his fellow-countrymen by framing sound laws and writing stirring homilies. It was not enough: when Æthelred and his son Edmund both died in 1016, Cnut, a Danish prince, was the uncontested claimant to the English throne.

As king of England from 1016 to 1035, Cnut astutely emphasised continuity over change, to the extent of marrying Æthelred's widow Emma, in spite of having a wife already. His generous ecclesiastical patronage supported those cults most favoured by his new subjects, including that of St Peter. English archbishops continued to visit Rome, Lyfing and Æthelnoth of Canterbury in *c*. 1015 and 1022 respectively, followed by Ælfric of York in 1026. According to the *Anglo-Saxon Chronicle*, Æthelnoth was particularly well received, obtaining episcopal consecration from the pope himself, in addition to a pallium.[9] Benedict VIII (1012–24) and John XIX (1024–32), the pontiffs with whom these English prelates dealt, were brothers, heads of the noble house of Tusculum (Tuscolani), who defeated rival dynasties for control of the papacy thanks to the support of successive emperors, Henry II and Conrad II. As king of both England and Denmark, Cnut wielded greater influence than any of his predecessors in either kingdom, and it was a measure of his significance that he attended Conrad's imperial coronation in Rome in 1027. He then headed to Denmark, dispatching a letter to his English subjects to assure them of his achievements on their behalf, which included the abolition of dues associated with the granting of pallia and a reduction of the tolls paid by the English in Rome.[10]

Macbeth, who reigned as king of Scots between 1040 and 1057, was so secure in his realm that he felt able to leave it in 1050 to undertake the only Roman pilgrimage made by any reigning Scottish monarch. However, the example of Cnut can be seen more clearly elsewhere in the British Isles, among that king's fellow Scandinavians. In 1028 Sihtric, king of Dublin, made his pilgrimage to Rome, as did Thorfinn (II) Sigurdson, earl of Orkney, in 1046. The parallel went further. Just as the episcopate contributed to the stability of Cnut's English regime, so it inspired Sihtric's foundation of a bishopric at Dublin and Thorfinn's of one in Orkney.

What Cnut could not influence was the English royal succession. After his death in 1035, his sons Harthacnut and Harold failed to rule jointly and died without issue, leading in 1042 to the succession of Edward, the long-exiled son of Æthelred and Emma, with Godwine, earl of Wessex, as the power behind the throne. Godwine duly doubled up as Edward's father-in-law, and when the king sought to break free from the stranglehold of his wife's family it had an ecclesiastical and, indeed, a papal dimension. The pope in question was the imperial kinsman Leo IX. At issue was the see of Canterbury, to which a relative of Earl Godwine was elected in March 1051. Edward overruled this election, appointing instead the bishop of London, Robert of Jumièges, who was swiftly dispatched to Rome to receive his pallium. According to the distinctly partisan *Vita Ædwardi regis*, it was Robert's hostility which drove the Godwine family first into rebellion and then into exile.[11] The archbishop certainly favoured papal over royal policy when he refused to consecrate Edward's candidate as bishop of London, arguing that the translation was simoniacal and had been expressly opposed by the pope. In September 1052 the tables were turned when the Godwines returned and Archbishop Robert fled. Whether Robert went to Rome and received papal support, in the manner of St Wilfrid, cannot be confirmed, but the papacy certainly rejected his replacement at Canterbury, on the grounds that the prelate in question retained the bishopric of Winchester in plurality. This was Stigand, whose precise status and authority was uncertain because he lacked papal confirmation and wore the pallium left behind by the fleeing Robert. If anything, matters became even more confused when another pallium arrived from Rome in 1058. The papacy was again in turmoil following the death of Leo IX, and a sequence of brief pontificates was punctuated by the latest attempt of the Tuscolani to monopolise the see of Peter. This time their figurehead was 'Benedict X': Stigand's pallium had been sent by an antipope.

As an alternative to the sorry saga of Stigand, the story of Anglo-papal relations in the mid-eleventh century could be told with reference to the fluctuating fortunes of a prelate who concluded his career as archbishop of York. In 1050 Ealdred, then bishop of Worcester, was sent by King Edward as one of two emissaries to Rome. Thereafter, his progress stalled because he was a supporter of the Godwines. In 1056 he added Hereford to Worcester, resigning the former when he was elected to York in 1060. The following spring he headed for Rome in a large party of pilgrims which included the bishops-elect of Hereford and Wells, whose purpose – in common with that of Ealdred himself – was to avoid potentially uncanonical consecration by Stigand. However, having retained Worcester, Ealdred was just as much a pluralist as Stigand, so Nicholas II (1059–61) refused him a pallium and deprived him of his episcopal status. Thus, after centuries of papal gratitude for unwavering English support, the pilgrims were wrongfooted by an assertion of Petrine authority. The senior layman among them was Tostig, earl of Northumberland, son of the late Earl Godwine. He had evidently brought with him the latest instalment of Romescot, and retaliated by threatening to withhold it. The English began their return journey, but had not advanced far along the Via Cassia when they were attacked by a band of robbers led by the uncle of 'Benedict X'.[12] This misfortune seemed to rebalance the relationship between the pilgrims and Pope Nicholas: Ealdred was recognised as archbishop, received his pallium and agreed to resign Worcester. While doubt still attached to Stigand, it was Ealdred who went on to anoint Kings Harold II and William I at either end of 1066.

During the long imperial minority after Emperor Henry III's death in 1056, Pope Nicholas determined that future papal elections would see the initial choice made by cardinal bishops, with their selection then confirmed by the Roman clergy, including the cardinal priests and deacons. A non-cardinal, Anselmo da Baggio, was presumably elected by this means after Nicholas's death. He became Alexander II (1061–73). That choice of papal name had far-reaching consequences, for King Malcolm III of Scotland (1058–93) and his saintly wife Margaret of Wessex are said to have called their fifth son after Pope Alexander. He became king of Scots in 1107. Nicholas and Alexander consciously presented themselves as strong papal monarchs, while 'Benedict X' was sidelined as a relic of Rome's anarchic past. One indication that this strengthened papal authority was exercised as far afield as England came in 1062, when Ermenfrid, bishop of Sion, and his colleague Hubert became the first legates to be sent across the Channel since 824. From the English side the Anglo-papal relationship retained its traditional, strongly Petrine character. The childless King Edward's reign concluded with the consecration of his abbey church of St Peter at Westminster, while his heir, Harold Godwineson, is thought to have presented hair from St Peter's beard to the secular canons at Waltham Holy Cross.

Harold's rival for the English crown, Duke William of Normandy, was no less pious, but his was a piety shaped by the reformers, whether that was expressed in the foundation of monastic houses or – taking his cue from the emperors – in his realisation that strong popes and strong princes could work in harmony with one another. William's closest clerical confidant, the Italian-born monk Lanfranc, accompanied Leo IX from France to Rome in 1050, and maintained excellent relations with Leo's successors. According to the contemporary chronicler William of Poitiers, one of those successors, Alexander, demonstrated his support for the duke at a particularly significant moment, sending him a banner to take on his English campaign in 1066.[13] If Christ's vicar really had favoured one side over the other, then it was a poor reward for King Harold's comparatively old-fashioned devotion to St Peter.

Ecclesiastical reform was not William the Conqueror's top priority when he became king of England and it was only after the death of Archbishop Ealdred in 1069 that dramatic changes were set in motion. In the spring of 1070 Cardinals Giovanni Minuzzo and Pietro Orsini travelled to Winchester, where they re-crowned the king, who was fresh from countering a Danish invasion in the north and unrest on the Welsh border. For any would-be rebels, there could be no clearer sign that William's rule in England was sanctioned by the pope and, implicitly, by God. A legatine council then deposed the pluralist Stigand from Canterbury and Winchester, together with those bishops who had accepted consecration from him. It was a very obvious and equally effective purge. Lanfranc was William's candidate for Canterbury, but he hesitated to accept the office until Pope Alexander commanded him to do so. The close relationship between pope and archbishop was most clearly in evidence when Lanfranc visited Rome in 1071 and, exceptionally, received two pallia, one of which had been habitually worn by the pope himself. William's choice for the archbishopric of York, Thomas of Bayeux, received his pallium on the same occasion. Much of our information about Thomas comes from Lanfranc's letters and concerns their rival claims for primatial authority, Canterbury's over York and York's over its province, including dioceses disputed with Canterbury. Thomas raised these matters during the archbishops' visit to Rome, but Alexander ruled that they could be resolved in England. According to Lanfranc's version of what happened next, Thomas cited Bede on Gregory the Great's vision of two equal provinces. Lanfranc countered this with a wealth of documentary material, issued by popes from Gregory to Leo IX, though its reliability has been a matter of considerable subsequent debate.[14] Thomas conceded and, by Pentecost 1072, Lanfranc's victory was complete: Thomas made a written profession and a public oath of obedience to his brother archbishop. York failed to secure the disputed Midland dioceses but at least its provincial authority was said to extend 'to the furthest limits of Scotland', while the archbishop of Canterbury was confirmed as 'primate of the whole of Britain'. The legate Hubert witnessed their agreements on behalf of the papacy.[15]

The Norman colonial elite – clerical and lay – fared exceptionally well during Alexander II's pontificate. This cosy Anglo-papal arrangement came to an abrupt end with that pope's death in 1073, for the next pontiff, Gregory VII, not only had an unprecedentedly exalted view of papal authority, but also saw no reason to seek accommodation with powerful princes. Early in his pontificate, Gregory reminded King William of the latter's subservient role as a collector of the 'dues of St Peter', which he should administer as if they were his own.[16] This was a prelude to papal demands for William to swear an oath of fealty to Gregory and for Lanfranc to present himself at the curia. The pope was rebuffed on both scores.[17] This rapid deterioration of what had previously been

a constructive relationship was far from exceptional and reflected developments elsewhere, for papal–imperial relations had completly broken down, to
the extent that Gregory and Emperor Henry IV excommunicated and deposed
one another respectively, with Henry installing the archbishop of Ravenna as
'Clement III'. While Gregory fled south, this antipope created a new regime in
Rome, complete with a full complement of cardinals. Many princes and prelates
transferred their allegiance to Clement. Lanfranc's enduring antipathy to
Gregory made him a potential supporter of the Clementine cause, but his
correspondence suggests that he was unconvinced of its legitimacy and bided
his time by adopting a position of studied neutrality.[18] For his part, William
refused to admit papal legates to England unless they were on secular business,
which left the ecclesiastical hierarchy to its own devices. It was in these
circumstances, without papal involvement, that the episcopal map was
redrawn: bishops' thrones were moved from Selsey to Chichester, Elmham to
Thetford (and later to Norwich), and (temporarily) from Lichfield to Chester,
while the dioceses of Ramsbury and Sherborne were united at Old Sarum.
England remained uncommitted at the deaths of Gregory in 1085, William in
1087, and Lanfranc in 1089.

In 1093 the conqueror's brutish and anticlerical successor William Rufus
(1087–1100) lay ill near Gloucester. Fearing the worst, he confessed his sins to
Anselm, the visiting abbot of Bec in Normandy, and nominated him to the
long-vacant see of Canterbury, forcing a crosier into his hand. The king then
recovered and found himself encumbered with an archbishop possessed of
unwavering convictions, for Anselm maintained that his primacy extended
throughout the British Isles, that he possessed legatine powers by virtue of his
office, and that papal leadership of the Church was effectively an article of faith.
Elsewhere, the tide was turning against the imperialist antipope and in favour of
Gregory VII's indirect successor Urban II, who managed to enter Rome. Anselm
found himself in a bind: his authority was limited without a pallium, but he
could not travel to Rome for one because the king failed to acknowledge Urban
as pope and therefore denied Anselm permission to leave. In the spring of 1095
William Rufus finally relented and sent two agents on a mission to Urban. They
returned with Gualterio, cardinal bishop of Albano, who presented Anselm
with his pallium. There was, however, no meeting of minds, because Anselm
believed that, as archbishop, he was a permanent papal legate, whereas
Gualterio pointed out that the manner of Anselm's appointment constituted
lay investiture with an ecclesiastical office, a practice which Urban and his
recent predecessors had expressly forbidden. By 1097 Anselm's determination
to travel to Rome was so strong that he left without the king's sanction and
remained in exile for the rest of the William Rufus's reign. According to Eadmer,
the archbishop's biographer, Urban could hardly have greeted Anselm more
fulsomely, 'as one to be venerated almost as our equal', because he was

'apostolic patriarch' of the *alter orbis* that was the British Isles.[19] This seemed to confirm and even augment the status which Anselm believed he enjoyed.

Urban died at the end of July 1099 and the electors, including Gualterio of Albano, chose a sometime legate to France and Spain as Paschal II (1099–1118). Early in his pontificate, Paschal sent Guy de Bourgogne, archbishop of Vienne, as legate to England, but the latter appears to have abandoned his mission within a matter of months.[20] Anselm moved to France, so was able to make a swift return to England within weeks of William Rufus's sudden death on 2 August 1100 and Henry I's seizure of the crown. Word of these events appears to have reached Paschal by means of the king's eldest brother Robert of Normandy, who launched an invasion of England in July 1101. Paschal dispatched an embassy headed by the cardinal bishop of Tusculum, but was probably motivated less by any hope of composiing dynastic differences and more by the prospect of collecting Peter's Pence, the post-Conquest term for Romescot. The surviving evidence suggests that little was achieved. Meanwhile, on the matter of investitures Anselm stood firm and would permit neither himself nor any other English prelate to accept investiture from the king or to perform homage to Henry for their estates, the possession of which made them powers in the land and did not involve cure of souls. Embassies shuttled to and fro in the hope of breaking this deadlock, Anselm's own return to Rome resulting in a second period of exile. Finally, in 1107, Henry surrendered his claim to invest bishops with their rings and crosiers, providing that he nominated them in the first place and received their homage. Paschal had no hesitation in accepting this compromise and that was how matters stood when Anselm died.

By 1109 Henry of England had negotiated the marriage of his daughter Matilda to the uncrowned emperor Henry V, though the union itself did not follow until 1114. In the meantime, Paschal renewed his opposition to lay investiture and the emperor appeared in his Italian domains with a large army. A deal was hammered out whereby Henry renounced his claim to invest, in exchange for imperial coronation by the pope and dominion over all Christendom, but the terms were so one-sided that Paschal refused to crown him when they met in St Peter's on 12 February 1111. In a scene witnessed by David the Scot, a future bishop of Bangor, Paschal was taken prisoner and forced to agree another set of terms.[21] Only then was the emperor crowned. His actions surely emboldened Henry of England, who irritated the pope across a range of issues, including refusal to permit his archbishops to travel to Rome for their pallia. In 1115 Paschal relented and sent Anselm's eponymous nephew, the abbot of S. Saba in Rome with a pallium for Ralph d'Escures of Canterbury, together with a list of grievances directed towards the king. Among the outstanding issues was the consecration of Thurstan, Henry's candidate for York, who refused to make a profession of obedience to Archbishop Ralph.

If Thurstan went to Rome he might be consecrated by Paschal, who was supportive of him, and a point of principle would have been lost. In 1117 Ralph was permitted to go there and explain the matter in person. He arrived to find that Paschal had fled southwards because the emperor, accompanied by his English wife, was back in the city.

At Paschal's death his cardinals turned unanimously to the long-serving papal chancellor Giovanni Caetani, but the emperor reacted swiftly to any potential papal resurgence and Gelasius II (1118–19) was driven from Rome, where another imperialist antipope was installed. The weakness of Gelasius's position was reflected in papal appeals on behalf of the still unconsecrated Thurstan, which went unheeded by Archbishop Ralph. There was nothing weak about the next pope, Calixtus II (1119–24), chosen by the nine cardinals who were with Gelasius when he died at Cluny. This was Guy de Bourgogne, the archbishop of Vienne who may or may not have crossed the Channel in 1100. Calixtus belonged to the ruling elite of Burgundy and its neighbours, his kinship network extending to Scotland and, in the form of Henry I and Matilda of Scotland's offspring Matilda and William (d. 1120), to the Holy Roman Empire and England. Calixtus was therefore not afraid of kings, as he demonstrated in a meeting with Henry at Gisors in 1119; he could mediate between monarchs, as he proved in the Anglo-French peace of 1120; and he was well-placed to strike a deal with the emperor over investitures, as he did in the Concordat of Worms (1122). The Church's dividend from his ability to deal with the secular world was the restoration of the papacy to Rome. Thurstan was the one outstanding English beneficiary of this pontificate, remaining with the pope from the latter's election until March 1120. During that period he was consecrated by Calixtus before the English bishops were able raise objections and obtained letters instructing the Scottish bishops to profess obedience to him. After seven years Henry relented and Archbishop Thurstan finally entered York. The dispute with Canterbury nevertheless remained. When the next primate, William de Corbeil, went to Rome for his pallium in 1123 Thurstan was of the party. Canterbury's claim to primacy over York was examined on that occasion and found wanting. Missions from Rome to England took place regularly throughout this relatively brief pontificate, but they were not necessarily paralleled by pilgrimages from England to Rome, for William of Malmesbury assures his readers that Englishmen who made two pilgrimages to the considerably nearer destination of St Davids could receive the same benefits and blessing as those who made one journey to Rome.[22] Towards the end of his life, Calixtus assented to the marriage of Henry's rebellious nephew William Clito to Sibylla of Anjou, a union that threatened Henry's position in Normandy from two directions, because the young man was based in Flanders. This threat could only be neutralised by a papal annulment, to which end Henry lifted his opposition to legates operating in England. The calculation worked perfectly, for Calixtus wasted no time in confirming the annulment once it was recommended to him by his new representative.

December 1124 witnessed one of the most extraordinary episodes in the history of the papacy. Calixtus II died; his successor had been elected unanimously and announced his papal name when the Roman patrician Roberto Frangipane broke into the cardinals' assembly and insisted on the election of his candidate. Celestine II resigned and a new ballot secured Frangipane's objective: the bishop of Ostia became Honorius II (1124–30). Honorius was a man of genuine ability, rather than merely the puppet of a faction-leader, and was ably represented in England by Cardinal Giovanni da Crema, who exercised greater authority than any legate since the post-Conquest mission of 1070. He travelled widely: to Llandaff, in connection with Bishop Urban's desire to expand his diocese at the expense of Hereford and St Davids, and to Roxburgh, where he met the Scots king David I (1124–53). In the course of Honorius's pontificate David failed in his bid to have St Andrews recognised as a metropolitan see. On the other hand, Thurstan of York finally persuaded Rome to overrule Canterbury's claim to primacy.

Another dramatic contest followed in 1130, when two rival popes were elected within a matter of hours: Innocent II and Anacletus II. Backed by the Frangipani dynasty, Anacletus controlled much of Rome, while Innocent enjoyed widespread support beyond the Alps and went into exile in France. Thus it was that Innocent's council at Reims remitted the Llandaff case to judges-delegate in 1131. Anacletus was briefly succeeded by another claimant in 1138, but it was Innocent's longevity that allowed him to be regarded by posterity as the legitimate pope (1130–43), thereby consigning 'Anacletus II' and 'Victor IV' to the annals of antipopery. Western Christendom was still effectively divided when Henry I of England died in 1135, leaving a similar rivalry between his daughter, the widowed empress Matilda, and his nephew, Stephen of Blois. At Henry's death Matilda was in Anjou and Stephen at Boulogne, so it was Stephen who crossed the Channel and made good his claim to the English crown, with vital support coming from his brother Henry of Blois, bishop of Winchester. Crucially, Innocent accepted Stephen as England's legitimate king.

Innocent reinforced his own position by creating over seventy cardinals and by convening the Second Lateran Council (1139). Among the former was Albéric, abbot of Vézelay, who became cardinal bishop of Ostia in 1138. Albéric was immediately sent as legate to England. During a relatively brief visit he brokered a peace with David I and held a legatine council at which Theobald, abbot of Bec, was elected to the archbishopric of Canterbury, a move designed to thwart the ambitions of Henry of Blois, who had designs on Canterbury or, as an alternative, wanted his Winchester see raised to metropolitical status. Albéric then returned to Rome and attended the ecumenical council.

That assembly heard Matilda's appeal, which argued that Stephen was a perjurer and a usurper and should therefore be deposed, but Innocent had no pressing need to decide against him, so allowed matters to drift. Meanwhile, Henry of Blois was compensated with a standing legation in England, which effectively undermined Archbishop Theobald's authority but was not intended to imply papal support for Stephen. Indeed, Anglo-papal relations were seriously strained in 1139–40 by Stephen's arrest of the bishops of Ely, Lincoln and Salisbury. In 1141 events took a different turn when Stephen was captured in battle. The legate Henry thereupon negotiated with Matilda, 'lady of England and Normandy', and made plans for her coronation. Archbishop Theobald, the potential consecrator, refused to renounce his allegiance to Stephen, so Henry sought advice from Innocent and was ordered to remain loyal to his brother. Sure enough, Stephen was released from captivity and restored to power before the end of the year, justifying the pope's caution. Towards the end of the pontificate, Stephen's interference in the election of a new archbishop of York became the source of protracted difficulties with Rome. His intruded archbishop was William Fitzherbert, who may have been no more or less worldly than many another Anglo-Norman prelate, but who failed to meet the standards of the reformed monastic communities which had recently been established in Yorkshire. The Cistercian abbots of Rievaulx and Fountains were among William's opponents when the case was heard in Rome. Innocent referred the matter to judges-delegate, including Henry of Blois, only for their authority to lapse when the pope died in September 1143.

It was during the brief pontificate of Celestine II (1143–4) that the English theologian Robert Pullen became known in curial Rome, thanks to his bishop, Ascelin of Rochester, objecting to Pullen's absence at the Parisian schools. By the time Pullen presented his appeal Celestine had been succeeded by Lucius II (1144–5) and it seems to have been Lucius who made Pullen a cardinal and appointed him as chancellor of the Church. The first English cardinal was therefore in a position to influence papal policy towards his nation, so can potentially be glimpsed behind the English legation of Cardinal Imar in 1145.

The Cistercian Eugenius III (1145–53) was a pope on a misson, to reform the Church along the lines established by his mentor Bernard of Clairvaux. To this end he convened a council at Reims in 1148, his Roman flock having driven him into exile. This was too good an opportunity to wash English ecclesiastical linen in public, so Stephen sought to counter any difficulties by sending three 'safe' bishops to Reims, while denying safe-conducts to all the others. His strategy failed: Archbishop Theobald defied the king and Eugenius suspended those bishops who failed to follow Theobald's heroic example. The battle for reform was nowhere more apparent than in the diocese of York. Eugenius had already suspended William Fitzherbert from the archbishopric. Now Fitzherbert's supporters attacked the Cistercians at Fountains, which was the pope's cue to deprive him of his office altogether. Meanwhile, Stephen and his brother Henry sought to influence the election of a new bishop of Lincoln, their first choice being Stephen's illegitimate son Gervase, abbot of Westminster. Eugenius blocked this. In these circumstances it is not surprising that Eugenius seemed to be interested in the proposal that St Davids become an archbishopric: St Davids was not Winchester and, more significantly, its bishop, Bernard, was not Henry of Blois. However, Bernard died and the campaign lapsed.

In 1150 Eugenius returned to Rome, from where he dispatched a legate to Ireland. Cardinal Giovanni Paparoni's route took him via Northumbria, which was then ruled by a son of David I. David consciously built up the episcopate as a buttress to his regime and the legate was persuaded to lobby for St Andrews being raised to metropolitical status. Again, nothing came of this, though when Paparoni reached Ireland and presided over the Synod of Kells (1152) he did divide the Irish Church into four provinces – Armagh (the primatial see), Dublin, Cashel and Tuam – thereby freeing Ireland from the influence of Canterbury. Distance did not make the pope look any more favourably on Stephen of England, who sought papal permission for the coronation of his legitimate son Eustace, to indicate the intended line of succession, and the bishopric of Durham for his nephew Hugh du Puiset. According to the contemporary historian Henry of Huntingdon, Stephen's perjury prevented Eustace from inheriting the crown, though this was not necessarily the view taken among the pope's advisers, while Archbishop Murdac of York was so resolutely opposed to Hugh's election that he excommunicated the Durham chapter and appealed to Rome.[23] Eugenius died in July 1153. At least in the secular sphere his temporising bore fruit, the English succession being fixed in November so that Stephen retained the crown for life, after which Matilda's son Henry, duke of Normandy, would succeed.

During his brief seventeen-month pontificate (1153–4) Anastasius IV's dealings with the British Isles were centred on York, for hardly had he restored Fitzherbert to the archbishopric than the latter was allegedly murdered and his successor, Roger de Pont l'Évêque, appeared in Rome to claim his pallium and forestall further controversy. It did not create much in the way of regional variation when Anastasius settled another source of contention by consecrating Hugh du Puiset as bishop of Durham. At the pope's death in December 1154 the cardinals swiftly elected the man who seemed to be his most direct replacement, for Anastasius had been abbot of Saint-Ruf, Avignon, and his successor, Adrian IV (1154–9), was a member of that community of Augustinian canons regular. It fell to Adrian to crown Frederick Barbarossa in 1155 but, once crowned, this emperor proved to be an unreliable protector and the pope was forced to come to terms with his menacing southern neighbour, William I of Sicily. Western Christendom had no shortage of strong rulers, for

Henry of Normandy succeeded to the Angevin Empire, including England, in October 1154. Within the next four years he received the homage of the young king Malcolm IV of Scotland (1153–65), redrew the border between their kingdoms in favour of England, and undertook two campaigns against the Welsh, all within the span of Pope Adrian's relatively brief reign. No action was taken against Ireland at that stage, for although Adrian's bull *Laudabiliter* (1155) assumed that the pope was its overlord and gave Henry permission to invade and hold it in fee from the papacy, it was explained to the king that the provisions of the purportedly fourth-century Donation of Constantine regarding papal overlordship of islands might apply just as easily in his English realm as it did to Ireland, so it was wiser not to invoke them at all.[24] Adrian's relations with the British Isles were a minor matter in comparison with the pressures he faced from the emperor and from Sicily, so the fact that he was the only English pope to date could reasonably be regarded as incidental.[25]

Adrian died at Anagni on 1 September 1159. Six days later the cardinals emerged from their deliberations with both a pope, the former chancellor Orlando Bandinelli, who took the name Alexander III (1159–81), and a pro-imperial antipope, another 'Victor IV'. The emperor maintained his opposition to Alexander by means of further antipopes, until the two men were formally reconciled at Venice in 1177. In the meantime, such was the strength of imperial control over Italy that Alexander was obliged to seek protection from Louis VII of France. Logically, Henry II of England (1154–89) might have sided with the imperialists, but he had more to gain from keeping the contending parties guessing which way he might jump. For his part Alexander needed English support and sought it in 1161 by canonising King Edward (the Confessor), a cause that had been rejected by Innocent II in less fraught circumstances. Two years later, the newly installed archbishop of Canterbury, Thomas Becket, was invited by Alexander to present a petition for his predecessor Anselm's canonisation, indicating yet more papal favour for the English.[26] It is not entirely clear what happened to this cause thereafter, because Anglo-papal relations were swiftly overtaken by the saga of Becket's high road to martyrdom, though Anselm's feast was celebrated at Canterbury by c. 1165.[27]

As a former royal chancellor, Becket lacked his predecessor's otherworldliness, but was nevertheless inspired by Anselm when he took a stand against the king's assaults on ecclesiastical liberties. It was a lonely stand, for his brother bishops had no appetite for a fight and Becket soon appealed for papal support.[28] In January 1164 he joined the other bishops in assenting to Henry's Constitutions of Clarendon, which endeavoured to set limits on ecclesiastical jurisdiction, including appeals to the papal curia.[29] Rejecting his own action in this episode as not merely weak, but sinful, Becket imposed penance on himself, fled into exile and sent the pope an account of what had happened.[30] Alexander duly condemned ten of the sixteen royal articles, but was not prepared to antagonise Henry by supporting Becket. It did not follow that Henry was beyond discomfiting the pope, which he did by threatening to ally with the emperor. In 1165 his ambassadors to the imperial diet at Würzburg were said to have gone so far as to swear that Henry would transfer his ecclesiastical allegiance to the imperialist antipope. At this point Alexander journeyed from France to Rome, from where he was soon forced to retreat further south, to Campania. His physical distance from the later stages of the Becket dispute meant that he was never up to date with its latest developments. At Becket's request, he conceded an English legation to the archbishop, who interpreted this as the authority to excommunicate his enemies. Learning of this, Alexander suspended the legation for a limited period, but as soon as the deadline was reached, in March 1169, Becket issued further excommunications, with the promise of more to follow. Alexander then suspended the excommunications, only for Becket to reimpose them as soon as the pope's latest action expired. With subordinates like that, who needed schismatics?

The deadlock was finally broken by Henry, who sought to have his eldest son crowned king, confirming the royal succession in the very manner that had eluded King Stephen. Since 1161 Henry had possessed papal letters permitting the archbishop of York to perform such a ceremony, which was what Roger de Pont l'Évêque did at Westminster on 14 June 1170. Becket was outraged and wanted revenge on all the English bishops who had participated in the coronation. To that end he sought to hasten his return to England by meeting Henry in Touraine and making peace with him. There followed another pause, while Becket waited for appropriate authorisation from Alexander, but news that Archbishop Roger, together with the bishops of London and Salisbury, had gone to visit Henry in Normandy quickened Becket's resolve and he arrived in Canterbury on 2 December. The papal contribution to this sequence of events was necessarily limited, though it may be noted that the bishop of London, Gilbert Foliot, revived Gregory the Great's original scheme by suggesting that his own bishopric might replace Canterbury as the primatial see, thereby demoting and isolating Becket. It was February 1171 before Alexander heard of Becket's murder in his cathedral on 29 December. His reprisals were thorough.[31] The excommunicated king was genuinely contrite, but also managed to negotiate favourable terms before making his submission to the papal legates, at Avranches in May 1172.[32] The martyr's canonisation followed at Segni on 21 February 1173. This concluded the Becket episode, but it was not the last that Alexander heard from the tempestuous house of Anjou, for pope and king soon clashed over Henry's desire to have his illegitimate son Geoffrey confirmed as bishop of Lincoln and again after Henry asked Cardinal Ugo Pierleoni to annul his marriage to Eleanor of Aquitaine.

Pierleoni's legation took him to not only to England, but also to Scotland, where William 'the Lion' succeeded to the throne in 1165 and was among those select enemies of Henry II to whom the Plantagenet king happened not to be closely related. In 1174 William was taken prisoner and forced to pay homage to Henry. The ecclesiastical implication of this was that the Scottish Church was expected to submit itself to that of England. However humiliating, this might have been a relatively straightforward act, had the archbishops of Canterbury and York not quarrelled publicly over which of them should receive the submission. The Scots took advantage of this division to secure from Alexander the bull *Super anxietatibus* (30 July 1176), which suspended York's jurisdiction north of the border.[33] Alexander's last years also witnessed the opening of what turned out to be a lengthy tussle over the bishopric of St Andrews, between King William's candidate, Hugh, and the chapter's choice, Master John the Scot. Both claimants appealed to the pope, who consistently supported John. Alexander appointed the archbishop of York as legate in Scotland and warned William that the recent bull could easily be reversed. Under papal instruction, Archbishop Roger of York readily excommunicated the king and placed Scotland under interdict around the time of Alexander's death on 30 August 1180.

Alexander III's pontificate was the third longest in papal history to that date and had seen so many disputes involving secular princes that there was ample need of a contrasting character to succeed him. The cardinals elected their dean, Ubaldo Allucingoli, who came with a welcome reputation as a conciliator. As Lucius III (1181–5) he lifted the Scottish interdict in March 1182, supplementing this with the gift of a golden rose to King William. Elsewhere, Lucius gained a firm Irish supporter by consecrating John Cumin as archbishop of Dublin and readily sent a pallium to the Cistercian Baldwin of Forde, who was archbishop of Canterbury from 1185. Lucius wanted to move the papal agenda away from the problems that had afflicted the previous pontificate and towards an emphasis on rooting out Cathar, Waldensian and other heresies. He was, however, constrained by secular forces. In 1182 the commune forced him out of Rome, so Cumin and the Scottish envoys had to travel further south, to Velletri, in order to meet him. Scenting weakness, the emperor asserted himself in Italy, which meant that papal–imperial relations had deteriorated once more by the time of Lucius's death.

Hohenstaufen occupation of the Papal States continued throughout the next pontificate (1185–7), which the Milanese pope Urban III spent mostly at Verona. It was there that John the Scot revived his claim to St Andrews and there also that agents for Archbishop Baldwin and the monks of Christ Church battled over the primate's papally-sanctioned scheme to found a collegiate church at Hackington, outside the walls of Canterbury. Urban was the pope who sent a crown for the projected Angevin kingdom of Ireland and a cardinal to place it on the head of Prince John, though the request had originally been made to Pope Alexander. In the event, Henry II decided against a coronation and the legate, Ottaviano, was back in Italy in time to elect Gregory VIII at Ferrara in October 1187 and Clement III (1187–91) at Pisa two months later.

Twelfth-century bishops of Rome had tended not to be Romans by birth. Clement III bucked that trend and negotiated the return of the curia to his native city. He revived the cardinalate by creating thirty ecclesiastical princes in as many months, among them Alessio, a former legate to Scotland, whose promotion coincided with the king's candidate emerging victorious in the dispute over St Andrews. When Clement looked beyond the Alps, it was for potential crusaders, so his priority was to secure peace between the kings of France and England, to which end Cardinal Giovanni Conti was sent on legation in 1189. Richard I's succession to the Angevin realms in July that year meshed perfectly with this scheme. In addition to preaching the crusade, Conti arranged a compromise solution to Archbishop Baldwin's dispute with the Christ Church monks, and judged the validity of Prince John's marriage to Isabella of Gloucester, to which Baldwin had objected on the grounds of consanguinity.[34] The legate's mission had an unexpected outcome in that the frustrated archbishop himself took the cross and died at Acre the following year.

For most of Celestine III's pontificate (1191–8) King Richard was either on crusade, imprisoned by his Christian enemies, or campaigning in France. Rulers from the emperor downwards had no fear of this aged pontiff and his attempt to send Cardinals Ottaviano and Giordano di Ceccano into Normandy, never mind to England, was thwarted. He fared better in appointing the archbishop of Cashel as legate in Ireland, and secured his place in Scottish history by issuing the bull *Cum universi* (13 March 1192), by which the Scottish Church was declared to be a 'special daughter' of the Holy See, immediately subject to the pope, with no intermediary.[35] Only the see of Galloway remained within the province of York. Relations between England and Rome were initially entrusted to William de Longchamp, bishop of Ely, who doubled as the king's chancellor and the pope's legate, but he fled when Richard's illegitimate half-brother Geoffrey returned to England as the papally authorised archbishop of York. A similar combination of secular and ecclesiastical responsibilities was assumed by the next archbishop of Canterbury, Hubert Walter, who served as resident legate from 1195. One thing remained unchanged in Walter's time: the sheer quantity of curial business generated by Archbishop Geoffrey, who was a master of the art of making enemies. By 1194 this prelate had been the source of so many appeals to Rome that Celestine played his Scottish card again and declared York to be under his direct protection.

After one of the oldest popes, the cardinals elected the youngest among them as his successor. Some of the electors had dealt directly with Henry II, particularly in Normandy, but their choice, Lotario dei conti di Segni, had already ventured as far as Becket's shrine at Canterbury during his time as a student in Paris. Raised to the cardinalate by his kinsman Clement III, Lotario was only thirty-seven at the time of his election. He became Innocent III

(1198–1216), the pope who – more than any other – managed to put the theory of papal monarchy into practice.

Innocent III's overarching policy was a new crusade, the fourth, which involved a temporary reunion of the Eastern and Western Churches, but only at the cost of westerners sacking Constantinople in 1204. Rather than join the crusade, King Richard's successor, John (1199–1206), chose to continue his brother's war against Philippe II of France. By the time they called truce in 1206, John had lost most of his continental inheritance. From 1201 to 1203 Innocent was represented in Scotland, Ireland and the Isles by Cardinal Giovanni di Salerno, who also dealt as best he could with English problems, such as Archbishop Geoffrey's continuing dispute with the York chapter. Innocent preferred to have a permanent representative on the ground and a vacancy at Canterbury provided his opportunity to realise this. The man he chose to fill it was his Parisian contemporary Stephen Langton, who had remained at the university, so was certainly not one of John's tame clerics. Innocent consecrated Langton in June 1207, to which John responded by seizing the archiepiscopal estates and exiling the monks of Christ Church. Innocent then raised the stakes further: if the king could not be persuaded to accept Langton, then the bishops of London, Ely and Worcester were to publish an interdict in England, under the terms of which the administration of sacraments was limited to the baptism of infants and confession of the dying.[36] John remained obdurate, so the interdict was imposed in March 1208, after which the three bishops fled abroad and their property was confiscated by the Crown. Other bishoprics and abbacies went unfilled but nevertheless acquired income from their estates, income that went into the king's exchequer, giving him no incentive to negotiate. Further talks came to nothing and the king's excommunication was published in November 1209. After another twenty months a papal agent, Pandolfo Verraccio – whose name has been anglicised as 'Pandulf' or 'Pandulph' – met John at Northampton, but again no progress was made towards healing the breach.

It was 1212 before the tempo finally increased, with Innocent once more taking the initiative. The Scots and Welsh were papally absolved from their allegiance to the excommunicate king and Innocent authorised a French invasion of England. Philippe obliged and prepared to cross the Channel. Suddenly John had good reason to talk. Innocent's terms remained unchanged and he gave the king a deadline of 1 June 1213 by which to comply.[37] With the French invasion imminent, the nuncio Pandolfo returned, landing at Dover on 13 May. His arrival sparked the most extraordinary turn of events. First John announced his acceptance of Innocent's terms; then, two days later, he surrendered to 'God, the apostles Peter and Paul, the Holy Roman Church our mother, and to our lord pope Innocent III and his catholic successors the kingdoms of England and Ireland, with all rights and appurtenances for the omission of our sins and of all our race, living and dead.'[38] The twist was that he immediately received them back as papal fiefs, swearing to perform homage to the pope when circumstances permitted. This unexpected move came at a cost of 1,000 marks per annum – 700 for England, 300 for Ireland – in tribute to his new overlord, but John calculated that it was a price worth paying to acquire the most influential ally in Christendom, while wrongfooting his French enemy. Innocent declared that John now held his kingdoms by 'a more exalted and surer title than before'.[39] The king was formally absolved on 20 July and made his promised oath of fealty in St Paul's Cathedral on 3 October, placing his hands between those of Innocent's new legate, Cardinal Nicola de Romanis, and undertaking to 'help in maintaining and defending, to the utmost of my power, against all men, the patrimony of Saint Peter'.[40]

So effective was John's *coup* that near neighbours attempted to emulate his example, with differing results. Finding himself under attack from Norway, Rǫgnvaldr, king of Man and the Isles, first sought secular protection by becoming John's liegeman. After the latter's death he played the papal card, requesting that the Isle of Man be accepted as a papal fief. For what it was worth, he received such protection from Honorius III in 1223. Two decades later, Dafydd, the self-styled prince of Wales, tried to pull off the same trick, his oppressor being Henry III of England. The pope of the day, Innocent IV, had too great a need of English taxes to fund his anti-imperial ventures and of English benefices with which to reward his followers, so Dafydd's attempt to become a papal vassal was frustrated.

Nicola de Romanis remained in England until June 1214. Thus Pandolfo was the principal papal representative in the realm when John attempted to execute another pro-papal coup, by taking the cross in March 1215. Although there was no tangible sign of him going anywhere, it would certainly have helped him had his rebellious barons swallowed the bait and themselves gone on crusade. In May they renounced their fealty to John, offered the crown to Louis, the French king's heir, and drew up the articles known as Magna Carta, the first of which declared the freedom of the English Church, by which they meant freedom from interference by the monarch.[41] Accompanied by Pandolfo, John played for time by assenting to the charter at Runnymede on 15 June. It took approximately two months for communications to travel between Rome and England, so it was 24 August before Innocent aided his vassal by declaring the charter to be null and void, though he had excommunicated the rebels in the meantime.[42] Langton refused to publish the excommunication and was consequently suspended from office.

Thereafter, a number of leading clerics – Irish and Scottish, as well as English – left for the Fourth Lateran Council, Pandolfo attending as the king's representative and as bishop-elect of Norwich. In contrast to their previous dealings, there was now complete agreement between king and pope over appointments in the English Church: Innocent confirmed Archbishop Langton's suspension and quashed the election of Langton's brother Simon by the chapter of York, favouring instead the king's candidate Walter de Gray.[43] Far from being free of royal interference, as Langton and the barons asserted, the king was now a vassal and favoured son of the pope, so could interfere more easily than ever before. If John could do no wrong in Innocent's eyes, it was not merely because he appeared to be a changed character, but because the French still defied the papal will, as did Alexander II, king of Scots since 1214, who actively encouraged the ongoing English rebellion. Though he did not live to know it, Innocent effectively outwitted them all: his next legate to England, Cardinal Guala Bicchieri, evaded French attempts to block his mission and, on 29 May 1216, pronounced sentences of excommunication on Alexander, Louis and the rebels. Innocent died on 16 July.

The legate Guala was inevitably among the absentees when Honorius III (1216–27) was elected at Perugia, and the suspended Langton was unlikely to have been in the vicinity of Innocent III's deathbed, though he was in Italy. The new pope came with vast curial experience, having served as *camerlengo* and vice-chancellor, heads of the Camera and the Chancery respectively. Honorius's initial priority was the crusade launched in 1217. This determined the relative ease with which he crowned Emperor Frederick II in 1220, even though Frederick had inherited Sicily from his mother, so potentially threatened the Papal States from two directions. Like Sicily, England was a papal fief and received close attention from the curia, doubly so from October 1216 when King John died, leaving his nine-year-old son, Henry III (1216–72), as a papal ward. This combination of circumstances made the legate the most powerful man in England. Guala's commission was confirmed by Honorius and in 1218 he was succeeded by the returning Pandolfo, who led the minority government alongside the justiciar and the bishop of Winchester.

Innocent and his successors exercised a 'plenitude' of power over the Universal Church, much of which they gained at the expense of bishops who had previously acknowledged no superiors in the governing of their dioceses. So much legal, administrative and financial weight now attached to the papacy – not to mention pastoral responsibilities across Western Christendom – that the burden had to be shared, whether with the cardinals, who were now recognised as a 'college', or with legates *a latere*, who were sent 'from the side' of the pope and exercised quasi-papal powers in specific regions. Lower-status nuncios were dispatched more routinely and concentrated on financial matters, including the collection of Peter's Pence. In the course of the thirteenth century popes took further steps to secure control over appointments to bishoprics, as when Innocent IV (1243–54) reserved all German appointments to himself.

Alexander IV (1254–61) took this tendency further, insisting that newly-elected abbots receive papal confirmation from him personally, which Simon of Luton and Richard of Ware did following their abbatial elections at Bury St Edmunds and Westminster respectively. These popes also acquired a new type of patronage when universities began competing with one another for papal recognition of their rights and privileges, the only insular example from this period being Oxford, which received confirmation of its statutes from Innocent IV in 1254. It could be argued that the bureaucratisation and centralisation of the Church reflected the work of God in that it was a means of bringing order out of chaos, but it came at a price, whether in the annual tribute imposed on papal fiefs, the supposedly regular collection of Peter's Pence, or the subsidies and clerical taxation levied to meet the demands of extraordinary expenditure, which all too frequently involved hostility towards the secular powers of Christendom. This burden increased as the thirteenth century advanced, and so did the reactions against it, the earliest and most far-reaching of which was the rapid growth of the mendicant orders – Franciscans and Dominicans – which offered a striking alternative to the corporate wealth of the monasteries and had no property that could be taxed.

For Gregory IX (1227–41) monarchy of the papal variety meant leading a series of interconnected crusades, against infidels, heretics and the emperor. With Henry III having attained his majority, England was of marginally less significance to the papacy, and it was the king who requested a new legate *a latere* in 1236. Gregory obliged by sending Cardinal Oddone di Monferrato – otherwise referred to as Otto – whose previous experience as a nuncio in England and skill as a conciliator helped to engineer an Anglo-Scottish peace. Following the extension of his mandate, he visited Scotland in 1239. The most awkward Anglo-papal disputes were still generated by episcopal elections, as examples from this pontificate illustrate. In the case of Richard le Grant, Gregory 'provided' the king's candidate to Canterbury and quashed that of the monks, but in others, such as at Winchester in the 1240s, the pope confirmed the monks' candidate, forcing the king to back down. The most extreme case of papal intervention in an insular election followed the death of Archbishop Richard in 1231, when Gregory quashed three capitular elections before settling on the scholarly Edmund of Abingdon.

Just fifteen years later Edmund, who died in 1240, was declared a saint. Innocent III had ensured that the making of saints was strictly controlled by the curia. An English case established a new, higher standard, the original dossier of the miracles of Gilbert of Sempringham, a cleric from Lincolnshire, being rejected and Innocent canonising him only after a more thorough investigation had taken place.[44] The second Englishman to meet the standard was Bishop Wulfstan of Worcester (d. 1095), canonised in 1203. A geographical survey reveals that two-fifths of the individuals canonised between that point and the papal interregnum of 1268–71 were British or Irish by birth or association, rising to half among the saints made by Honorius III (Hugh of Lincoln, Laurence O'Toole, Alexander III's legate in Ireland, and William Fitzherbert of York), Alexander IV (the pilgrim William of Perth, murdered in Kent on his way to the Holy Land) and Urban IV (Richard of Wyche). Even the eighth-century bishop Vergilius of Salzburg – one of Gregory IX's new saints – was of Irish birth. The total may have included Queen Margaret of Scotland (d. 1093) and would have included Bishop Osmund of Salisbury (d. 1099) if the enquiry into his miracles commissioned by Gregory had reached a definite conclusion.

At Pope Gregory's death in August 1241 the former papal auditor (judge) Robert of Somercotes (in Lincolnshire) was the most junior of the cardinals in Rome. With imperialist forces threatening the city, the senator of Rome sought to hasten an election by locking the cardinals *cum clave* ('with a key': hence 'conclave') in the ancient Septizodium. A number of cardinals fell ill, though Robert was the only one to die in the enclosure, before the election of Goffredo da Castiglione as Celestine IV. Celestine himself survived only seventeen days, after which there was electoral deadlock until June 1243. Hardly had the Ligurian Sinibaldo Fieschi taken the name Innocent IV than imperial pressure forced him out of Rome. Much to the satisfaction of France's crusading king Louis IX, the curia settled at Lyon and remained there until after the death of Frederick II in 1250. Innocent's Council of Lyon (1245) was convened with a view to deposing the emperor, but the western Europeans who dominated this assembly had other agendas. In the case of the English it was to complain about papal taxation and the rising tide of non-resident Italians enjoying the fruits of English benefices. Robert Grosseteste, the erudite bishop of Lincoln, raised these concerns to a higher level by addressing the council on what such practices implied for the papal office itself. If the pope placed administration, taxation and the interests of his family before pastoral care, Grosseteste argued, Christians were bound to oppose him.[45] Innocent did not change his ways. In 1250 he granted Henry III a tax of one-tenth on English clerical incomes in order to fund a crusade. The king's envoy to the pope on that occasion was his brother Richard, earl of Cornwall. A personal connection having been established, Richard was subsequently invited by Innocent to invade Sicily: if he could oust Frederick's sons, the kingdom would be his. Richard declined the offer, but Henry rashly accepted it on behalf of his ten-year-old son Edmund.

After Robert of Somercotes, the next English cardinal was the Spanish-educated Cistercian known as John of Toledo. His first conclave occurred at Naples in December 1254 and elected Alexander IV. Although Alexander belonged to the same dynasty as Innocent III and Gregory IX, he inherited Innocent IV's unrealistic hope that the Plantagenets could save the papacy from Hohenstaufen power in Italy. Thus Henry readily undertook not merely to invade Sicily, but to pay for the papacy's earlier campagns there, all with a view to acquiring a kingdom for young Edmund. It came to nothing, just like attempts to get the earl of Cornwall elected emperor or, at least, as senator of Rome. Such miscalculations came at a price: by means of the Provisions of Oxford (1258) Henry was forced to share power with his baronial critics, led by Simon de Montfort, earl of Leicester. The barons effectively saved Henry from himself by asking Alexander for a series of concessions, including mitigation of the Sicilian commitment. Alexander conceded nothing and cut his losses by cancelling the grant of Sicily to Edmund. One of the pope's last acts was to absolve Henry from the oath he had taken in relation to the power-sharing arrangement.[46] At least in theory, this restored the king's untrammelled authority and ensured that any baronial opposition counted as rebellion.

In 1261 seven cardinals who endured a three-month conclave at Viterbo before assenting to the election of the patriarch of Jerusalem, Jacques Pantaléon, as Urban IV (1261–4). Montfort tried and failed to persuade Urban to reverse Henry's absolution, though the practical limitations on papal support for the king were evident when the papal legate to England, Cardinal Guy Foulquois, could get no nearer than Boulogne. In his absence, Foulquois was elected to the papacy by a college that still included John of Toledo. After suffering a string of rebuffs from the Montfortian rebels, Foulquois had an exceptionally clear idea of what the Church ought to achieve beyond the Channel and, as Clement IV (1265–8), promptly dispatched Innocent IV's nephew, Cardinal Ottobono Fieschi, as legate to England. Montfort himself was killed while Fieschi was *en route* and the king's loyalists exacted revenge on the rebels. The legate operated more carefully, first excommunicating the Montfortians for their rebellion, and then absolving them in order to promote reconciliation. Alongside this he issued a comprehensive set of canons for the regulation of the English Church and preached the crusade with such success that Henry's heir, the Lord Edward, took the cross in 1268.[47] Taken together, Fieschi's achievements could be said to represent the most complete harmony ever attained between England and the papacy, the culmination of efforts that can be traced back to the beginnings of the reform movement in the tenth century and far more convincing than the breathtaking opportunism exhibited by King John in 1213.

CHAPTER 3

ROME, CAPITAL OF THE WORLD?

Between the thirteenth and the fifteenth century Christendom shrank and its centre of gravity shifted westwards. The fall of the Christian strongholds of Tripoli and Acre in 1289–91 signalled the end of serious attempts to recover the Holy Land and paved the way for Ottoman expansion in Asia Minor and the Balkans, though the city of Constantinople held out defiantly until 1453. Only in Iberia did the tide turn in the opposite direction, the Christian reconquest of the peninsula culminating in the fall of Granada in 1492. The popes of the later thirteenth century made frantic efforts to shore up the dwindling crusader states, costing both money and manpower, the very resources which secular princes sought to tap for their own non-crusading enterprises; in the case of England's Edward I (1272–1307) this meant military campaigns against the Scots and Welsh. The fourteenth-century popes retreated towards Western Christendom's French heartland, transferring the papal capital from Rome to Avignon. They were justifiably accused of favouring the French nation, and that at the same time as Edward III of England (1327–77) was asserting his claim to the throne of France. After the schism between Roman and Avignonese claimants to the papal throne, the fifteenth-century popes were obliged to rebuild the Church from one of its lower ebbs and did so by centralising it in their much-neglected city of Rome. That also cost money. A substantial proportion of the papacy's income came from French benefices. Although England contained far fewer dioceses, their average wealth was higher. In terms of official taxable values, five of the fifteen wealthiest bishoprics of Latin Christendom were English.[1] Ireland's wealthiest, Cashel, was on a par with Bordeaux, Bourges and the Hungarian primatial see of Esztergom, while Scotland's, St Andrews, was rated higher than the major economic centres of Lyon and Milan. In short, it was in Rome's financial interest to cultivate good relations with the English and Scottish monarchs. The kings' devotion to the papacy tended to be in proportion to the degree of opposition they encountered at home. In an era when half of the deaths of English kings were by violent means and only half of the Scottish kings died in their beds, instability was the norm and support from an external authority was particularly valued. This was not only the period in which Edward II (1307–27) and Henry VI (1422–61, 1470–1) fell victim to their enemies, but also that in which Richard II (1377–99) and Henry VII (1485–1509) appealed to the popes to have those same royal predecessors canonised. On the other hand, antipapalism thrived in proportion to the king's strength and was most apparent during the long reign of Edward III.

The longest interregnum in papal history lasted from 29 November 1268 until 1 September 1271, with the cardinals at Viterbo split between pro- and anti-French factions. The Englishman known somewhat confusingly as John of Toledo made his most notable contribution to the agonisingly protracted electoral process with a wry comment made when the roof was removed from their palace as an encouragement to reach a decision: it provided better access for the Holy Spirit, the only elector who really mattered. The election was eventually made by delegation to a committee of six cardinals, three of whom had been created by the French pope Urban IV and three by his Italian predecessors. Although John of Toledo was not among the delegates, their choice was acceptable to the English: as archdeacon of Liège, Tebaldo Visconti had accompanied Ottobono Fieschi on his successful English legation in 1265–8 and was in Acre with Henry III's crusading son Edward when news reached him of his election. Given the nature of that election, it is little wonder that the new pope, Gregory X (1271–6), devised comprehensive regulations for the conduct of future conclaves. Although there were eight more conclaves before the end of the thirteenth century, only one English cardinal voted in any of them: Hugh of Evesham was among the electors of Honorius IV in 1285, but died when malaria struck the conclave enclosure in 1287, months before the survivors finally elected Nicholas IV (1288–92).

The centrepiece of Gregory X's pontificate was the Second Council of Lyon (1274), which he called as a means of unifying the Church in preparation for a new crusade. As an experienced crusader, Edward I's contribution was keenly anticipated by Gregory, but the king disappointed him by choosing to assert his new authority at home, rather than in the Holy Land. The council's impact was nevertheless felt as keenly in the British Isles as anywhere else, for it consented to papal taxation of the clergy to finance the crusade. Gregory's bull *Cum pro negotio* (1274) then set out detailed arrangements for the collection of one tenth of the clergy's income in each of six consecutive years, instructions that provided the model for all subsequent papal exactions. From the start they met with opposition.

Gregory's two immediate successors, Innocent V (January–June 1276) and Adrian V (July–August 1276) came with strong English connections, Adrian having been none other than the legate Fieschi and Innocent Fieschi's assistant

Pierre de Tarentaise. Both died soon after election, though Adrian made testamentary provision for a hospice in his native Liguria, on the pilgrim route from England to Rome, which was to be dedicated to St Thomas (Becket) of Canterbury. The next pope, John XXI (1276–7), was Portuguese and survived little longer than his predecessors. None of them created cardinals.

Nicholas III (1277–80) revived the Sacred College by creating nine new cardinals, including Archbishop Robert Kilwardby of Canterbury, the Dominican chosen by Gregory X in preference to the candidates of both Prince Edward and the Christ Church monks. Kilwardby's promotion meant that the latest Canterbury vacancy was of the pope's own making, and Edward – now king – again sought to have his chancellor, Robert Burnell, translated from Bath and Wells. As in 1272 Burnell was thwarted: Nicholas quashed his election and selected John Pecham, a Franciscan who had been teaching in Rome. The pope was no less interventionist in his dealings with York, rejecting a capitular election in order to provide William de Wickwane to the archbishopric in 1279. Nicholas had a particularly keen interest in the York chapter because a number of its prebends, which were among the richest in England, were held by members of his family, the Orsini. This connection began in the 1250s when the future pope, then Giovanni Gaetano Orsini, obtained the prebend of Fridaythorpe. It continued with his brother Giordano and nephew Matteo as successive prebendaries of Fenton, and another nephew, Napoleone, as prebendary of South Cave. This was precisely the sort of Italian invasion to which English clerics had been objecting for decades, but it was during Nicholas's pontificate that these objections were translated into the secular sphere, when Edward began to chafe at the annual tribute imposed on England by his grandfather King John. The pope firmly rejected Edward's proposal to amend it.

In that it took five months to elect his successor, Nicholas was a hard act to follow. His bequest to the English Church was the zealous Pecham, who created business in Rome for the Orsini pope and for his French successor, Martin IV (1281–5) by challenging the reforming bishop of Hereford, Thomas de Cantilupe. Each prelate was well aware of his rights and privileges, not least when they clashed. Cantilupe's first appeal to Rome was made in 1280, a year after Pecham's return to England. In February 1282 the archbishop declared Cantilupe to be excommunicate. By June the bishop was in Orvieto, appealing in person to Pope Martin. He died before a decision had been reached regarding his appeal. His remains were then returned to Hereford and the first miracles connected with them were recorded at Easter 1287, at a time when the English bishops again felt threatened by their authoritarian metropolitan.

After two more relatively short pontificates and the panic-inducing fall of Acre, the twenty-seven-month papal interregnum of 1292–4 was particularly disorderly. Accumulating business included confirmation of Robert

Winchelsey's election to Canterbury, which was only achieved once a reluctant eighty-six-year-old hermit was thrust onto the papal throne as Celestine V (July–December 1294). Celestine's abdication and the subsequent election of Benedetto Caetani as Boniface VIII (1294–1303) was an exclusively Franco-Italian affair, though it had an Anglo-Welsh consequence in that Celestine had delegated to Archbishop Winchelsey the choice of a new bishop of Llandaff, only for Boniface to rescind the acts of his predecessor. For two years, therefore, doubt remained over the validity of John of Monmouth's appointment, though it was finally confirmed.

Like the Orsini, the Caetani acquired ecclesiastical wealth from York. When Benedetto Caetani was still a cardinal, his nephew Francesco became prebendary of Knaresborough. From 1295 Francesco was a cardinal and later staked a claim to the deanery of York. A thaw in relations between York and Rome was evident when the pope consecrated Thomas of Corbridge as archbishop in 1300 and Cardinal Caetani acquired the lucrative archdeaconry of Richmond in 1301. This turn of events meant that the archbishop was the most eminent visitor from the British Isles to Rome in 1300, Pope Boniface's holy year, the first in Christian history, when pilgrims to the city received a special indulgence remitting the penalty for their sins and Rome's visible economy received a boost from the increased number of visitors.

No pope was as imperious as Boniface VIII, but not even he could inspire peace among the Christian powers and divert their energies into a new crusade. His strategy for bringing peace to the realms of England and France, which had been at war since 1294, meant attempting to starve Edward I and Philippe IV of clerical taxation. The bull *Clericis laicos* (1296) named neither kingdom, but warned all secular powers, great and small, not to tax the clergy without papal permission and encouraged ecclesiastics to stand firm in the face of lay aggression.[2] Archbishop Winchelsey was certainly emboldened, refused to pay the king's extraordinarily high tax on the clergy, and was safe from Edward's wrath as long as Boniface lived. War nevertheless continued, so the pope dispatched two of his most senior cardinals – Bérard de Got and Simon de Beaulieu – as legates to negotiate a peace. Both of them died in 1297 without making much progress.

Thanks to a Franco-Scottish alliance made in 1295–6, Edward faced war on two fronts, but whereas Boniface was even-handed in his condemnation of the French and English kings, he tended to sympathise with the Scots, whose king, John de Balliol, surrendered to Edward in 1296, leaving the English king as self-proclaimed overlord of Scotland. The Scottish Church was equally leaderless when Bishop Fraser of St Andrews died in 1297 and Wishart of Glasgow was temporarily imprisoned by the English. However, it was still immediately subject to Rome and could look to the pope for support. Boniface initially demonstrated this by appointing William Lamberton, an ally of the freedom fighter William Wallace, to St Andrews. Then, in 1299, he insisted on the deposed King John being transferred from English to papal custody, and sent a strongly-worded bull, *Scimus, fili*, to King Edward, reminding him that Scotland was ecclesiastically subject to Rome and feudally subject to no-one.[3] In the longer term, papal support proved to be conditional and, when an Anglo-French treaty was signed in 1303, one of Boniface's last acts was to instruct the Scottish bishops to reach an accommodation with Edward.

Benedict XI (1303–4) did little more than favour his fellow Dominicans before expiring after a pontificate of less than nine months. His two new cardinals were Niccolò Alberti, another of Boniface's unsuccessful legates to France and England, and Walter of Winterbourne, King Edward's confessor. After an eleven-month interregnum, Walter was among the fifteen cardinals who elected a new pope in June 1305, their choice falling on a non-cardinal, the archbishop of Bordeaux. This choice was crucial for Anglo-papal relations because the prelate in question – Bertrand de Got, brother of the sometime legate Bérard – was a subject of Edward I as duke of Aquitaine and, beyond him, of the French king Philippe IV.

Between 1305 and 1312 Clement V (1305–14) created twenty-four new ecclesiastical princes, only one of whom was not French. The odd man out was Thomas Jorz (or Joyce), a direct replacement for Walter of Winterbourne in that he was another of Edward I's Dominican confessors. Like Walter, Jorz received the title of S. Sabina, but had no opportunity to enjoy that church's favourable position on Rome's Aventine hill, because Clement based the curia first at Poitiers and then at Carpentras, besides calling a council at Vienne to address the accusations of heresy made in France against the now underemployed crusading order of Knights Templar. That Jorz flourished in the new climate of close co-operation between the pope and the English king can be confirmed by the papal provision of his brothers Walter and Roland to the archbishopric of Armagh, in 1307 and 1311 respectively, though he was by no means the only cardinal involved in English business. In 1306 Pedro Rodríguez helped to negotiate the marriage of Edward's heir, Edward of Caernarfon, to Philippe IV's daughter, Isabelle. By 1309 the younger Edward was king and his exchequer was paying annual pensions to Jorz and five other cardinals. In 1312 Edward and Isabelle's eldest son, a third Edward, was baptised at Windsor by the nuncio Cardinal Arnaud Nouvel. In the same year Guillaume Teste was serving as collector of papal taxes in England when he too was made a cardinal.

Although the Anglo-papal relationship was undoubtedly close, whether in terms of red hats or by any other measure, it was almost entirely one-sided, because Clement indulged Edward I and received precious little in return. After Clement's election Edward moved first, asking the pope to suspend Archbishop Winchelsey from office, ironically enough for being a particularly faithful executor of Pope Boniface's policy against rapacious princes. Clement obliged in February 1306 and Winchelsey headed into a French exile that lasted until after the king's death. In the absence of a primate at Canterbury, Clement asked Archbishop Greenfield of York and Bishop Bek of Durham to lead an investigation into the Templars in England. There was, however, no insular enthusiasm for action against the knights and little was achieved. Even more decisively, Edward took such advantage of his previous authority over the former archbishop of Bordeaux that he went beyond merely objecting to payment of the annual tribute; he ceased to pay it entirely. There could be no more telling sign of the reversal of English and papal fortunes in the decades since King John's submission. Only in one area did Clement venture to stand up to Edward, and that related to Scotland. Robert Bruce led a rebellion by the king's Scottish vassals and was crowned king of Scots in March 1306. Bishops Wishart and Lamberton were captured by the English and their parallel cases tested the lengths to which the Gascon pope was obliged to go for the now ailing king, for this time Clement followed the pattern set by Pope Boniface, defending the bishops, demanding their release and, in the case of Wishart, welcoming him to the papal court.

Wishart and Lamberton eventually returned to their dioceses, but relations between the Holy See and its Scottish subjects took a marked turn for the worse after the election of Pope John XXII (1316–34). This followed a twenty-eight-month three-way struggle between Italian cardinals, whose priority was to return the papacy to Rome, Pope Clement's fellow Gascons, who sought to maintain their favourable situation, and other French electors. The eventual victor, Jacques Duèse, was a canon lawyer from Cahors who had been bishop of Avignon, near Clement's base at Carpentras. He was a man of immense energy and determination, though hardly a master of diplomacy, which had consequences throughout the secular and ecclesiastical spheres. As pope he transferred the papal administration to Avignon, where it acquired a more settled character. Early in the pontificate, the English sought John's help regarding their Scottish war. In response, John sent his nephew and vice-chancellor Gauscelin de Jean and the Genoese cardinal Luca Fieschi as legates to England, Scotland and Ireland. The legates struck a partisan note when they attempted to negotiate a truce with 'Robert Bruce now governing the kingdom of Scotland', rather than with King Robert I (1306–29). For their refusal to make peace, Bruce and his followers were excommunicated by John on 28 May 1318, a sentence published by the legates at Nottingham on 13 August. The Scottish barons responded with the letter, addressed to John, now known as the Declaration of Arbroath, in which they recounted their travails at the hands of the English and the relief brought by their 'most tireless prince, King and lord, the lord Robert'.[4] It was the pope who gave way, from 1324 acknowledging Robert as king, lifting excommunication in 1328, and granting permission for future kings to be anointed in the manner of those in France, England and elsewhere. The last was John's legacy to King David II (1329–71) and his successors.

John's relations with England were the inverse of those with Scotland, starting reasonably well and then deteriorating. In 1317 the visiting papal *nipote* acquired the archdeaconry of Northampton, the revenue from which followed him back to Avignon, and the university at Cambridge was confirmed as a *stadium generale*, which cost the pope nothing.[5] Anglo-papal relations still appeared to be good in 1320, when John canonised Thomas de Cantilupe (d. 1282). Compared with thirteenth-century popes, those of the fourteenth century were much less ready to create new saints, making their choices all the more interesting. During his eighteen-year pontificate John canonised only three individuals, the other two being the Dominican theologian Thomas Aquinas (d. 1274) and the Franciscan Louis of Toulouse (d. 1297), who belonged to a cadet branch of the French royal family with which John claimed a dynastic connection. By 1320 Philippe V was king of France and his sister Isabelle was long established as queen consort of England. She had a track record of getting the pope to favour her candidates for English bishoprics, in preference to those of her husband, so the canonisation of the late bishop of Hereford could be interpreted as a French pope and a French queen scoring a final victory for the Anglo-Norman elite over Cantilupe's rival, the humbly-born Archbishop Pecham. Indeed, the interests of pope and queen continued to converge: during the 1320s Edward II's rule was not only undermined by his wife's political rebellion, but repeatedly challenged by the pope when Edward nominated his chancellor Robert Baldock for the sees of Coventry and Lichfield (1321), Winchester (1323), and Norwich (1325), only to be thwarted on each occasion. It is little wonder that the king made no effort to send the annual tribute to Avignon. Edward III sent a token payment in 1333, after which no more was dispatched and the king's status as a papal vassal was simply ignored.

Pope John's legal training did not prevent him from venturing opinions on theological matters and his naturally forceful character ensured that his interventions provoked serious controversy. Throughout their corporate existence the Franciscan friars had been divided between those who mitigated the rule of their founder by living in communities and building their own churches, independent of episcopal control, and a minority of hardline Spirituals, who rejected all forms of property. John sought to enforce order by condemning the Spirituals as heretics, but then overplayed his hand by rejecting the view of most Franciscans that, regardless of contemporary ecclesiastical practices, Christ and the Apostles espoused absolute poverty. He had managed to pick a fight with friars of all nations, among whom two English examples can illustrate the greater whole. In 1322 William of Alnwick was present when the Franciscan general chapter drew up the decree *De paupertate Christi* to counter the pope's position and defended it in his

Determinationes. Rather than face the legal consequences, William sought sanctuary with the king of Naples. A more dramatic flight was that of the Oxford master William of Ockham from Avignon to Aigues-Mortes during the night of 26 May 1326. He had been at the papal court since 1324 to defend himself against charges of heresy and dangerous teaching. The case against him had reached no conclusion when he decided that John's views on Christ's poverty were heretical, rendering the pope unfit to judge the teachings of others. William eventually found a sanctuary in Munich, where he was protected by the emperor, Louis IV, who was in the process of marshalling opposition to John and briefly backed an antipope in 1328–30, the first for a century and a half.

When John died in 1334 it was relatively easy for the cardinals to elect a contrasting figure, the Cistercian inquisitor Jacques Fournier, as their next pope. The papacy had lost so much prestige that Benedict XII (1334–42) had his work cut out regulating and codifying the Church's internal structures and practices. His stand against nepotism and corruption alienated so many curialists that he was not entirely master of his own house, the Palais des Papes, from which his lack of influence over distant princes may be inferred. One failure was Benedict's attempt to heal the rift with the emperor, whose schism persisted, and another was his plan for a joint Anglo-French crusade, which had to be abandoned in 1336 as war between those powers looked increasingly likely. Hostilities did indeed break out the following year when Philippe VI forfeited Edward III's French titles. Benedict responded quickly, dispatching two cardinals to negotiate a settlement, but their mission was frustrated when Edward met Louis IV at Koblenz and was made vicar-general of the Holy Roman Empire. By allying with the excommunicate emperor Edward did himself no favours in Avignon, giving rise to fanciful stories that Edward II had not been murdered, that he was being protected by Benedict and could be employed at any moment to threaten his son's legitimacy as king.

It can safely be assumed that the French king was as much in favour at Avignon as his English counterpart was out of it. Nevertheless, during the papal interregnum of 1342 Philippe took no chances and lobbied for the election of his former chancellor, Pierre Roger. He need not have worried: in just two days Roger acquired the requisite number of votes and became Clement VI (1342–52). Clement was well versed in the ways of courts and allowed courtly trappings to flourish in Avignon. The conclave was followed by an outbreak of diplomatic exchanges, as the new pope sought to negotiate an Anglo-French peace. His agents included Cardinals Étienne Aubert, Annibaldo Caetani and Pierre des Près, while the brothers Andrew and John Offord were among the English diplomats to whom dealings with the papacy were most regularly entrusted.[6] In England Clement was not regarded as an honest broker, an impression confirmed by the fact that only one of the thirteen cardinals he created in 1342–4 was not French.

By the 1340s at least seven non-English cardinals held English benefices, including the archdeaconry of Nottingham and the deaneries of Salisbury and York. This was merely the apex of a system that saw 'aliens' provided to benefices across Western Christendom. As it happened, no 'aliens' were papally provided to English, Irish or Welsh bishoprics during that decade. Rather, Clement habitually asserted his authority by quashing capitular elections and royal nominations, only to provide the very same candidates himself. In some cases he overreached himself due to ignorance of the local circumstances, as when he provided bishops to Leighlin and Llandaff even though the incumbents were still alive. For once Canterbury was not a cause of contention, all the interested parties being frustrated by forces beyond their control. After the death of Archbishop Stratford in 1348, the king's candidate was the diplomat John Offord, but he seems to have died of plague in May 1349, before he could be consecrated. The chapter then secured papal approval of their candidate, the eminent scholar Thomas Bradwardine, only for the plague to kill him in August. In September the monks fixed on Simon Islip. True to form, Clement quashed that election, but provided him anyway. When the crisis of the Black Death had passed, the English government reacted against previous collusion in papal provisions, clarifying its position with an overtly antipapal policy embodied in the Provisors Act (1351), 'provisors' being the clerics who procured or received benefices. The statute declared that the king and other lords, 'and not the bishop of Rome', would henceforth appoint to benefices in the realm of England. In reality this proved to be sabre-rattling that made no immediate difference to Anglo-papal relations, because Clement made a number of English and Welsh provisions or translations in the autumn of 1352, all of which proceeded without incident.

Clement VI was a strong pope, if a worldly one, and in 1352 the cardinals in conclave reacted against his excesses by drawing up an election 'capitulation' designed to increase the powers and income of their college at the expense of those enjoyed by the next pontiff. All promised to abide by the terms of this document in the event of being elected, but the man who became Innocent VI (1352–62), the former legate Étienne Aubert, promptly rejected it as a curtailment of his papal power. Curtailing that power was precisely what the English government had in mind when a second Statute of Provisors was enacted in 1353. It was accompanied by another statute, that of Praemunire, which sought to prevent litigants taking their cases to the papal courts, a practice which was said to undermine the king's justice.[7] This was a decided novelty and went against the centralising trend of the previous few centuries. Measures were taken to obstruct the passage of some of the king's more discontented subjects, but they tended to evade capture and were then obliged to remain in Avignon, where the wheels of papal justice turned slowly.

Financial constraints helped to ensure that Innocent's was a relatively quiet pontificate. Its most notable achievement was the campaign led by the warrior prelate Gil de Albornoz to restore control over the Papal States. In 1359 war threatened to come to the Comtat Venaissin, the region adjacent to Avignon, in the shape of an attack by the English commander Sir Robert Knolles, but that plan was abandoned, leaving Innocent's role in the Anglo-French conflict as one of intercession and peace-making, culminating in the 1360 Peace of Brétigny.

Urban V (1362–70), the sixth successive French pontiff, was elected at the height of Edward III's dominance in Western Europe: Jean II of France was Edward's prisoner and although David II of Scotland was at liberty he owed the king of England an impossibly large ransom. Edward's next target was the county of Flanders and its exceedingly eligible heiress. By the end of 1362 lack of a papal dispensation was all that stood between the marriage of Margaret of Flanders and Edward's fourth surviving son, Edmund, earl of Cambridge. There matters still stood when Jean II died in 1364 and was succeeded by his eldest son, Charles V, who exerted sufficient pressure on Urban to ensure that no dispensation was issued. Rubbing salt into the wound, Charles later secured Margaret's marriage to another fourth son, his own brother, the duke of Burgundy, thereby laying the foundation of Valois Burgundy as a significant power in its own right. Once Urban had shown himself to be in the pocket of the French king, the papacy could be regarded as a legitimate target for English attacks. Assaults on it had the benefit of protecting and potentially increasing sources of patronage for the king's key supporters while preventing portions of the nation's wealth draining away to Provence. Thus the English Parliament passed a new Statute of Provisors in January 1365. Besides confirming the previous statutes, this one extended the measures to cover a wider range of benefices, thereby protecting the interests of more lay patrons. The next Parliament went further, declaring King John's 1213 submission to papal overlordship to have been invalid in the first place.[8]

Urban had previously been a legate in Italy and, after more than four years in Avignon, he resolved to return the papacy to Rome. This move was fiercely opposed by many of the French cardinals; it also upset the *status quo* in Italy, where Bernabò Visconti, lord of Milan, had resisted Cardinal Albornoz and retained control of Bologna, the second city of the Papal States. Urban declared war against Milan and employed some of the English soldiers who had gravitated towards Italy after the Peace of Brétigny, but matters were complicated by the marriage of Visconti's niece to Edward III's son Lionel, duke of Clarence, which was celebrated in the summer of 1368. That September Urban sought to placate the English while strengthening his own support by naming a fellow Benedictine, Archbishop Simon Langham, Edward's chancellor, as one of eight new cardinals. There was a precedent for this in that the French chancellor had been raised to the same status in 1361. The sudden death of Duke Lionel then caused Edward's Italian policy to implode, so it is little wonder that the king reacted badly to Langham's promotion and delayed his departure for some months. Next to unravel was the Peace of Brétigny, leading Edward to reassert his claim to the French crown in 1369. Finally, Urban's vision of the papacy restored to Rome and inspiring a wide range of Christian endeavour from scholarship to crusading, ended in tatters when he retreated to Avignon in 1370 and, true to the saintly Bridget of Sweden's prophecy, promptly died.

French electors dominated the ensuing contest, but Langham's involvement meant that, for the first time in sixty-five years, there was an English cardinal in the conclave. Their choice fell on Pierre Roger de Beaufort, a nephew of Clement VI. His education and diplomatic experience drew him towards Italy, so it was hardly surprising that, as Gregory XI (1370–8), he followed Urban's example in seeking to restore the papacy to Rome. More immediately, though, the Anglo-French conflict called for papal mediation. Gregory had a family connection with it in that his brother was held captive by Edward's son John of Gaunt, duke of Lancaster, which may help to explain why Gaunt gave his four illegitimate children the surname Beaufort. Gregory's initiatives began with peace talks at Calais in February 1372, which resumed early the following year but made no decisive progress. This nevertheless provided the context for Anglo-papal negotiations over ecclesiastical matters, specifically papal provisions to benefices in lay patronage and the pope's request for a heavy subsidy from the English clergy to meet extraordinary expenditure. Gregory calculated that he could take advantage of disunity around the ailing Edward and bind the English government more closely to the papacy while dividing it from the antipapalism regularly expressed in Parliament. A concordat was finally agreed at Bruges in 1375. Both sides made concessions, but Gregory got what he needed most, an immediate levy of 60,000 florins on the clergy, with the promise of another 40,000 to follow.[9]

It was during the winter of 1376–7 that Pope Gregory made the journey from Avignon to Rome, following the recent example set by Queen Margaret of Scotland, the rejected wife of David II, who defended her marriage at the curia before dying in Rome in 1375. His path was also in some measure prepared by the English *condottiere* Sir John Hawkwood, who had been employed by the papacy as part of a campaign to pacify the peninsula. Once in Rome, Gregory survived only fourteen months, during which time the most significant piece of insular business was his condemnation of the views propounded by the Oxford theologian John Wycliffe, particularly in *De civile dominio* (1375–6), which argued that clergy could be removed from their benefices by the secular power. This was brought to the pope's attention by Adam Easton, a monk of Norwich, and by other Benedictines at the curia. Gregory's bulls of 22 May 1377 instructed Archbishop Sudbury of Canterbury and Bishop Courtenay of London to investigate Wycliffe's views and, if necessary, cite him to appear before the pope.[10] However, Wycliffe had support within the university and a powerful patron in John of Gaunt, and the process encountered such delays that Gregory had died before Wycliffe appeared at Lambeth to answer the charges against him.

Progress against Wycliffe may have been diplomatically sluggish, but events in Rome were moving apace. The conclave of April 1378 was the first to be held there since 1303 and the people of Rome were determined to influence the selection of their bishop. Under pressure from the mob, the cardinals, most of whom were still French, elected a non-cardinal, Bartolomeo Prignano, archbishop of Bari. Urban VI (1378–89) was the first non-French pope since Benedict XI at the beginning of the century and Easton predicted that his election would be welcomed in England as an anti-French development. It was certainly not welcomed among the cardinals who had remained in Avignon. The reaction did not end there, for many of those who had participated in Urban's perfectly canonical election soon regretted their decision, escaped from his irrational behaviour and tyrannical rule, and declared the election invalid. Urban simply replaced them, appointing twenty-four new cardinals on 18 September. Bishop Courtenay would have made it twenty-five, but rejected the honour. At Fondi the fugitive cardinals, fortified by a message of support by the king of France, elected one of their number, Robert of Geneva, as 'Clement VII'. By the summer of 1379 Clement and his alternative court was established at Avignon and the secular powers had formed two 'obediences', Clementine and Urbanist, according to whether they were pro- or anti-French. Scotland's French alliance was well established, so the fault line lay in part through the British Isles. This division was not merely between Scotland and England, for the schism also divided the sprawling diocese of Sodor and Man, the Hebrides declaring for Clement while the Isle of Man identified with England and the Urbanist cause.

In this bizarre world of rival popes, rival cardinals and rival ecclesiastical jurisdictions, Scotland was suddenly able to punch above its weight, so much so that it acquired its first cardinal, Walter Wardlaw, bishop of Glasgow, who was promoted by Clement in December 1383. Similarly, England and the English enjoyed more influence in Rome than had previously been the case. Adam Easton channelled his curial experiences into a dialogue on the nature of papal power, the now incomplete *Defensorium ecclesiasticae potestatis*, in which he expressed an arch-papalist line.[11] It was dedicated to Urban as nothing less than 'monarch of the world'. During the course of its composition Easton was called upon to testify to Castilian and Aragonese ambassadors concerning the origin of the papal schism and agued strongly for the legitimacy of Urban's election.[12] His reward came in December 1381, when he was named first, ahead of five Italians, among new cardinals created to bolster Urban's position. In the political sphere England's adherence to Urban was nowhere more apparent than in the marriage he facilitated between Richard II and Anne of Bohemia, whose brother Wenzel, king of the Romans, was another Urbanist.

During the early years of the pontificate English enthusiasm for Urban was even shared by Wycliffe, who thought of the dynamic pope as a potential reformer. His antipapalism developed in response to Urban's actions, which demonastrated some of the worst excesses of autocratic government. In 1385, while the pope and his court were at Nocera in the kingdom of Naples, Easton and five of his fellow cardinals were accused of conspiring against the pope, arrested and deprived of their offices. The others also lost their lives; Easton was saved only because Urban could not afford to lose England's support. That support did not necessarily need to come from the king himself; it could be from whoever happened to exercise power in England at the time. Thus, when Urban was drawn into the power struggle between Richard and the so-called 'lords appellant' in 1388 it was to side with the king's critics, his contribution being to demote Richard's favourites from the sees of Durham and Salisbury and promote Thomas Arundel, brother of the appellant earl of Arundel, from Ely to York. That particular crisis passed, Richard regained the reins of government and once more controlled England's dealings with the papacy.

Easton was still imprisoned when Urban died in 1389, so took no part in the ensuing conclave. The thirteen electors, all of them Italian, chose the Neapolitan Pietro Tomacelli. As Boniface IX (1389–1404), one of Tomacelli's first acts was to release and reinstate the Englishman, who went on to live in semi-retirement until his death in 1397. From Easton's compatriots Boniface nevertheless faced a reaction against Urban's reliance on England, parliamentarians provocatively revising the Statutes of Provisors and Praemunire in 1389–93.[13] The next conclave occurred in 1394 and brought together prelates from various nations, but it met in Avignon and elected a successor to 'Clement VII', signalling that there would be no quick resolution of the schism. Walter Wardlaw had died in 1387, so there was no Scottish dimension to this election. The victor, 'Benedict XIII', clung on tenaciously for the next twenty-nine years, despite losing French support in 1398. While Boniface and Benedict survived as heads of their respective obediences, Scotland and England experienced changes of leadership in 1399. Robert III (1390–1406) was excluded from the government of his kingdom by his closest kinsmen, and Richard II was ousted by his cousin Henry, duke of Lancaster. Boniface was supportive of Richard in the period of crisis leading up to his deposition, providing Roger Walden to Canterbury when Richard exiled Archbishop Arundel, and granting a concordat in November 1398, among the terms of which was a relaxation of the Statutes of Provisors.[14] The pope was by no means so accommodating to Richard's successor, Henry IV (1399–1413), clashing with him over an episcopal vacancy at Rochester in 1404.

The bishopric of London was also in the balance when a former collector of papal taxes in England, Cosimo de' Migliorati, was elected as Boniface's successor later that year. Like Boniface, Innocent VII (1404–06) took a stand against the usurper king, providing Richard's former protégé, Walden, to London in preference to the new king's choice, Thomas Langley. In June 1405 Henry finally conceded that Walden should be bishop of London, but only as a sop to the papacy, for word was about to reach Rome that the archbishop of York, Richard Scrope, had been summarily executed for treason. The king need not have worried for, according to the eye-witness record of the Welsh chronicler Adam Usk, so tenuous was Innocent VII's hold on power that an urban revolt forced him out of Rome for seven months of his twenty-five-month pontificate.[15] Once it was apparent that he was no threat to anyone, the English took such advantage of Innocent's weakness that his excommunication of the lords responsible for the execution of Archbishop Scrope was simply not published. Meanwhile, the Welsh rebels led by Owain Glyn Dŵr declared for 'Benedict XIII'. Usk was among those who changed sides, travelling to Avignon, where he was provided to the see of Llandaff. During the same year, 1407, Benedict also provided Gruffudd Young first to Bangor and then to St Davids. The position of these Welshmen was, however, as compromised as that of their patron and neither was able to make good his claim.

After Innocent's death on 6 November 1406 thirteen Italian cardinals and a solitary Frenchman elected the Venetian Angelo Correr just twelve days later. He became Gregory XII (1406–15) and was not necessarly any stronger than his predecessor. Through Sir John Cheyne and the up-and-coming canon lawyer Henry Chichele, King Henry managed to dictate terms to Gregory in the matter of episcopal appointments, achieving his greatest success when the pope was forced to translate/demote his own choice for York, Robert Hallum, to Salisbury so that the king's candidate and former curial proctor, Henry Bowet, could enjoy the archbishopric, which had remained vacant since Scrope's execution.

There was talk of Gregory and Benedict meeting in northern Italy and resigning simultaneously as a means of ending the schism, but it came to nothing. Gregory's absence from Rome encouraged Ladislas of Naples to invade the Papal States and the pope's authority crumbled even further. In an attempt to bolster his position. In 1408, in an attempt to bolster his position, Gregory created fourteen new cardinals, three of whom were chosen with a view to cultivating secular princes. This calculation failed spectacularly, for the Aragonese and German prelates soon died and Philip Repingdon, bishop of Lincoln, remained in England, where his promotion was not recognised. The year ended with Henry IV withdrawing English obedience from Gregory and appointing a delegation to the council called to meet at Pisa by cardinals from both sides. This body declared both Gregory and Benedict to be deposed, after which the cardinals went into conclave and elected the Cretan Pietro Filargis as their pope. Over in Rimini, Gregory fumed impotently and, in a vain attempt to counter English acceptance of Alexander V, named King Henry's illegitimate brother Henry Beaufort, bishop of Winchester, as legate in England and Ireland. Alexander died less than a year after his election and Baldassare Cossa was chosen to succeed him. The English government acknowledged Cossa as 'John XXIII' (1410–15), but did not go as far as to accept his selection of the former Pisan delegates Langley and Hallum for the cardinalate.

John was no nearer commanding pan-European respect than either Gregory or Benedict, so the emperor, Sigismund, persuaded him to summon a general council at Konstanz in 1414. This assembly made light work of John, after which Gregory finally submitted his resignation in July 1415. That left Benedict, whose shrivelled obedience still included the Scots, for whom he had recently confirmed the foundation of St Andrews as Scotland's first university.[16] Under Hallum's leadership, the English delegation was active throughout the council, and never more so than in Benedict's formal deposition on 26 July 1417, but it was a 'pilgrim', rather than a delegate, who then ushered the fathers towards a papal election. This was Henry Beaufort, who was then at the height of his influence with his nephew Henry V (1413–22). The new king's priority was to stake a claim to the French throne by striking at that kingdom while it was weakened by civil conflict, and for that he desired support from a pope who was recognised by all sides.

The conclave of 1417 was unique in papal history in that the twenty-three cardinals were a minority of the electors, outnumbered by representatives of the English, French, German, Italian and Spanish 'nations'. Henry V's personal reputation as the victor of Agincourt helped to secure England's separation from the rest of the German nation and his six electors were Richard Clifford, Nicholas Bubwith, John Catterick, John Wakering (all bishops), Thomas Spofford (abbot of St Mary's, York) and Thomas Polton (dean of York). It was easily the greatest concentration of Englishmen in any conclave. The man they helped to electe in the king's interest in 1417 was the Roman patrician Oddone Colonna. However, if Henry imagined that he could exercise influence over the revived papacy in exchange for the gratitude of Pope Martin V (1417–31), he underestimated the new pontiff. Like Gregory XII, Martin had his sights set on securing control over the English Church by means of Bishop Beaufort, who was named cardinal and legate to England on 18 December, months before any similar promotions in other nations. The fact that Martin left Beaufort's name unpublished, while the man himself went on pilgrimage to the Holy Land, left time for Henry to take his cue from previous English kings who had refused to be bridled by legates and threatened his absent uncle with forfeiture of his bishopric. While everyone waited for Beaufort's reappearance, Martin asserted his right to provide to vacant bishoprics. Those at Armagh, Bangor and St Davids gave him opportunities to overturn capitular elections or challenge the English government, opportunities which he took and which the secular authorities allowed to pass without incident. The real target, Beaufort, finally returned to England in 1419 and was threatened with a charge of praemunire if he published Martin's bulls relating to the cardinalate, legateship and Winchester's proposed exemption of the authority of Canterbury.[17] Henry's will prevailed: Beaufort, held on to his bishopric but lost everything else.

Relations between the papacy and Scotland were difficult as long as the duke of Albany, regent for James I (1406–37), maintained a stubborn adherence to the deposed 'Benedict XIII', even while individual prelates sought confirmation of their appointments from Martin. Crucially, the University of St Andrews made its submission to Martin in August 1418, after which Albany bowed to the inevitable. Diplomatic and financial relations were resumed.

It was 1420 before Martin returned to Rome. From that point onwards, he made his home city integral to the revived papal monarchy, announcing a holy year for 1423, rebuilding some of Rome's much-neglected infrastructure and making it the centre of a more thoroughly administered state. Martin's initiatives constituted such an obvious break with the recent past that the Renaissance papacy can be said to date from his return to the city. However, no break could be entirely clean and the terms under which he had been elected obliged him to call general councils 'frequently'. Any such assembly represented a potential threat to papal power so, instead of summoning one to meet in the decayed Lateran palace, he arranged for it to congregate in distant Pavia in 1423. There was no chance of Henry V's indirect influence at Konstanz being repeated because the charismatic king had died in 1422, leaving his brothers to govern and his infant son, Henry VI, with an unrealistic claim to the French crown. Conciliarism was now so low a priority that the English delegation to Pavia, which was initially led by the bishop of Lincoln, Richard Flemming, steadily dwindled, leaving only one bishop, William Barrow of Carlisle, in attendance at its second venue, Siena, by November 1423.

Beyond the Papal States, Martin asserted his rights as they had been understood before the rise of conciliarism. Thus English ecclesiastical wealth was once more siphoned off to support the regime in Rome. In this instance it meant that Martin's nephew Prospero Colonna held the archdeaconry of Canterbury for a decade from 1424. The man most directly undermined by this was Archbishop Chichele, who tried to cling on the the enhanced authority he had enjoyed while there was no meaningful papal power. Chichele's sheer longevity frustrated any Roman desire to be rid of him. Thus the most conspicuous conflict over a major benefice was occasioned by the death of Archbishop Bowet of York in 1423. The chapter elected Philip Morgan, who had been papally provided to Worcester and was the candidate of the regency council, but Martin insisted on translating Flemming from Lincoln. Both sides stood their ground until a compromise was reached in 1425, when John Kemp was translated from London to York.

One of the curialists involved in the negotiations behind Kemp's translation was William Swan, whose letter-book – surviving in two manuscript copies – is an important source for Anglo-papal relations in this period.[18] Swan served many masters, who were better represented at the curia than was the king, for Thomas Polton left Rome when Morgan appeared to have created an attractive vacancy at Worcester and was not replaced as the royal proctor until 1429. Martin, on the other hand, was amply represented in England, whether by the envoy Giuliano Cesarini or collectors such as Simone da Teramo and Giovanni Obizzi. The pope's determination to impose his authority across the English Channel could not have been clearer: in 1426 Cesarini was commissioned to persuade the government to revoke the Statutes of Provisors and Praemunire, and Obizzi brought an order suspending Archbishop Chichele's legatine status.[19] Chichele and his ally Humphrey, duke of Gloucester, had the advantage of fighting on home turf: in 1427 Obizzi was arrested on the duke's order.[20] It was surely no coincidence that the king of Scots was emboldened to introduce his own antipapal statutes in 1427–8.

Cesarini's mission presented an opportunity for Henry Beaufort to restore his reputation by ingratiating himself with a papal representative, so much so that Cesarini was able to report that Beaufort favoured revocation of the contentious statutes. Consequently, Beaufort was among the beneficiaries when Martin tried a different approach to the English problem: in 1426 a quarter of the pope's twelve new cardinals came with English connections of some sort. Besides Beaufort, the others were the papal *nipote* Prospero Colonna and the sometime envoy Cesarini. This time Beaufort enjoyed the honour without losing his benefices, but his political adversaries had not finished in their efforts to thwart both the cardinal and his papal master. In 1427 he was appointed to a central European legation with a view to raising an army and leading it against the Hussite heretics in Bohemia. Desparate for troops to throw into their efforts to retain Henry V's conquests in France, the English government took over payment of Beaufort's army, diverted it to France and destroyed any hope of a crusade. It was the end of any mutually beneficial relationship between Pope Martin and the English cardinal.

As Beaufort knew from the more active phases of his career, an able ecclesiastic could exercise greater power and dispense more patronage in the king's service than he could as part of the Sacred College, in which power, influence and income was shared, whether between a few ecclesiastical princes if the pope happened to be weak, or many if he was strong. Thus no English cardinals voted in the remaining seven conclaves of the fifteenth century. Martin V's immediate successor was elected by a predominantly Italian college, though the absence of three French and two Spanish cardinals served to make Beaufort's non-participation appear less remarkable. The new pope, Eugenius IV (1431–47), was a nephew of Gregory XII and came with both curial and conciliar experience, but his instincts were for the religious life and created the impression that he could be treated with contempt, whether by the secular powers, hardline conciliarists, or Romans who resented the very existence of a Venetian pope. With a patience cultivated as a canon regular of S. Giorgio in Alga in the Venetian lagoon, Eugenius calmly waited for each storm to blow itself out.

Still bound by the decree *Frequens* (1417), Martin had summoned a general council to meet at Basel. His death then delayed its assembly. By the early 1430s there was enough of a reaction against Martin's interventionist brand of papal monarchy, particularly in France, to take advantage of a new council, and the first assault on Eugenius's authority came from Basel, where the fathers disobeyed his instruction to dissolve. Instead, they championed a reformist agenda to the extent of dealing with the excommunicated Hussites, and mirrored papal diplomacy by dispatching their own envoys to the secular powers. The English government responded to one such embassy by sending two successive delegations to Basel. The first included the former royal proctor Thomas Polton and the second was led by Polton's curial successor, Bishop Robert Fitzhugh of London, but there was no serious danger of England's regency government pursuing an overtly antipapal agenda or of breaking off relations with Eugenius, who represented considerably less of a threat to their interests than had his predecessor. James of Scotland, on the other hand, was a mature monarch at the height of his power. That he was more inclined towards antipapalism was indicated by the fact that his right-hand man, the chancellor John Cameron, headed the Scottish delegation to Basel in 1434.

Eugenius could do little about the Basel conciliarists as long as he was beset by enemies closer to home. The Colonna family resented the diminution of power and patronage that followed the death of their papal kinsman and revolted against the new Venetian pope. Prospero Colonna, the archdeacon of Canterbury, took part in their rebellion and was briefly deprived of the cardinalate in 1433. By June 1434 popular opposition to Eugenius was so intense that he was forced to flee from Rome. The organs of papal government were re-established in Florence, where the English agents Andrew Holes and Adam Moleyns flourished in the melting pot of scholars both curial and Florentine. This was the context in which Moleyns was required to lobby for Beaufort's kinsman Thomas Bourchier to become bishop of Worcester, regardless of the fact that Eugenius had already provided the dean of Salisbury, Thomas Brouns, to the vacancy. Moleyns persisted and, in 1435, Eugenius overruled his own decision in order to provide Bourchier, while Brouns received compensation in the form of Rochester, one of England's poorest sees. If Christendom's ultimate fount of patronage could be made to bend so easily, there was no real incentive for the English elite to side with the conciliarists of Basel.

Although Eugenius remained in Florence until 1443, papal authority was soon restored in Rome, from where it spread slowly but steadily during the remainder of the pontificate. In 1435, for example, it was with assistance from papal intermediaries that France and Burgundy composed their long-standing differences at the Congress of Arras. England's recent European prominence had been due as much to its Burgundian alliance as it was to Henry V's military prowess, so this realignment of the powers presented an opportunity for the papacy to seek reassurance that England was not about to find new friends by siding with the conciliarists. To that end the Venetian cleric and arch-papalist Pietro del Monte was sent as collector of papal taxes though, in practice, financial matters were left to a sub-collector. Instead, del Monte ingratiated himself with the ruling elite, particularly the king's uncle Humphrey of Gloucester, and Anglo-papal relations proceeded with relative ease. Meanwhile, under the continuing influence of John Cameron, James of Scotland committed himself neither to Eugenius nor to the council, but was in contact with both. Cameron visited the curia in 1436 and requested a legate for Scotland. Antonio Altan, bishop of Urbino, was appointed and arrived in the kingdom at the end of the year. However, within a matter of weeks, the king was assassinated and any meaningful negotiations stopped. Altan was on hand to provide papal support for the six-year-old James II (1437–60), but was soon sent on a separate mission to Germany.

In September 1437 Eugenius ordered the Basel fathers to transfer to Ferrara, where he convened an ecumenical council of the Eastern and Western churches to address the plight of beleaguered Constantinople. Most complied, but a hard core stayed put. The latter included the Scottish Cistercian Thomas Livingston, whose family was among those who contended for power during the royal minority. Livingston was also closely involved with the conciliarists' 'deposition' of Eugenius in June 1439 and their subsequent election of the duke of Savoy as 'Felix V'. In gratitude, Felix provided him to the bishopric of Dunkeld. The eletion of an antipope caused Eugenius to assert himself as never before: on 18 December 1439 he responded to the election of a rival by creating seventeen new cardinals, selecting a geographically diverse range of prelates from throughout Christendom. Four of the new cardinals had insular connections – not all of them positive – though only Archbishop Kemp was native to the region.[21] Gerardo Landriani had been the conciliar envoy to England in 1432, but the really clever touch came in balancing Louis de Luxembourg, administrator of Ely and archbishop of Rouen in English-occupied Normandy, against Guillaume d'Estouteville, bishop-elect of Angers, whose family had lost their Norman estates to the English invaders. The next step after an Anglo-French balancing act with red hats was an Anglo-French peace, which Eugenius clearly approved when his nuncio in France, the former collector del Monte, presided over the betrothal of Henry VI to Marguerite, daughter of Duke René of Anjou, in 1444. To underline the Anglo-papal harmony that prevailed towards the end of the pontificate, Henry became the first English recipient of a golden rose, nearly three centuries after Lucius III's gift to Scotland's William the Lion.

When news of Eugenius's death reached Basel supporters of 'Felix V' hoped that their cause would flourish. To that end Livingston was sent on a legatine mission to Scotland. The eighteen Roman cardinals knew that they could give no ground to their opponents and rapidly elected one of their number, Tommaso Parentucelli of Sarzana, to the papal office. Nicholas V (1447–55) proved to be a pope who could do business with secular powers, among whom Charles VII of France made his submission to the papacy. Without that king's support, the council dissolved and Felix abdicated. 1450 was declared a holy year, so offered an opportunity for reconciliation on a grand scale, but Rome's infrastructure was unable to cope with the mass influx of pilgrims and Nicholas devoted the later years of his pontificate to urban regeneration, of which the rebuilding of St Peter's Basilica was merely the most prominent example. His message to the outside world was that Rome was now a permanent capital where ecclesiastical authority was firmly centralised in the person of the pope.

England's experience during this pontificate was of interconnected military defeats, political crises and popular uprisings. The loss of Normandy in 1450 triggered calls for Richard, duke of York, to be given a leading role in government, King Henry's confidants having manifestly failed; the loss of Gascony in 1453 heralded the king's mental collapse, leaving England without a functioning monarch. A succession of royal proctors kept business ticking over at the curia, but records for this period are so thin that there are no surviving details of Archbishop Marino Orsini's brief English mission in 1451. The papal connection was somewhat stronger in Scotland: William Turnbull, formerly James I's curial proctor, obtained a bull authorising the foundation of a university in his diocese of Glasgow.[22] Such a development hardly posed a threat to Nicholas's ambition to make Rome the world capital of learning. On the other hand, the Ottoman Turks threatened Christian culture in its entirety. After the fall of Constantinople to the forces of Sultan Mehmet on 29 May 1453, Nicholas made frantic efforts to bring the secular powers together in a new crusading initiative. To England he dispatched a Greek exile, Nicolas Agolo, and a future cardinal, Bartolomeo Roverella, but neither could make any impact in a realm descending into civil war.

Crusading fervour so motivated Nicholas's successor, the aged Catalan Calixtus III (1455–8), that he had a medallion struck to record his life's mission: the destruction of the enemies of the Christian faith. Most of the Christian powers were stubbornly deaf to his appeals for united action, the only significant result being the Hungarian defence of Belgrade in 1456. No support could be expected from England, where Lancastrians fought Yorkists at

St Albans on 22 May 1455, after which the duke of York's sole concern was maintaining control of domestic government. In the light of such diverging priorities, it is all the more remarkable that Calixtus was the only Renaissance pope to canonise an Englishman. A campaign by the king's agents in Rome finally reached fruition after four decades, when the eleventh-century bishop Osmund of Salisbury was canonised on 1 January 1457.[23]

As his autobiographical *Commentaries* attest, Pius II (1458–64) came to the papacy with a post-schism Italian's antipathy towards Frenchmen and a mainlander's aversion to Venetians. His impressions of England and Scotland were formed in 1435, when he was sent on a mission to James I. He had reached the 'rich and populous' city of London before being denied a safe-conduct to Scotland and sent back to the Channel by way of Canterbury.[24] When he finally reached the remote and barbarous northern kingdom he made a ten-mile barefoot pilgrimage to Whitekirk, discharged his mission to the king, and then took the risk of returning to Basel via Durham, York and London.[25] Over the following years, this young adventurer, Enea Silvio Piccolomini, became a prolific and versatile man of letters. By the time of his papal election in 1458, England had produced similar *literati*, including John Tiptoft, earl of Worcester, who conveyed the king's obedience to the new pope by means of a Latin oration so eloquent that it reduced Pius to tears. However, as Calixtus had known and Pius now had to admit, such learning could not restore Christianity in the former Byzantine Empire. To that end the new pope invited representatives of the secular powers to meet with him in Mantua. An English delegation to this diet was named but went nowhere because the political elite was again descending into armed conflict. Eventually, in September 1459, a small delegation led by the curial proctor Robert Flemming arrived in Mantua: it was an insult to Pius's grand design and he refused to receive so unimpressive an embassy. This makes a neat enough story but, in truth, England was not exceptional, for France, Burgundy and the other larger powers had no greater intention of supporting the pope's crusade, even if they had the means to do so.

Another strand of Pius's campaign for a crusade saw an envoy, Francesco Coppini of Prato, dispatched to Burgundy and England. Coppini relished a political situation in which Yorkists cultivated Duke Charles of Burgundy in opposition to Henry VI's French queen. In 1460 Coppini threw in his lot with Richard Neville, earl of Warwick, and the other Yorkist lords holed up in Calais. When they crossed the Channel he accompanied them to Northampton, so was present at their capture of King Henry on 10 July. Coppini inaccurately assumed that he possessed legatine powers, but departed from the practices of previous legates, who had consistently supported kings against rebellious and over-mighty subjects, rather than the other way round. At least Coppini managed to pick a winner, for the eighteen-year-old Edward, duke of York, declared himself king in March 1461 and roundly defeated the Lancastrians at Towton. A legate was finally nominated for England and Scotland later that year, though in practice the wily bishop of Arras, Jean Jouffroy, devoted himself exclusively to French concerns. None of this could contribute anything to the papal crusade, which got no further than Ancona, where Pope Pius died on 15 August 1464.

As one of the Venetians despised by Pius, Paul II (1464–71) offered a clear contrast with his predecessor. Pius had broken with papal precedent by marrying his nephew into a ruling dynasty, that of Naples; Paul confined himself to clerical dynasticism. Pius had created a rural retreat in the Tuscan countryside, outside the Papal States; when Paul built it was a vast palace in the heart of Rome. Most significantly, Paul made no attempt attempt to coordinate crusading ventures into some sort of unified whole. Meanwhile, so loyal were Pius's cardinals to their patron's memory that they could not conceal their hostility towards Paul, who lacked a similar body of loyal lieutenants. His response was to develop the practice of his kinsman Eugenius IV and look for support from beyond the Alps. Thus he created cardinals who could connect Rome with the most powerful secular princes of the day, King Mátyás of Hungary, Louis XI of France and Charles the Bold, duke of Burgundy. Paul's 'Burgundian' was actually Thomas Bourchier, Kemp's successor at Canterbury, who suddenly became useful in 1467 because the twice-widowed Charles was about to be betrothed to Margaret of York, sister of Edward IV (1461–70, 1471–83). Edward used Bourchier's promotion as a stick with which to beat the pro-French Nevilles, particularly George Neville, archbishop of York, whose Roman contacts were evidently not strong enough to see him raised to the cardinalate. Between 1469 and 1471 the Nevilles rebelled against Edward, first taking the king's brother, George, duke of Clarence, with them, and then restoring Henry VI to the throne while Edward fled to Burgundy. The papal dimension of this episode emerged when Clarence required a dispensation to marry Richard Neville's daughter Isabel because they were related within the prohibited degrees of consanguinity. It was obtained by the king's proctor, James Goldwell, who remained in Rome throughout Paul's pontificate, but was relatively under-employed when it came to securing benefices for the king's candidates. By the mid 1460s this process had acquired another layer, with cardinals acting as 'relators' or sponsors of candidates. Each 'relation' earned the cardinal a fixed-rate fee or *propina*. It fell to proctors such as Goldwell to cultivate friendly cardinals. During Paul's pontificate this system was still developing, so there are relatively few signs of geographical specialisation, though the Breton Alain de Coëtivy sponsored two Scottish candidates and Latino Orsini – no friend of Burgundy – appears to have been Goldwell's patron of choice for English clerics.[26] Orsini was already the longest-serving Italian-born cardinal and achieved even greater prominence in 1471, when Sixtus IV (1471–84) appointed him as camerlengo. Goldwell benefited personally from the connection, Orsini acting as his sponsor to the bishopric of Norwich in 1472.

There was much jockeying for patronage at the beginning of Sixtus's pontificate and detailed lists of cardinals' familiars reveal that even the non-curial Bourchier supported sixteen clerics in Rome, none of whom were English.[27] The same source has a 'Johannes Blakader' among the familiars of Guillaume d'Estouteville. This surely refers to Robert Blackadder, the envoy of James III (1460–88). In August 1472 Blackadder realised the long-held objective of Scottish curial diplomacy: St Andrews was raised to metropolitical status, thereby eliminating any lingering claim by the archbishops of York over the Church in Scotland. The incumbent bishop, Patrick Graham, had the honour of becoming the first Scottish primate. Cardinal d'Estouteville's anti-English interest in Scottish benefices pre-dated his patronage of Blackadder but was clearly sustained by that relationship and included sponsorship of the orator himself to the see of Aberdeen in 1480. Other Francophone cardinals related candidates to Scottish bishropics and abbacies, but the prelate who came closest to d'Estouteville in exhibiting a sustained interest was the Mantuan Francesco Gonzaga, a kinsman of James III's Danish queen.

When viewed from Rome, Scotland was essentially an adjunct to its French ally, whereas Yorkist England was emerging as something more significant than an offshoot of Valois Burgundy, particularly after the death of Charles the Bold in 1477. However, when viewed by Pope Sixtus IV himself, both nations were on the periphery of a world centred on his own extended family, who were celebrated by poets, buried in classically-inspired Roman monuments, and married into Italian princely families, for Sixtus played Italian power politics on a scale only faintly foreshadowed by Pius II. The best that England could offer to the court culture of Sistine Rome was a visit by Edward IV's cultured brother-in-law Anthony Woodville, who went on pilgrimage during the holy year of 1475 and returned as 'defender and director of papal causes' in England, and Robert Flemming's Latin hexameter poem *Lucubratiunculae Tiburtinae*, written in praise of the pope and printed in 1477. Sixtus's instinct for dynasticism worked well in his dealings with monarchies and princely states, making it no coincidence that the most notable of his wars were against republican Florence and Venice. War came at a cost, which could only be met – if it was met at all – by income from lucrative benefices. In this respect England was so much more useful than it had been while weakened by civil conflict and, accordingly, steadily became more of a papal priority. In 1480–1 there was a very particular military crisis to which Sixtus hoped that the princes of Christendom might respond: after years of campaigning in the Balkans, Ottoman troops had crossed the Adriatic and occupied the city of Otranto in the heel of Italy. It was at this point that Sixtus chose to send a blessed sword and hat to Edward IV, the first such gift to a king of England, though there was no realistic chance of him campaigning so far from home.

For his part, King Edward spent the early 1470s cultivating a range of diplomatic relationships in preparation for his invasion of France in 1475.

In Italy this meant overtures towards Federico da Montefeltro, one of the vicars in the Papal States, and King Ferrante of Naples, in whose realm were various Orsini estates and benefices; to the north an Anglo-Scottish treaty was signed in 1473 and an Anglo-Danish one in 1475. These alliances provided the context for Cardinal Gonzaga's sponsorship of candidates to bishoprics in northern England in 1476–8. However, that was not the whole picture. In 1478 alone, English episcopal candidates were related by five cardinals, of whom only one, Paul II's kinsman Marco Barbo, developed an enduring relationship with the English nation. It was Barbo who secured the English collectorship for Giovanni Gigli in 1476, thereby initiating that agent's long financial and diplomatic career in Anglo-papal relations. The vast majority of Barbo's relations to English bishoprics occurred from that point onwards, coinciding with the period when John Shirwood was Edward's representative at the curia. Shirwood had before him the model of Goldwell's cultivation of Latino Orsini, and perfected it. The bond that united Shirwood and Barbo was classical literature, for Shirwood was among the foremost Greek scholars of his day and could compose elegant Latin prose as a matter of course. The most direct literary connection between the two men was Shirwood's *Liber de ludo arithmomachia*, which he dedicated to Barbo as 'protector anglorum'.[28] Not surprisingly, Barbo was the relator when Shirwood became bishop of Durham in 1484. In that year Richard III (1483–5) also recommended Shirwood for the cardinalate, but had missed Sixtus's final promotion, even had the pope been minded to create a cardinal who could make no obvious contribution to the war he was then waging against the Venetians. Meanwhile, the most committed red-hatted friend of Ireland was Cardinal Giovanni Arcimboldi of Milan, who sponsored to seven vacancies between 1478 and 1484. This somewhat surprising connection was established when Arcimboldi proposed the Florentine Ottaviano Spinelli, then nuncio in Ireland, to the archbishopric of Armagh. It is logical to assume that Spinelli then maintained the connection with his patron.

If Rome gained so much by maintaining good relations with wealthier powers, why did monarchs still consent to clerical taxation leaving their kingdoms, to legal cases being heard in the papal courts, and to Italians holding bishoprics that could have gone to royal favourites? One abiding reason was provided by regulations relating to marriage. In the ordinary course of events, members of the ruling elite married within their own narrow caste and, as the Clarence–Neville example illustrates, that frequently required a dispensation which only the pope could supply. Equally, a marriage could only be terminated by an annulment, such as the duke of Orléans demanded of the pope when he inherited the French throne in 1498.[29] On that occasion Orléans was the undoubted heir to the kingdom, but a prince whose claim was contested could bolster his case by citing the support of the reigning pope. In England in 1485 the change of ruling dynasty passed smoothly because

Henry Tudor's agent, the exiled bishop of Ely John Morton, had visited Rome, preparing the papacy for Richard III's defeat and Tudor's intended marriage with Elizabeth of York. Hardly had Tudor become King Henry VII than a legate – Giacomo Passarella, bishop of Imola – was sent to England, listened to the arguments and issued a dispensation, allowing the couple to marry two days later. So grateful was Henry for continued papal support during the period when Yorkist pretenders sought to challenge his title that he sent a large embassy, led by Thomas Millyng, bishop of Hereford, to tender his obedience to Innocent VIII (1484–92), as Cardinal Barbo had cause to observe in correspondence on 20 May 1487.[30] Barbo, the 'protector anglorum', died in 1491. He proved to be a stepping-stone to the first formal recognition of a cardinal protector of England or, indeed, of any nation. England being an offshoot of the German nation, the man chosen for this role in 1492 was a specialist in German affairs, the Sienese cardinal Francesco Todeschini-Piccolomini.[31]

Cardinal Gonzaga died in 1483, so in Innocent's time the Scots' relations with Rome were again mediated by their French allies. In practice this meant Cardinal Jean Balue, who displayed little interest in Scottish affairs until after the murder of James III, when the accession of the young, unmarried James IV (1488–1513) raised the northern kingdom's diplomatic profile. The precedent created by Blackadder and d'Estouteville was repeated when the latest Scottish ambassador to the curia, Blackadder's kinsman Andrew Forman, took up residence in Balue's household. Blackadder's predecessor as bishop of Aberdeen had succeeded in having his diocese exempted from the jurisdiction of the new archbishop of St Andrews, so Blackadder played exactly the same card after his translation to Glasgow and received a similar exemption. Buoyed by this, he then tried something more audacious, returning to Rome in 1491 to argue that Glasgow should itself be a metropolitan see. Innocent meekly complied, granting Glasgow its enhanced status on 9 January 1492. No less remarkably, Innocent was persuaded to send two golden roses to Scotland in just five years, the second in anticipation of James IV's future defence of the faith, rather than in recognition of any past achievements. Thus did Blackadder and Forman prove to be masters of the art of managing a relatively weak pope, an art that was lost by Scots and English alike in the course of the sixteenth century.

CHAPTER 4

OF SWORDS AND ROSES

The parameters of this chapter were determined by the election of Pope Alexander VI in 1492 and the death of Pope Urban VIII in 1644. They correspond reasonably closely to the outbreak of the Italian Wars (1494) and the conclusion of the Thirty Years War (1648), a period of European history in which the clearest fault line was between France and the Habsburg lands of Spain and the Holy Roman Empire. In terms of the insular chronology, the chapter begins in the reign of the first Tudor monarch, Henry VII, and ends before the execution of Charles I (1625–49). Its title draws attention to continuity in papal gift-giving, from the blessed swords and hats sent to James IV of Scotland and Henry VIII of England to the golden roses dispatched to Mary, queen of Scots, and Charles I's consort Henrietta Maria, for there was a concentration of such gifts in this period, but no more after 1625. Such continuity contrasts with the idea of the sixteenth century marking a clean break in British history, between subservience to the papacy in a benighted 'medieval' past and a nation becoming great and realising its destiny precisely because it had broken free from those papal shackles. When the Protestant nation told its own story it emphasised the Acts of the English Parliament by which the unilateral break with Rome was created in the 1530s, and the papal excommunication of its heroine Elizabeth I in 1570. The pope was cast as the arch-villain and anyone who exhibited loyalty to the papacy was a traitor. This story of heroes and villains was consolidated over the following centuries, but the reality in the long sixteenth century was not so clear cut, there being relatively few pontificates when there were no high-level contacts or desire to heal the breach, whether for religious or political reasons. By the 1640s the most striking division was not between Britain and Rome, but between Charles I's courtiers, many of whom were attracted to Catholicism and had no particular problem with the papacy, and the Puritans, to whom the pope was nothing less than the Antichrist.

By 1492 the Sacred College of Cardinals had been so thoroughly politicised and Italianised that the conclave which opened after the death of Innocent VIII soon reached a deadlock between the 'Milanese' faction's Neapolitan candidate and the 'Neapolitan' faction's Venetian candidate. It was broken by both groups voting for the Aragonese vice-chancellor Rodrigo Borgia. As Alexander VI (1492–1503), Borgia's rebalancing of the college saw the promotion of marginally more Spaniards than Italians, contributing to the xenophobia that soon disfigured his reputation, but he was adept at currying favour with monarchs in general, as was demonstrated by his promotion of a Polish prince and the Hungarian chancellor. Henry VII's chancellor, Archbishop John Morton, was also among Alexander's new cardinals. Morton was firmly non-curial, so in 1503 the pope compensated for that by promoting to the cardinalate the bishop of Hereford, Adriano Castellesi, who had been sent on a mission to Scotland in 1488 and succeeded Giovanni Gigli as papal collector in England two years later. With regard to official protection by a cardinal Alexander's pontificate witnessed no change to the existing arrangements: between 1490 and 1503 Todeschini-Piccolomini sponsored candidates to thirty-two English and Welsh episcopal vacancies, together with seven in Ireland.[1]

Further down the hierarchy came proctors and nuncios. In the case of Castellesi this was the same person, depending on whether he happened to be representing the English king in Rome or the pope in England. Along with Gigli, Castellesi was keen to inherit the diplomatic mantle of John Shirwood. Death removed Gigli from this competition in 1498, his embassy and the bishopric of Worcester being inherited by his nephew Silvestro, of whom Castellesi became an implacable enemy. A new Italian entered the Anglo-papal story in 1502 when the scholarly Polidoro Virgili – Polydore Vergil to the English – became sub-collector of Peter's Pence. Ordinary business was conducted as before. Even the extraordinary business between Rome and the royal courts of England and Scotland had a traditional character to it. Thus Henry VII received a blessed sword and hat from Alexander, and James IV was sent the sceptre which still survives among the Honours of Scotland. More rare, but no less traditional, was the request made by William Elphinstone for papal permission to found a university in his bishopric of Aberdeen. The bull of foundation, dated 10 February 1495, was the last such document granted by a pope to a British university. Alexander was also called upon to umpire the Anglo-Scottish 'perpetual peace' of 1502, in the sense that a military attack by one party upon the other would lead to the aggressor being excommunicated.

During Alexander's pontificate the vicissitudes of war in the Italian peninsula and the alliances behind that conflict brought a new dimension to papal relations with the secular powers, even those as far afield as the British Isles. The first foreign invasion was that of Charles VIII of France, who laid claim to the kingdom of Naples in 1494–5. That triggered a military response from the king of Aragon on behalf of his ousted kinsmen. In 1498 Charles was succeeded by his cousin Louis, duke of Orléans, who thereupon opened another

Italian front by claiming the duchy of Milan. By 1503 Spain was in possession of Naples, as France was of Milan. Henry VII was steadily drawn into Fernando of Aragon's anti-French diplomacy, first as a rather distant member of the Holy League formed in response to the first French invasion, and later through the marriage in 1501 of his son Arthur with Fernando's daughter Catalina. When Arthur died within five months of their (unconsummated?) union, the parties' determination to retain this dynastic alliance by means of a marriage between the new English heir, Prince Henry, and his brother's widow required a papal dispensation. This matter was still pending in 1503.

In August that year Castellesi secured his place in the Borgia legend by hosting the dinner at which Alexander and his son Cesare were said to have been poisoned. They probably contracted malaria. After Alexander's death on 18 August none of his Spanish protégés stood any chance of election to the papacy, but nor was there much appetite for a French pontiff. Todeschini-Piccolomini's German and English connections made him politically neutral as far as control of Italy was concerned and he was elected as Pius III on 22 September, but the rigours of his coronation ensured that he died after a reign of just twenty-six days.

Cardinal Giuliano della Rovere made the most of that stop-gap pontificate and secured unanimous election in a matter of hours on 31 October– 1 November. After a twenty-year apprenticeship and a decade of frustrating exile from Alexander's Rome, Pope Julius II (1503–13) could hardly have been better prepared. He set about securing his state methodically and ruthlessly. The coffers emptied by Alexander were steadily filled. The Roman baronial families alienated by the Borgia were tied by marriage to the Della Rovere. Overmighty subjects were subdued, not by a papal kinsman but by the pope himself. Any neighbouring state that dared to use superior military forces to occupy papal territory learned to its cost that Julius would stop at nothing to exercise his authority over the Papal States in their entirety. The Julius who went to war against the Venetians or the French was the same combative Julius who is denied entry to heaven in a lively dialogue written for an erudite English readership, presumably by the Dutch scholar Erasmus.[2]

James IV could hardly have been more peripheral to Julius's italocentric priorities, which adds a certain irony to the fact that Scotland's sword of state was originally half of the traditional sword and hat blessed by the pope. Julius's interest in England was essentially financial. The archbishopric of Canterbury required filling three times between 1500 and 1503, suggesting that England could be a convenient source of income for a curial cardinal sponsoring candidates to such vacancies. It is little wonder that Julius gave the English protectorship to his nephew Galeotto Franciotti della Rovere. Castellesi hoped to secure the appointment, but had to be content with translation from Hereford to the more lucrative bishopric of Bath and Wells. When the protectorship became vacant again it went to Julius's henchman Francesco Alidosi. At his death in 1511 it fell into abeyance, leaving the Rome-based archbishop of York, Christopher Bainbridge, to fill the role in all but name.

Henry VII's dealings with Julius were never anything other than businesslike. The principal item of English business was Henry's request for a dispensation for the marriage of Prince Henry to his widowed sister-in-law. Julius was initially uncertain how to proceed, eventually issuing a brief, which stated that the first marriage had been consummated, and a bull, which permitted the princess's remarriage 'even if' her first union had been consummated. Both were backdated to 26 December 1503. The intermediaries in this episode included Richard Bere, abbot of Glastonbury, who led the English embassy to Rome in 1504, and Silvestro Gigli, who conveyed the dispensation to England. The man sidelined in all of this was Castellesi, who felt so threatened by Gigli that he insisted on the members of Bere's mission lodging with him in his palace near the Vatican. Even when Gigli was safely in England, Castellesi still felt vulnerable: in 1507 he fled from Rome and was deprived of the collectorship, as was Virgili of the sub-collectorship.

Henry VII had been superfluous to the requirements of the anti-Venetian league of Cambrai in 1508, but Henry VIII (1509–47) was useful to Julius because of his potential to draw French forces away from northern Italy. In 1511 Henry followed his father-in-law into the anti-French Holy League. This time the intermediary was Bainbridge, who served as Henry's curial ambassador from 1509 and found such favour with Julius that he was raised to the cardinalate in 1511 and appointed legate to the papal army. If the pope and his cardinals could so forget themselves as to become warriors, then a king could fill the spiritual void by summoning a general council of the Church, which is precisely what Louis XII did. By the time Louis's essentially French council assembled at Pisa in September 1511, Julius had called a technically valid one to meet in Rome the following year. The Fifth Lateran Council was part of a co-ordinated anti-French strategy, according to which Fernando and Henry undertook to invade France from the south-west and, on condition that Louis was defeated, Julius promised to transfer the title 'Most Christian King' to Henry. Although English forces proceeded no further than Fuentarrabía, in Italy Louis was defeated by Swiss arms in the summer of 1512, retreating back over the Alps and into his own kingdom. The French king's Pisan schism imploded just as easily but, again, it was no thanks to Henry, whose representative, Gigli, arrived in Rome five months after the opening of Julius's council. Most of its sessions were held during the next pontificate.

English cardinals had excluded themselves from conclaves for more than 140 years when Bainbridge voted in March 1513. Inside the enclosure he made his mark quite literally, scratching onto the bottom of his dinner plate the names of Cardinals Giovanni de' Medici and Raffaele Sansoni-Riario as a message to the outside world regarding the likely result. Medici was indeed elected, becoming Leo X (1513–21). The Medici of Florence had grown rich on French trade and French benefices, and papal policy towards the secular powers changed accordingly. France's more recent ally James IV had breached the 'perpetual peace' by attacking England, so the resolutely anti-French Bainbridge ensured that James was excommunicated before Leo could show clemency. This had few consequences, because James was killed at Flodden in September 1513. Henry, meanwhile, was cultivated with a sword-and-hat gift combination, and was introduced to Leo's pro-French policy by the legate Gian Pietro Carafa. On the other side of the diplomatic coin, Henry's ambitious almoner Thomas Wolsey employed Gigli in Rome to undermine Bainbridge, so when the cardinal died suddenly in 1514 Gigli was accused of ordering his murder. With Bainbridge out of the way, Leo revived the English protectorship for his cousin Giulio de' Medici, who added Ireland to his portfolio in 1517. Like Franciotti della Rovere, Giulio was vice-chancellor of the Church, so this was quite a coup, and Henry demonstrated his appreciation by favouring Giulio's appointment to the bishopric of Worcester in 1521.

Scotland acquired its first cardinal protector towards the end of Leo's pontificate and the man chosen was another Florentine, Pietro Accolti. Leo also selected his own nephew – and Innocent VIII's grandson – Cardinal Innocenzo Cibo, for the primatial see of St Andrews. This appointment was contested by Andrew Forman, who wanted St Andrews for himself and had sufficient curial experience to cut an appropriate deal. Thus Leo agreed that Forman should resign the archbishopric of Bourges to Cibo, so that the Scot could be provided to St Andrews and serve as legate *a latere*; only his ambition for a red hat remaining unrealised. Forman spent his last years in Scotland, where the governing elite acquired a papal connection to trump anything enjoyed by their English counterparts. In 1518 the French sister-in-law of the duke of Albany, regent for James V (1513–42), married Leo's nephew Lorenzo, duke of Urbino. Albany took advantage of this dynastic link by requesting that the pope take the young king under his protection. Hardly had Leo done so than he acquired a similar responsibility much closer to home: Lorenzo and his wife died suddenly, leaving a baby daughter, Caterina.

In 1515 a new French king, François I, appeared to represent a greater threat to the Italian states than had his cousin Louis. With a French army once more in Italy Leo panicked and, on 10 September, conceded a red hat to Wolsey, in the hope that England would break its new French alliance and provide a military distraction to the north. By 1518 Leo needed another favour from England, which had the resources to contribute to his proposed crusade against the Ottoman sultan Selim, whose rapid conquests of Syria and Egypt boded ill for chronically disunited Christendom. Leo proposed a five-year truce, during which the Christian powers would seek to recapture

Constantinople. Legates were appointed to preach the crusade, with Cardinal Lorenzo Campeggi being selected for England. Wolsey was now Henry's all-powerful lord chancellor and had no intention of involving England in a crusade, so Campeggi was kept waiting at Boulogne while concessions were extracted from Rome. This time Leo granted legatine powers to Wolsey and deprived the futigive Castellesi of both the cardinalate and the bishopric of Bath and Wells, the administration of which was assumed by the English cardinal. Only then was Campeggi permitted to cross the Channel. Nowhere did the proposed crusade inspire much enthusiasm, but only Wolsey managed to incorporate the pope's plan into a grander scheme of his own devising, which was for a 'universal peace', agreed in London that October and ratified by Leo with considerable reluctance.

From 1519 onwards the Anglo-papal relationship was coloured not only by the connections of both parties with France, but also with a new emperor, Charles V, from the house of Habsburg, who already ruled the Low Countries, Castile, Aragon and Naples, and whose imperial election Leo had sought to prevent because of the imbalance of power that would result. Pope and emperor were, however, thrown together by the need to contain the Lutheran revolution that was rapidly taking hold in the German states, and formalised this in a treaty of May 1521. Following Leo's rejection of François as an unreliable ally, England also tacked towards the emperor. In the Treaty of Bruges Charles and Henry pledged themselves to protect the pope, Henry's commitment being reinforced when his ambassador John Clerk presented Leo with the king's anti-Lutheran tract, *Assertio septem sacramentorum*.[3] Henry might have failed in his attempt to be 'Most Christian', but the text was enough to earn him, his heirs and successors an alternative title, 'Defender of the Faith', granted by Leo in October 1521.

In its determination to prevent Leo's cousin Giulio becoming the second successive Medici pope, the conclave of 1521–2 elected *in absentia* the imperial councillor Adriaan Florenszoon Dedel. There was no English dimension to the election, because Henry VIII's agent arrived too late and even the disgraced Castellesi was murdered *en route* to Rome. It was small compensation that Margaret of York, duchess of Burgundy, had been an early patron of the new pope, Adrian VI (1521–3). Throughout 1522 Adrian maintained a policy of strict neutrality, rebuffing Wolsey's invitation to support an anti-French alliance. In December the fall of Rhodes to Sultan Suleiman reinforced the pope's determination to reconcile the Christian powers and encourage them to unite against the infidel, to which end he conceded an extension of Wolsey's legatine powers. Adrian's resolve was repeatedly tested and, by July 1523, he was sufficiently exasperated by François to join Charles and Henry in an anti-French league. This abandonment of papal neutrality caused the pope's health to break down immediately and he did not live to see the allies' spectacular failure to dismember the French kingdom.

French efforts to block the imperial candidate, Giulio de' Medici, delayed his election for seven weeks in the autumn of 1523. The cardinal protector of Scotland, Accolti, had form as a pro-French anti-imperialist, whereas the English protector, Campeggi, had diplomatic experience in the Empire. The English envoys John Clerk and Thomas Hannibal talked up Wolsey's candidature in their dispatches from Rome, but were instructed to lobby for Medici, with Wolsey as Henry's second choice. Realistically, an absentee Englishman was not a likely successor to an absentee Dutchman and it was an experienced curial operator who became Pope Clement VII (1523–34).

England's previous cultivation of Giulio de' Medici paid dividends in the post-conclave period, for Henry received a golden rose and Wolsey gained the lifelong legatine powers denied him by Leo, followed by papal approval for the foundation of Cardinal College, Oxford. Clement was no less obliging towards the Scottish regency government, at its request removing the archbishop of Glasgow from the jurisdiction of the primate, Archbishop James Beaton of St Andrews. This balancing of English and Scottish requests shadowed the pope's appreciation of the need to balance imperial and French ambitions in Italy. By the beginning of 1525 power had tipped decisively in favour of Charles, so Clement entered into an anti-imperial league with Florence and Venice, but it was not enough to assist French forces at Pavia, where they were roundly defeated on 23–24 February, with François himself being taken prisoner. Upon gaining his liberty the king wasted no time in joining Clement, Florence, Venice and the Sforza of Milan in the anti-imperial League of Cognac (22 May 1526). The pope who had been elected as an imperialist made it clear that Habsburg power in Italy had to be curbed.

Seeking to take advantage of French vulnerability, England tacked back towards the emperor and two envoys, Sir John Russell and Sir Thomas Wyatt, were sent to Italy in the hope of mediating between Charles and Clement. On 8 February 1527 they presented the pope with a gift of 30,000 ducats from their king. It was enough neither to buy off the imperial army which was making its way south towards Rome nor to defend the city from the impending assault, which began on 6 May. While Rome was sacked and occupied, Clement was effectively a prisoner in Castel S. Angelo, until he escaped to Orvieto in December. News of the sack did not reach England until 1 June. In the meantime, Henry was aware that Clement had annulled his sister Margaret's marriage to Archibald Douglas, earl of Angus, on the grounds that Douglas had been precontracted to marry someone else.[4] If the Scottish queen dowager could obtain an annulment, then the English king could presumably be rid of his barren consort, for their lack of a son surely proved that God was displeased by Henry's marriage to his brother's widow (as indicated by Leviticus 20:21) and Julius II had therefore been in error when he dispensed for it. Wolsey looked for a quick fix: if other cardinals joined him in Avignon to govern the Church during Clement's imprisonment, they could pronounce the marriage to be invalid and free Henry to marry the presumably fertile Anne Boleyn. Katherine countered by assuring the pope and her devoted nephew the emperor that her first marriage had not been consummated, so was no impediment to the second, which even followed a biblical injunction to marry a deceased brother's widow and father children on his behalf (Deuteronomy 25:5). The citing of Old Testament texts reflected the biblical interests then fashionable at the English court, but was utterly irrelevant to the practice of canon law.[5]

The right language could produce results, even if they were limited ones. Between December 1527 and March 1528 two English embassies reached Clement at Orvieto. The first envoy, William Knight, asked for – and obtained – a dispensation that effectively permitted Henry to marry the sister of his ex-mistress, Mary Boleyn, while making no reference to his marriage to Katherine. On the second occasion Clement conceded little more than he had before: another dispensation for the king to marry Anne Boleyn and a commission for Wolsey and Campeggi to hear the annulment case in England. This was followed on 8 June by the granting of legatine authority to Campeggi. All the while the military initiative in Italy was with Odet de Foix, vicomte de Lautrec, whose anti-imperialist campaign was designed to restore Clement to Rome. However, at the height of summer Lautrec's army was more than decimated by disease, the commander himself dying in August. Clement did return to his capital in October, but it was against the backdrop of uncontested Habsburg strength in the peninsula, so his extreme caution in the case of the emperor's aunt was perfectly understandable. Campeggi arrived in England with long-standing doubts about the strength of Henry's case and secret instructions from Clement to reach no definite conclusion. In this he was assisted by Katherine's acquisition from Spain of Julius II's original brief of 26 December 1503, with its uncompromising wording concerning the validity of her marriage to Henry, rather than the copy on which she had hitherto relied.

1529 opened with Clement falling seriously ill. This imposed a further delay on attempts to resolve the 'king's great matter', for Henry's latest envoys, Sir Francis Bryan and the cleric Pietro Vanni, did not receive an audience until April. Meanwhile, Wolsey sent his trusted agent Stephen Gardiner an annotated list of cardinals to use in the event of a conclave, only for Clement to recover. Efforts to secure the annulment centred on a new resident ambassador to the curia, William Benet, together with the opening on 31 May of Wolsey and Campeggi's much-anticipated legatine court, held at the London Blackfriars. Neither of these developments made a scrap of difference, for the revived pontiff confronted the reality of French failure to break Habsburg power in Italy by signing the Treaty of Barcelona with Charles on 29 June. Almost immediately, France renounced its Italian ambitions: at least formally, Clement, Charles and François were all on the same side. Far from balancing the powers, England was completely isolated, so the pope was merely reflecting diplomatic reality when he advoked the annulment case to Rome.

Wolsey's failure to secure the annulment precipitated his fall from power, after which the campaign was taken up by others, including Anne Boleyn's uncle, the duke of Norfolk, who had no clear strategy about how to proceed. A petition dated 13 July 1530 and signed by more than eighty of the realm's leading men, from the archbishops downwards, requested Clement to grant the annulment, but the weight of numbers – and that of their accumulated seals – made no difference. Benet remained in Rome, though priority was given to the mission of Edward Carne, whose instructions were to temporise, which he did ingeniously for the next two years. Of more immediate concern to the pope was the fate of his native Florence, where the so-called 'last republic' capitulated in August after a ten-month siege by imperialist forces. The emperor decided what form of government the Tuscan state would then adopt and chose a compromise that left it a republic, albeit with the teenage Alessandro de' Medici as its *capo*. Two years later Alessandro became the first duke of Florence. By advancing the cause of the pope's kinsmen, Charles calculated that Clement would be suitably grateful. That it frustrated Henry of England was a convenient by-product.

Driven by a combination of religious zeal and the astute management of Henry's new councillor Thomas Cromwell, the English Parliament – the 'Reformation Parliament' – then took the initative, systematically rejecting papal authority and in effect nationalising the Church in England and Wales. The clergy were collectively charged with praemunire, which they acknowledged by paying an extremely large fine to the Crown, and submitted themselves to the king's authority with regard to the formation of canon law.[6] Asserting that 'this realm of England is an Empire', independent of 'the authority of any foreign potentates', Parliament passed the Act in Restraint of Appeals, according to which anyone taking legal appeals to courts outside the kingdom – in practice, those of the pope – would incur the 'dangers, pains, and penalties' contained in the Statutes of Provisors and Praemunire.[7] This conveniently made it impossible for Henry to submit his own case to Rome. Meanwhile, as far as the Roman curia was concerned, everything carried on as normal: Pietro Vanni was appointed as collector of taxes that were unlikely to be forthcoming, and Campeggi proposed Henry's undistinguished candidate for Canterbury, Thomas Cranmer, regardless of having been dismissed by the king as protector of England. Safe in the knowledge that he was protected by the recent legislation, Cranmer declared the king's marriage to Katherine to be null, leaving Henry married to his new wife, Anne. Clement was more vexed than ever and resolved to excommunicate Henry. However, instead of sailing off into uncharted ecclesiastical waters, Henry responded in the manner of monarchs considerably more powerful than he happened to be and issued an ill-judged appeal to a general council of the Church.

There was a significant royal marriage in 1533 and it was not that of Henry and Anne. Clement was so keen to see his niece Caterina safely married to François's younger son that he travelled to Marseille to perform the ceremony himself. There François argued in the interest of his fellow monarch that Henry's excommunication should be deferred for six months, only to be frustrated when he chanced upon the English cleric Edmund Bonner presenting Clement with Henry's request for a council. In their headlong dash into isolation, the English had managed to alienate a king whose example demonstrated that it was possible to control the Church in a particular realm without breaking from Rome.

By the end of March 1534 further antipapal legislation had been passed by the Parliament, including measures to deprive the papal exchequer of annates, which were levied on benefices, and Peter's Pence, which was paid by laymen, and to remove the absentee bishops of Salisbury and Worcester, Campeggi and Girolamo Ghinucci.[8] The Act of Succession excluded Katherine's daughter Mary, while favouring Anne's daughter Elizabeth. This was not an explicitly antipapal measure, but acceptance of it was by means of an oath, and that came with an overtly antipapal preamble. Alongside these events, on 23 March, the Roman authorities finally reached a definitive conclusion about Henry's marriage to Katherine: it was unquestionably valid. That was how matters stood at Clement's death in September. Any Act of Parliament can be repealed, but momentum was now with England's religious reformers and their king was sufficiently relieved by the pope's demise to make no attempt to reverse what had been done.

When the next conclave opened, on 11 October, its outcome was so obvious to informed observers that the French and imperial ambassadors were not required to apply pressure one way or the other. Henry's long-serving Roman agent Gregorio Casali was left to his own discretion when lobbying in England's interest. A unanimous election was secured in just two ballots, meaning that Alessandro Farnese, the widely respected dean of the college, received the votes of the Scottish protector Benedetto Accolti – who had succeeded his uncle Pietro in that capacity – and the (former) English protector Campeggi. As Pope Paul III (1534–49), Farnese's nepotism was something that all the princes could appreciate; they parted company when he proved to be a determined ecclesiastical reformer who would not be deflected from his resolve to summon an ecumenical council to address the continuing divisions in the Church. The new pope had no previous interest in England and began with suitably conciliatory words, but the Reformation Parliament was not to be stopped in its revolutionary tracks and, a month after Paul's election, the Act of Supremacy passed into law, declaring a new form of papalism without the pope, that of the king as 'supreme head on earth of the Church of England'.[9] The Act was reinforced by an oath requiring the holders of public offices, secular or ecclesiastical, to swear that 'no forraine Prince, Person, Prelate, State or Potentate, hath or ought to have any Jurisdiction, Power,

Superiorities, Preeminence or Authority Ecclesiasticall or Spirituall within this Realme.' Its meaning could not have been clearer.

While waiting for his conciliar plans to reach fruition, Paul concentrated on reform of the curia and on strengthening the Sacred College with men who had proved their commitment to the Church or possessed talents worth harnessing to the cause of ecclesiastical reform. In 1535–6 three out of his eighteen new cardinals represented a direct response to Henry's schism and an assertion of papal authority in the king's realm. First, in addition to the deprived Ghinucci, Paul selected John Fisher, bishop of Rochester, who was convicted for misprision (knowledge) of treason in 1534 and then refused to take the oath of supremacy precisely because it meant repudiating papal authority. Denying Henry's claim to supreme headship constituted treason itself. Henry asserted his new authority by having Fisher executed on 22 June, only a month after he was named a cardinal. The bishop's case was paralleled by that of the former lord chancellor Thomas More, who followed Fisher to the block on 6 July. Alongside these executions, the Parliament of June–July 1536 rushed through a measure for the 'utter abolition' of papal jurisdiction in England, fulminating against

> The pretended power and usurped authority of the Bishop of Rome, by some called the Pope [...] which did obfuscate and wrest God's holy word and testament a long season from the spiritual and true meaning thereof, to his worldly and carnal affections as pomp, glory, avarice, ambition and tyranny.[10]

Before the end of the year Paul responded by creating a third English cardinal, and raised the stakes by selecting Henry's kinsman Reginald Pole. Pole had previously taken it upon himself to defend in writing the unity of the Church, so notoriously fractured by his own cousin.[11] Now he was sent as legate to support the traditional Christians of northern England who had risen in the Pilgrimage of Grace. However, the rebellion was quashed before he got anywhere near the Channel.

A long-prepared bull of excommunication against Henry was finally published on 17 January 1538. When viewed from Rome he was a nuisance who would have been better employed aiding the defence of Christendom in the Mediterranean. To that end Paul travelled to Nice for a peace congress with the emperor and the French king. Henry and Cromwell thereupon exaggerated their own significance by assuming that this trio was plotting an anti-English crusade. They launched a pre-emptive attack by fabricating a plot against the king and arresting Cardinal Pole's closest relatives, including his elderly mother, the countess of Salisbury. This spurred her dutiful son during a second mission to depose Henry, though it proved to be just as futile as the first.

In a new development, the English elite's attitude towards the pope acquired a cultural expression in John Bale's play *Kynge Johan*, which was performed at Archbishop Cranmer's residence on 2 January 1539. In the sole surviving manuscript of this work Innocent III and his agent 'Pandulphus' appear among the speakers, while King John himself is presented as a proto-Protestant hero who withstands Rome's tyranny, even if historical fact then obliges him to submit himself to papal authority – a dastardly Roman trick? – resign his crown and sceptre, and pay the annual tribute of a thousand marks.[12]

Paul displayed a few tricks of his own in 1539 by opening up an Irish dimension to the on-going battle with King Henry: Adrian IV's pro-English bull *Laudabiliter* was revoked, Conn O'Neill, earl of Tyrone, was declared to be 'king of our realme of Ireland', and Ghinucci became Ireland's first cardinal protector. However, if the wider Protestant schism was to be healed, that could hardly be achieved by tinkering on the periphery that was Ireland. In 1541 the Venetian cardinal Gasparo Contarini – who happened to be Paul's nominal adminis-trator of the Salisbury diocese – led a serious attempt at reconciliation with the German Protestants at Ratisbon/Regensburg. These negotiations collapsed, though not without expressions of regret that a conciliator such as Contarini had been sent too late to heal Western Christendom's breach. From that point onwards the religious divisions became institutionalised, whether in the refoundation of the Roman Inquisition to root out heresy in central Italy or in the origins of Calvin's theocratic regime in Geneva. Insular counterparts were found in the countess of Salisbury's execution, in Henry's assumption of headship of the Church in Ireland, and in the earliest use of the derogatory term 'papist'.

At least there was some consolation for the pope in Scotland, but only as long as the pro-French party retained its dominance. In 1537–8 Paul demonstrated his support for James V by sending him a blessed sword and hat, and buttressed the anti-Protestant cause by appointing David Beaton, nephew of Archbishop James Beaton, as Scotland's second cardinal. At King James's death in December 1542 Cardinal Beaton asserted his leadership of the pro-French faction in a realm now nominally ruled by the baby Mary Stewart (1542–67), but was imprisoned by the pro-English regent James Hamilton, earl of Arran. Learning of this, Paul sent Marco Grimani, patriarch of Aquileia, to strengthen what can begin to be identified as the 'Catholic' cause. By the time Grimani set foot in Scotland, in October 1543, Beaton and the regent had been reconciled. The threat from Henry VIII's England remained, though, and Grimani employed generous hospitality in an effort to inspire unity among the Scots.[13] At Grimani's departure Beaton was left with legatine authority and, under his leadership, Scotland briefly identified as closely with the papacy as it did with France, until a group of Protestant lairds killed him at St Andrews in 1546.

In England the governing elite took a decisively Protestant turn after Edward VI's accession in 1547. In the absence of any diplomatic or ecclesiastical connections with Rome, the current pontiff was reduced to a literary existence. Thus William Thomas's *Historie of Italie* culminates in the rumour that the aged Pope Paul was 'for the most part [...] nourished with the sucke of a womans breast' and was so cold that two girls lay in his bed to keep him warm at night.[14] Their ministrations were evidently insufficient and he died on 10 October 1549, the 'wonderful news' of which could soon be read in a decidedly partisan account of his 'abominable actes' and 'most mischeuous life'.[15]

The military dimension of the Habsburg–Valois conflict had moved to non-Italian theatres, but Paul's death meant that it could again be played out in a conclave. The imperialists selected Pole as their candidate and made strenuous efforts to elect him before the French cardinals arrived in Rome. Another man might have lobbied to secure the final two or three votes needed for election, but Pole chose to remain in his cell writing about the pope as a martyr who does not desire his exalted office.[16] The French arrived and deadlock ensued, until Giovanni Maria Ciocchi del Monte was elected in February 1550.

The centrepiece of Julius III's relatively brief pontificate (1550–5) was the second phase of the council that had first opened at Trent in 1545. It did not represent Catholic Christendom as a whole, for subjects of the emperor dominated this assembly and the French boycotted it. Relations between France and Scotland were now so close that one cardinal, Giovanni Domenico de Cupis, protected both nations. Among Scottish ecclesiastics, the French alliance was personified by another member of the Beaton dynasty, James, archbishop of Glasgow, who received episcopal ordination in Rome in 1552. England was a low papal priority until Edward VI died and Mary (1553–8) defied her late brother's wishes by claiming the throne. The opportunity to reconcile England and Rome was now so clear that Julius appointed Pole as legate for that purpose, but there followed more than a year of frustration while Charles V secured the marriage of his son Philip to the new queen. Not until Philip was safely established in England was Pole permitted to cross the Channel. When he did so, events moved rapidly: between 22 and 30 November 1554 his attainder was lifted, he addressed Parliament and formally reconciled England to the papacy.

Word of Julius's death reached England on 6 April 1555, the day after the conclave opened to elect his successor. Wisely, Pole made no attempt to travel to Rome, for the pro-Habsburg cardinals rapidly saw off a Francophile challenge and the *intransigenti* stood characteristically firm against their more worldly colleagues. By the end of April Pole was able to congratulate Marcello Cervini, whom he knew well from a joint legation in 1544, and trusted that the 'most deformed kingdom' of England would be reformed by the new pope.[17] It was not to be: Marcellus II died just two days later.

The absent Pole and his ally Giovanni Morone both came close to being elected as pro-Habsburg candidates in the ensuing conclave, but their chances evaporated when the pro-French Cardinal Farnese advanced the candidature of their seventy-nine-year-old dean, the sometime legate to England, Gian Pietro Carafa. Since the onset of the Italian Wars there had been popes from Tuscany, Liguria and the Papal States, but not until the election of Carafa had there been one from Spanish-ruled Naples. Paul IV (1555–9) was an implacable enemy of Spain, the government of which was abdicated by Charles V in favour of Philip at the beginning of 1556. Within months Spanish troops invaded the Campagna and periodically threatened Rome, until the pope consented to peace terms in September 1557.

Paul's dealings with England are to be understood in relation to his war with Spain. They began smoothly enough when an embassy consisting of Bishop Thomas Thirlby of Ely, Viscount Montagu and Sir Edward Carne received papal approbation of the terms by which Pole had negotiated England's reconcilia-tion. Carne remained in Rome as resident ambassador – up to and beyond his recall in 1559 – while Thirlby and Montagu returned home with various signs of papal favour: a golden rose for Mary, confirmation of Pole's legation, and the bull *Ilius* (7 June 1555), which confirmed Ireland as a kingdom, rather than a lordship, with Philip and Mary as its monarchs. Pole's fortunes only took a turn for the worse when Philip arrived in England half way through the Hispano-papal conflict in Italy. He stayed away from court, rather than deal directly with the pope's enemy, but was nevertheless deprived of his legatine powers in April 1557. Two months later Paul announced that Pole's successor was the Observant Franciscan William Peto, who was raised to the cardinalate on the same occasion. This was a panic measure that went nowhere, for Peto rejected the legation and died as he had lived, unobtrusively.

Aside from his Neapolitan inheritance, Paul IV also brought to the papacy his experience as an inquisitor, flushing out any suspicion of heresy. In the 1540s Pole's circle had included individuals who subsequently fled from Italy and identified themselves as fully-fledged Protestants, so it came as no surprise when Paul announced that the English cardinal was under suspicion. Mary protected her kinsman, who remained in England until the day they both died, 17 November 1558. Thereafter, Paul was the pope against whom Elizabeth I's first English and Irish Parliaments aimed the Act of Supremacy and its accompanying oath, which essentially revived that of 1535.[18] Nor was solace to be found in Scotland, where the nuncio, John Row, was helpless to assist the regent, Mary of Guise, while pro-English noblemen, known as the Lords of the Congregation, sought to further the Protestant cause.

Bread and circuses were in short supply in the Rome of this austere, uncompromising pontiff, and his death in August 1559 was the trigger for a sudden explosion of violence. Rioters freed the inmates of the Inquisition's prison, among them an Englishman, Thomas Wilson, and a Scottish Dominican, John Craig, who was just hours from being burned for heresy. The Milanese cardinal Giovanni Angelo de' Medici went into the conclave as one of the favourites, but it still took more than three months of inconclusive voting before his unanimous election provided a welcome release for the prisoners of the red-robed variety. Pius IV (1559–65) could hardly have presented a starker contrast to his immediate predecessor: a protégé of Giovanni Morone and a natural conciliator, he enthusiastically revived the council. Morone had claimed the protectorship of England and Ireland after Pole's death and this, in turn, attracted Pius's attention westwards. Indeed, Pius was so keen to draw a line under the schism that he hoped English representatives would make their way to Trent. Papal agents reached Ireland, but neither Pole's former secretary Vincenzo Parpaglia nor the experienced diplomat Girolamo Martinengo managed to cross the Channel and make the pope's case in England. The council reconvened at Trent in 1562. In the absence of any English participation the Anglican bishop of Salisbury, John Jewel, took this as his cue to compose a robust defence of the reformed Church, complete with condemnation of the 'yoke and tyranny of the Bishop of Rome'.[19] Jewel then joined other members of the Church of England's Convocation to declare, among their thirty-nine articles of belief, that 'The Bishop of Rome hath no jurisdiction in this Realm of England', and the secular elite made its own antipapal gesture by extending to MPs and graduates the obligation to swear the oath of supremacy. On the papal side Parpaglia began to prepare for Elizabeth's excommunication, though intermittent communication was maintained, including by means of the queen's kinsman Thomas Sackville, who met the pope in 1564.

Pius was mindful that Mary, the young queen of Scots, was heir presumptive to the English throne and, while she was still with her in-laws in France, he sent her a golden rose. Once she had returned to Edinburgh he sent further assistance, in the form of a nuncio, the Dutch Jesuit Nicholas Floris of Gouda, though a face-to-face meeting with the queen had to be delayed until Mary's Protestant courtiers were preoccupied at one of John Knox's regular sermons. It was difficult for Rome to keep abreast of developments in Scotland, where Catholic worship was banned, permitted and then banned again in relatively quick succession. On one matter there was no equivocation, for the infatuated monarch was determined to marry the English Protestant Lord Darnley and that required a dispensation. Beyond supplying it was precious little that Pius could do for her.

With France convulsed by civil war, Mary of England's widower Philip II of Spain gave the cardinals a relatively free rein when they elected the next pope. In January 1566 they chose the Dominican Michele Ghislieri, who exercised an inquisitor's determination to eliminate heresy. What Pius V (1566–72) lacked was political or diplomatic experience. Among his earliest acts was the dispatch of a nuncio to Scotland, one of the front lines in the battle against Protestantism. The situation was delicate, to say the least: in December 1566 Mary and Darnley's son (Charles) James was baptised a Catholic, but five months later his mother contracted a Protestant marriage to the earl of Bothwell, and that lost her the pope's trust. Compromise failed miserably. The nuncio withdrew, Mary was forced to abdicate in favour of her infant son, and a firmly Protestant regency government banned Catholic worship throughout the kingdom. The battle for Scottish Catholicism had been lost.

If Scotland represented an outpost of the French religious wars, then Philip regarded England as belonging to his sphere of influence, which meant that Pius's attempts to bring it back into the Catholic fold contributed to a more extensive test of wills between the zealous pope and the cautious king, whose focus was on bringing to heel his rebellious subjects in the Low Countries. With regard to the island kingdom Philip opted for the long haul, supporting William Allen's foundation of an English seminary at Douai to train priests for future work in England, whereas Pius sent money to the Florentine merchant Roberto Ridolfi to aid the earls of Northumberland and Westmorland in their 1569 rebellion against Elizabeth. That rebellion was crushed, but the earls' appeal for Elizabeth's excommunication was realised after Pius undertook a formal enquiry into her support for heretics. The bull *Regnans in excelsis* excommunicated 'the pretended queen of England', deprived her of her title, absolved her subjects from any oaths or duties she claimed from them, and declared excommunicate anyone who obeyed her orders.[20] Philip had not been informed. In view of the fact that there was no means of conveying the document to Elizabeth herself, approved copies of the text were held to carry the weight of the original. The resourceful Ridolfi helped to smuggle such copies into England. In its next sitting, Parliament responded with 'A Bill against bringing in and putting in Execution of Bulls, Writings, or Instruments, or other Superstitious Things from the See of Rome'. Elizabeth did not favour such knee-jerk patriotism and let it be known through diplomatic channels that she would simply prefer to see the sentence lifted.

In 1571 a league of Mediterranean states was formed to defend Venetian-held Cyprus from the Ottomans. Its much-celebrated naval victory at Lepanto crowned one pontificate and provided inspiration for the next, for Pius died on 1 May 1572 and the Bolognese canon lawyer Ugo Boncompagni was elected twelve days later. A new generation of Catholic crusaders was forged in the national colleges founded in Rome by this pope, and Germany witnessed a sustained revival of Catholic fortunes, but the fact that Boncompagni was inspired by Gregory the Great when he chose his papal name suggested that some of his zeal would be channelled northwards and westwards. Flanders was the closest that Gregory XIII (1572–85) had been to the British Isles and his former student Pole was the atypical sort of Englishman with whom he was acquainted, so his vision of toppling heretics and reviving insular Catholicism had no firm foundation. Throughout the later 1570s English and Welsh Catholic exiles in Rome and the Low Countries devised invasion schemes, each of which required a Spanish fleet. Nothing came of them because England and Spain entered into a two-year commercial treaty. Then Philip's government was declared 'bankrupt' for the third time in less than two decades, and the death of his brother, Don John of Austria, deprived the king of his most successful and inspirational commander. That left Gregory as the principal backer of an Irish rebellion in 1579 led by James Fitzmaurice Fitzgerald.

At the height of the rebellion Elizabeth teased Rome and Madrid by activating long-contemplated negotiations for an Anglo-French marriage alliance, which had the potential to make the duke of Alençon and Anjou as powerful in England as Philip had been during Mary's reign. Gregory responded by entering into an alliance with Philip and the grand duke of Tuscany, the purposes of which were to depose the Elizabeth as the heretical product of an illegal marriage, to set the queen of Scots at liberty, and to allow England's Catholic nobles to elect a king of their choice who would hold office under papal authority. Gregory's military commitment was set at 10,000 infantry and 1,000 cavalry. Hardly had the terms been drawn up than the Irish rebellion was crushed, which boded ill for any enterprise in England. By 1583 Gregory had been reduced to imagining that Elizabeth could be deposed and replaced by James VI of Scotland (1567–1625), who would somehow revert to his baptismal Catholicism as he crossed the border.

If Gregory's English policy was a resounding failure politically, on the missionary front he had the distinction of being the pope who authorised the transformation of the moribund English hospice in Rome's Via di Monserrato – a fourteenth-century foundation – into a seminary, even if his original intention was to employ its products in Italy.[21] After the earliest students rebelled against their rector, Gregory placed the college under Jesuit leadership. His commitment to the institution was reinforced in 1580 when he appointed his nephew Filippo Boncompagni as protector of England. Direction of the English mission was entrusted to William Allen, who requested that English Jesuits lead the way, the first wave of 'seminary priests' following thereafter. The Jesuits Robert Persons and Edmund Campion were selected. Gregory specifically released them from the terms of *Regnans in excelsis*, which meant that they were not required to seek Elizabeth's deposition. It was a detail conveniently overlooked by the English authorities in their determination to expose papist spies and traitors. Persons soon fled to France, but Campion managed to make contact with many Catholics in England before being caught.

The second half of Gregory's pontificate witnessed a glut of publications, across a range of genres, inspired by the current state of relations between the papacy and the British Isles. At the firmly Catholic end of the spectrum, John Leslie, bishop of Ross, wrote a Latin history of Scotland to assure the pope that

Scots had ever been loyal to the Church.[22] From the Protestant elite a pamphlet by William Cecil described the means by which successive popes had sought to undermine the rule of Elizabeth, England's national icon.[23] Quite which side of the Catholic/Protestant divide the playwright Anthony Munday inhabited has been a matter of debate. His brief residence at the English College coincided with the student rebellion of 1579, making his lively memoir a particularly significant source of information about the *inglesi* in Rome.[24]

One of the pontificate's more extreme examples of insular antipapalism was opposition to reform of the calendar. The Julian calendar was flawed and the Council of Trent declared it to be a problem that the papacy was best placed to solve. Thus it was Gregory who introduced the necessary reform, causing ten days to be lost.[25] The resulting 'Gregorian' calendar was too papal to be accepted by Protestant states, which meant that England and Scotland fell ever further out of step with their continental neighbours, chronologically as well as ecclesiastically.

The papal election of 1585 was almost exclusively an Italian affair, contested by Alessandro Farnese and Ferdinando de' Medici and won by the latter in the sense that his candidate, Felice Peretti Montalto, was elected unanimously. Montalto became Sixtus V (1585–90). He had tended to avoid the curia during Gregory's pontificate and could consequently present himself as a new broom. His many reforms proved to be enduring and had their greatest impact on curial cardinals, who served on an expanded range of Roman congregations, and on bishops, who were required to go periodically *ad limina apostolorum* to keep Rome informed about the health of their dioceses. The same energy and organisational skills were applied to extensive building works throughout Rome, which are all the more remarkable for being the products of a relatively short pontificate. Such a natural leader as Sixtus was unimpressed by Philip II's dilatoriness and regarded Henri III of France as a lightweight who betrayed the Catholic cause by negotiating with Huguenots. On the other hand, Elizabeth genuinely impressed him because she had managed to make her small realm the arbiter of Europe, holding the balance of power between Spain and France. So great was her potential that Sixtus was prepared to rescind *Regnans in excelsis*, invest her with the kingdom and provide her with amenable bishops, if only she would renounce Protestantism. That hope was expressed repeatedly, including in the final months of his life, when he assured the Venetian ambassador that an English agent was even then making his way to Rome.[26] Elizabeth's conversion would have been the easy option, for the alternative had been presented by William Allen in a memorial of September 1586 and necessitated the invasion of England by Catholic forces which, for all practical purposes, meant Spain. Allen was Philip's candidate at the next creation of cardinals, but Sixtus was so set on Elizabeth having a change of heart that he ignored the request. Matters only changed after the queen of Scots was executed in 1587 and a new figurehead was deemed necessary for the English Catholics. Thus Allen received his promotion on 7 August, though his dream of becoming both archbishop of Canterbury and lord chancellor sunk with the Armada the following summer. He had to be content as mere 'prefect' of the English mission.

It was never part of the plan that Allen would end his days in Rome, where he struggled to master the vernacular, or vote in a single conclave, let alone participate in four of them in sixteen months. On each occasion the English cardinal, together with the English and Irish protectors Enrico Caetani and Nicolas de Pellevé, was part of the large but relatively uncoordinated Spanish party.[27] In September 1590 an electoral consensus was reached with relative ease, for the Genoese Giambattista Castagna had served as legate to both France and Spain. This pope, Urban VII, died just twelve days after his election. Finding another unifying figure proved to be considerably more difficult and the next conclave descended into chaos as cardinals reacted against Philip's open opposition to thirty of their number: there were fifty-three in the enclosure. France offered no counterweight because its king since 1589, Henri IV, was a Protestant. After nearly two months the electors settled on the bishop of Cremona, Niccolò Sfondrati, who was one of Philip's Milanese subjects but regarded as the least objectionable option by the anti-Spanish grouping. Gregory XIV found roles for Allen that required a better knowledge of Latin than of Italian, whether as prefect of the Vatican library – housed in Sixtus V's magnificent new *sala* – or as a member of the commission charged with revising the Vulgate text of the Bible. At Gregory's death in October 1591 Philip acknowledged that he could acquire a congenial pontiff by more subtle means than had been applied previously and was satisfied with the result, which was the rapid election of Giovanni Antonio Facchinetti as Innocent IX. Innocent's piety, learning and simple lifestyle inspired much admiration, but his constitution was fragile and the pontificate lasted a mere two months, leading to Cardinal Allen's fourth conclave.

On that occasion the cardinals chose particularly wisely, for the Florentine canon lawyer Ippolito Aldobrandini had assisted Pius V's *nipote* Michele Bonelli on a mission to Spain, Portugal and France in 1571–2, and later achieved distinction as legate to Poland, where his objective was to settle a dispute with the Habsburgs. Henri IV was first to recognise the opportunity for a Franco-papal rapprochement, though the new pope, Clement VIII (1592–1605), initially suspected that the king's politic rejection of Protestantism was no more than a ruse suggested by Elizabeth and delayed his formal acceptance of the king's submission until 1595. From that point onwards, whether by creating new cardinals or by sending a legate to the Franco-Spanish peace negotiations at Vervins in 1598, Clement consciously built up the French Church as a counterweight to Spain. Elsewhere, Catholic fortunes revived apace, particularly in Poland and the German states, contributing to the vast numbers of pilgrims who were welcomed to Rome during the holy year of 1600.

Elizabeth's subjects were still officially banned from visiting Rome, but that did not deter young men from venturing there and making literary use of their experiences. Among those who visited in the 1590s, the poet Robert Tofte supplied the Anglican bishop Richard Bancroft with an account of the 'five laste popes' (Sixtus to Clement), Henry Wotton honed his diplomatic skills with a pen portrait of Clement as an 'imperious prelate', and Edwin Sandys – son of the eponymous archbishop of York – developed a vision of Christian unity that was partly inspired by the pope's personal piety.[28] Formal diplomatic relations were not on the agenda, but the way to an improved relationship was heralded by the inveterate traveller Fynes Moryson, whose interest in the antiquities unearthed in Clementine Rome had the advantage of being doctrinally neutral.[29]

A similar glut can be found in theatrical treatments of the Anglo-papal relationship, though not all are as benign as Shakespeare's references to the pope and treatment of the legate Henry Beaufort in *Henry VI, Part 1* (1591). Exchanges between the king and the legate Pandulph in the anonymous *Troublesome Reign of King John* (1590–1) provide excuses for patriotic antipapalism with a distinctly Tudor twist:

> Know, Sir Priest, as I honour the Church and holy churchmen, so I scorn to be subject to the greatest prelate in the world. Tell thy master so from me, and say, John of England said it, that never an Italian priest of them all, shall either have tithe, toll, or polling penny out of England, but as I am king, so will I reign next under God, supreme head over both spiritual and temporal; and he that contradicts me in this, I'll make him hop headless.[30]

Shakespeare's *King John* smooths some of the *Troublesome Reign*'s sharper corners and his characters confine themselves to political antipapalism, rather than indulging in the religious antipopery that went down well with Protestant audiences. Marlowe's *Edward the Second*, on the other hand, combines the issue of papal overlordship with a swipe at Catholic munbo-jumbo, and that in a single speech:

> Why should a king be subject to a priest?
> Proud Rome, that hatchest such imperial grooms,
> For these thy superstitious taper-lights,
> Wherewith thy antichristian churches blaze,
> I'll fire they crazed buildings, and enforce
> The papal towers to kiss the lowly ground,
> With slaughter'd priests make Tiber's channel swell,
> And banks rais'd higher with their sepulchres![31]

In *Doctor Faustus* Marlowe went further and entertained his audiences with both a power-crazed pope and an imperialist antipope.

Back in the real world, Cardinal Allen's death in October 1594 left the English secular clergy leaderless. They descended into bitter disputes, among themselves and with the English Jesuits, who had a well-connected figurehead in the former missioner Robert Persons. There was no attempt to fill the void until 1598, when an archpriest, accountable to the nuncio in Flanders, was appointed by the English protector, Cardinal Caetani, to exercise authority over the secular clergy of both England and Scotland. Persons' influence could be discerned behind this appointment, for the archpriest was required to work closely with the Jesuit missioners and the man chosen, George Blackwell, was Persons' literary collaborator. It was not an appointment designed to conciliate. The unreconciled seculars appealed over Caetani's head by petitioning the pope for a bishop, rather than an archpriest. Clement VIII was certainly no partisan of the Jesuits, but he chose to uphold the authority of Rome by confirming Blackwell's appointment. The dispute played straight into the hands of Bishop Bancroft, who took it upon himself to ensure that patriotic Englishmen were aware of Fr Persons' belief that the king of Spain was Elizabeth's lawful heir and of Blackwell as Persons' agent in England. Blackwell continued to overreach himself by suspending priests who opposed his promotion, which prompted further appeals against him. The final group of appellants were four priests released from prison and 'banished' by the secular authorities precisely so that they could make the journey to Rome. After four months Clement saw through the government's ruse and the priests were sent home, but at least the episode persuaded him to take more decisive action about England. Towards the end of 1602 he reversed Blackwell's original instruction about close consultation with the Society of Jesus and, in another blow to the Jesuits, permitted the English Benedictines to join the mission.

While the Scottish Benedictines remained in their German monasteries, Scottish Catholics gained a permanent presence in Rome when Clement formally established a college for them towards the end of 1600. Scottish Catholicism was a threadbare remnant, dependent on families such as the Erskines, Gordons and Ogilvys. The only surviving member of the hierarchy was the younger James Beaton, who continued to act as James VI's ambassador in Paris, though William Chisholm, bishop of Vaison, appears to have been the king's candidate for promotion to the Sacred College in 1599. The Scottish Catholic elite was prepared to be patient, entertaining higher hopes of James's conversion than their English counterparts did of Elizabeth's, and were encouraged by his wife's discreet acceptance of Catholicism in the 1590s. The king's periodic communications gave Clement cause to share their hope, so much so that he offered to support James's succession to the English throne, in exchange for the king's elder son being educated in Rome. The offer was declined.

Among the English Catholics who rejoiced at Elizabeth's death and James's accession in March 1603, few were more exuberant than Sir Anthony Standen, who was sent on an unofficial mission to the Catholic states of Lorraine, Venice and Florence. In his excitement Standen suggested that the queen consort, Anne of Denmark, could act as a bridge between the pope and the English Catholics, and paid for this indiscretion with imprisonment. James, on the other hand, was so accomplished at sitting on the ecclesiastical fence that he could 'acknowledge the Roman Church to be our mother church, although defiled with some infirmities and corruptions', as he informed his first English Parliament.[32] That assembly passed severe anti-Catholic legislation, only for James himself to draw any sting by sending another envoy, Sir James Lindsay, to Rome to keep the pope in suspense as to his real intentions.

The death of Clement VIII on 3 March 1605 deprived the Church of a wise head. With the French Wars of Religion between Catholics and Protestants now concluded, the conclave was again the forum for Franco-Spanish rivalry and the role of a latter-day Charlemagne was contested by a wily ex-Protestant actively reviving his kingdom's fortunes and a young king who chose to abdicate the work of government. The election turned on anti-Spanish arguments made in print by the historian Cesare Baronio, who was consequently excluded by Felipe III, but this merely opened the way for the cardinals to elect Alessandro de' Medici, who was a kinsman by marriage of Henri IV. Leo XI's pontificate lasted only twice as long as the conclave that elected him and the cardinals were enclosed once more on 8 May. Eight days later differences of opinion were so intense as to descend into violence, which so shocked the electors that they immediately settled on a candidate: Camillo Borghese, the cardinal-protector of Scotland. Scottish Catholic exiles in Paris hailed Borghese's election in poetry and a thesis on the superiority of popes over councils.[33] In Rome it was more a case of electing in haste and repenting at leisure, for Borghese was aged only fifty-two and reigned, as Paul V, for nearly sixteen years. By far the most powerful cardinal in Pauline Rome was the papal nephew Scipione Borghese, who left in the shade men such as the English protector Oduardo Farnese, the Irish protectors Pompeo Arrigoni and Fabrizio Veralli, and even the new Scottish protector Maffeo Barberini, whose neglect of the Scots College helped to place it under Jesuit direction in 1615. Among the English religious, the Benedictines emerged from this pontificate most obviously strengthened, with their new identity as an independent congregation and their new monastery at Douai, which was under the patronage of that papal apostle to the English, Gregory the Great.[34]

Pope Paul's interest in England was initially so muted that English Catholics were said to be disappointed by his lack of support.[35] He continued to enjoin civil obedience following the discovery of the notorious 'powder plot' by Catholics in November 1605. Then came the defining episode of

Paul's pontificate, at least as far as relations with the secular powers were concerned. In April 1606 he imposed an interdict on the Venetian republic, the last time that a pontiff excommunicated an entire state.[36] In the unrealistic hope that Venice was about to turn Protestant, Anglo-papal relations reached a parallel crisis. In May the English Parliament passed a new Act against recusants, which required the king's Catholic subjects to take an overtly antipapal oath of allegiance formulated by Richard Bancroft, who was now archbishop of Canterbury.[37] Naturally enough, Paul condemned the oath. Characteristically, James took a more circuitous approach, recalling Clement's invitation to him to submit to Rome and insisting that he would only declare his true opinion on papal supremacy to a legitimate council of the Church.[38] Many English and Welsh Catholics wanted a quiet life and favoured the oath of allegiance, but papal opposition to it was renewed after the arrest of George Blackwell, the archpriest, in June 1607. Under pressure from Bancroft, Blackwell took the oath and urged others to follow his example. When Paul heard of this he sent another brief, dated 22 September, condemning the oath and ordering non-compliance with it. At this James declared Paul to be ill-disposed towards the kingdom and hostile towards him personally.[39] Early the next year pope and king again responded typically to the difference between them: Paul acted decisively, deposing Blackwell and replacing him with George Birkhead, a man unknown to the government; James went into print, his *Triplici nodo, triplex cuneus* being a defence of the oath. The distinguished Jesuit controversialist Roberto Bellarmino responded on behalf of the papacy, leading James to reply in 1609 with *A Premonition to All Most Mightie Monarches, Kings, Free Princes and States in Christendom*, in which he denied the Petrine primacy and presented a novel argument about the Holy Ghost, rather than the pope, as Christ's vicar on earth. The book was prohibited in Rome, where there was nevertheless a feeling that sensitivity was required because, for all its doctrinal errors, it was still the work of a 'great prince'.[40] Neither side chose to pursue the matter any further. Indeed, throughout the 1610s James was motivated by a vision for the reunion of Christendom by means of marriages for his children, most of which would have required a papal dispensation for the other parties. Savoy, Tuscany and France were all considered, but in each case it was clear that Paul intended to refuse the request. By the time of the pope's death a Spanish match for Prince Charles had become something of a diplomatic fixture and the word was that Paul was inclined to relent, though no decision was made.[41]

The Venetian interdict and its far-reaching consequences were still topical when another pope made his appearance in English drama. The play was Barnabe Barnes' *The Devil's Charter*, performed before King James at Candlemas 1607, and the pontiff was Alexander VI, whose depiction as a necromancer, poisoner and sodomite stoked Protestant antipopery without venturing into political antipapalism.[42] The crisis has long passed and the king had entered a period of more positive engagement with Catholic powers when next a pope walked on a London stage, at the Red Bull Theatre, Clerkenwell, in 1612. In *The White Devil*, Webster presents Cardinal Montecelsi – subsequently 'Pope Paul IV' – as more of an authority figure than anything else, leaving the dramatic intensity focused on other characters. This pontiff should not be confused with the Carafa pope, for the historical events from which the plot derives involved a nephew of Sixtus V. One nice distinction between the two plays and the purposes served by their respective popes is that Alexander's election is conveyed by a suggestive tableau in which money and plate changes hands, whereas Paul's is announced in a fair approximation of the traditional 'Annuntio vobis gaudium magnum [...]'[43]

Even a critic such as Barnabe Barnes, son of an Anglican bishop, could allude to the buildings of Rome and the traditions they witnessed, for the city represented a shared heritage to educated men and women of all nations. Barnes' compatriots thoroughly embraced revived Antiquity, whether in terms of physical remains, such as the earl and countess of Arundel viewed in Rome in 1614, or neo-Latin literature, as in Charles Aleyn's translation of Pius II's *Historia de duobus amantibus*.[44] Public expression of a shared culture was perhaps most evident when the Arundels' protégé Inigo Jones took the catafalques made for Sixtus V and Paul V as his models for the hearse created for James VI and I's laying-in-state in 1625.

In 1621 it took only two days to elect Alessandro Ludovisi as Paul's successor. The ensuing pontificate was also brief, lasting little more than two years, but the impact of Pope Gregory XV and his dynamic nephew Ludovico Ludovisi endured, especially through their revised rules governing conclaves, which remained in force for nearly three centuries, and the foundation of the Congregation for the Propagation of the Faith – Propaganda Fide – to direct the Church's global missionary work, including in Protestant Europe. The prefects and secretaries of Propaganda became important points of contact for generations of British Catholics, some of whom received priestly formation at its Roman college. In England, Gregory's election revived hope of a papal dispensation for the Infanta María Ana to marry Prince Charles. To that end the Catholic George Gage was sent on two missions to Rome and a congregation of cardinals determined a set of conditions relating to the king's Catholic subjects. James wrote directly to Gregory in the course of these negotiations and, with the dispensation safely secured in 1623, Charles did likewise, assuring the pope of their commitment to the peace and unity of Christendom.[45]

Attempts to secure the Anglo-Spanish marriage continued into the next pontificate but soon fizzled out, making the dispensation a dead letter. The Infanta eventually married her cousin, the future emperor Ferdinand III, thereby reinforcing bonds between the Spanish and imperial Habsburgs at the height of the Thirty Years War, a conflict that entirely enveloped the twenty-one-year reign of Pope Urban VIII (1623–44). A pontificate of such length was no more intended by the electors in 1623 than it would have been by those in any other conclave, but sickness broke out in the enclosure, forcing the parties led by Cardinals Borghese and Ludovisi to reach a hasty compromise. The man whose candidature happened to be under consideration at that point was the fifty-four-year-old canon lawyer Maffeo Barberini, a Florentine whose prior experience included an extraordinary legation to France. In the conclave Barberini set a precedent by openly canvassing for himself. As pope he was no less reluctant to advance the interests of his family, red hats being granted to his nephew Francesco, who became responsible for relations with secular powers, the pope's brother and Francesco's brother, both of whom were called Antonio.

Francesco Barberini inherited the Scottish protectorship from the newly elected pope and retained it until his death in 1679, adding England to his portfolio in 1626. The Church in Scotland remained extremely weak, dependent on Irish missioners in the Gaelic-speaking west and a network of interconnected families in the north east. It was a small world, in which the Capuchin friar George Archangel Leslie, who undertook missionary work in Scotland in the 1620s and '30s, was related to the wandering scholar and 'living library' Thomas Dempster, as well as to the historian and papal diplomat George Conn. Leslie corresponded with the future pope, Dempster was knighted by Urban, and Conn joined the household of Francesco Berberini. In 1625–6 Conn accompanied Barberini on what proved to be fruitless peace legations to France and Spain, and his publications in this period were dedicated to Urban and to Cardinal Francesco.[46]

In 1633 Propaganda Fide received a report from another missioner, David Chambers, requesting a bishop for the Catholics of Scotland. This would have put them on a par with England, which had received its first post-Reformation bishop a decade earlier. This was a Warwickshire man, William Bishop, who had been an ardent opponent of the archpriests, the last of whom died in 1621. Bishop achieved little beyond establishing a chapter of secular priests – later known as the Old Chapter – before death overtook him. Cardinal Richelieu, Louis XIII's chief minister, then persuaded Rome to send his client Richard Smith as Bishop's replacement. Upon his arrival in England in 1625 Smith claimed episcopal jurisdiction over seculars and regulars alike, rather than the more limited authority conceded by Rome. All the regulars, not least the Jesuits, revolted against him and were supported by many lay Catholics. Smith was suspended from office in 1628, at which his supporters and detractors indulged in a war of words until Urban enjoined silence on them by means of the brief *Britannia* (9 May 1631). Smith retreated to France, where he died in 1655.

Resistence to episcopal authority extended beyond the existing religious orders, for the Yorkshirewoman Mary Ward was determined to create a Jesuit-inspired 'institute' that answered directly to the pope. Houses of her 'English Ladies' opened on the continent but, far from receiving papal support, Ward's initiative was condemned by Urban in the bull *Pastoralis Romani pontificis* (13 January 1631). Undaunted, she travelled from Munich to Rome, where her personal appeal to the pope resulted not only in a charge of heresy being dropped but in the opening of a papally protected house and school in the city.

Among female contributors to this phase of the Anglo-papal story none could compare with the French princess Henriette Marie. So avidly was her marriage to Charles encouraged by the pro-French pope that it was rumoured Urban's brother, the elder Antonio, would be sent as legate to England for the wedding.[47] Initial expectations were thwarted by the king's inability to suspend the anti-Catholic laws and by the support of his Protestant subjects, led by the duke of Buckingham, for France's Huguenot minority. In 1628 Buckingham's assassination created an opportunity for more positive relations, as Urban was not slow to recognise, though nothing happened immediately.[48] That anything happened at all was due to the succession of agents who served Henrietta Maria in Rome and kept open a line of communication. In 1633, with Urban's sixth creation of cardinals in the offing, the queen's used that channel to inform Francesco Barberini that George Conn was her candidate. Charles supported the proposal, but Rome exercised caution, prepared to consider a hat only if there was clear evidence that Charles would convert. To that end Barberini requested from the Benedictine monk Leander Jones a report on the current condition of Catholicism in England. Jones took to his task with gusto, putting an unrealistically positive spin on the significance of the oath of allegiance and taking the opportunity to minimise the Church of England's differences with Rome, though he was on safer ground when he assured Barberini that it would not be appropriate to send another bishop to England. The report was enough to take the relationship a stage further and, in December 1634, Gregorio Panzani arrived in London as a papal minister accredited to the queen. A year later the Venetian ambassador expressed astonishment at Panzani's continued presence at court, where he was favoured by the king, protected by the queen and no-one succeeded in troubling him.[49]

Panzani asked for another agent to further his discussions regarding the reconciliation of Anglicans, the less 'squeamish' of whom agreed that the pope was superior to other bishops and possessed the authority to convoke general councils.[50] In what was presumably a concerted move, the queen requested that George Conn be Panzani's replacement. Conn took up his post in the summer of 1636, bringing with him a jewelled cross decorated with a design of Barberini bees, but such was Urban's determination to be the pope who brought

England's heretical monarch back into the fold that Panzani did not leave until early the following year.[51] Even from England the Venetian ambassador could report that 'No nation is made more of at Rome just now than the English, where in the past the subjects of this crown went about incognito and in great danger.'[52] The ambassador's point can be illustrated by the contrasting fortunes of the Scottish adventurer William Lithgow, who was obliged to hide from 'blood-sucking Inquisitors' in 1609, and the equally Protestant John Milton, who enjoyed Francesco Barberini's hospitality during his Roman sojourn of 1638–9.[53]

Though Conn was not a natural courtier, he inspired numerous conversions, including that of the 'clever pirate' Sir Kenelm Digby, who served as Henrietta Maria's Roman envoy in 1639. That Conn's Catholicising activities fell during the period of Charles I's 'personal rule' only added to the charges being stacked up for future use by the king's critics. When a new prayer book was issued in Scotland in 1637, the false rumour circulated that Conn had brought it from Rome. During the resulting rebellion his contribution was to assure Charles of Catholic support, including the possibility of a papal loan. By 1639 Conn was ailing and replaced by Carlo Rossetti, whose period in office witnessed not only the revival of the Puritan-dominated English Parliament, but his summons before it when he failed to honour a promise to leave the country. Within a matter of months he was in Cologne.

Although there was no serious papal attempt to intervene in the Scottish Bishops' Wars of 1639–40, the Irish uprising of 1641 was a different matter. During the pontificates of Clement VIII and Paul V, Hugh O'Neill, earl of Tyrone, had kept alive the notion of papal overlordship of Ireland, so much so that an rumour spread in England in 1609 that Paul had make the fugitive O'Neill king of Ireland.[54] Urban's real legacy to Ireland was the appointment of active protectors: Gregory XV's *nipote* Ludovico Ludovisi, who founded the Irish College in Rome, and the younger Antonio Barberini, who doubled up as prefect of Propaganda Fide. Urban was impressed by the Irishmen who made their way to Rome to express loyalty to the Holy See and support was sent to them in the form of dynamic bishops, led by Hugh O'Reilly, the first resident archbishop of Armagh in nearly four decades. It was O'Reilly's 1641 synod at Kells that precipitated the formation of the Kilkenny-based Irish Catholic Confederation, which assumed aspects of government while the English became distracted by their civil war. From 1643 the confederation received direct papal support in the person of the priest Pierfrancesco Scarampi.

Of all the clerics who featured in this phase of relations between Britain and the Holy See only Carlo Rossetti emerged with a cardinal's red hat. England's most eminent churchman, Archbishop William Laud, remained firmly ineligible for such an honour. 'Advancing popery' was nevertheless among the charges on which Laud was tried from 1641. Writing after the archbishop's execution, the Puritan William Prynne emphasised that the trial had been a means of

> discovering to the world the severall secret dangerous plots, practises, proceedings of the Pope and his confederates [...] to undermine the Protestant religion, usher the whole body of popery into our church, and reduce all our realms to their ancient vassalage to the Sea of Rome.[55]

Prynne was also painfully well aware of the 'insensible steps and degrees' by which a post-Reformation Anglo-papal reconciliation had begun. In the event, neither the execution of a schismatic archbishop nor that of a king was enough to halt a process that became increasingly 'sensible' and public over the following centuries.

CHAPTER 5

CONVERGING INTERESTS

The limits of confessional hostility were realised during the Thirty Years War (1618–48), which began with a localised revolt by Protestant Bohemians against the Catholic emperor and ended as a wide-ranging power struggle between the Catholic powers of France and Spain. Thereafter, wars between seventeenth- and eighteenth-century European powers were sparked by economic, political and territorial/colonial motives, rather than religious ones, with princes routinely forming alliances across confessional lines. In the case of England and Scotland before and immediately after the Union of 1707 that tended to mean siding with the enemies of France – be they Dutch Protestants or Catholic Habsburgs – in order to contain the power of Louis XIV. The War of the Spanish Succession (1701–14) resulted in Britain becoming a naval power in the Mediterranean: Gibraltar and Minorca were ceded by Spain, giving Britain geographical interests considerably closer to the Papal States than ever before. In the 1740s, as in previous centuries, Italy was once again a theatre of war for non-Italian powers. British ships bombarded the city of Naples, and Britain's Austrian allies engaged a Spanish/Neapolitan army in battle at Velletri in the Papal States. Eighteenth-century rulers measured their power in terms of ever larger armies, which left the poorly-defended pope being treated with contempt, an attitude that extended into ecclesiastical matters. Superior military power finally overwhelmed the papacy in the century's final decade, when Rome succumbed to French forces. At the same time Britain strengthened its regional position by taking Malta from its French occupiers. Precisely how papal and British interests gradually converged can be seen in the contributions of individual players in each of the fifteen pontificates between 1644 and 1799.

The Barberini family accumulated so much power during Urban VIII's twenty-one-year reign that the papal nephews Francesco and Antonio went into the conclave of 1644 fighting for their political survival. They enjoyed firm support from Europe's strongest power, France, but were thwarted when Spain vetoed their preferred candidate, Giulio Cesare Sacchetti. At the height of the malaria season, sickness took hold in the conclave, with Francesco Barberini one of the cardinals forced to leave the enclosure. Those who remained, including the former envoy to England Carlo Rossetti, determined on a quick election, which ensured that Giovanni Battista Pamphili became Pope Innocent X (1644–55) before Cardinal Mazarin, the French chief minister, could take steps to prevent his elevation to the papal throne. The knives were out for the Barberini. A post-conclave investigation into their expensive conflict with the Farnese family over the duchy of Castro resulted in Francesco, Antonio and their brother Taddeo fleeing to France, where Taddeo soon died and Antonio remained until 1653; Francesco was pardoned and returned to Rome in 1658. Consequently, although Francesco remained protector of England and Scotland, as Antonio did of France and Ireland, the Roman colleges were left without effective patronage at a time when economic hardship threatened their very survival. At least the Scottish secular clergy filled the gap by employing a highly effective Roman agent, Will Leslie, from 1650 onwards, and the English Benedictines had a long-serving Roman procurator in Dom Wilfrid Selby.

Innocent X was in no position to spearhead a principled reaction to the extreme nepotism of the previous regime, because he was no less zealous in promoting the interests of his relatives. Unconventionally, though, his *nipoti* were merely frontmen for his sister-in-law, Olimpia Maidalchini Pamphili, the most prominent woman in papal Rome since the tenth century. As Rome gained a leading lady, Britain had just lost one, Queen Henrietta Maria seeking refuge in France shortly before the death of Pope Urban. From there she acted on behalf of her beleaguered husband Charles, and did so by playing the Catholic card. In 1645 her chancellor, Kenelm Digby, was sent back to Italy to raise funds for the royalist cause. His prospects were limited by the fact that he was representing a French princess at a time when Spanish interests were dominant in Rome. He obtained 20,000 crowns, but his promise of Charles's conversion came to nothing. Thereafter, Stuart appeals to Rome became increasingly desperate. In 1647 Charles was under house arrest but still hoped to gain Catholic support with an offer of religious toleration; this came to nothing when Innocent rejected the proposed oath of allegiance which Catholics would have been required to take. By August 1649 the king was dead and his exiled son, also Charles, sent Fr Robert Meynell from Paris to Rome with a letter of introduction to anyone who might be willing to help. The initiative came to grief when Meynell committed to paper an assurance to the pope that Charles was willing to convert. In reality, conversion was not a price that the prince could pay if he wished to claim his English and Scottish thrones.

In the absence of any meaningful diplomatic relationship, royalists could at least fall back on papally-inspired publications. *The Cardinal*, a tragedy by the Rome-leaning Laudian James Shirley, had been performed in 1641, but now appeared in print, as did translations from Italian of two works about papal Rome.[1] *The Scarlet Gown* presents anecdotal biographies of sixty cardinals alive in the later 1640s, though there is only one future pontiff in the collection: Benedetto Odescalchi, who 'will alwaies be of the Austrian Faction'.[2] *The Court of Rome* lists scores of offices in the papal household and Roman curia, and describes uniquely papal ceremonies, including conclaves, consistories and canonisations.[3] Dedications to two staunch royalists – John Manners, earl of Rutland, and Sir Justinian Isham – confirm that the translations were aimed at a sympathetic readership, rather than being antipapal ammunition for the Stuarts' enemies.

In competition with Stuart appeals to Rome were those from the Irish confederates, beginning in 1645 with Richard Bellings' request that the papal agent Scarampi be replaced by a higher-status nuncio. The Florentine archbishop of Fermo, Giovanni Battista Rinuccini, was selected for this mission. Rome was not awash with relevant expertise and Rinuccini's principal qualification was as the biographer of the wonder-working Scottish Capuchin George Archangel Leslie.[4] He had no prior diplomatic experience, as was confirmed by his refusal to accept the peace negotiated between the earl of Ormond and the confederates, which would have allowed Irish Catholics to fight for Charles against the combined forces of the English Parliament and the Scottish covenanters. When Ormond's peace was finally promulgated in July 1646, Rinuccini set about destroying the treaty, its authors and adherents. Armed with little more than righteous indignation, he advocated an attack on Dublin by those confederates who rejected the peace deal. It failed spectacularly. However, with the royalist cause in freefall and the king a prisoner, Ormond could no longer hold out and, in June 1647, he arranged an orderly handover to parliamentarian forces. This was surely not the outcome Rinuccini desired, but it was one he could have prevented. In 1648 another Irish mission made its way to Rome. The emissaries were Nicholas French, bishop of Ferns, and Nicholas Plunkett, whose young kinsman, Oliver, had left Ireland with Scarampi and was studying at the Irish College. The objective was to seek papal approval of a royalist–confederate accord then under negotiation in Paris. Innocent had no intention of doing a deal with the Stuarts as long as they failed to convert, so the Irishmen came away with nothing more than a papal knighthood for Plunkett. In their absence Catholic Ireland descended into civil war, triggered by Rinuccini's excommunication of those confederates who supported the peace policy. The Confederation's supreme council threw in their lot with what remained of the royalist cause and ordered Rinuccini to leave the country, which he did in February 1649. By then it was too late to stop the Cromwellian conquest of Ireland and the systematic destruction of the Church there. So little could Rome help that after three of the four archbishops died between 1651 and 1654 their sees remained long vacant.

Rinuccini's zeal for the Church was too blunt a weapon and his example was one that subsequent generations of papal diplomats chose to reject when dealing with British elites. None were more conscious of that rejection than the Irish, who felt betrayed by any hint of an Anglo-papal alliance. The former nuncio sought to vindicate his actions by writing an account of recent Irish history, but it was the pope who had greater cause to regret the policy they had both followed.[5] Innocent lived long enough to see his old adversary, Mazarin, pull off a spectacular coup by allying France with the English Commonwealth and containing its formidable military strength in wars against the Protestant Dutch (1652–4) and Catholic Spain (1654–60). This turn of events obliged Charles to leave France for the Rhineland and then appeal to Spain as the power best placed to return him to his kingdoms. Spain had secured Innocent's election and he was considered to have remained partial to her, but if he had second thoughts regarding the Stuarts it was too late for him to act on them.

There was no possibility of Mazarin leaving France to partipcate in the conclave occasioned by Innocent's death in January 1655, so the process was kept on hold while his opinion was sought. As in 1644, Sacchetti was the French candidate vetoed by Spain. He broke the deadlock by advocating the election of Fabio Chigi, who became Alexander VII (1655–67). As a former nuncio in Cologne and papal secretary of state, Chigi was a not unreasonable choice to steer a course through the continuing Franco-Spanish conflict, though his personal dealings with Mazarin resulted in the latter bearing a grudge that determined French policy towards Rome. Across the Channel, the leaders of the Cromwellian Protectorate (1653–9) felt secure as long as France and Spain were at war, but feared that a new pope would seek to compose their differences and unite those states against the republican regime. In what appeared to be a clever ploy, they sent a Catholic priest to spy in Rome. It proved to be too clever, because the agent travelled to Italy at the government's expense and then disappeared. Meanwhile, the royalist exiles had to wait upon events, and were encouraged first by the death of Cromwell in 1658 and then by Franco-Spanish peace negotiations. Mazarin ensured that the pope was denied any mediatory role in the Peace of the Pyrenees (1659), from which Louis XIV emerged with a Spanish bride and Charles left as empty-handed as he had arrived.

Patience paid off and, from May 1660, Charles II (1660–85) was finally in possession of his kingdoms. Before he could take the initiative in looking for a consort the Portuguese regent proposed her daughter Catarina. As Portugal and Spain were still at war this arrangement suited France, but the negotiations stalled until after Mazarin's death in 1661, at which point Charles began to display greater enthusiasm for all things French. After their marriage the pious Catherine of Braganza sought to lobby the pope in the interest of her husband's Catholic subjects, though she proved to be of less consequence than her mother-in-law Henrietta Maria had been in that respect. In October 1662 it was reported that Richard Bellings, son of the eponymous emissary of 1645, was going to Rome to propose that the queen's grand almoner, Ludovic d'Aubigny, be made a cardinal.[6] It was a vain hope, for the next creation of cardinals did not happen until January 1664, when Alexander made a point of not promoting the candidates of secular powers. Some time later Cardinal de Retz assured Venice's curial ambassador that English hostility towards Rome, demonstrated by the presence of their frigates in the Mediterranean, was due to the pope's failure to provide either a dispensation for the royal marriage or a hat for d'Aubigny.[7] That would indeed have been to follow the French example, for Louis had recently occupied Avignon in a show of force designed to intimidate the pope.

If Alexander VII made relatively little direct impact on the British Isles, he acquired at least one insular admirer, the Anglican poet Philip Ayres, who translated an Italian account of the pope's piety and learning, his aversion to nepotism and patience in adversity, in order to convey a minority view that even a pope could be entirely admirable.[8] On the other hand, Alexander's architectural patronage left an abiding impact on subsequent generations of British travellers, who entered Rome via the Porta del Popolo, which was refashioned in 1655, and proceeded to the Vatican by means of the colonnaded Piazza S. Pietro, commissioned from Bernini by the Chigi pope.

The conclave of June 1667 took place shortly after France and Spain went to war over rival claims in the Spanish Netherlands. Further north, it coincided with an audacious Dutch raid that destroyed many of Charles's ships lying at anchor in the river Medway. Alexander's secretary of state, the Tuscan Giulio Rospigliosi, quietly gained support from all parties within the Sacred College and became Pope Clement IX (1667–9) on 20 June. It was accurately predicted that this sixty-seven-year-old would live for only two or three more years. During that time Europe witnessed a remarkable outbreak of international diplomacy, including a papal initiative that resulted in the Franco-Spanish peace of Aix-la-Chapelle (1668). The same season brought peace between Spain and Portugal, but only after one of the English queen's brothers was deposed and exiled by another. Besides international peace, Clement's relatively brief pontificate witnessed a spate of notable conversions from Protestantism, including those of Marshal Turenne, Louise Hollandine of the Palatinate and James, duke of York, who were respectively the military hero, cousin and brother of Charles II, whose own sympathies were as Catholic as they could be without risking the loss of his throne. At ministerial level the prospects for improved Anglo-papal relations were in place because Charles's secretary of state for the southern department – the first holder of that office – was the pro-Catholic earl of Arlington. With these various pieces in place, it was the queen who tested the potential for a new Anglo-papal relationship when she requested, and received, a series of papal briefs in connection with a cause close to the pope's heart, the defence of Venetian-held Candia (Crete) from assault by the Ottomans. Catherine's line of communication was via the Venetian ambassadors in London and Rome. Her initiative could proceed no further than warm words, because Charles was not prepared to jeopardise England's lucrative Levantine trade by sending ships to Candia. If nothing else, Clement was grateful for news from that quarter when the English ambassador to Constantinople passed through Rome in 1669.[9]

Among the English Catholics, members of the Old Chapter of secular priests used this window of conciliatory opportunity to petition Rome for a bishop. Their candidate was Philip Thomas Howard, a grandson of the earl and countess of Arundel who visited Rome in 1614. As a youth Howard had been so determined to become a Dominican friar, in defiance of his grandfather's wishes, that he appealed directly to Innocent X. The pope summoned him to Rome, was satisfied as to his vocation and apparently recognised the potential of this illustrious youth to revive the Catholic cause in England. More recently, Howard had succeded d'Aubigny as the queen's grand almoner. The choice of Howard as bishop for England was a shrewd move because it had the potential to settle the long-standing differences between secular and regular clergy, and to do so without involving the Jesuits, who remained resolutely opposed to the creation of a hierarchy. Nothing came of it, however, because Charles preferred not to antagonise his Protestant subjects. However, the pope's attention had been drawn to the British Isles and, in the course of 1669, he ensured that all four vacant Irish archbishoprics were filled, and that with the king's approbation. The new primate was Oliver Plunkett, whose long residence in Rome meant that he came with genuine papal approval.

After Clement IX's death in December 1669 it took over four months for the various factions to agree on a candidate. A French phyisician in London, Theophilus Garencières, took this as his cue to publish an account of a previous conclave, that of January 1592, with suitable emphasis on the 'intrigues and cunning devices of that [...] assembly'.[10] In April 1670 the final ballot saw fifty-six out of fifty-nine electors vote for the octogenarian Emilio Altieri. As a cardinal of just ten days' standing at the death of his predecessor, Altieri had little choice but to become Clement X (1669–76). This was the pope who named St Margaret (d. 1093) as co-patroness of Scotland. Contacts between the papacy and the Stuart kingdoms certainly intensified during this pontificate, even if there was no formal relationship. They began with a chance opportunity created by the death of Grand Duke Ferdinando II of Tuscany just weeks after the conclave. The king's condolences were conveyed to Florence by James Hamilton, who then proceeded 'out of curiosity' to Rome, where Clement presented him with devotional objects for Queen Catherine.[11] The following year Clement took a further step towards linking the two regimes at the highest level when the death of the Irish protector Antonio Barberini created an opportunity for Paluzzo Altieri, the pope's adopted nephew and secretary of state, whose knowledge of Ireland came from his Dominican confessor, John Baptist Hackett.

Clement X's own extra-Italian experience was of Poland and he maintained his predecessors' emphasis on the need for co-ordinated action against Ottoman incursions into eastern and central Europe. It was not an emphasis shared by Louis XIV, who was set on war against the United Provinces and acquired English naval support by subsidising his impecunious cousin Charles. In the spring of 1672 Charles sought to distract more extreme Protestants from the fact that he was supporting Catholic France against the Protestant United Provinces by granting religious liberty to non-Anglicans – both Protestant and Catholic – by means of a 'declaration of indulgence'.[12] Further Catholic benefits included the Howard family's restoration to the office of earl marshal and a revival of plans for granting Philip Thomas Howard episcopal authority. By 1673 Charles was struggling in the war and was forced to bow to Protestant demands: the indulgence was withdrawn and, in its place, the holders of public offices were required to assent to the decidedly anti-Catholic Test Act (1672). The duke of York's resignation from all his offices confirmed his Catholic allegiance.

In this fluid situation a marriage was arranged between the widowed duke and Maria Beatrice d'Este of Modena, its Francophile backers including Cardinals Rinaldo d'Este, the girl's uncle, and Francesco Barberini, who still protected England and Scotland. So mixed were the messages coming from London that Rome could not be certain that the young princess would be as free to practice her faith as the Stuarts' previous Catholic brides had been. At the height of the confusion, in September 1673, Clement issued a brief approving the marriage, only to change his mind just as the wedding ceremony was about to take place. York's proxy for the wedding, the earl of Peterborough, declared that any delay might leave the duke with no choice but to marry a Protestant, so the duchess of Modena ensured that the ceremony went ahead, only informing the pope once it was a *fait accompli*. Although Clement personally favoured the match, the duchess's actions suggested that disrespect for the papacy was spreading from France to its allies. More than a year later Barberini was still trying to regularise the marriage. In the meantime, England was forced out of the war, which continued as a conflict of the traditional Franco-Spanish variety, Spain entering the fray in order to save the United Provinces from extinction.

An explosion of antipapal books and pamphlets accompanied the Este marriage and the breakdown of the king's pro-French, anti-Dutch policy in 1673–4. At the scholarly end of the range the Herefordshire poet Thomas Traherne ventured well beyond the famous case of the Donation of Constantine when he accused various popes of the 'sin of forgery'.[13] Among more popular genres, dialogue allowed all-purpose popes to converse with the devil, and a spurious papal letter encouraged English Catholics to 'pluck the Crown from the Princes head [...] or blow up [...] an Heretical Parliament'.[14] With regard to the second instruction, it may be noted that, before 1673, the anniversary of the 1605 Gunpowder Plot passed without incident. Only then, for the first time, heightened tensions found release in the burning of papal effigies.[15]

Antipapalism and Anti-Catholicism did not stop there, as a new wave of persecution broke throughout Charles's realms. Even the highly-favoured Philip Thomas Howard was forced to retreat from England to Flanders. Clement offered what support he could, adding Howard's name to those of five Italians promoted to the cardinalate in May 1675, though there was a distinct danger that this move could backfire and end up doing more harm than good to Charles's Catholic subjects. The new cardinal did not have to wait long to influence the course of papal history: Clement X died in July 1676 and Innocent XI (1676–89) was elected two months later. Gregorio Leti's account of papal elections had been available in English since 1671 and reappeared as *The New Pope*, interest in the conclave enhanced by the presence of an English elector for the first time since 1592.[16] The pope himself, Benedetto Odescalchi, was a saintly ascetic who deplored the nepotism of his predecessors and came to the papacy with a carefully constructed programme of reform. As even the better-informed English reader knew, he also came with a reputation for partiality towards the emperor, which was useful at a time when central Europe was under particularly severe threat from the Ottomans. This put him on a collision course with Louis XIV, who had blocked Odescalchi's election in 1669–70 and was now at his most Gallican and most absolutist.

Far from either Rome or Versailles, Cardinal Howard's brother Henry, earl of Norwich, employed one Titus Oates as chaplain to the Protestant members of his household in 1676. The arrangement was soon terminated and it was the closest Oates came to the 'cardinal of Norfolk' and the English Catholics in Rome. For reasons that remain obscure, Oates then embarked at breakneck speed on a Catholic career, being received into the Church and admitted to the English Jesuit colleges in Valladolid and St Omer, all within a matter of months. It was soon clear that Oates would be even less employable as a Catholic than he had been as a Protestant: he was expelled from St Omer in June 1678. Again wasting no time, he used his recent experiences to fabricate an elaborate international Catholic plot to kill King Charles. By the end of October he had appeared before the Privy Council and the House of Commons, implicating all and sundry in his 'popish' plot. Among the accused was the duchess of York's secretary, Edward Colman, imagined by Oates to be in correspondence with Louis XIV's Jesuit confessor, François de La Chaise. On the basis of Oates's spurious evidence Coleman was found guilty and executed as a traitor. The 1673 pamphlet *Room for News* was quickly reissued as *The Plot Discover'd*, but when a court of law could accept blatant lies as facts there was really no need for the printers to resort to something as overtly fictional as a dialogue between the pope and the devil.[17]

Emboldened by his 'success' with Colman, in 1679 Oates decided to aim higher and take a shot at Cardinal Howard. Knowing nothing of Roman affairs, he made the accusation as English as he could, alleging that plans were afoot to make Howard archbishop of Canterbury and to place some of his fellow Dominicans in other English bishoprics. This time the London printers were not caught on the hop and milked the papal connection for all it was worth, their output extending to popish plot playing cards. The prolific anti-Catholic author John Oldham imagined the pope and the devil discussing the plot and, in another pamphlet, the two usual interlocutors were joined by 'the Jesuit Ignatius' and 'Cardinal Barbarin' to analyse its failure.[18] Seizing the moment, the playwright Nathaniel Lee channelled antipapalism into a tragedy about Alexander VI's son Cesare Borgia, though he took care not to present the pontiff himself on stage.[19] The uncensored world of public processions was another matter and, in November 1679, a papal effigy was paraded through the Sussex town of Lewes.[20] It duly became a tradition.

Members of the political elite had always harboured doubts about Oates and his curiously adaptable plot. They dropped him in the winter of 1679–80, even as Charles recommended one of his prime targets, Cardinal Howard, to succeed another of them, Francesco Barberini, as protector of England and Scotland. Popular antipopery could not be so easily suppressed and, in the case of staunchly Protestant London, could even have a useful social function. Thus a mock procession through the city's streets, led by a 'pope' and 'cardinals', was permitted in November 1680.[21] In terms of pamphlet publications, the dialogue format continued to flourish, though another genre was attempted in 1683, when the 'eminent pen' of Independent minister Christopher Ness was employed in a scurrilous biography of the current pope. *The Devils Patriarck* identified Innocent XI, the 'Master of all Misrule', as the originator of the famous plot, with Cardinal Howard, the Jesuit general Giovanni Paolo Oliva and Louis XIV's confessor among the ringleaders.[22] To suggest that Innocent was somehow in league with the Jesuits, let alone with the French king, indicates the level of ignorance that was being peddled. On the other hand, there was nothing lightweight or entertaining about a London jury convicting Archbishop Plunkett of treason or a London crowd watching his execution at Tyburn in 1681. The line was finally crossed in the spring of 1683 when a group of Protestants with aristocratic contacts plotted to kill both the king and the duke of York at Rye House in Hertfordshire, with a view to placing the former's squarely Protestant illegitimate son James, duke of Monmouth, on the throne. Such a direct threat to the monarchy effectively eased the duke of York's previously contested succession in February 1685.

In power James II (1685–8) was every inch the Catholic monarch his critics had feared, but what had not been anticipated was that a minister such as Robert Spencer, earl of Sunderland, the secretary of state for the southern department, which dealt with the Italian states, would acclimatise himself so well as to convert to Rome. Business with the Holy See suddenly intensified. At the Roman end it was in the safe hands of Cardinal Howard, who was assisted by his secretary John Leyburn. This meant that the fraught question of reintroducing a hierarchy into England was addressed by means of a compromise: Leyburn was appointed vicar apostolic, a cleric of episcopal rank in extra-diocesan mission territory. He travelled to England, accompanied by a nuncio, Ferdinando d'Adda. By way of reply, James sent Roger Palmer, earl of Castlemaine, on an embassy to Rome.

The externals of this embassy – the earl's suite and itinerary, the hospitality of Prince Pamphili at Piazza Navona, Castlemaine's initial meeting with the pope in April 1686, his official entry into Rome the following January, and subsequent lavish entertainments – were carefully recorded by John Michael Wright, the earl's chief steward.[23] The Palazzo Pamphili was decorated with the papal arms and symbols of Britain on 24' high boards. Crowds cried 'Viva il grand Re d'Ingelterra' as the earl made his way to the Palazzo del Quirinale, and the elite enjoyed a musical tribute to the king hosted by ex-Queen Kristina of Sweden.[24] However, behind the elaborately decorated facades, Castlemaine was every bit as undiplomatic as his king in seeking to promote causes at variance with those of the pope. James took his cue from France, where king and pope were in dispute over appointments to bishoprics and Bishop Bossuet's recently formulated Gallican Articles neatly embodied the tenets of antipapal conciliarism. Avignon remained an easy target and French ambassadors in Rome asserted theselves by acting with extremely bad grace. James's diluted version of this multifaceted conflict was to request that his Jesuit confidant Edward Petre be raised to the episcopate. Innocent refused. There was, however, room for compromise, because James also requested a red hat for his brother-in-law Rinaldo, the first Cardinal Rinaldo d'Este having died in 1672. As it happened, a list of new cardinals favourable to many of the secular powers had been prepared, so Rinaldo was added as the twenty-seventh and last name. His maternal uncle was Cardinal Carlo Barberini, which made him a kinsman of some of Innocent's early patrons. There was a tenuous English connection elsewhere on the list, for the Portuguese candidate Verissimo de Lencastre was clearly identifiable as a descendant of John of Gaunt. The new cardinals were created on 2 September 1686. Thereafter Castlemaine achieved nothing more and was withdrawn. James continued to make unacceptable proposals, including requests for Petre to be made a cardinal, which were consistently rebuffed. On the other hand, the birth of Prince James Francis Edward in 1688 permitted Cardinal Howard to demonstrate how the Anglo-papal relationship might be cultivated by more subtle means: he hosted a banquet at his palace adjacent to the English College and invited the pope to be the baby's godfather. Howard's sensitivity to conditions in his homeland was also in evidence when

England was divided into four districts (London, Midland, Northern and Western), each with a vicar apostolic, rather than a bishop.

Hardly had this new arrangement been established than James was forced out of his realms: the political elite brought his safely Protestant daughter Mary and her husband William of Orange from the United Provinces and forced James to flee to France in December 1688. The nuncio Adda was back in Italy by March 1689, William declared war on France at the beginning of May, and Innocent died on 11 August. These developments kept the presses busy and, true to form, the pope featured prominently, whether he was 'in a passion' or once more conversing with the devil.[25] In keeping with the sort of confessional flexibility illustrated by the earl of Sunderland, there was also greater subtlety than had previously been on offer, for T.D. recognised Innocent's personal qualities, distinguishing this 'Faultless prelate, if e'er Pope was so' from the corrupt body of which he was head, and T.L.'s life of the pontiff is as balanced as it is informative, attributing the failure of Castlemaine's mission to a combination of the ongoing Franco-papal differences and Innocent's opposition to the Jesuits' power over princes such as James.[26]

Thanks to his brother-in-law Rinaldo d'Este, James was the monarch most closely connected to the conclave of August–October 1689. The interests of his erstwhile subjects in England and Scotland were still protected by Cardinal Howard and those of Ireland by Altieri, who doubled up as prefect of Propaganda Fide. Once again, voting took place in the context of war, and one reason the cardinals elected their seventy-nine-year-old sub-dean, Pietro Ottoboni, was his acceptability to powers on both sides of the conflict. In practice Alexander VIII's Venetian patriotism made him wary of Venice's imperial neighbour and open to improved relations with France. Indeed, the sole non-Italian among the fourteen cardinals he created was Louis's candidate. A red hat also went to the former nuncio Adda. The earl of Melfort represented the Stuarts in Rome for most of Alexander's sixteen-month pontificate and the pope was as supportive as he could be in the circumstances: financial aid was provided for the Catholics of Britain and Ireland, and a congregation of cardinals was commissioned to address insular affairs in the context of a wider European peace. All of this stands in stark contrast to the oft-repeated assertion that when the Williamite and Jacobite armies met at the Boyne on 1 July 1690 the pope was an ally of the Protestant leader, rather than the Catholic one.[27] This is a myth. Such a claim might have been valid had Innocent yet lived, but Alexander was not bound by his predecessor's policies and was clearly committed to the cause of peace.

Apart from the addition of Adda, British and Irish connections were unchanged when the next conclave opened in February 1691. The Irish protector Altieri was among the party leaders. After five frustrating months the electors settled on the archbishop of Naples, Antonio Pignatelli, a former nuncio to Poland and Austria. Pignatelli was sufficiently inspired by the Odescalchi pope as to choose the name Innocent XII (1691–1700), but differed from him in seeking better relations with France. In the context of continuing war that objective generated serious suspicion in Vienna. Far from taking sides, Innocent was committed to a negotiated peace, yet Louis was emphatic that no papal intermediary would be involved in talks between the powers. Paris was the closest that any papal diplomat got to the peace negotiations at Rijswijk in 1697. Among the resulting terms, Louis recognised William as king of England, Scotland and Ireland, while nevertheless continuing to provide practical support for the exiled Stuarts.

Innocent XII's pontificate was not notable for any significant developments in the Anglo-papal relationship. There was not even much in the way of ecclesiastical business. Dublin and Cashel acquired new archbishops, while in England three of the original vicars apostolic remained in post, ministering to their beleaguered flocks as inconspicuously as possible from bases in London, Wolverhampton and north Yorkshire. The exception was Philip Michael Ellis, who deserted the Western District and settled in Rome. He sought to make himself indespensible to King James and Cardinal Howard, but when the latter died in 1694 Ellis was not asked to fill the Howard-shaped void. Instead, the English clergy acquired a Roman agent in the person of George Witham. It was on his watch and in the interest of his fellow secular priests that Innocent instructed the regular clergy to seek the approval of the vicar apostolic in order to operate in a particular district. Howard's death also necessitated revised provision for Scotland: James asked Archbishop Alessandro Caprara to provide what protection he could to the Scots College, while the Scottish clergy acquired their first vicar apostolic, the scholarly convert Thomas Nicolson. Even these relatively modest developments were enough to contribute to a sense in some quarters that 'there has beene of late a much greater Resort into this Kingdom than formerly of Popish Bishops Priests and Jesuits', in response to which William's government asserted itself with an Act for 'preventing the growth of popery'.[28] It came into force in 1700.

Cardinal Altieri's death in 1698 left the protectorships of all three kingdoms in abeyance. By 1700, therefore, connections between the College of Cardinals and the British Isles were limited to Carlo Barberini as prefect of Propaganda Fide and Ferdinando d'Adda's increasingly distant nunciature. Rinaldo d'Este had succeeded to the dukedom of Modena and resigned the cardinalate in order to marry and perpetuate his dynasty. That autumn's conclave was over-shadowed by the long-anticipated death of Carlos II of Spain on 1 November. In a dramatic extension of Bourbon power endorsed by the late pope, Louis XIV's sixteen-year-old grandson Philippe inherited the Iberian kingdom. Emperor Joseph I argued for an Austrian Habsburg alternative, a proposal supported by William, whose maritime interests were most directly threatened by the new arrangement. In previous conclaves the election of experienced diplomats had been presented as a means of proceeding from war to peace. This time, as the possibility of a major conflict loomed, the cardinals deliberately wanted a pope lacking the merest hint of a connection to any of the potential combatants. They chose Giovanni Francesco Albani, a native of Urbino whose career had never taken him beyond the Papal States. He took the name Clement XI (1700–21).

Europe was at war for most of this pontificate. The War of the Spanish Succession was faught on many fronts, including in Italy, where imperial forces occupied all the Spanish possessions in the name of their claimant to the throne. Among these, Naples remained a papal fief and so insistent was the emperor that Clement invest his candidate with the southern kingdom that Joseph declared war against the pope in 1708. A British fleet, which was principally engaged in transporting imperial troops, came close to bombarding the papal port of Civitavecchia, but Joseph intended merely to frighten the pontiff and a direct assault was avoided. From this it can be inferred that pope and emperor were on opposite sides with regard to Europe's other contested thrones, those of England, Ireland and Scotland: Clement recognised James Francis Edward Stuart as James VIII and III, whereas Joseph was allied with James's Anglican half-sister Anne (1702–14). In 1711 the deaths of Emperor Joseph and the dauphin resulted in the Habsburg claimant to Spain being elected as emperor and Louis XIV's great-grandson becoming heir apparent to the throne of France. This dynastic reshuffling helped to propel the warring powers towards three negotiated settlements, at Utrecht (1713), Rastatt and Baden (both 1714). Felipe V retained the Spanish throne, while his rival, now Emperor Charles VI, took up where Charles V had left off in the 1550s, ruling the previously Spanish Netherlands, together with Milan, Naples and Sardinia. Britain emerged from Utrecht as a major European player, forcing the Stuart 'Pretender' out of France, while the pope was a helpless bystander throughout the entire process.

In order to defeat or at least contain the Bourbon powers, Britain was obliged to ally with a range of Protestant and Catholic states, the latter including Savoy and Portugal. A certain amount of religious flexibility was required, so it helped if government ministers had travelled in Catholic countries, particularly those within the remit of the secretary of state for the southern department. Here a gradual shift can be perceived during Clement's pontificate. None of William's secretaries came with prior experience of Rome. Among those of Anne's reign, William Legge, earl of Dartmouth, was the first to have travelled to Rome. Those who served George I (1714–27) in the 1710s invariably had experience of travel in Italy, though only Joseph Addison had been as far as Rome. The envoys in Florence were still the only British diplomats in central Italy and were increasingly inclined to employ diplomacy of the cultural variety. One of them, the antiquary Sir Henry Newton, maintained a correspondence with Pope Clement himself. At the same time, a thaw in papal attitudes towards Britain can be glimpsed in the words of one former secretary of state for the southern department. Charles Talbot, duke of Shrewsbury, was an opportunistic Catholic convert to Anglicanism who lived in Rome for over three years at the height of the war. In 1704 noted that 'a year ago I was so ill in the opinion of the Pope that it was thought a crime to go near me; now that they fear the D[uke] of M [arlborough] and his red-coats should come into Italy, his Holiness does nothing but commend me.'[29]

In the context of war new arrangements were made for British and Irish Catholics. New cardinal protectors were appointed in 1706: Alessandro Caprara for England, Giuseppe Sacripanti for Scotland, and Giuseppe Renato Imperiali for Ireland. In practice, their supervision was limited to the national colleges, which existed in a much reduced state, with the Scots College a particular cause for concern. In 1707, the year that the Act of Union between England and Scotland took effect, Propaganda Fide proposed to unite the three colleges, but the scheme was vetoed by James VII and II's widow and the institutions continued their parallel lives. Meanwhile, the English and Scottish clergy received new Roman agents and the long-absent Ellis was instructed to resign his vicariate, but was not replaced until 1713.

At Queen Anne's death in August 1714 the Act of Settlement (1701) ensured that the elector of Hanover, an ally of the emperor, became George I of Great Britain and Ireland. At a technical level it was a smooth transition. However, within a year of George's arrival, Tories ousted from power by overtly Hanoverian Whigs made common cause with Scots resentful of the Union and looked to the Pretender for leadership. With tacit support from France, James travelled from his refuge in Lorraine, landing in Scotland on 22 December 1715. For six weeks in the depths of winter his poorly-equipped forces struggled in difficult conditions, before being abandoned by their king in early February. Only at that point did the rebellion later known as 'the Fifteen' acquire its indirect papal dimension, when James was denied permission to return to Lorraine and sought sanctuary in Avignon. Thereafter his options became steadily more limited: in 1717 Britain entered into a triple alliance with France and the Dutch republic, which became a quadruple alliance with the emperor the following year, all the powers pledging to support the Hanoverian succession. At first James had little choice but to retreat to the Papal States, where Clement gave him use of the Palazzo Ducale in Urbino. The allies' common enemy was Spain, where the king's principal minister, Cardinal Giulio Alberoni, sought to revive Felipe V's international standing. By 1719 this included plans for a two-pronged Spanish invasion of Britain, led by Jacobite commanders. James hastened to Spain in anticipation of gaining possession his kingdoms. However, the scheme was not merely vaguely reminiscent of 1588;

Plate 1 St Peter-on-the-Wall, Bradwell-on-Sea (Historic England).
Anglo-Saxon churches dedicated to St Peter, the first pope, can be found along the east coast of England, at Bradwell-on-Sea, Barton-upon-Humber and Monkwearmouth. Of these, the seventh-century chapel of St Peter-on-the-Wall, Bradwell-on-Sea, is the most venerable, having been built in the remains of the Roman fort.

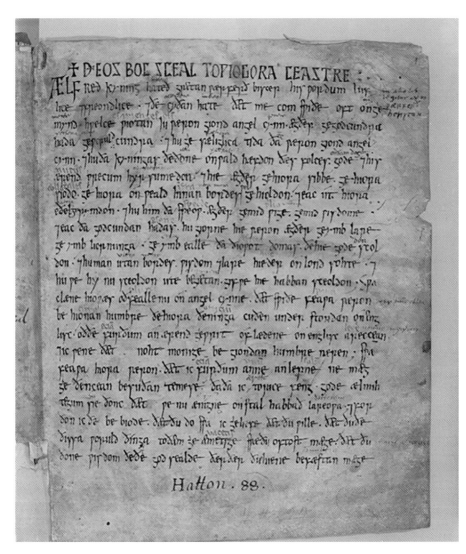

Plate 2   Gregory the Great, *Pastoral Care*, King Alfred's West Saxon version,
c. 890–897 (Bodleian Library, Oxford).

In the preface to his translation of Pope Gregory's *Liber regulae pastoralis* – known
in English as the *Pastoral Care* – King Alfred explains that the missionary
Augustine of Canterbury first brought the text to England. Alfred rated it as one
of those 'books which are the most necessary for all men to know'.

Plate 3 Detail from the Bayeux Tapestry (Universal History Archive/UIG/ Bridgeman Images).

According to William of Poitiers, who lived through the events of 1066, Pope Alexander II sent a banner to William of Normandy before the duke's expedition to England. Although there is no reference to it in the text of the Bayeux Tapestry, the banner is depicted at various points, including in the thick of the battle at Hastings.

Plate 4 Sarcophagus of Pope Adrian IV (Alinari/Bridgeman Images).

The only English pope, Adrian IV, is thought to have been born in or near St Albans. He died at Anagni on 1 September 1159. His body was carried to Rome and buried in this ancient granite sarcophagus, which is now located in the Grotte beneath St Peter's Basilica.

Plate 5 King John pays homage to the papal legate, 1213 (Private Collection/Ken Welsh/Bridgeman Images).

Whether in near-contemporary chronicles, sixteenth-century plays or modern histories, King John has proved to be a controversial figure. His excommunication and subsequent submission to the papacy made him both a hero and a villain to patriotic English Protestants. This depiction of John performing homage for his realm is taken from Cassell's *History of England* (*c*.1901).

Plate 6 Tomb of Cardinal Adam Easton (Julian Gardner).

Imprisoned by Urban VI and restored to the cardinalate by Boniface IX, Adam Easton died in 1398 and was buried in his titular church, S. Cecilia. His sepulchral monument brings a bit of England to Trastevere, being an English table-tomb on which the royal arms are flanked by those of the cardinal himself.

Plate 7   Pinturicchio, *Enea Silvio Piccolomini as an ambassador to the court of King James I of Scotland* (DeAgostini/Getty Images).

In 1435 Enea Silvio Piccolomini visited Scotland on behalf of the Council of Basel and also travelled through England. As Pope Pius II he recalled the expedition in his autobiographical *Commentaries*. These, in turn, inspired Pinturicchio's fresco cycle of 1502–8 for the Piccolomini Library in the cathedral of Pius's home city, Siena.

Plate 8 Scottish sword of state (Crown Copyright Historic Scotland reproduced courtesy of Historic Scotland).

Between 1482 and 1537 two English and two Scottish kings received ceremonial swords and mitre-like hats blessed by popes. In 1507 Julius II sent James IV a sword decorated with Della Rovere acorns and oak leaves, in a scabbard bearing the papal coat of arms. It became the Scottish sword of state.

Plate 9 Friedrich van Hulsen, *The pope's bull against the queen* (Private collection/Bridgeman Images).

This engraving by a seventeenth-century Dutch printmaker recalls Pius V's excommunication of Elizabeth I by means of the bull *Regnans in excelsis* (1570). In keeping with the partisan spirit of the times, the warlike pontiff instructs an English Catholic to initiate 'every evil', including the assassination of the queen.

Plate 10 Thomas Cockson, *The revells of Christendome*, *c.* 1609 (Private collection/Bridgeman Images).

Games of chance stand for power politics in this satirical engraving, in which Britain's James VI and I, Henri IV of France, Kristian IV of Denmark and Maurits of Nassau are getting the better of some friars. Pope Paul V makes an undignified grab at the winnings while James attempts to dislodge the papal tiara.

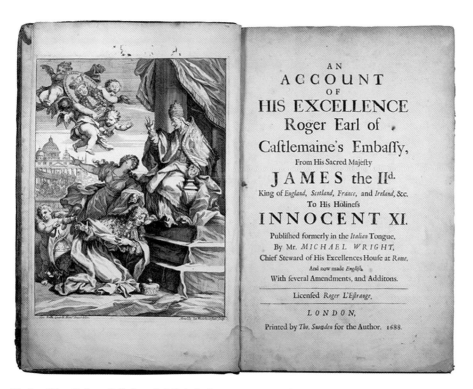

AN
ACCOUNT
OF
HIS EXCELLENCE
Roger Earl of .
Caſtlemaine's Embaſſy,
From His Sacred Majeſty
JAMES the IId.
King of *England*, *Scotland*, *France*, and *Ireland*, &c.
To His Holineſs
INNOCENT XI.
Publiſhed formerly in the *Italian* Tongue,
By Mr. *MICHAEL WRIGHT*,
Chief Steward of His Excellences Houſe at *Rome*.
And now made *Engliſh*,
With ſeveral Amendments, and Additons.

Licenſed *Roger L'Eſtrange*,

LONDON,
Printed by *Tho. Sowden* for the Author. 1688.

Plate 11 John Michael Wright's account of the earl of Castlemaine's Embassy to Innocent XI, 1688 (University of Aberdeen).
The frontispiece of this extensively illustrated work depicts Roger Palmer, earl of Castlemaine, kissing the foot of Pope Innocent XI on behalf of his royal master, James VII and II, whose portrait is held aloft by putti. Castlemaine's mission to Rome took place in 1686–7 and Wright's first, Italian edition appeared in 1687.

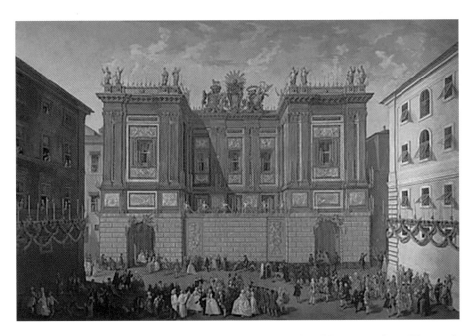

Plate 12 Paolo Monaldi(?), *Prince James receiving his son, Prince Henry, in front of the Palazzo del Re* (*c.* **1747–8**) (National Galleries of Scotland).
During the Roman exile of James Francis Edward Stuart, the 'Old Pretender', British observers were less interested in what happened at the city's papal palaces than in comings and goings at the Palazzo Muti (or 'del Re'), near SS. Apostoli. Here James greets his twenty-two-year-old son Henry on the occasion of the latter's appointment as a cardinal.

Plate 13   Sir Thomas Lawrence, *Pope Pius VII*, **1819** (Royal Collection Trust/
© Her Majesty Queen Elizabeth II 2015).

Following the defeat of Napoleon in 1815, Lawrence was commissioned to
paint the leaders of the anti-French coalition. His portraits of Pius VII and
Cardinal Ercole Consalvi, the papal secretary of state, hang in the Waterloo
Chamber at Windsor Castle, alongside those of the other monarchs and their
ministers.

Plate 14 'HB' (John Doyle), *Absolution, a Retrospective Sketch*, 1835 (© National Portrait Gallery, London).

As home secretary Robert Peel introduced the 1829 government bill conceding Catholic emancipation. In November 1834 he was on holiday in Rome when word reached him that William IV wanted him to form an administration. Doyle's lithograph shows Sir Robert being blessed by Pope Gregory XVI and was published in January 1835.

THE GUY FAWKES OF 1850
PREPARING TO BLOW UP ALL ENGLAND !

Plate 15 'The Guy Fawkes of 1850', *Punch* (Look and Learn).
The restoration of the English and Welsh hierarchy in the autumn of 1850 initiated a glut of pamphlets, cartoons and cries of 'Papal aggression'. In November *Punch* marked the anniversary of the gunpowder plot by depicting the pope preparing to blow up the British Establishment with mitres rather than powder kegs.

Plate 16 'The Pope', *Vanity Fair*, (1878) (Private collection).
After Pius IX's reign of nearly thirty-two years, relations between the papacy and
the secular powers were in need of some refreshment. Leo XIII's election in
February 1878 provided that opportunity, though it could hardly have been
expected that this sixty-seven-year-old would himself reign for more than a
quarter of a century.

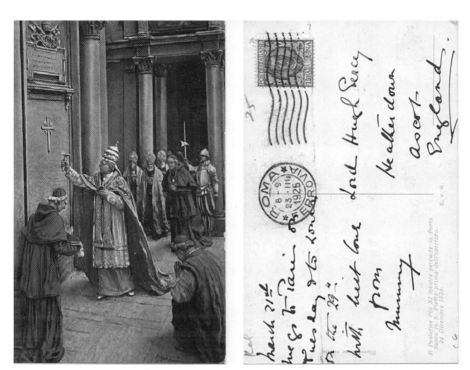

Plate 17 Pius XI opening the Holy Door at St Peter's Basilica, 24 December 1924 (Private collection).

This postcard, written on 21 March 1925, was sent by Helen, duchess of Northumberland, to her young son, Lord Hugh Percy, the future tenth duke, during Pius XI's holy year. The duchess experienced Rome before the height of the pilgrimage season. In April and May 200 pilgrims joined the Scottish National Pilgrimage, with 1,200 more on its English counterpart.

Plate 18 Visit by Princess Elizabeth and the Duke of Edinburgh to the Vatican, 13 April 1951 (Popperfoto/Getty Images).

This private visit followed that of Edward VII in 1903 and George V's audience in 1923. As queen, Elizabeth paid state visits to Popes John XXIII in 1961, John Paul II in 1980 and Francis in 2013, a number exceeded only by her visits to France, the United States, Germany and Italy. The state visit to Italy in 2000 provided the context for a second audience with John Paul II.

Plate 19 Sir Mark Heath presenting his credentials to John Paul II, 1 April 1982 (*L'Osservatore Romano* ©, all rights reserved).

After Rome became the capital of a new Italian kingdom in 1871 Britain chose to maintain diplomatic relations with Italy, rather than with the papal prisoner in the Vatican. An extraordinary legation to the Holy See operated from 1914 and became a permanent mission in 1926, but full diplomatic relations were not established until 1982.

Plate 20 Benedict XVI at the Birmingham Oratory, 19 September 2010
(*L'Osservatore Romano* ©, all rights reserved).
On the final day of his state visit to Britain, Benedict beatified John Henry
Newman at a mass in Cofton Park, close to Newman's grave at Rednal, to the
south west of Birmingham. Afterwards he visited Newman's rooms at the
Birmingham Oratory.

it managed to surpass both 1588 and 1715 in failing to achieve its objective. Once more James retreated to Italy.

There were few marital options available to an exiled mendicant king. Poland's elective monarchy presented more dynastic possibilities than most and a potential bride was identified in Maria Clementina Sobieska, who was named in honour of her godfather, the still-reigning pope. The emperor obliged his British ally by arresting the girl and her mother at Innsbruck, with a view to preventing the marriage, but she was spirited away by Irish Jacobites and met her husband in September 1719, shortly after his return from Spain. The pope never ceased to accord James the honour due to a reigning monarch and he now took a paternal interest in the couple, providing them with an urban palace near SS. Apostoli and a rural one at Albano.

The years 1714–15 marked a decisive shift in British domestic politics: Tory defenders of Anglicanism were firmly out of office while Whigs used their new-found power to promote liberal religious policies. Here was an opportunity for some of Britain's more enterprising Catholics to assert themselves. On behalf of his co-religionists, Thomas Howard, eighth duke of Norfolk, did precisely that. His uncle, the seventh duke, a nephew of Cardinal Howard, had followed the example of the duke of Shrewsbury and repudiated his Catholic faith in order to hold public office, which he did seamlessly under Kings Charles, James and William, but the eighth duke sought to make Catholic talent available to the Crown without compromising Catholic views of papal authority. This Catholic Whiggery was not an exclusively secular phenomenon and its clerical adherents were no less determined to secure potentially influential positions. Thus, in 1716, another Catholic Whig, John Talbot Stonor, became vicar apostolic of the Midland District. With Bonaventure Giffard of the London District ailing and in need of a coadjutor (assistant), this looked like a second opportunity to advance the cause. However, Thomas Strickland failed in his efforts to gain the appointment. Instead, he became Norfolk's emissary, first to King George in Hanover and then to Rome. The proposals he conveyed for Anglo-papal cooperation were attractive to both sides, but the Roman authorities stalled, out of respect for their unfortunate guest, the Pretender. On the other hand, George had use for a man of Strickland's talents and sent him to Vienna in 1719 to negotiate a papal–imperial accord, which the British government viewed as a roundabout means to winning papal support for a deal involving Catholic toleration, an acceptable oath of allegiance and a comprehensive rejection of Jacobitism. There was even talk of a cardinal's hat for Stonor. The scheme was undoubtedly clever and forward-thinking, but receptiveness to the message was marred by the character of the messenger, for Strickland could not conceal his arrogance and ambition.

Clement XI lived long enough to have the cannon of Castel S. Angelo fired in celebration of the birth of Charles Edward, the Jacobite prince of Wales, on 31 December 1720. The Jacobite artist Antonio David's depiction of the prince's baptism, which took place the same day, was painted in 1725 but conveniently includes those cardinals who were close to the Stuart court: the protectors Sacripanti, Imperiali and Filippo Antonio Gualterio, together with Francesco Acquaviva, Francesco Barberini, Fabrizio Paolucci and Pietro Ottoboni.[30] All seven voted in the conclave that followed Clement's death in March 1721, as did James's sometime ally, the now-disgraced Alberoni. When Michelangelo Conti was elected on 8 May, James and Clementina were on hand to congratulate him and witness the cardinals' *adoratio* of the new pope, Innocent XIII (1721–4).

A humbler witness of the *sede vacante* and papal coronation of 1721 was the Jacobite antiquarian Richard Rawlinson, whose unpublished journals provide useful insights into Anglo-Roman life in the early 1720s.[31] Rawlinson was a nonjuror, a Jacobite of the Anglican variety, and duly became a bishop among that fast-dying breed. If his episcopal profile was lower than his antiquarian one, it was with good cause, because he had before him the unfortunate example of Francis Atterbury, bishop of Rochester and dean of Westminster. Atterbury's Jacobitism evolved out of a Tory fear that the Whigs' grip on power – reinforced by electoral success in 1721 – was imperilling the Church of England. He became convinced that the only remedy was a foreign invasion and Stuart restoration. Atterbury was connected to a number of such schemes but only the plot of 1722 bears his name, even though he was resigned to its futility before any action could take place. At the Italian end, James had planned to take ship from Genoa and make his way to Britain, all the while using correspondence with the pope to make his whereabouts known and divert attention from his real intentions. He had got no further than Bagni di Lucca in Tuscany when the plot was discovered. The conspirators played into the hands of prime minister Robert Walpole, who ensured that Britain's Catholics suffered harsher financial penalties for their faith. Atterbury was humiliated and forced to live the remainder of his life in exile.

Jacobite exiles created expenditure for the papacy, but at least they posed no doctrinal dilemmas. This contrasted with challenges that had been coming from France since the mid-seventeenth century, for Rome was much exercised by the rigorist, Augustinian-inspired teachings of Cornelius Jansen (d. 1638) and the Jansenists associated with the Parisian convent of Port-Royal. Opposition to Jansenism was maintained by the Jesuits. Papal condemnations by Urban VIII and Innocent X failed to suppress the movement, which gained more adherents in France and the Low Countries, prompting Clement XI's anti-Jansenist bull *Unigenitus* (1713).[32] Speculation that Innocent XIII would repeal the bull came to nothing, though it did inspire a sudden intensification of the anti-Jansenist witch-hunt. This time there were allegations by the Jesuit rector of the Scots College in Rome about the danger to Scottish students travelling there via Paris. The withdrawl of *Unigenitus* was one offer among many made by candidates or their backers during the highly-politicised papal election of March–May 1724. Compared to the French and imperialists, the Pretender was a relatively minor player, but enjoyed greater influence than he had in 1721, for the electors now included his client Melchior de Polignac. Not to be outdone, even the British employed an agent in Rome, the Brandenburger Philipp von Stosch, who intrigued on the imperialist side while the Stuarts pinned their hopes on France. The Holy Spirit confounded them all and the century's least political pope was elected. Vincenzo Maria Orsini had managed to vote in six conclaves without becoming tainted by the experience; as pope his focus remained fixed on his spiritual responsibilities, which included presiding over the jubilee of 1725 and canonising ten of the century's twenty-nine new saints.

By becoming Benedict XIII (1724–30), rather than XIV, Orsini finally determined that Scotland had supported an antipope over three centuries earlier. As far as contemporary Scotland was concerned, Benedict listened to his fellow priests, rather than to James VIII. At Sacripanti's death in 1727 he overruled James and appointed one of his own cardinals, Alessandro Falconieri, as protector. In the same year Rome recognised the geographical and linguistic challenges of the Scottish mission by dividing it into Lowland and Highland vicariates. As far as Benedict's dealings with England were concerned, what emerges most clearly is devotion to his own order, for the sole vacancy among the vicars apostolic was filled by the Dominican Thomas Dominic Williams, who was sent to the Northern District. Williams was a product of the English Dominican house founded by Cardinal Howard at SS. Giovanni e Paolo on Rome's Monte Celio. Uniquely among the English vicars he was consecrated by the pope himself. Although Williams and his colleagues continued to encounter practical difficulties when ministering to their flocks, overt persecution of Catholics evaporated once the Atterbury Plot had served Walpole's purpose.

So assiduously did Benedict attend to his spiritual responsibilities that there was a void at the heart of papal government. Much business was entrusted to his Beneventan favourite, Niccolò Coscia, a man who could be bought. The emperor and the king of Sardinia took full advantage of this weakness, which had knock-on effects throughout the hierarchy. By way of illustration, the Abbé Strickland appears to have purchased the emperor's support for his elevation to the see of Namur in the Austrian Netherlands. British elites, many of whom witnessed the unimpressive reality of papal power during their grand tours, ceased to regard the pope as any sort of threat. Indeed, so unthreatening was he that the Anglican bishop of London, Edmund Gibson, could become known as 'Walpole's pope' without his career ending in Laud-like tragedy.

For Benedict's dealings with the Stuarts the British government could refer to Stosch's reports. As these relate, all began harmoniously, with the ascetic pope giving the king and queen ornate furniture made for his predecessor. In 1725 he baptised their second son, Henry Benedict, duke of York, but before the end of the year James's decision to entrust his elder son to a Protestant governor caused Clementina to snap. She retreated to the convent of S. Cecilia in Trastevere. Benedict took her side and cut James's pension, forcing him to economise by moving to Bologna in 1726. A reconciliation was effected, but it was not until 1729 that all four members of the family returned to Rome and relations with the pope were restored: James received his papal pension once more, his candidate became protector of England, and Benedict was given a relic of St Edward the Confessor. In the interim, James had been distracted by the possibilities offered by George I's death, only to be frustrated by Louis XV's minister, Cardinal Fleury, and a reinforced Anglo-French alliance.

Secular influences, including Spain's anti-Austrian veto of Cardinal Imperiali, kept the electors enclosed for almost four months in 1730. The external consideration that finally determined an election was the prospect of Gian Gastone de' Medici dying without issue and grand ducal Tuscany being swallowed up by one of the larger powers. A Tuscan pope might act in the interests of his home region. The secretary of state, Antonio Banchieri of Pistoia, was a strong candidate, but too obviously supported by France. The Florentine Alamanno Salviati suffered a similar limitation in that he had been raised to the cardinalate as the Stuart candidate, though in no sense was he regarded as *papabile*. That left the venerable Lorenzo Corsini, who was elected.

Pope Clement XII's pontificate lasted throughout the 1730s, during most of which he was blind and otherwise incapacitated, his physical weakness reflecting the contempt with which even Catholic princes regarded his temporal power. First, papal claims to the overlordship of Parma and Piacenza were ignored when Don Carlos of Spain claimed the dukedoms through his mother Elisabetta Farnese. Then the War of the Polish Succession (1733–8) was fought on Italian soil, Spanish troops passing through papal territory in order to reclaim Naples by force. Gian Gastone finally died in 1737, leaving Clement with new neighbours virtually all round: Spanish Bourbons in Naples, the emperor himself in Parma, and the imperial son-in-law in Tuscany. Although Britain had entered into a new alliance with the emperor in 1731, Walpole ensured that she remained neutral in the conflict because the balance of her interests now lay outside Europe. The Stuarts, on the other hand, had a genuine interest in the Polish succession, for both James and his patron Louis XV had Polish wives. As usual, the Stuarts failed to achieve their objective: Louis's father-in-law was not restored to the Polish throne and had to be content with the duchy of Lorraine. There was, however, a Catholic Whig footnote to this conflict, for the Abbé Strickland visited Charles VI in Vienna and then played on divisions in Walpole's ministry to agitate in favour of British military support for her imperial ally. In response, Walpole had no difficulty in engineering the destruction of the interfering Strickland, whose extreme ambition and disreputable personal life were quite enough to undo him.

What Strickland wanted above all else was an imperial recommendation for the cardinalate. This was impossible as long as Clement deliberately avoided creating crown cardinals, though he then made a bizarre exception for the eight-year-old Infante Luis of Spain and promoted Portuguese, French, Austrian, Spanish and Polish candidates in 1737, three years before Strickland's death. James III's position was quite distinct from that of a *de facto* monarch, but papal recognition of him as a king nevertheless gave him the right to nominate cardinals and he acquired new allies among the red-hatted elite with the promotions of Domenico Riviera in 1733 and Pierre-Guérin de Tencin in 1739. When the protectorship of Scotland fell vacant in 1734, it was Riviera who filled it. The next such vacancy was for Ireland in 1737. In a masterly stroke, it was filled by the pope's nephew Neri Corsini, who was perfectly familiar with Britain, having paid his first visit to London 1711, returning in 1718 as the Tuscan ambassador.

In 1731 the indefatigable Stosch claimed that his life was threatened in Rome and fled to Florence, but was determined to retain his income by dispatching a stream of reports on British travellers and their connections with the Stuart court, even if that meant competing with the British envoys to Tuscany. There were three successive such ministers in Florence during Clement's pontificate, but only one of them ventured as far as Rome: in 1735 Charles Fane undertook the journey in order to further Anglo-imperial relations by meeting the emperor's man in the Sacred College, the Spanish-born Cardinal Cienfuegos. The Jacobites then resident in Rome included Sir Thomas Dereham, whose eponymous cousin had been the British minister in Florence in the 1680s. The advent of a Florentine pope made the younger Dereham an exceptionally useful contact for the Stuarts, who benefited financially, ecclesiastically and even in terms of military protection during the Corsini pontificate. At Clementina's death in 1735 the Apostolic Camera paid the funeral expenses and the pope accorded her the highest honours, culminating in her burial in St Peter's.

While the Stuarts and their court were increasingly settled and accepted in Rome, a more recent British import into Italy was 'condemned and prohibited [...] for ever' by Clement in the bull *In eminenti* (1738).[33] This was Freemasonry, which had long since abandoned its craft roots and acquired a religious dimension: Deism. Clement's condemnation applied universally and had implications in many countries, but it certainly reinforced the distinction between generations of Catholics and non-Catholics in British society. On the Catholic side, the ultimate Society within a society was still that of Jesus, no less international than the Freemasons and easily more controversial in the eighteenth century. In the first half of that century the Jesuit rectors of the insular colleges in Rome were suspected of diverting students from the mission for which they were being trained and into the Society of Jesus, even if the accusations were found to be without foundation. Anti-Jesuit hostility on the part of the secular clergy reached a climax in the 1730s, so the Jesuits responded with accusations of Jansenism, which was a test of loyalty to the pope by those who had taken the Society's famous fourth vow. Such was the level of suspicion among English Catholics that when Matthew Pritchard, the Franciscan vicar apostolic of the Western District, visited Rome in 1736 it was thought that he went as an agent of the Jesuits. The prosaic reality was concern about the finances of his district, which had recently received papal support, and the appointment of a coadjutor, which could be a thorny business.

When the long-ailing Clement finally expired, on 6 February 1740, one of the century's most colourful grand tourists happened to be in Rome. This was Sir Francis Dashwood, who got into the spirit of the *sede vacante* by organising a mock conclave, in which he took the part of Pietro Ottoboni, dean of the Sacred College, while votes were cast by other foreign visitors. The real Ottoboni died eleven days into what turned out to be the century's longest conclave. It took 255 scrutinies to obtain the required two-thirds majority for any candidate, the one who finally broke through being Prospero Lambertini, the humane, learned and hard-working archbishop of Bologna. He became Benedict XIV (1740–58), the 'enlightened' pope beloved by scholars of his own and subsequent generations. Appropriately enough, this was the pontificate during which Britain finally adopted the Gregorian calendar: a shared calendar provided the context for steadily converging political and cultural interests.

The economic and cultural achievements of this relatively long reign were many and varied, from agricultural reform to the indexing of the Vatican archives, but there was much to be done precisely because it followed decades of weak papal leadership. Benedict's strength was matched by his esteem for the Society of Jesus, which meant that attempts by the English vicars apostolic to remove the Jesuit rectors from the Roman colleges were not pursued during this pontificate. Instead, some of the vicars returned to tried and tested methods of containing the regulars. This strategy resulted first in the brief *Emanavit nuper* (1745) and then in the bull *Apostolicum ministerium* (1753), both of which reinforced the 1698 instruction about the regulars requiring approval from the vicar apostolic in order to minister in a particular district. The Jacobite exiles were also left in no doubt of their place. Benedict had developed an affection for the Stuarts during their sojourn in his Bolognese diocese and, as pope, demonstrated it by means of improvements to their palaces in Rome and Albano, together with a new tomb for Clementina, to which her remains were translated in 1745.

All the while, the Roman curia had far more pressing matters to deal with, not least the imperial election triggered by the death of Charles VI in October 1740.

His daughter Maria Theresa's inheritance of the Habsburg lands was contested by Austria's French and Prussian enemies. Once again Italy was a convenient battlefield for the belligerents. From 1744 the war became more of an Anglo-French conflict which, in turn, opened up the possibility of yet another Jacobite plot, a previous attempt having been abandoned on the death of Clement XII. This time, Charles Edward Stuart left Rome for France early in 1744, arrived in Scotland in the summer of 1745, advanced as far as Derby by December, and then retreated northwards. His momentous defeat at Culloden followed on 16 April 1746, ending any hope of a Jacobite restoration in Britain. Predictably enough, Stosch assured London that the pope had helped to fincance the expedition, but the evidence suggests that Benedict had no expectation of its success and maintained a suitable distance.[34] Again, the fate of the Empire was of greater import in Rome: Charles VII's death triggered another contest in 1745, which saw Maria Theresa's husband, hitherto grand duke of Tuscany, elected to the imperial throne. When peace finally came, in the shape of the Treaty of Aix-la-Chapelle (1748), it brought what turned out to be a lasting settlement of non-Italian interests in the peninsula and an equally lasting French rejection of the Jacobite cause.

War frequently caused difficulties for popes who wished to create new cardinals, and that of the Austrian Succession was no exception. In this case, there was a vaguely British dimension in that the duke of York's promotion was delayed by his absence in France, but when it occurred in 1747 it represented a financial lifeline for what remained of the exiled dynasty. Papal honours kept coming the duke's way: diaconal and priestly ordination at the pope's hands, together with the offices of archpriest and prefect of the fabric of St Peter's Basilica. Even for a prince it was too much too soon and the pope was repeatedly called upon to intervene in domestic disputes between the sensitive young cardinal and his melancholic father.

From 1756 the European powers were at war once more. Land warfare in Germany, North America, West Africa and India, together with naval action in European waters and the Caribbean, made the Seven Years War a conflict of global proportions, yet its impact on the conclave of May–July 1758 was minimal. By a combination of design and accident, Protestant Britain was allied with Protestant Prussia against Catholic France and Austria. Among the Catholic monarchies, only Portugal sided with Britain, but neither of her cardinals participated in the election. Stuart influence in Rome was now so negligible that the protectors of Scotland and Ireland could lead rival factions, Giuseppe Spinelli co-ordinating the *zelanti*, who opposed secular interference in the conclave, and Neri Corsini leading the long-serving *anziani*. In contrast to the unanimity with which Benedict XIV had been elected, the Venetian Carlo Rezzonico limped over the two-thirds threshold with the century's narrowest margin of victory. His administrative and pastoral experiences were limited to Rome, the Papal States and his Paduan diocese.

Cardinal York – as Duke Henry Benedict was known – enjoyed the favour of Pope Clement XIII (1758–69), acquiring a palace in Frascati when he became bishop of Tusculum and the vast Palazzo della Cancelleria upon his appointment as vice-chancellor of the Church. This was a Ruritanian fantasy compared with the real power being wielded by his counterparts in the British government. These men also knew Rome, for the prime ministers had routinely experienced the Grand Tour and one of the chancellors of the exechequer in this period was none other than the notorious former papal elector Sir Francis Dashwood. This political generation happened to enjoy greater power than its predecessors because Britain had an expanding population, prospered from healthy trade, and enjoyed spending its surplus wealth, though only Dashwood went so far as to have himself painted as Pope Innocent III.[35] The Peace of Paris (1763) greatly increased Britain's overseas colonies, which now included Florida and Canada. With regard to the latter, the treaty stated that Britain would permit freedom of worship to her new Catholic subjects, thereby effectively opening a chapter in relations between London and Rome that would endure as long as Britain remained a colonial power.

This new political reality coincided with the Pretender's physical incapacity and the continued absence from Rome of his dissolute elder son, Charles. Whatever the religious shortcomings of the House of Hanover, their capacity to reproduce – in contrast to the tenuous Stuart line – suggested that they were a political fixture. George II's eldest grandson succeeded to the throne in 1760 and the next eldest, Edward, duke of York, toured Italy in 1763–4. Much to the disgust of the red-hatted Stuart claimant to that title, the duke was feted by Clement and took part in the Holy Week observances. With the ground thus prepared it can have come as no surprise that, at the Pretender's death on 1 January 1766, the papacy recognised George III (1760– 1820) as king of Great Britain. James was honorably buried in St Peter's, but the papacy accorded no further political support to the Stuarts. When the Jesuit rectors of the English and Scots colleges joined other Jacobites in hailing Charles, the Young Pretender, as their king they were promptly dismissed on papal authority.

Before Clement XIII's election the Portuguese minister Pombal had initiated a campaign against the over-powerful Jesuits in South America, but it was during this pontificate that the Society was expelled from Portugal, France and Spain. Most of the British and Irish Jesuit-run colleges on the continent survived *in situ*, albeit under the control of secular clergy, while the British Jesuit community at St Omer moved to Bruges in the Austrian Netherlands. It was a measure of Rome's weakness *vis-à-vis* the Catholic powers that death alone saved Clement from consenting to the unconditional suppression of the Society. John Thorpe, Roman agent for the English Jesuits, watched at the pope's deathbed and reflected the gravity of the situation by sending a lock of the pope's hair to Lord Arundell of Wardour: a relic, rather than the works of art he generally dispatched.

Much confusion attended the election of a successor to Clement XIII in the spring of 1769, the result of which was ultimately determined by the Bourbon powers of France and Spain, rather than by cardinals with Jacobite or even Hanoverian connections. Versailles wanted a pope who would suppress the Jesuits, but even once the election of the Franciscan Lorenzo Ganganelli had been secured it was still not certain that the new pontiff, Clement XIV (1769–74), would oblige. While Clement vacillated, the anti-Jesuit cause in Rome was spearheaded by Cardinal Mario Marefoschi, a former auditor of Cardinal York and secretary of Propaganda Fide, who filled the first insular protectorship to arise after the death of the Old Pretender. Unsurprisingly, Marefoschi's visitation of the Irish College in 1772 resulted in its withdrawal from Jesuit control. Early in 1773 the imperial government acquiesced in the Society's suppression and the papal brief to that effect was signed on 21 July. When the last Jesuit rector of the English College was arrested, the efficient new protector, Andrea Corsini, assumed *de facto* leadership of the institution. Among the English Jesuits, the Society's suppression was felt most forcefully at their college in Bruges. Some members of that community were imprisoned before they reassembled in the prince-bishopric of Liège. Clement's reputation was then contested in print, the barbs of bitter ex-Jesuits being countered by the secular priest Charles Cordell, whose knowledge had been gained through making translations of Clement's life and letters.[36]

Jesuit missioners existed in Britain but exercised no authority and were obliged to keep low profiles, so perhaps it is no surprise that Clement was partial towards British visitors, who could offer welcome relief from the contentious issues with which he was beset. The Herveys of Ickworth in Suffolk had been regular visitors to Rome since the 1710s, but no member of that family was more addicted to the city than Frederick Augustus, bishop of Derry and earl of Bristol. Even as he formulated an uncompromisingly antipapal oath of allegiance to be taken by Irish Catholics, his cultural interests endeared him to the pope, enabling him to declare that he was one of the 'few heretics' who were in papal favour.[37] In the diplomatic sphere, Sir William Hamilton was the second British envoy to Bourbon Naples and, in 1772, the first to meet a pope. The fourth earl of Rochford, veteran of a lengthy Italian tour, was serving as southern secretary when two more brothers of George III, the dukes of Gloucester and Cumberland, were received by the pope, who cultivated them in the hope of securing 'une plus grande tolerance aux catholiques' in Britain and Ireland.[38] Cumberland was honoured with three audiences in five weeks and the facade of St Peter's was illuminated for both princes. Meanwhile, the Young Pretender and his bride Louisa of Stolberg-Gedern were acknowledged by the papacy with no title higher than Baron and Baroness Renfrew. Disgruntled, they left Rome for Florence in 1774.

By the 1770s the Anglo-Roman artistic community was sufficiently well-established as to venture beyond producing works for wealthy travellers and look to the papacy for patronage. The Yorkshire-born architect Thomas Harrison proffered a design for turning the Vatican's Cortile del Belvedere into a sculpture gallery and the London-based Roman Giuseppe [Joseph] Bonomi designed a sacristry for St Peter's. Neither was built. The Irish sculptor Christopher Hewetson fared better, preserving Clement XIV's vigorous features in a portrait bust of 1771. Clement and his successor Pius VI – the former Giovanni Angelo Braschi, elected in a five-month conclave in 1774–5 – are both recalled in the Vatican's Museo Pio-Clementino, which was created to house antique statues unearthed from sites throughout the Papal States. For these popes, archaeological discoveries and their display provided relief not merely from deciding the fate of the Jesuits, but also from Emperor Joseph II's anticlericalism and successive partitions of Catholic Poland by its 'enlightened' neighbours. Archaeology had positive diplomatic and economic functions. Most notable in this respect was the visit to Rome by the Lutheran monarch Gustav III of Sweden in 1783–4. Few of the *inglesi* who visited Rome were genuinely cultured, but they were numerous and came with large disposable incomes, so any defects of manners or religion could be conveniently overlooked. Among British visitors, the most notable collectors were the Lancastrian Catholics Charles Townley and Henry Blundell. In the course of his four visits to Rome, Blundell had a number of dealings with the pope, acquiring a set of marble-topped tables from him but losing *Phaeton before Helios*, a recently discovered sculpture from the Villa d'Este at Tivoli, which Pius desired for the papal collection.

Elsewhere in the cultural sphere, Pius was the only pope who inspired a musical dimension to the Anglo-papal relationship, even if it was limited to a single composition. Samuel Wesley, son of the prolific Methodist hymn-writer Charles, marked his adolescent conversion to Catholicism by dedicating his *Missa de spiritu sancto* to the pontiff: a presentation copy was sent to Rome in 1784. This proved to be a passing phase and, at the age of twenty-two, Samuel became a Freemason.

Pius's lengthy pontificate overlapped with the premierships of five British statesmen. Of these Rockingham and Shelburne had visited Rome before attaining high office, North and Portland did so after resigning it, and the younger Pitt had no time for anything as frivolous as a grand tour. The last southern secretary and (from 1782) most of the early foreign secretaries had already been to Rome. In 1775 the duke of Gloucester returned there and stayed for sixteen months, including a period of *villegiatura* at Castel Gandolfo as the guest of Cardinal Alessandro Albani. The pope welcomed the duke and his morganatic wife, who gave birth to their only son while in Rome, and Gloucester entered into the spirit of the age by taking an interest in archaeology. The year 1786 saw the couple back in the city, albeit with the duke's mistress, and honoured with another papal audience. Such indulgence of George III's brother contrasted with the last days of Charles Edward Stuart, who separated from his flighty wife and was cared for at the Palazzo del Re (now Muti) by his illegitimate daughter. Just as the papacy had failed to recognise his claim to the throne, so he was denied burial in St Peter's alongside his parents. Instead, at Charles's death on 31 December 1788, Cardinal York took his brother's body to his cathedral church at Frascati and began to style himself Henry IX. It made not a whit of difference in papal Rome, where another Hanoverian prince was feted in the 1790s. Augustus, duke of Sussex, sixth son of George III and no closer to his father than any of the others, first appeared there in 1791. The climate suited this somewhat sickly prince and he resided in the city in 1792–3, when he entered into a clandestine marriage, and again in 1794–6. The longer he stayed, the more he devoted himself to archaeological excavations, first at Ostia and later at Velletri with the pope's nephew Luigi Braschi-Onesti.

Pius did not cultivate Protestant princes from a position of strength, benignly welcoming lost sheep back to the fold, but because Catholic elites were increasingly inclined to ignore papal authority and sideline papal adminis-tration. They could distinguish between being in communion with the bishop of Rome and being subject to him, between running their own ecclesiastical affairs relatively efficiently and waiting for the wheels of curial bureaucracy to turn. If this trend was most obvious in Joseph II's Austria, it spread to Italy, where Joseph appointed a new archbishop of Milan in 1784 without any reference to Rome. Elsewhere in the peninsula, there were attempts to establish state churches in Naples, Venice and Tuscany: the pope's authority was directly challenged by his nearest neighbours. This was in effect Gallicanism translated to meet the aspirations of states other than France. In Britain the poet Alexander Pope had identifed himself as a Catholic but not a papist during the first half of the century, and the distinction acquired institutional form when the first Catholic Committee was formed in 1782 by laymen whose careers had been thwarted by the 'papist' label. They campaigned for the abolition of civil disabilities imposed on Catholics, in exchange for the creation of a clerical hierarchy independent of Rome and therefore of no threat to the secular authorities.

Catholic 'relief' was a live political issue in Britain from the 1770s onwards. With their emphases on landowning and inheritance, oath-taking and the harbouring of 'mass-priests', the Relief Acts of 1778 saw the Protestant gentry in Parliament coming to the aid of their Catholic neighbours. The vicars apostolic were not consulted regarding this legislation, which meant that there was not so much as an indirect papal connection. Ironically, there was a papal dimension during the riotous anti-Catholic reaction of 1779–80, when Charles Walmesley, vicar apostolic of the Western District, was spied in his vestments, sparking a cry that the pope himself was in Bath. Only with the passing of the 1791 Relief Act did it cease to be unlawful to celebrate mass in England, after a period of 232 years. The clergy dropped their opposition to an amended oath of allegiance and British Catholics were finally free of the penalties that had been imposed on 'papists' for longer than anyone could remember.

Such dramatic developments were only possible because, from 1789, the political initiative in France had been seized by men who rapidly moved beyond Gallicanism to the systematic destruction of the Church and, beyond that, to the dechristianisation of France. The abolition of papal taxes came early in this frantic national convulsion, and was followed by the long-threatened elimination of papal government in Avignon in 1791. A 'civil constitution' was imposed on the clergy, most of whom refused to take the accompanying oath, particularly after Pius condemned it in the spring of 1791. Priests were killed in large numbers, religious houses dissolved, and ecclesiastical property was secularised, though some of the colleges and religious communities of British Catholics managed to secure immunity. For the French clergy there was no such protection and from 1792 they began to seek refuge in Britain. In total, 10,000 of them crossed the Channel, numbers that could only be supported through broad public sympathy and practical assistance in their plight.

Britain joined Austria, Prussia and other states in a coalition to limit the revolutionary contagion. Pius was not part of this alliance, but nevertheless appreciated that his survival depended on its success. France responded with declarations of war. This had immediate consequences for the British expatriate colleges and religious houses at Douai, St Omer and elsewhere, which now lost their immune status. Successor establishments were soon established in Britain, including St Edmund's College at Old Hall Green, Hertfordshire, and Crook Hall in County Durham. The Jesuit college at Liège was transferred to Stonyhurst in Lancashire, retaining all its privileges as a pontifical institution and making it exempt from the authority of the vicar apostolic, who protested vehemently.

On the day that France declared war against Britain, 1 February 1793, the MP for Sudbury, John Coxe Hippisley, arrived in Genoa, having witnessed the trial of Louis XVI when he passed through Paris. He and his party proceeded to Rome, where he remained on and off for more than two years. Turning the war to his advantage, Hippisley presented himself as a well-connected Englishman who could help the pope in his time of need, though he had no formal role or diplomatic authority. With Hippisley's encouragement, Pius sent Mgr Charles Erskine to Britain with a wide-ranging brief. He was to compose differences between the vicars apostolic and the laymen of the Cisalpine Club, successor to the Catholic Committee, to further the cause of political emancipation for

Catholics, to express the pope's thanks for Britain's hospitality towards the French exiles, and to explore the possibility of a formal diplomatic relationship between Britain and the papacy. In view of the fact that Catholic 'relief' and support for the French exiles had been achieved without any papal involvement, none of the relevant parties felt a pressing need to accommodate either the pope and or his agent. While Pius waited for news of Erskine's progress, Hippisley introduced him to other British visitors, though the most striking record of Anglo-papal relations in this period is surely James Northcote's painting of three British officers receiving medals from the pope as a mark of his appreciation for the good conduct of their regiment, the 12th Light Dragoons, during their time ashore in Civitavecchia. Erskine had been withdrawn by the time Pius made another intervention with a military connection. In 1796 he appointed Thomas Hussey as his vicar to the Crown's potentially disloyal Catholic soldiers in Ireland. Hussey had recently been made president of St Patrick's College, Maynooth, an institution funded by the British government with a view to securing the loyalty of Irish priests and seminarians. Thus, if anyone embodied the real potential of the Anglo-papal relationship it was Hussey, rather than Hippisley or Erskine.

In 1796 northern Italy became a Franco-Austrian battleground, the brilliant general Napoleon Bonaparte repeatedly getting the better of his adversaries. His conquests were reconfigured as the Cisalpine Republic, a French client state centred on Milan. After humiliating terms were imposed on the papacy in February 1797, that state also included the Romagna. At the beginning of 1798 news reached Rome that the revolutionary army, commanded by General Berthier, was preparing to head south. It arrived on 10 February and occupied Castel S. Angelo. A republic was declared and all ecclesiastical bodies suppressed. Pius was escorted to Siena, where he remained under house arrest until May, receiving visits from well-wishers of any nationality prepared to antagonise his French captors. Some of these were British. Thereafter he was moved to greater seclusion at the Carthusian monastery south of Florence. Cardinals fled in all directions: York, Albani, Romualdo Braschi-Onesti, protector of the English College, and the ex-secretary of state Ignazio Busca to Naples, Hyacinthe Sigismond Gerdil, the prefect of Propaganda Fide, to Turin, and his successor Stefano Borgia to Padua. Lack of communication between Pius, Gerdil and Borgia meant that the Midland District was without a vicar apostolic for two years after the death of Charles Berington in June. At least the Irish protector Carlo Livizzani stayed put in Rome, but there was precious little left to protect when all the colleges were closed and their properties sequestered by the French. The Scots agent, Paul MacPherson, took responsibility for twenty-two English, Irish and Scottish students, conveying them safely to London, while the English agent, Robert Smelt, sought refuge in Pisa. By the end of the year Naples had also fallen to a republican faction and the cardinals who had fled there were on the move once more. Austria was the nearest anti-French power, so they gravitated towards Austrian-held Venice, where Hippisley found Cardinal York in penury and poor health. His intervention resulted in the British government awarding the Jacobite 'king' a generous annual pension, though the arrangements were not completed until the winter of 1799–1800.

Between March and July 1799 'Citizen Braschi', as Pius was known among the revolutionaries, was moved from Florence to Parma, Turin, Grenoble and, finally, to Valence. The physical demands of the journey combined with the emotional strain of his exile meant that he survived only a few weeks thereafter, dying on 29 August. News of his passing took another month to reach London, and requiems were duly celebrated in the Portuguese embassy chapel on South Audley Street and the Sardinian chapel at Lincoln's Inn Fields. Erskine was not content: Britain and the Holy See were both under attack from 'enemies to the Christian Religion' and he recognised himself as the personification of their shared interests. Thus he took it upon himself to pay for a more elaborate mass at St Patrick's, Soho Square, on 16 November. The liturgy was celebrated on a scale not seen in Britain since before the Reformation and in a manner that was decidedly ornate:

> The whole interior of the walls, from the ceiling to the ground floor, was hung with black cloth [...] The pulpit, the altar steps, the floors of the sanctuary and body of the Chapel were also clothed in a sable livery; and in the centre was erected a magnificent Sarcophagus, Mausoleum or Tomb, supposed to contain the remains of the Holy Pontiff [...] On the tomb was laid a velvet cushion, superbly embroidered with gold, supporting a splendid model of the Tiara, or Papal Triple Crown, covered by a canopy elevated about twenty feet, and forming an obtuse angle at the top, on which were placed nine superb plumes of Ostrich feathers, rising in a pyramidal order, from the lower to the uppermost part of the roof.[39]

It was a foretaste of the Italianate features that came to characterise nineteenth-century British Catholicism, and was all the more improbable for appearing in the heart of as traditionally Protestant a city as London.

CHAPTER 6

'GOD BLESS OUR POPE, THE GREAT, THE GOOD'[1]

There are surprisingly few papal portraits in the Vatican's Pinacoteca. Those of secular princes are limited to Titian's posthumous depiction of Doge Nicolò Marcello and Sir Thomas Lawrence's full-length portrait of George, prince of Wales, in his Garter robes. The latter is dated 1816, when George III still lived and his son acted as regent; the crown itself is on display and the prince points to a letter from Pope Pius VII (1800–23). Somewhat less incongruous is Lawrence's portrait of that weary pontiff at Windsor Castle, but only because it is part of a series of anti-Napoleonic princes and their ministers created for the Waterloo Chamber, where it still hangs. The lands over which the Georges ruled remained Catholic mission territory where antipapalism was deeply ingrained, but the existence and positioning of the two portraits suggest that monarchs who had survived the revolutionary turmoil could rise above confessional differences. Between 1800 and 1914 the monarchical dimension of the relationship between Britain and the papacy grew ever stronger, even while the supranational character of papal monarchy continued to pose problems for the political class and 'No popery!' was never far from the lips of nationalistic demagogues. In an era of sporadic revolutionary outbursts, the Church's 'eldest daughter', France, was at her most capricious and demanded the utmost patience from her holy father. Neighbouring Britain was relatively straightforward, being more of a prodigal son. The pope knew one thing about such a child: he returns. Men and women in nineteenth-century Britain returned to the Catholic fold in such numbers that it amounted to a 'second spring', but few were inspired by the undemonstrative cisalpinism of eighteenth-century British Catholicism. Instead, their devotion to the papacy made Britain a bastion of overtly Italianate ultramontanism.

The interregnum after the death of Pius VI had lasted more than six months, and the conclave in Austrian-occupied Venice more than three, when the

Benedictine bishop of Imola, Barnaba Gregorio Chiaramonti, was elected on 14 March 1800. He honoured his unfortunate predecessor by becoming Pius VII. The task of resurrecting the papacy's fortunes from their exceptionally low ebb was given to Cardinal York's protégé Ercole Consalvi, who served as Pius's secretary of state until 1806 and again from 1814. Lacking Austrian support, the new pope left Venice and had reached Ancona when news reached him of the decisive French victory over Austrian forces at Marengo on 14 June. In another swipe at his enemies, the victorious general, First Consul Napoleon Bonaparte, declared himself willing to act as defender of the Church. It was an offer that Pius could not afford to reject. A papal envoy was dispatched to Paris to negotiate the terms on which Catholicism would be restored in the republic. Britain's challenge to the new pope was lightweight in comparison. After the fiasco that was his union with Caroline of Brunswick, the prince of Wales renewed his relationship with Maria Fitzherbert, who wanted papal assurance that their Anglican marriage of 1785 was canonically valid. Consequently, ten weeks after Pius's election, Fitzherbert's confessor John Nassau, together with Gregory Stapleton of St Edmund's College at Old Hall Green, left London on a secret mission. Their arrival in Rome coincided with that of the pope. Stapleton made a particularly good impression: before the end of the year he was appointed vicar apostolic of the long-vacant Midland District. As for the marriage, its validity was soon confirmed. At least in private, a more fitting postscript to Henry VIII's 'great matter' could hardly be imagined: the Catholic wife was vindicated and the Protestant interloper ignored. In public, however, the prince chose to be bound by the Royal Marriages Act (1772), not to mention those of Settlement and Union.

On 1 January 1801 the Union was extended to include Ireland, which lost its own parliament and was represented by Protestant MPs at Westminster. At a stroke, the number of Catholics in the United Kingdom increased dramatically, with the majority of Irish citizens sharing the civil disabilities of Britain's Catholic minority. Thus the scene was set for decades of Irish discontent, matched by entirely justified fears that the 'occupying' power wanted to use the papacy to preach a message of paying tribute to Caesar. A possible solution presented itself almost as soon as the problem was created, for the Franco-papal concordat, signed on 15 July, ensured that the Church could once more teach the faith to France's Catholic majority, in exchange for a redrawn episcopal map, a new set of bishops, and an obligation on all clerics to swear an oath to the State, which paid their stipends. In such circumstances the pope could no longer defend the French clerics who had fled to Britain. In London the recently promoted Cardinal Erskine informed Archbishop Dillon of Narbonne that the pope had ordered him to resign. Dillon and some of his fellow exiles were outraged, defied the order and stayed put. Erskine took this as his cue to retreat to Rome.

Many of the French exiles returned home in 1802, when the Anglo-French Peace of Amiens briefly facilitated travel across the Channel. British priests took this opportunity to reclaim deserted properties in France. Gregory Stapleton died on such a mission to St Omer, leaving another vacancy in the Midland District. A natural diplomat, Stapleton had been appointed in order to scupper the promotion of a contrasting character, the controversial John Milner, who accused the prefect of Propaganda Fide of failing to endorse his valid election. In 1802 Milner's name was again put forward and again encountered delay, until Erskine's patronage finally secured its confirmation. At the death of Cardinal Gian Francesco Albani in September 1803 Erskine became protector of the Scottish nation and Cardinal York dean of the Sacred College. These developments were entirely unremarkable, the sort of things that made the sheer scale of papal favours towards France stand out all the more prominently, for the archbishops of Tours, Paris, Rouen and Lyon were all created cardinals on 17 January 1803. Then, after the renewal of hostilities with Britain, Pius meekly played the part of Leo III, anointing a new Charlemagne, Napoleon I, in Paris on 2 December 1804. The emperor crowned himself.

It was April 1805 when the pope left France and May when Lord Grenville and Charles James Fox moved parliamentary resolutions to remove Catholic disabilities. That the votes were lost in both the Commons and the Lords can be partially explained by the international situation, for the pope appeared to be in Bonaparte's pocket. In reality, Pius recognised the significance of Britain and Russia as counterweights to France and sought to maintain a neutral position between France and the anti-Napoleonic Third Coalition. However, on 2 December Napoleon's crushing victory over the Russians and Austrians at Austerlitz created an obvious imbalance of power. In order to maintain its independence, the papacy was again forced to bow to French demands, which included Consalvi's resignation as secretary of state.

Antipapalism was so strong in Britain at the height of the Napoleonic Wars that it boded ill for the authors of works relating to papal history. Two such appeared in 1806: John Lingard's *Antiquities of the Anglo-Saxon Church*, which sought to rebut Protestant nationalism by emphasising the Roman connections in England's early Christian history, and William Roscoe's *Life of Pope Leo X*. Neither work was likely to appeal much beyond their authors' broadly Whig, anti-war circles. Confirmation that the tide was against them came in the 'No popery!' election of 1807, called after George III refused to support Grenville's proposal for Catholics to serve in the army and navy. What the popular cries failed to acknowledge was that Pius resisted Napoleon as far as he could, by not adhering to the continental blockade against Britain and by refusing to endorse Joseph Bonaparte's claim to the kingdom of Naples. Rome itself was occupied by French troops from February 1808 and the pope was imprisoned in the Quirinale for the next seventeen months. This stand-off finally ended when the French goaded Pius into excommunicating those in authority (meaning Napoleon), inspiring an ambitious young officer, Etienne Radet, to launch a daring assault on the palace and kidnap the pope. Accompanied by his secretary of state, Bartolomeo Pacca, Pius then endured weeks of discomfort and indignity all too reminiscent of Pius VI's sufferings, before being billeted in Savona.

Thus began the wholesale break-up of the papal regime. Its treasures could be transported to Paris easily enough, but many of the cardinals went there under duress. Erskine survived only a year, dying in 1811. From April 1810 there was a division between the eleven 'red' cardinals who attended Napoleon's wedding to Marie Louise of Austria and the thirteen 'black' cardinals who refused to do so and were banned from wearing their distinctive robes. The 'blacks' included Michele di Pietro, who was unable to function as prefect of Propaganda Fide. The impact on insular appointments was minimal: only one of the Irish archbishoprics required filling and the system of coadjutors helped to ensure continuity of leadership in England and Scotland. With regard to Catholic education, including priestly formation, the continuing struggle between France and the papacy was seen most clearly in the new seminaries at Oscott and Ushaw, both of which opened in 1808. Their foundation helped to account for Spencer Perceval's formation of a 'No popery!' ministry in 1809, regardless of the fact that the pope himself could hardly have been less of a threat to anyone. Behind the scenes, even Perceval's administration attempted to assist Pius, by means of a scheme to spirit him out of Savona on a British frigate. The French government learned of it and the pope was moved to landlocked Fontainebleau, where he remained until the fall of Napoleon and the restoration of the Bourbon monarchy in 1814.

In the meantime Catholic 'relief' continued to be debated with some regularity in the British Parliament, a distinguishing feature of Henry Grattan's 1813 Bill being that it recognised the reality of Pius's exile by referring to the 'pope', rather than the 'bishop of Rome', the title preferred by parliamentarians since the sixteenth century. Grattan's text also reflected years of debate by stating that the government should enjoy the power of veto over appointments to the Irish bishoprics. British and Irish Catholics were themselves divided between 'vetoists' and 'anti-vetoists', so demanded direction from Rome. This was supplied on 16 February 1814 by the secretary of Propaganda Fide, Giovanni Battista Quarantotti, in a rescript which agreed to the governmental veto. It solved nothing: Archbishop Troy of Dublin and most of the English vicars apostolic accepted the decision, while Milner and most of the Irish bishops condemned it. Milner sped to Rome, arriving there shortly after the newly-released pontiff, and secured a revocation of the rescript on 25 June. William Poynter, vicar apostolic of the London District, hastened after him in order to present the counter-argument. Poynter need not have worried, for

Pius's secretary of state, the restored Consalvi, was in London for five weeks of negotiations prior to the Congress of Vienna and was determined to remain on good terms with Britain. On 5 July the foreign secretary, Viscount Castlereagh, introduced Consalvi to the regent, who was singularly impressed and thereafter maintained a correspondence with the cardinal. Leaving the prince behind, the two ministers continued their association in Vienna. The powers represented at the congress collectively responded to the undignified plights of two successive popes by confirming papal sovereignty over central Italy. By this means Castlereagh and his colleagues contributed to the maintenance of a regime condemned as autocratic and illiberal by Britain's next political generation. Milner was convinced that Castlereagh and Consalvi also struck a private deal which he interpreted as unfavourable to the Catholic community in Britain. The evidence for this duly appeared in April 1815, when Pius had fled from Rome during what turned out to be Napoleon's Hundred Days. In his Genoese exile the pope provided Poynter with written confirmation of his support for the governmental veto. Britain's special status in papal eyes was confirmed by a parallel case, the worldwide re-establishment of the Jesuits, sanctioned by the bull *Solicitudo* (1814) but then qualified by a letter to Poynter explaining that it was conditional on the consent of secular governments, consent that the British government was not minded to give.

One measure of the wartime strain placed on Britain's elites was the readiness with which so many of them travelled to Rome as soon as they were able to do so. Caroline of Brunswick was received by the pope in 1816, though when she returned in 1820 Pius obliged George IV (1820–30) by declining to meet her. Elizabeth, duchess of Devonshire, daughter of the earl-bishop of Bristol, became a permanent resident in Rome and befriended Consalvi. Together they facilitated the transfer of the Stuart archive to Windsor, Cardinal York's death in the midst of war having prevented any earlier organisation of his papers. Similarly, John Coxe Hippisley helped to secure paintings from the cardinal's collection and dispatch them to the regent. There was cultural traffic in both directions: in addition to sending Lawrence to Rome to paint the portraits of Pius and Consalvi, the prince contributed £50 towards the cost of Canova's Stuart monument in St Peter's Basilica. The pope had little to offer in exchange, so hoped that the prince, who had not been on the Grand Tour, would be content with casts of sculptures in the Vatican collections and that London's Catholic community would appreciate a gift of plate for their new church of St Mary Moorfields, in Finsbury Circus, which opened in April 1820.

Even had there been a suitable candidate, there was no clamour for a British cardinal after the death of Erskine. With Pacca as protector of the Scots from 1814 and Consalvi protecting the reopened English College from 1818 and serving as pro-prefect of Propaganda Fide from 1822, the British could hardly have had more powerful friends in Rome. Either side of an understandable gap from 1807 to 1816, Pius VII created a total of ninety-nine cardinals, only one of whom came with British ancestry. Carlo Odescalchi inherited a mixture of Irish (Mahony) and English (Clifford) blood, besides having a connection with the Scottish earldom of Newburgh. His was among Pius's last promotions, for the pontiff died five months later, on 20 August 1823.

All but two of the forty-nine cardinals who voted in the resulting conclave had been promoted by Pius VII. There was, however, little for them to react against in the character of their saintly patron, so instead they rejected Consalvi and his 'enlightened' policies by electing his long-term rival, the ultra-conservative Annibale della Genga. The new pope, Leo XII (1823–9), had diplomatic experience in Lucerne and Cologne, at the imperial diet and in France, but the closest he came to a British connection was receiving his episcopal consecration from Cardinal York in 1794. The previous regime finally ended with Consalvi's death in January 1824, which left Propaganda Fide in the hands of Giulio Maria della Somaglia and the English College under the protection of Placido Zurla, both of whom were conservative *intransigenti*. Leo's priority was the restoration of order – the old order – whether in terms of improving the papal finances or celebrating a holy year in 1825. More specifically, in 1826 the Irish College was re-established in new premises and acquired its first post-revolutionary cohort of students, Scotland was divided into eastern, northern and western vicariates, and the Society of Jesus was formally restored in England on 1 January 1829.

When viewed from an insular perspective, Leo has become the pope who possibly created the historian John Lingard a cardinal *in petto* in October 1826, but it is a claim that cannot be verified one way or the other. As it happened, one of the new cardinals created on that occasion did have a British connection, but it was far removed from Lingard's humble origins and therefore better reflected the interests of this pope. Giacomo Giustiniani was the uncle of Cardinal Carlo Odescalchi, so therefore half British/Irish. It was Giustiniani's brother who inherited the earldom of Newburgh. Between Giustiniani's promotion and Odescalchi's entry into the Society of Jesus in 1838 these kinsmen of the Clifford family effectively represented British ecclesiastical interests in the Sacred College. As the leading British Catholic families tended to be inter-related, so the Cliffords provided their more distant kinsmen with *entrées* into Roman society, and those kinsmen came in strength. At Easter 1828, for example, the pope sent a fatted calf to the English College, and the rector, Robert Gradwell, had no trouble assembling a dinner party of English and Irish gentlemen, headed by Lords Arundell of Wardour, Gormanston and Dormer.[2]

Leo was impressed by the academic standards set at the English College and it was a measure of Gradwell's success that his star students, Nicholas Wiseman and George Errington, became rector and vice-rector in 1828. No less impressive was Paul Cullen of the Collegium Urbanum, who publicly defended his doctorate before the pope: to the best of his knowledge, he was the first Irishman ever to have been thus honoured. These were the non-aristocratic prelates of the future. More immediately, the humbly-born Lancastrian who hoped to break the glass ceiling in Leonine Rome was Peter Augustine Baines, the Benedictine vicar apostolic of the Western District, who spent the late 1820s in the city and ingratiated himself with the pope. That meant bypassing Gradwell, with whom Baines had a difficult relationship, including with regard to rival claims over which of them had been entrusted by the British government to negotiate the re-establishment of diplomatic relations with the Holy See.[3] Leo's death in February 1829 effectively ended whatever hopes of preferment Baines may have entertained.

In Britain the campaign for Catholic emancipation remained a hot political issue throughout the 1820s. The resolutely anti-Catholic Lord Liverpool managed to thwart it until he suffered a stroke in 1827, after which George Canning's brief premiership was stymied by his commitment to emancipation. Matters then came to a head when the Catholic Daniel O'Connell was elected as MP for County Clare in June 1828, forcing the Tory leaders Wellington and Peel to embrace a traditionally Whig cause and steer a Catholic relief bill through Parliament. As with Catholic relief in the eighteenth century, what these developments conspicuously lacked was a papal dimension.

Five of the cardinals who voted in the conclave of February–March 1829 had British connections: Odescalchi and Giustiniani were of British descent, Pacca and Zurla protected the Scottish nation and the English College respectively, and Mauro Cappellari was the principal point of contact for the English and Scottish vicars apostolic by virtue of being the prefect of Propaganda Fide. On 31 March Cardinal Francesco Castiglioni, a friend of Consalvi, recalled his own and his predecessor's imprisonment by becoming Pius VIII (1829–31). The conclave coincided with George IV's futile last-ditch attempt to prevent Parliament passing the Catholic Relief Bill, which had its first reading in the Lords on the day of Pius's election. It received royal assent on 13 April and a Catholic MP – not O'Connell – took his seat three weeks later.[4]

These stories of papal patronage and British politics finally coincided on 15 March 1830, when Pius created his first non-Italian cardinal, the widowed Dorset gentleman and firmly non-resident Canadian bishop Thomas Weld, whose promotion was designed as a gesture of gratitude for Catholic emancipation. Weld and his daughter had both married Cliffords, so could claim a degree of kinship with Cardinals Odescalchi and Giustiniani. Indeed, they lived in the Palazzo Odescalchi, close to Carlo Odescalchi's titular church, SS. Apostoli, and to Weld's at S. Marcello, where the new English cardinal had custody of Consalvi's tomb. Rome was not short of British Catholics with claims to nobility, but what caused Weld to outrank the others was his royal connection, for he was related to Maria Fitzherbert (previously Mrs Edward

Weld) and, as far as the curia was concerned, she was married to King George, even if he had long since broken with her. Baines could not compete and had already returned to his hitherto neglected Western District.

If the character of nineteenth-century English Catholicism is identified with any one of those districts it was surely the Midland, from where two socially prominent converts made their way to Rome in 1828–30. The Romantic enthusiast Ambrose Phillipps (later de Lisle) was still in his teens when he received his first papal audience, with Leo in 1828. In turn, Phillipps influenced the conversion of George Spencer, son of the second Earl Spencer, who was already an Anglican cleric when he became a Catholic in 1830. Spencer's Roman ordination followed two years later, at S. Gregorio Magno, on the site of Gregory the Great's monastery. Their Roman experiences brought Phillipps and Spencer into contact with a Passionist priest whose vocation was to convert the English, though it was not until the 1840s that the missionary known in Britain as Dominic Barberi was able to realise that vocation from a base in Staffordshire. What these pioneers created was a cultural hybrid, for these Italian elements and influences were contained in the Gothic churches of A.W.N. Pugin, not least those built in the Midlands for Phillipps and the earl of Shrewsbury.

Towards the end of 1829 a Mr and Mrs Edward Casaubon – also from the Midlands – were said to have honeymooned in Rome: he immersed himself in the Vatican library, she was diverted by art and artists, but neither of them met the pope.[5]

Nothing was as British about the next pontificate as the means by which it came into being. Odescalchi, Giustiniani and Weld voted in the fifty-day conclave of 1830–1. At one point Giustiniani received twenty-one out of the twenty-nine votes needed for election, but was vetoed by Spain. Pacca, the Scots' protector, was dean of the Sacred College and Zurla, who still protected the English College, was the friend of his fellow Camaldolese monk, Cappellari, who was elected as Gregory XVI (1831–46). After leaving his native Veneto for Rome, Cappellari had been a long-serving abbot of the Camaldolese community at S. Gregorio, so was aware of its significance for the conversion of England, and had also been prefect of Propaganda Fide since 1826.

The previous pontificate had concluded with a revolution in France, where the elderly, authoritarian Charles X was forced to abdicate and Louis Philippe of Orléans emerged as a constitutional monarch; the new pontificate began with insurrection in the Papal States. Now that monarchy existed on a sliding scale, from the despotic to the democratic, Gregory veered towards the former, even if that meant siding with the Russian Orthodox czar against his rebellious Polish Catholic subjects. One of this pope's more subtle messages to the secular powers was the beatification in 1839 of Boniface of Savoy, a stout defender of ecclesiastical liberties. If this was essentially a message to the contemporary house of Savoy, which ruled the Turin-based kingdom of Sardinia as a liberal monarchy, perhaps there was also a message for liberal Britain, where Boniface had been archbishop of Canterbury. As for France, Bl. Boniface had the foresight to die on 14 July, his feast thereby clashing beautifully with what became the republic's national day.

Compared with France or the Papal States, British society was characterised by stability, which the country's political elite attributed to such a combination of material prosperity with civil and religious liberty as to make it a model for the rest of Europe. Gregory's pontificate coincided with the ministries of Earl Grey (1830–4), Viscount Melbourne (1834, 1835–41) and Sir Robert Peel (1834–5, 1841–6). Grey was the last premier to have visited Rome as part of a pre-revolutionary grand tour, and Peel was holidaying there when word arrived that William IV (1830–7) wanted him to form his first ministry, so these prime ministers were characteristic of their class in being familiar with the city. Under the Whigs Grey and Melbourne foreign affairs were the preserve of Viscount Palmerston; they were centred on a strategic *entente* with Louis Philippe's France, and were interventionist in nature, whether in Iberia, the Low Countries or Greece and the Ottoman Empire. In 1831–2 the Great Powers – Austria, Britain, France, Russia and Prussia – jointly sought to intervene in the Papal States, with a view to improving the administration and avoiding revolts of the sort that accompanied Gregory's election. Britain's particular priority was trade, and parliamentary democracy was among the island nation's latest exports. However, the pope displayed no desire to inject life into a stagnant economy, while the central Italian market for parliamentary democracy was limited to educated opponents of the papal regime. The only tangible result of Palmerstonian intervention in that region was the presence in Rome of a low-ranking British diplomat, Thomas Aubin, from 1832 onwards. Questions over the legality of entering into a diplomatic relationship with the pope were avoided by attaching Aubin's post to the British embassy in Tuscany.

Liberalism extended well beyond the political sphere and into that of the Church, for this was the period in which the liberal triumvirate of Lamennais, Lacordaire and Montalembert argued for an alliance between Church and People, as opposed to the traditional alliance of Church and Crown. Their works were condemned by Gregory in the encyclical *Mirari vos* (1832). For the most part British Catholics cut themselves off from such essentially continental disputes. The rector of the English College, on the other hand, had a ringside seat and did not like what he saw. Wiseman's memoirs provide ample evidence of his 'deep veneration' for Pius VII, his 'warm gratitude' to Leo XII, and his 'sincere respect' for Pius VIII, but become noticeably more selective about Gregory, emphasising the cultural life of Rome as a means of avoiding more contentious subjects.[6] Like the artists and writers who gravitated there, Wiseman was inspired by Rome's past; indeed, he was attracted by the entire Romantic package, including some of its 'liberal' ideas, and that was where he diverged from the arch-conservative pope. If Wiseman was the front men for the Anglo-papal relationship – such as it was – then much of the day-to-day work was undertaken by his vice-rector, Charles Baggs, who doubled up as a papal chamberlain. Baggs expressed his devotion to the papacy in publications about papal supremacy and Roman liturgy.[7]

The elaborate papal liturgy was an acquired taste and quite alien to British visitors of any denomination, as one confirmed after watching Pope Gregory in the church of S. Maria sopra Minerva in 1833:

> There is much unedifying dumb show [...] nor can I endure the Pope's foot being kissed, considering how much is said in Scripture about the necessity of him that is greatest being as the least, nor do I even tolerate him being carried in on high.[8]

The writer was John Henry Newman, vicar of the university church of St Mary the Virgin in Oxford. The fervently anti-Whig, anti-liberal Newman came from evangelical roots, so was naturally repelled by what he glimpsed of the papal cult. However, whether or not they could bring themselves to acknowledge it, some Anglicans found themselves in greater sympathy with the conservatism of Pope Gregory than with the liberalism of their compatriots and fellow-churchmen, and Newman was of this persuasion. If, as they maintained, the Church was divinely created, how could a portion of it be nothing more than the religious arm of the British State, subject to legislation enacted by laymen? In their preaching and publications this Oxford Movement reacted accordingly, so that Pope Gregory's fifteen-year pontificate embraced John Keble's sermon on National Apostasy in 1833, all ninety *Tracts for the Times* (1833–41), and the logical development that was Newman's reception into the Catholic Church in 1845. Critics of these so-called Tractarians too readily accused them of popery: not all converted to Rome and, even among those who did, not all were wildly enthusiastic ultramontanes.

Like Newman, William Ewart Gladstone received an evangelical upbringing before choosing the path of Anglican high churchmanship. A member of Parliament from the age of twenty-two, he differed markedly from the clerics Keble and Newman on the relationship between Church and State, arguing for the closest of connections. His thoughts on the subject were published in 1838, the same year that he holidayed in Rome with his clerical friend, the recently-widowed Henry Edward Manning.[9] Like Newman, Gladstone was appalled by the reality of what he encountered in the Papal States, but his emphasis was political: he was repelled by the pope's autocratic rule, a relic of another age. Nationalism loomed so large in his thinking that he considered it only natural that each nation should have its own church, each a part of the Catholic whole. The supranational power of the papacy represented the very opposite of this vision. From 1842 Gladstone served in Peel's administration and found his view of the world tested by the realities of government, particularly Peel's policy of permanently endowing the seminary at Maynooth as a means of creating cohorts of pro-British priests in Ireland. Even when Gladstone looked for a way out it illustrated a certain obsession with the papacy, for he volunteered to quit as president of the Board of Trade in order to succeed Aubin as the British envoy in Rome. Peel was not minded to lose one of his closest associates or to raise the profile of the Anglo-papal relationship beyond its existing status, so sent someone who would blend in more easily, the Catholic William Petre. Gladstone resigned anyway.

The English Catholic clergy could not avoid Rome altogether and, in 1837, two of the vicars apostolic, Thomas Griffiths and Thomas Walsh, went there to propose that a full diocesan structure be created to meet the needs of a rapidly expanding Catholic population, which was particularly evident in the large industrial towns of northern England. What they received was a redrawn map, the four districts becoming eight in 1840. Wiseman duly became Walsh's coadjutor in the new Central District and Baggs was appointed to the Western District, where he lectured on papal supremacy but died before he could convert his flock to a more Italianate style of worship. Wiseman's departure left Paul Cullen as the dominant figure among the British and Irish in Rome. He had been rector of the Irish College since 1832 and moved it to a new home at S. Agata dei Goti. Like previous rectors, Cullen represented the interests of the Irish bishops, but they were so divided between pro- and anti-British factions that he would have been hard pressed to represent them equally. In practice, he supported the anti-British campaigns of John MacHale, archbishop of Tuam. So closely did Cullen side with MacHale that, in December 1844, he spread a rumour that Britain and the Holy See were about to establish full diplomatic relations, a rumour designed to inflame anti-British feeling in Ireland and inspire contempt for those bishops who collaborated with the occupying power. Rome had no desire to antagonise Britain: as in its relations with Russia and Poland, the papacy sided with the non-Catholic establishment against its Catholic subjects. Gregory gave Cullen a severe dressing down. MacHale was less easy to contain, and his campaign against the British plan for non-denominational Queen's Colleges of higher education was in full swing when Gregory died.

By the time of Gregory's death in June 1846 the Sacred College included cardinals named Carafa, Castracane, Fieschi, Mellini, Piccolomini, Riario-Sforza and Spinola, so gave the impression of being stuck in Renaissance period. It should come as little surprise, therefore, that the 1840s witnessed a surge in Borgia-related fiction by British authors.[10] The Cambridge-educated Charles Januarius Acton voted in the conclave, but counted as more of a Neapolitan than a Briton in what can therefore be regarded as an exclusively Italian contest. In a break from the tradition of protracted conclaves, the electors reached a result in just four scrutinies, thereby asserting their independence from any possible outside influence. In Giovanni Maria Mastai Ferretti, the fifty-four-year-old bishop of Imola, they chose a pastoral pope who came with no curial baggage: his only extra-Italian experience was a mission to Chile and Peru in the 1820s.

The new pontificate opened with an entirely traditional amnesty for political prisoners and proceeded with the introduction of political, social and economic reforms, some of which were prompted by nothing more than practical necessity. Italy's liberals were nevertheless ecstatic and cries were heard for the dynamic new leader to head a federation of Italian states, free from foreign occupation. Appropriately enough, the Irish 'liberator' O'Connell headed for Rome, but died at Genoa. At least he had lived long enough to witness Pius's first significant extra-Italian intervention, an encyclical in support of victims of the Irish potato famine.[11] In Britain Pius's election coincided with the formation of a new Whig administration; Palmerston returned to the Foreign Office and there was soon talk of establishing diplomatic relations with this apparently liberal pope. In April 1847 Sir William Temple, Palmerston's brother and Britain's ambassador in Naples, had exploratory talks with Pius and his secretary of state, Cardinal Gizzi. Meanwhile, the pope's subjects grew restive when he failed to present himself as leader of a united Italy, and Austria sent troops into Ferrara and Comacchio on the northern periphery of the Papal States. Rome could only imagine how useful British naval power might have been to deter the invaders, so when Nicholas Wiseman arrived in July to propose the restoration of the English and Welsh hierarchy, he was soon sent back to London on a diplomatic errand. In response, the government argued that, regardless of his spiritual role, the pope was an Italian prince, with whom it would be entirely appropriate to have diplomatic relations, the prelude to offering him assistance, naval or otherwise. The prime minister, Lord John Russell, dispatched his father-in-law, the earl of Minto, to open up a channel of communication with the curia. Minto was not the most fleet of travellers, which gave the Irish in Rome opportunity to secure papal condemnation of the Queen's Colleges while the envoy was still *en route*. Events elsewhere in the peninsula moved so quickly that the crisis had passed by November, when Minto finally arrived in Rome. The government was still on course to normalise relations with the Holy See, and Parliament duly debated the Diplomatic Relations with the Court of Rome Bill. This triggered the airing of Protestant arguments about it being illegal for Britain to conduct such business with the papacy, but the bill nevertheless passed into law. There was, however, no longer any immediate need to put its measures into practice nor, for a short while, any court in Rome to which an ambassador could have been sent.

Rome was one of the last places to experience the widespread revolutions of 1848. When it did so, Pius's recently-appointed prime minister – a complete novelty in the Papal States – was assassinated, the Quirinale was surrounded by a threatening mob, and the pope made a daring escape with the aid of the French and Bavarian ambassadors. He found refuge in Gaeta and waited for the latest Roman republic to follow the example of its predecessors and fizzle out, which it did when the city was taken by French troops sent by the new emperor, Napoleon III. British support for the beleaguered pontiff was limited to an unrealistic offer of asylum in the Crown colony of Malta and sympathetic words from Queen Victoria (1837–1901). If any of Victoria's subjects emerged with credit from the short-lived republic it was Paul Cullen, who provided curialists with sanctuary at the Irish College. MacHale therefore played a particularly shrewd game when he recommended Cullen for the see of Armagh, which became vacant in April 1849. Cullen was duly entrusted not merely with the primacy but, as apostolic delegate, with convening a national synod, the first in Ireland since the twelfth century. It was held at Thurles in 1850.

When Pius returned to Rome and Cullen to Ireland they were part of a wider phenomenon of post-revolutionary travel. Indeed, although John Murray's *Handbook for Travellers in Central Italy* first appeared in 1843, a second edition was not required until 1850; regular revisions were required thereafter. One Englishman who made the journey to Rome in 1850 was George Townsend, a canon of Durham, whose mission was to persuade the pope to participate in a 'General Council of the West', in which he would be accorded 'the first place of order, though not of juridiction', with a view to achieving the reunion of Christendom.[12] For a man who had always been an avowed 'enemy' to Roman Catholicism, Townsend's impression of the pope was decidedly positive:

> No Quaker could have received us with more simplicity than Pio Nono, – no sovereign with more dignified courtesy, – no Presbyterian with more plainness [...] He seemed to be about sixty years of age, of a fresh complexion and most benevolent countenance. He gazed at us, as we might have expected, with intent curiosity as we approached him. It was the first time, perhaps, that a Protestant clergyman, accompanied by his wife, had ever ventured to enter the Vatican upon such an errand as that which had brought us from England.[13]

Townsend conspicuously failed in his objective, leaving the way open for ecumenists of a different stamp. Of these the most conspicuous were the Catholic Ambrose Phillipps de Lisle and the young Anglican Frederick George Lee, who together founded in 1857 the Association for the Promotion of the Union of Christendom. The Association's gradualist approach to the reunion of the Roman, Anglican and Orthodox traditions involved concession, compromise and acknowledgement of catholicity outside the Church of Rome. That made it a characteristically British way to heal the divisions of Christendom.

By the time Pius fled to Gaeta arrangements were far advanced for the ailing Thomas Walsh to be translated from the Central to the London District and to become England's first post-Reformation Catholic archbishop. Then everything stopped because Propaganda Fide ceased to operate during the pope's exile. Wiseman's right of succession to the London District was realised at Walsh's death in February 1849 and, for the next eighteen months, he entertained the hope of becoming the first metropolitan of a restored hierarchy. There matters stood until he once more journeyed to Rome in the late summer of 1850. The unadorned version of what happened next was that the bull *Universalis ecclesiae* (29 September) replaced the eight vicariates with one archiepiscopal and twelve episcopal sees, their geographical titles carefully avoiding duplication of any Anglican ones.[14] Wiseman was appointed to Westminster and given administration of adjoining Southwark. Over the following days he was created a cardinal and assigned the titular church of S. Pudenziana. The exuberant version of all this was what Wiseman dispatched 'out of the Flaminian Gate' on 7 October, in a letter to be read in the churches of Westminster and Southwark. From its emphasis on St Peter and the allegedly part-British family of the senator Pudens – father of Pudenziana – through to Wiseman's 'sincere attachment and unflinching devotion to the Holy See', this text is the supreme expression of British ultramontanism. Unfortunately, it also lapses into the sort of high-handed turns of phrase that could be wilfully misinterpreted among Britain's antipapal majority:

> [...] at present, and till such time as the Holy See shall think fit otherwise to provide, we govern, and shall continue to govern, the counties of Middlesex, Hertford, and Essex as ordinary thereof, and those of Surrey, Sussex, Kent, Berkshire, and Hampshire, with the islands annexed, as administrator with ordinary jurisdiction.[15]

Parliament was not sitting, so *The Times* acted as the principal forum for Protestant outrage at this act of 'papal aggression'. There was no immediate reaction from the government, which had expressed no objection to the creation of an Australian Catholic hierarchy in 1842 and happened to be looking once more at the possibility of a diplomatic relationship with Rome. When Lord John Russell did intervene in early November he caught the public mood on the anniversary of the Gunpowder Plot but tarnished his own and his party's credentials for toleration, assuring the bishop of Durham that 'No foreign prince or potentate will be permitted to fasten his fetters on a nation which has so long and so nobly vindicated its right to freedom of opinion, civil political and religious'.[16] Still appealing to patriotic mainstream Anglicans, Russell's more specific criticisms were reserved for Tractarians, who led their flocks Romewards by stealth. Wiseman returned to England and immediately penned a response, emphasising that the restoration of the hierarchy involved no temporal implications.[17] Lawyers for and against the cardinal nevertheless had a field day, for here was an apparent clash of jurisdictions such as they knew well enough from their history books but not as a present reality.[18] The new bishops had committed no offence, so the government played to popular opinion by introducing the Ecclesiastical Titles Bill, with a view to creating a law that Wiseman and the others could then be found to have infringed by assuming English episcopal titles. Neither front bench was enthusiastic about this: Russell had painted himself into a corner. The bill passed into law in August 1851, though no prosecutions were brought and Gladstone repealed it two decades later.[19]

One Tractarian who had been inching Romewards was Gladstone's friend Manning, by then archdeacon of Chichester. What tipped him over the edge was the 1850 judgement by the Judicial Committee of the Privy Council in favour of the Reverend G.C. Gorham, whose understanding of the faith had been found wanting by his bishop. The judgement confirmed the Church of England's subservience to the State, even in matters of doctrine. When Gladstone had argued for a close relationship between Church and State, he had not envisaged laymen determining what did or did not constitute heresy. At least a return to government kept his mind suitably occupied. Manning was no less distraught and took decisive action: within the space of a few months in 1851 he was received into the Catholic Church, ordained by Wiseman, and sent to Rome. In the course of this process he lost Gladstone's friendship, but won the pope's confidence and returned to England as Wiseman's right-hand man.

A period of relative calm followed the fall of Russell's administration and Palmerston's removal from the Foreign Office in 1852. There was still no diplomatic relationship with Rome, but at least Petre was replaced by a career diplomat, Richard Lyons, and an Anglo-papal commercial treaty was signed, both in 1853. Pius commissioned a screw-propelled steamship from a British firm: it was launched on the Thames in 1859 and named the *Immaculate Conception*, after the popular Marian belief which the pope had controversially accepted as dogma earlier in the decade.

Pius IX's exceptionally long pontificate was punctuated by three major crises. After the revolution of 1848, the second was caused by the speed of Piedmontese expansionism in 1858–61. Thanks to Piedmont's military alliance with Napoleon III, Austria was forced to cede Lombardy in 1859. The last Habsburg duke of Tuscany had already fled, leaving the way for the Piedmontese premier Cavour to engineer plebiscites there and in the neighbouring duchies of Parma and Modena, all of which were duly annexed to Piedmont in May 1860. As that year's campaigning season was still young, Garibaldi and his volunteer army landed in Sicily and rapidly secured the island's fall, followed by that of Naples. Further Piedmontese machinations ensured that the largely peasant populations of Romagna, Marche and Umbria voted for annexation, leaving the pope in control of nothing more than the Lazio region around Rome. This delicate balance was secured by the French emperor, who personally supported the cause of Italian nationalism, but was mindful of his subjects' abiding allegiance to the pope. Thus French troops remained in Rome.

When this sequence of events began Britain's foreign secretary was the Conservative earl of Malmesbury, whose wife's uncle was the French ambassador in Rome. Towards the end of 1858 Britain acquired a new *attaché* there: Odo Russell remained in post until 1870 and developed an effective working relationship with the long-serving secretary of state Giacomo Antonelli. The policy Russell was initially required to mediate was traditional in that it advocated political and economic reform in the Papal States, but was novel in proposing the partition of that territory and the loss of papal temporal power north of the Apennines. The Tory administration fell in June 1859 and was replaced by a Whig–Liberal one, with Palmerston as prime minister and Lord John Russell, Odo's uncle, as foreign secretary. Even the chancellor of the exchequer, Gladstone, was an expert on the iniquities of papal government, having translated a recent history of the Papal States.[20] It was a formidable grouping, as the pope readily admitted. According to Odo, Pius lamented that 'England is ever at work against us [...] favouring and assisting revolution. Your people hate the Pope, your Parliament hates the Pope, your ministers and especially your uncle hate the Pope.'[21] The much-reduced Papal State of 1860 was not far removed from Lord John's vision of the pope ruling a city-state consisting of 'Rome and 15 miles around'. Logically enough, Britain emerged as a staunch ally of the kingdom of Italy, which became a reality in 1861.

Whig–Liberal antipapalism was more strident than Conservative antipapalism, but both political elites strove to reflect mainstream British opinion. However, the events of 1858–61 forced the parties to reappraise their attitudes towards Britain's Catholic minority and Ireland's Catholic majority. 'Papal aggression' had broken the previous alliance between Whiggery and Catholicism, leaving Catholic votes available to the Tories. Malmesbury instructed Odo Russell to emphasise 'conservative principles' in his meetings with Antonelli and the Irish Tory vote certainly increased in 1859, even if it was not enough to prevent a change of government. From the autumn of that year there was evidence of a rising tide of popular support in Britain and Ireland for the beleaguered pope, countering the Italian nationalism championed by political and intellectual elites. Wiseman, Cullen and other members of the hierarchy visited Rome during the winter of 1859–60. Returning to their provinces they set about coordinating financial assistance for the pope's defence. Cullen's ultamontanism bore particularly remarkable fruit, his poor flock immediately raising £80,000 and continuing to send annual donations of Peter's Pence for decades thereafter. Even before Garibaldi's campaign got under way, more than 1,000 Irishmen headed to the Papal States, where they formed the Battalion of St Patrick and saw considerable action before being forced to capitulate at the end of the campaigning season. This time the Liberal government sought to conciliate Catholic public opinion by bringing the men safely home.

The crisis of 1858–61 revealed yet another British position on the papacy, a minority one limited to Queen Victoria and her consort. Their 'German' policy stemmed from sympathy for Austria and implacable opposition to upstart Piedmont. Thus the queen asked successive foreign secretaries, Malmesbury and Russell, to tone down their antipapal statements. As the crisis deepened, Victoria requested the strengthening of Britain's naval power in the Mediterranean and Odo Russell repeatedly assured the pope that, if necessary, he could be evacuated on a British vessel, but most revealing of a distinct royal policy was Victoria and Albert's insistence that the prince of Wales pay a three-month educational visit to Rome in 1859. They were no less insistent that the prince be accorded a papal audience. In the event he received two, and appears to have developed a lifelong interest in the papacy somewhat at odds with his future Anglican responsibilities, but entirely in keeping with the spiritual trends of that era.

With the rallying cry 'Rome or death', in 1862 Garibaldi attempted to extinguish what remained of the pope's temporal power, but pressure from France caused the campaign to be aborted. It was 1866 before Austria's military defeat by Prussia allowed Italy to absorb the region of Venetia, leaving Rome as the sole remaining target for Italian nationalists. At that point the Conservatives returned to power in Britain, leaving the workaholic Gladstone under-employed. A curial cardinal, Karl August von Reisach, happened to be visiting Britain and encouraged the former chancellor to use his influence to mediate between the papacy and the Italian government in Florence. Consequently, on 22 October Gladstone had a forty-five minute audience with Pius, after which he informed the Italian premier Ricasoli that the pope appeared to have no theoretical objection to Italian unification or 'repugnance' towards parliamentary government, though he did argue that Italian elections were 'not really free'.[22]

In 1867 Garibaldi made another move against Rome, but was repulsed by French and papal troops at Mentana, only ten miles from the papal capital. Among the casualties in that encounter was seventeen-year-old Julian Watts-Russell, who came to be regarded as an English martyr for the papal cause. For his part, the pope mustered an army of bishops, hundreds of whom converged on Rome for the canonisation of Japanese martyrs in 1862 and again five years later for the 1,800th anniversary of the martyrdom of Sts Peter and Paul. The city acquired a string of fortresses in the shape of national seminaries: the construction of a new chapel at the English College and the complete rebuilding of the Scots College formed part of this wider campaign. From 1864 all the pope's men were armed with the encyclical *Quanta cura* and the accompanying 'syllabus' of eighty 'errors' which were said to be circulating in contemporary society. Traditional targets such as Protestant Bible societies appeared alongside topical concerns about 'modern liberalism' and criticism of the pope's temporal power. Britain's leading liberal Catholic, Sir John Acton – nephew of the late cardinal – found himself and his publications under sustained attack from Wiseman's close associates, so much so that his liberal Catholic quarterly, the *Home and Foreign Review*, folded even before the *Syllabus of Errors* was issued. This was also the point at which Catholic members – inevitably liberal types – were ordered to withdraw from Phillipps de Lisle and Lee's ecumenical association: there could be no compromise whatsoever with non-Catholics.

Throughout the 1850s and '60s, Pius's source on all things English was his chamberlain Mgr George Talbot, a convert originally sent to Rome as Wiseman's personal agent. Talbot was neither expert nor impartial. He had been rejected by Newman for the newly founded Birmingham Oratory and ensured that suspicions about Newman's orthodoxy developed in Rome. Elsewhere, Talbot intervened in a long-running dispute between Wiseman and his coadjutor George Errington, ensuring that Errington was deprived of his office. At Wiseman's death in February 1865, just two months after the *Syllabus* was published, there was a last-ditch assertion of anti-Roman cisalpinism. When the Westminster chapter compiled the three-man *terna* of candidates for the vacant archbishopric they named the ousted Errington as their first choice, followed by two equally congenial bishops. Pius took it as an affront and asserted his authority by ignoring the list and appointing Manning as the second archbishop of Westminster. Unlike Wiseman, Manning was an Englishman born and bred, yet, if anything, he exceeded Wiseman in his devotion to the person, spiritual authority and temporal power of the pope.

In Ireland ultramontanism acquired the additional objective of attempting to divert popular energies from the increasingly violent republican or Fenian cause. Appropriately enough, a story circulated that the pope had been the target of an assassination attempt, but justice prevailed and it was the assassin who met a sudden death.[23] Very much alive, the pope 'spoke warmly against Fenianism' during Gladstone's audience in 1866, 'and declared that his Irish clergy were decidedly hostile to it, and that he had always approved and seconded their hostility'.[24] As if to underline the point, Cullen had been made a cardinal three months earlier.

The scale of Irish immigration to Scotland overwhelmed the relatively modest native Catholic population, while spreading the urgent problem of Fenian agitation. Manning investigated the situation for Propaganda Fide and proposed restoring the episcopate, which would allow Roman-educated clerics to replicate the ultramontanism of England and Ireland. The man chosen in

1868 as apostolic delegate to oversee the transition, Charles Eyre, came from an English recusant family but had the requisite Roman qualification.

Ultramontanes were united by a fear that the process of Italian unification was about to be completed, at the expense of what little temporal power the pope retained. In a world where the amount of colour on a map was a reliable indication of power and authority, they assumed that the loss of what remained of the Papal States would threaten the pope's spiritual authority as well. Attention therefore focused on the precise definition of that spiritual authority: was the pope 'infallible' and able to dictate the Church's teaching in all matters and at all times or, as Gallicans argued, only when speaking in concert with a general council? When Pius convened an ecumenical council to meet in the Vatican from December 1869 and address a range of contemporary issues, observers anticipated that its concealed purpose was to define infallibility. The ultramontane majority argued that the Church was under threat from so many liberal and secular forces that formal definition of the pope's authority was essential, while the Franco-German-led minority either opposed definition outright or thought it 'inopportune' as long as Rome and Lazio remained contested territory. The English and Irish bishops divided along well-established lines. Manning orchestrated the 'infallibilist' party throughout the council and delivered a powerful speech when the issue was finally debated in May 1870, but most of the English bishops were 'inopportunists'. Similarly, Cullen argued vigorously for infallibility, while MacHale was not convinced. Beyond the episcopate, W.G. Ward set out the ultramontane argument in *De infallibilitatis extensione* (1869), while Newman thought that Rome was diverted by such flattery and that definition was unnecessary and irresponsible. To the newly minted Lord Acton defining papal infallibility was not merely 'inopportune'; it was immoral and had to be stopped.

Gladstone had certainly not lost his interest in the papacy when he formed his first administration at the end of 1868. Twelve months later the council opened and the British government was on the receiving of two completely separate and diametrically opposed lines of communication from Rome. Acton wrote to the premier directly, articulating the anti-infallibilist minority's need of diplomatic pressure from the secular powers. This Gladstone was only too eager to supply. To thwart any such intervention Pius permitted four bishops to communicate with the outside world. Manning was a member of this quartet, his role being to maintain contact with the foreign secretary, Lord Clarendon, by means of the *chargé d'affaires* Odo Russell, who doubled up as Clarendon's son-in-law. This ploy worked: Clarendon argued that the council's affairs were purely ecclesiastical and beyond the remit of secular government. Gladstone backed down, but it was a close-run thing: on 6 July 1870 Clarendon was replaced at the Foreign Office by Acton's stepfather, Earl Granville; twelve days later the decree on papal infallibility, *Pastor aeternus*, was accepted by the council. Acton and many of the 'minority' bishops had already left Rome. Russell did so in August.

Those who remained were suddenly overtaken by events. Napoleon III's declaration of war against Prussia in July had been followed by a rapid sequence of military encounters. On 2 September the emperor was taken prisoner at Sedan and the pope lost his protector. The Italian king seized this opportunity, his troops entering Rome on 20 September. Ultramontane enthusiasm was briefly channelled into defending the eternal city or, as in the case of a young Scot, David Hunter-Blair, caring for the wounded. The Union Jack was flown from the English College and the new British agent, H.C. Jervoise, did what he could to protect the colleges and their villas from the invading forces. There was talk of the infallible one leaving Rome, but Britain and most of the other secular powers advised him to stay. He did so and was effectively imprisoned in the Vatican for the remainder of his life, continuing to appoint to governmental posts in a state he no longer controlled. For all practical purposes, defending the temporal power was a lost cause. When the Italian state secularised ecclesiastical property throughout its new capital, the insular colleges appealed to the British government for help, but Granville cited the unpopularity of papal infallibility as grounds for declining to do so.

Elsewhere in Europe, the definition of papal infallibility caused anti-infallibilists to break with Rome and become identified as 'Old Catholics'. Suddenly it appeared that the patience of Anglicans was being rewarded and that they were acquiring new friends and allies throughout the continent. This invigorated the Anglo-Continental Society, which had been founded in 1853 to disseminate the principles of Anglicanism in mainland Europe, and now resolved:

> That the declaration of Papal Infallibility, followed by the fall of the Temporal Power of the Popes, presents an occasion of offering an earnest and affectionate appeal to members of the Roman Catholic Communion throughout the world, beseeching them to return from the novelties of modern doctrine and mediaeval discipline to the Scriptural Faith and Apostolic Order of the Primitive Church.[25]

It was 1874 before Gladstone again found himself in opposition and able to express views that he was obliged to contain while in office. Beginning with a magazine article in October and continuing at greater length in a pamphlet published on 5 November, he deplored efforts by Manning and others to 'Romanise the Church and people of England', which had happened because Rome 'has refurbished, and paraded anew, every rusty tool she was fondly thought to have disused.'[26] His concerns centred on the implications of Pius IX's 'Vaticanism' on the civil allegiance of Catholics, arguing that no one could convert to Rome 'without renouncing his moral and mental freedom, and placing his civil loyalty and duty at the mercy of another', becoming 'a Catholic first, an Englishman afterwards'.[27] *The Vatican Decrees* proved to be a bestseller, reinforcing as it did interpretations of the past to be found in patriotic antipapal histories. Catholic authors from across the liberal-ultramontane divide responded to Gladstone's challenge, though only Newman succeeded in drawing the sting by explaining the legal and theological limitations of papal infallibility, at a stroke countering not only the antipapalism of Gladstone but also the ultramontanism of Manning.[28]

For a centralising pope such as Pius IX to be denied a holy year in 1850 was ironic; for him then to live long enough to be forced to celebrate an unconventional form of jubilee in 1875 may suggest some divine purpose. As if to make up for what had been lost, the faithful congregated in Rome in 1877, this time to celebrate the pope's golden jubilee of episcopal consecration. The Scots were well represented and took the opportunity to make the case for a restored hierarchy. Among the laymen was David Hunter-Blair, by then a papal chamberlain, who brought along his impressionable Irish Protestant friend Oscar Wilde. John Strain, vicar apostolic of the Eastern District, had his Wiseman moment when reading the loyal address of Scottish Catholics to the Holy Father on 12 May:

> Distant Scotland, the Ultima Thule [...] once a most faithful hand maid of the Holy See [...] now begins again to put forth blossoms of faith and to produce seemly fruits, and when your Holiness shall be pleased to establish among us the Ecclesiastical Hierarchy [...] a fresh impulse will be given to religion, and many will return to the faith of their fathers.[29]

Propaganda Fide approved the restoration on 28 January 1878, but the pope's death ten days later meant that formal recognition was delayed until March. Strain duly became archbishop of St Andrews and Edinburgh, his province including the dioceses of Aberdeen, Argyll and the Isles, Dunkeld, and Galloway; Charles Eyre's archbishopric of Glasgow stood in splendid isolation. Although Episcopalian bishops resented a parallel hierarchy, there were no popular cries of papal aggression.

An unfamiliar calm was indeed descending on the British-papal relationship. The reasons for it were to be found around the globe. A fresh burst of colonial scrambling placed increasing numbers African and Asian Catholics under European rule, and no power scrambled more successfully than Britain. Within Europe the Vatican encountered increasing anticlericalism in the French Third Republic; it had strained relations with Austria–Hungary, none at all with encircling Italy, and was suitably horrified by the systematic anti-Catholicism of Bismarck's Kulturkampf. It was perhaps not entirely accidental that two new British cardinals were created in 1875–7: Manning, after nearly a decade as archbishop of Westminster, and the aristocratic curialist Edward Henry Howard. When they shared in the cardinals' collective responsibility for the government of the Church during the *sede vacante* of 1878, Manning went so far as to propose that the British government be asked to permit the conclave to be held on Malta, to prevent interference from the new Italian state. On the other hand, if the electors acted fast, any such upheaval could be avoided.

Elected after just three ballots, the next pope, Leo XIII (1878–1903), was chosen in part because he was an Italian who resolutely defended papal monarchy against the house of Savoy, more because he was not a member of Pius's inner circle and had spent three decades effectively exiled in his Perugian diocese, and mostly because he was reputed to be a natural conciliator who could build bridges – truly pontificate – where Pio Nono had alienated individuals and nations. Gioacchino Pecci came to the papacy with just one diplomatic posting to his name, as nuncio to Belgium in the 1840s. That kingdom gained its independence from the Netherlands in 1831, when its predominantly Catholic population suddenly found themselves ruled by a German Protestant king, Leopold I. In Belgium Pecci witnessed not only the rule of a liberal monarch in a parliamentary democracy, but also rapid industrialisation and its social consequences. This exposure set him apart from other Italian prelates of his generation. In terms of industrialisation, Belgium took its inspiration from neighbouring Britain, but there was also a dynastic connection, for Leopold had been George IV's son-in-law and was Palmerston's choice to rule the new kingdom. In turn, Leopold engineered the union of his nephew Albert of Saxe-Coburg to his niece, Britain's Queen Victoria, and the couple visited Belgium during Pecci's time as nuncio. When Pecci left Brussels early in 1846 he returned to Rome by way of London and Paris, which made him the first pope since Paul IV to have set foot on British soil. For their part, the non-Italian cardinals, including Manning and Howard – but not Cullen, who arrived too late – were among Pecci's most ardent supporters in the conclave.

The British government's interest in Leo was limited to his potential influence in Ireland. Gladstone remained determined to address the root causes of popular discontent there and, after his re-election in 1880, reverted to the traditional strategy of attempting to use the papacy as a means of bringing order to the island, which could not be achieved by the prime minister's other policy, that of imprisoning large numbers of nationalists. George Errington, nephew of the eponymous archbishop and 'an independent Catholic gentleman', went to Rome on 'a mission that was not a mission' but which was nevertheless in the government's interest.[30] This caused such a furore among Gladstone's political opponents that he was obliged to abandon the scheme. Thereafter, his third and fourth administrations (1886, 1892–4) brought attempts to introduce Home Rule in Ireland, a policy that would benefit the Catholic majority but foundered due to Protestant opposition. After the failure of the Errington experiment, it was attempted without attempting to involve the papacy.

Although Leo XIII remained imprisoned in the Vatican throughout the twenty-five years of his pontificate, lack of temporal power did nothing to diminish his sense of being a papal monarch and he was ever ready to establish diplomatic relations with the Court of St James. Indeed, monarchy itself provided the clearest thread running through his dealings with Britain. While there was no clear view among the British political class about whether diplomatic relations should or even could be established with the stateless pontiff, the celebration of Victoria's golden jubilee in June 1887 provided an entirely original opportunity for one monarch to congratulate another. Even as the Anglican service of thanksgiving was conducted at Westminster Abbey, a papal envoy, the princely Neapolitan Mgr Fulco Luigi Ruffo-Scilla, presided at mass in the Catholic pro-cathedral in Kensington. Elsewhere, Sheffield's Catholics were assured of the prince of Wales's remarkable attachment to Pius IX, not least in connection with his bout of typhoid fever in 1871:

> We rejoiced as we heard that, at the last most critical, well nigh supreme moment, there came the blessing of the Holy Father to his almost departing spirit, and that as soon as reviving strength could bear him, he hastened to Rome and received the paternal embrace of Pope Pius IX.[31]

Conveniently, Leo celebrated his golden jubilee of priestly ordination during the winter of 1887–8, so the queen was able to reciprocate by sending the duke of Norfolk to Rome with a gift of a golden ewer and basin. This level of amity could only renew suspicions of a papal–British accord at Ireland's expense, so Manning took the opportunity presented by Mgr Ignazio Persico's Irish mission in 1887 to persuade the pope's agent that 'the true *nunciatura* for England and Ireland is the episcopate': diplomatic relations were unnecessary.[32] By the end of that year another nationalist, Michael Logue, was appointed to the Irish primacy. Thus it fell to the pope to remonstrate with his rebellious Irish flock in the encyclical *Saepe nos*, which criticised 'those methods of warfare known as Boycotting and the Plan of Campaign', that is violent opposition towards British landlords.[33] Six months later, in a gesture that did nothing to appease rural discontent, the pope sent a second encyclical, accompanying a gift of 'vestments, vessels and ornaments' for use in Irish cathedrals.[34]

In 1889 British possession of Malta brought about the negotiation of a concordat between Britain and the Vatican – the Simmons–Rampolla agreement, named after the island's former governor and Leo's secretary of state – but its scope was so limited as to pass without much comment. Consequently, the next opportunity for high-level talks was Victoria's diamond jubilee in 1897, when the papal envoy, Mgr Cesare Sambucetti, met Lord

Salisbury at the Foreign Office. Still there was no sign of full diplomatic relations being established. However, the Catholic press emphasised royal interest in the visit, the queen standing to greet Sambucetti but remaining seated throughout audiences with other visiting dignitaries, and the prince of Wales intervening three days before the event to insist that the mass of thanksgiving be held at the more spacious Brompton Oratory, rather than at the pro-cathedral.[35] On 22 June Sambucetti took part in the carriage procession to St Paul's Cathedral, where the open-air nature of the thanksgiving service helped to avoid inter-denominational difficulties. One member of Sambucetti's suite who returned to London on subsequent occasions was the high-born Neapolitan and future cardinal Gennaro Granito-Pignatelli di Belmonte. At the time of Victoria's death he was nuncio in Belgium, so well placed to cross the Channel and convey the pope's sympathies. The pleasantries continued in 1902 when Edward VII sent the Catholic earl of Denbigh to congratulate Leo on the twenty-fifth anniversary of his election. By then the pope was ninety-three and increasingly vulnerable to the designs of ambitious curialists. One such was Rafael Merry del Val y Zulueta, the London-born and Ushaw-educated son of a Spanish diplomat, who had acted as Ruffo-Scilla's interpreter in 1887 and represented the papacy on the occasion of Edward's coronation.

In terms of relations between the papacy and the British monarchy, Leo's pontificate reached a suitable climax in April 1903 when King Edward expressed determination to meet the pope during a cruise around the Mediterranean. In the absence of British diplomatic representation at the Vatican, the practicalities were entrusted to Mgr Edmund Stonor, the highest-ranking British cleric in Rome. Perhaps mindful of criticism levelled at the Australian prime minister, Sir Edmund Barton, who had recently visited Leo, Balfour's cabinet feared an anti-Catholic reaction and advised the king to abandon his plan. Edward would not be deterred and the prime minister finally relented, insisting only that the meeting was seen to be at the pope's invitation. To this Rampolla objected that an invitation to a Protestant monarch was without precedent, so could not be issued. The British ambassador to Italy, Sir Francis Bertie, then headed down to Naples to meet the approaching monarch. He could only hope that his subordinates were resourceful enough to solve the problem, even though they had no accreditation to the Vatican. Fortunately for the ambassador, it happened that another kinsman of the duke of Norfolk, Esme Howard, was serving as honorary second secretary at the embassy and, in turn, was friendly with Merry del Val in the Secretariat of State. The two men discussed the problem on 21 April and fixed it for Leo to express 'a strong personal desire' to meet the king. An entirely private visit – the first such by a British monarch – was arranged for 29 April. The inside story of this remarkable episode is recorded in the memoirs of Rennell Rodd, the embassy's first secretary, but its externals were also observed by an Italian seminarian:

'A highly significant event this, of a heretical king of Protestant England, which has persecuted the Catholic Church for more than three centuries, going in person to pay his respects to the poor old Pope, held like a prisoner in his house.'[36] That student was Angelo Roncalli who, as Pope John XXIII, made history when he received an equally private visit from an archbishop of Canterbury, and a staunchly Protestant one at that. Edward VII, by contrast, repeatedly demonstrated sympathy towards Catholicism and sought to employ this personal interest in the cause of improved Anglo-papal relations.

If the monarchical element in that relationship grew stronger during the course of Leo's pontificate, it was at the expense of the aristocratic one. Manning ensured that clerical members of 'old' Catholic families were excluded from the English and Welsh episcopate, which was precisely why Howards and Stonors gravitated towards Rome. Henry Fitzalan-Howard held the dukedom of Norfolk from 1860 to 1917, so potentially provided a remarkable degree of continuity as *de facto* leader of Britain's Catholic minority, but his significance for Anglo-papal relations largely depended on his kinsman Cardinal Howard, who was particularly prominent early in the Leonine era. In 1881, Howard was made archpriest of St Peter's Basilica and, in 1884, cardinal-bishop of Frascati, but illness removed him from the scene just three years later. During that relatively brief window of opportunity, the Howards' influence can be seen most clearly in Newman's promotion to the cardinalate in 1879. Rome's attitude towards the allegedly 'liberal' Newman began to thaw after Mgr Talbot was removed to an asylum in 1869, but a question mark hung over his orthodoxy as long as Pius IX lived. Again, Leo's Belgian experience then made a crucial difference, for it had allowed him to meet Dominic Barberi and George Ignatius Spencer, to learn about the Oxford Movement and to be inspired by Newman's personal history. Meeting the new English cardinal in person had a profound impact on Leo, who readily waived any obligation on him to reside in Rome.

Besides personal loyalty to Newman, the Howards were custodians of the recusant tradition and knew what it was to be martyr's kin: Philip Howard, thirteenth earl of Arundel, was convicted of treason in 1585 and spent his last decade imprisoned in the Tower of London. Pius IX had turned down Wiseman's request that the English and Welsh martyrs of the Reformation era be honoured with a liturgical feast, but Leo's election presented a fresh opportunity to advance their cause. It was revived in 1884 with the rector of the English College as co-postulator. Behind the rector was the college's protector, Cardinal Howard. John Fisher, Thomas More, Margaret Pole and fifty-one other martyrs were duly beatified in 1886, appropriately enough on the feast of St Thomas of Canterbury.

Another nine martyrs were beatified in 1895. By then the character of the Anglo-papal relationship was being dictated by Herbert Vaughan, whose priorities were those of the present, not the past. Vaughan inherited the ultramontane tradition in all its exuberance and argued for a revival of the pope's temporal power. As bishop of Salford he made the point by asking his clergy to imagine the pope imprisoned not in the Vatican, but in Manchester Town Hall.[37] As Manning's successor at Westminster in 1892 and as a kinsman of Cardinal Weld, he clearly expected to receive a red hat, so devoted his energies into denying the cardinalate to the archbishop of Dublin. He succeeded, but when the list was announced in January 1893, Vaughan's precedence was established beneath both Logue of Armagh and Archbishop Persico, the former apostolic delegate to Ireland.[38] The new English cardinal then broke with tradition by doubling up as protector of the English College, a duplication facilitated by his close working relationship with Merry del Val. Whatever Vaughan wanted, the Vatican obligingly supplied. In 1895 it was papal permission for Catholics to attend British and Irish universities: a clear break with Manning's policy. For the English and Welsh hierarchy's joint pastoral letter for 1 January 1901 what Vaughan required was papal support for condemnation of 'liberal' Catholics, the very people towards whom Leo had been conciliatory through bestowing hats on scholars such as Newman. Merry del Val ensured that it was forthcoming.[39] Though never a liberal himself, in his extreme old age Leo was becoming a puppet manipulated by conservatives who might be 'noble' by birth, but who were not behaving like gentlemen. It should come as no surprise that Vaughan wanted Merry del Val to succeed him at Westminster and that his name appeared on the *terna* in 1903. At that point the duke of Norfolk asserted himself: a true aristocrat ensured that the 'Cockney Spaniard' remained in Rome.[40]

Elsewhere among the aristocracy, Charles Lindley Wood, second Viscount Halifax, was no less conscious of his responsibilities, which included presidency of the English Church Union, an Anglo-Catholic body within the Church of England. By the early 1890s Leo had undertaken a number of initiatives to reconcile the Catholic Church with Orthodoxy, and Halifax took this as his cue to interest the pope in the possibility of the Church of England's corporate reunion with Rome, possibly even in time for the thirteenth centenary of Augustine's mission to England (1897). The theological arguments were set out by his friend Abbé Fernand Portal, who received a sympathetic hearing from Leo and Rampolla in 1894. Halifax was similarly encouraged by a meeting with the pope at Easter 1895, an encounter to which the Vatican responded publicly by issuing the apostolic letter *Amantissima voluntatis*, known for convenience as *Ad Anglos*.[41] This recalls the solicitude of Gregory the Great, Celestine I and other pontiffs for the English people, the 'grievous wound' of the Reformation, and more recent global achievements: 'Every one knows the power and resources of the British nation and the civilizing influence which, with the spread of liberty, accompanies its commercial prosperity even to the most remote regions.' The pope's voice can be heard in his recollection of meeting George Ignatius Spencer in Belgium, but one of the hands was that of Merry del Val, who ensured that *Ad Anglos* offered no concessions to Halifax and his fellow Anglicans, and allowed only one route to Christian reunion, that of prayers to Gregory the Great, Augustine of Canterbury, St Peter and St George, and, above all, to the Blessed Virgin Mary. As in other matters relating to England, behind Merry del Val was the figure of Cardinal Vaughan, who knew that Halifax and Leo were deluding themselves if they imagined corporate reunion was a serious possibility: they had to be stopped. The letter generated positive comments in the British press, though Anglicans from the archbishop of Canterbury downwards were piqued by the all too obvious absence of any reference to their branch of the Church Catholic.

One particular point of contention between Rome and Canterbury concerned the validity of Anglican orders from the time of Edward VI onwards, a matter of obvious interest to the clerics on both sides. Many authors addressed the subject, including Portal in 1894.[42] Vaughan fixed on this because most Anglicans denied the sacramental power of priests to take bread and wine and mysteriously transform them into the body and blood of Christ. If there was no unity on this matter of faith, there could be no visible or structural unity between Anglicans and Roman Catholics. The cardinal instructed his pet historians, Dom Aidan Gasquet and Edmund Bishop, to compile anti-Portal arguments. These were but opening skirmishes; the real battle ensued in 1896, when a pontifical commission met to determine this limited question about the validity of Anglican orders. The pope's personal appointees, Abbé Louis Duchesne (another historian) and Pietro Gasparri (a canon lawyer), were favourable to the Anglo-Catholic position, but were outnumbered and outgunned by Vaughan's adherents, who included Gasquet, David Fleming OFM and Canon James Moyes of Westminster. The commission's secretary, with responsibility for drafting its conclusions, was Merry del Val. A foretaste of those conclusions appeared in the papal encyclical *Satis cognitum*, which emphasised papal primacy in the unity of the Church, the implication being that individual Anglicans would have to submit to Rome, rather than negotiate any sort of exclusive deal with it.[43] The commission's finished product was the bull *Apostolicae curae*, which pronounced Anglican orders to be 'absolutely null and utterly void'.[44] Halifax's dream was well and truly shattered.

Although the door was effectively closed to any immediate dialogue with sympathetic Anglicans, in 1898 the pope tried another angle when he used an encyclical to the Scottish hierarchy to express the responsibility he felt towards 'separated brethren'. Mgr James Campbell, lately rector of the Scots College, had suggested that unity with Presbyterians might be easier to achieve, because they were independent of the civil power, and Leo's encyclical therefore emphasised a shared love of Scripture as the basis for possible reunification.[45] There was no Scottish equivalent of Halifax.

While Manning showed no interest in any earthly monarch apart from the papal one and was positively antagonistic towards the English Catholic aristocracy, his genuine enthusiasms proved to be increasingly democratic in nature. His concern for the urban poor originated in the plight of the Irish immigrants for whom he had pastoral responsibility, and spread to the wider 'labour question'. It was not enough to condemn socialism or communism as anti-Christian creeds without offering a serious Christian answer to the challenges of industrial society. Most significantly, he gained heroic status by negotiating a settlement of the 1889 London dock strike. By his own admission, the pope had already been inspired by Manning when working on the encyclical *Immortale Dei*, on the Christian constitution of states, but when he switched his focus to social questions, that inspiration was all the more apparent.[46] During the preparation of Leo's most celebrated encyclical, *Rerum novarum*,[47] on the rights and duties of Capital and Labour, Archbishop Walsh of Dublin wrote to Manning from Rome: 'I think I trace your Eminence's Influence in this as in many other things that I have noted here during this visit.'[48] Whatever the residual impact of the pope's experience of Belgian industrialisation in the 1840s, it was then nearly fifty years past, which meant that Manning's more recent crusading zeal for workers' rights more directly inspired the foundation stone of all subsequent Catholic social teaching. Thanks to *Rerum novarum*, Leo XIII's posthumous impact was perhaps as great as any of his canonised predecessors. Britain may have lacked the fervour of Belgium or France when it came to disseminating his teaching and putting it into practice, but it can nevertheless be discerned in Charles Plater's foundation of the Catholic Social Guild in 1909. This rapidly acquired branches throughout Britain and Ireland, groups whose work came together in the Catholic Workers' College (subsequently Plater College) at Oxford.

If Leo was the 'people's pope' who communicated with his flock by means of encyclicals, then it was entirely appropriate that travel to Rome was effectively democratised during his pontificate. Thanks to the enterprising Baptist Thomas Cook, large pilgrim groups travelled from Britain for the pope's golden jubilee, for the holy year in 1900 and on other occasions in between. It was perhaps no less appropriate that a highly contemporary pontiff, 'Pius X', complete with long-lost son, should make an appearance in popular culture. Hall Caine's novel *The Eternal City* (1902) was rapidly turned into a stage play and film versions duly followed.

Like many of his predecessors, Leo XIII died in the sweltering heat of a Roman summer, on 20 July 1903. Through to the coronation of his successor twenty days later the ceremonies of the *sede vacante* proceeded in time-honoured fashion. Unusually, they had a strong Irish dimension.

Sir Thomas Esmonde represented the Irish Nationalist party at the papal exequies, and Logue became the first Irish cardinal to vote in a conclave. He was joined by the Irish-born Cardinal Gibbons of Baltimore; another Irishman, Cardinal Moran of Sydney, Cullen's nephew, arrived too late to vote. There was no English elector because Vaughan had died on 19 June, but a number of *inglesi* were informed observers of the electoral drama. Some of the papal chamberlains retained their offices at the pope's death, so witnessed everything up to the sealing of the enclosure. They included the convert Hartwell De la Garde Grissell, who kept a diary during the Interregnum.[49] Grissell's account of the twice daily *sfumate*, which indicated no election, can be compared with that of Rennell Rodd, who had again been left in charge of the embassy, but observed the Interregnum in a private capacity.[50] On 2 and 3 August Rodd was accompanied in Piazza S. Pietro by Sir John Harrington, the British minister in Abyssinia, who happened to be passing through Rome. Harrington gave up, but Rodd was there to witness the absence of smoke on the morning of 4 August, followed by Cardinal Macchi's announcement of the election of Giuseppe Sarto, patriarch of Venice, as Pope Pius X (1903–14). He telegraphed the Foreign Office accordingly. It was, however, Logue who witnessed the incident for which this conclave remains best known, the Austrian 'veto' of Cardinal Rampolla. Grissell learned of it soon enough and Rodd took a diplomat's interest in the technicalities. All the electors had sworn fidelity to Pius IX's bull against external interference and would have recorded a formal protest had a genuine veto been presented, so Rodd reasoned that Cardinal Puzyna had done no more than express the emperor's hope that Rampolla would not be elected. With regard to motivation, Rodd knew that Austria feared Rampolla as the French candidate, but thought it more likely that Franz Josef had not forgotten the secretary of state's opposition to the Christian burial of Crown Prince Rudolf, who apparently committed murder and suicide at Mayerling in 1889.

Pius X's prior experience of secular power was limited to Austrian rule in the Veneto until 1866 and the kingdom of Italy thereafter. Linguistically, he was limited to Italian, Latin and a smattering of French. The London-born Spaniard Merry del Val was therefore a logical choice to serve as his secretary of state, but this prelate's linguistic facility was not matched by natural diplomacy. As if to underline the fact that he was no Rampolla, in the first year of the pontificate the Vatican severed diplomatic relations with France. President Loubet had visited Rome in an attempt to woo Italy from its German alliance. His effort failed, leaving France reliant on Czarist Russia to contain Germany, but Loubet's mistake in the Vatican's eyes was his failure to visit the pope, who could hardly visit him. The diplomatic break proved to be a prelude to the republic's abolition of the century-old Napoleonic concordat in December 1905, a separation of Church and State with far-reaching social, financial and educational consequences. Another diplomatic relationship was lost when the Portuguese monarchy was overthrown in 1910 and an anticlerical republic created. With 'Catholic' powers falling away rapidly, the papacy turned increasingly to their 'Protestant' counterparts. Kaiser Wilhelm was particularly keen to ingratiate himself with the Vatican, in part through diplomatic representation, but also by facilitating international eucharistic congresses – hitherto francophone phenomena – in Metz and Cologne.

Edward VII exercised less power than his eldest nephew and thus remained wary of appearing too openly favourable towards the Church. In 1906 he approved the marriage of his niece Princess Victoria Eugénie of Battenberg to King Alfonso XIII of Spain on a personal basis, a technicality being found so that he could avoid approving of it officially, as the Royal Marriages Act required. The princess became a Catholic and lost her place in the British line of succession, so there was no point of contention with the papacy. High-ranking papal envoys were regularly sent to Britain and observed the diplomatic niceties to perfection. In 1904 Cardinal Vincenzo Vannutelli attended the consecration of Logue's cathedral at Armagh, tactfully dropping his legatine status when passing through England.[51] When he returned to London in September 1908 for the International Eucharistic Congress, Vannutelli therefore became the first papal legate to England since Reginald Pole in the sixteenth century. The congress itself posed a problem for the authorities, because it was not entirely held behind closed doors. The German government had suspended its law against Catholic processions so that the Blessed Sacrament could be carried through Metz the previous year. In Britain the corresponding law was thought (by Archbishop Bourne of Westminster) to have fallen into abeyance or was entirely overlooked (by the home secretary, Herbert Gladstone). During the days immediately prior to the procession through the streets around Westminster Cathedral the king and his senior ministers panicked at the prospect of it provoking anti-Catholic violence. The procession therefore went ahead without the sacrament or eucharistic vestments, Vannutelli made suitably diplomatic comments about 'English liberty', and the Anglo-papal courtly dance continued. The only significant British state occasion to fall during Pius's pontificate was George V's coronation in 1911, when the pope was again represented by Archbishop Granito-Pignatelli di Belmonte.

In Rome, Pius and his loyal lieutenants inaugurated a fresh wave of legal, administrative and doctrinal centralisation. The apostolic constitution *Sapienti consilio* (1908) reorganised the curia to meet contemporary realities, rather than hoping that the pre-1870 order could be restored.[52] For the three hierarchies of the British Isles – and others besides – this meant that they no longer answered to Propaganda Fide, but to the Consistorial Congregation and its powerful secretary Cardinal Gaetano De Lai.[53] More particular reorganisation followed in 1911, when the English bishoprics of Birmingham and Liverpool were raised to metropolitan status. Rome sent a French Servite friar, Alexis-Henri-Marie Lépicier, to oversee the transition. This was a sensible choice for Lépicier had joined his order in London and spent much of his earlier career there and at its house in Bognor. De Lai also took the opportunity to send Lépicier as apostolic visitor to Scotland. On the doctrinal front, this pontificate remains best known for the encyclical *Pascendi Dominici gregis*, which condemned agnosticism and other 'errors' under the blanket term 'modernism', and for the anti-modernist oath which the clergy were required to take from 1910.[54] For the ultramontane majority in Britain and Ireland, including the latest converts such as Aelred Carlyle and the monks of Caldey, this was precisely the sort of leadership they had expected from Rome. There was only one notable British target, the convert and former Jesuit George Tyrrell, who roundly criticised the encyclical, was excommunicated and died unreconciled in 1909.

Infinitely more picturesque was a man whose clerical career encapsulated the dilemmas of his age, as he veered between Catholicism and Anglicanism, depending on whether his doubts about Anglican orders or papal authority were uppermost. This was Arnold Mathew, who also failed to be contained by the Old Catholic Union of Utrecht and established his own denomination in 1911. His Catholic past caught up with him and he was excommunicated that same year, leaving his papal interests to be channelled into a history of Alexander VI's life and times.[55] Such an odyssey was stranger than fiction and set the bar high for the authors of papal-inspired literature. Perhaps it is no surprise, therefore, that the genre reached its zenith during Pius X's pontificate.

Frederick Rolfe, that highly idiosyncratic historian of the Borgia, returned to the Rome of Alexander VI for his 1905 romance *Don Tarquinio*, a considerably more original piece than the Borgia-inspired verse dramas of his contemporaries.[56] It was, however, a fictional pontiff who proved to be his greatest creation. In *Hadrian VII* (1904), Rolfe's alter ego George Arthur Rose receives the ordination that Rolfe himself had been denied, and that specifically in order to be elected pope. No serious attempt is made to disguise the cardinals who actually voted in 1903: Luigi Oreglia appears as Cardinal Orazzo, Serafino Vannutelli as Serafino Vagellaio, Vincenzo Vannutelli as Vincenzo Vagellaio, and so forth. Cardinal Mariano Ragna is not vetoed in the novel, as Rampolla may or may not have been in reality, but he does cause a scandal by voting for himself. The real Herbert Vaughan (of Courtfield in Herefordshire) is kept alive as Cardinal Courtleigh, so that he can regret his previous injustice to Rolfe/Rose. Far from being imprisoned in the Vatican, the fictional Pope Hadrian takes possession of the Lateran and is reconciled with the king of Italy. Not content with these achievements, he reorganises the global interests of all the secular powers, whose leaders are in his thrall. He remembers his patriotic duty by canonising Alfred the Great, Henry VI and Mary, queen of Scots, and by sending a golden rose to Queen Victoria's mausoleum at Frogmore.

The autobiographical nature of the piece means that Hadrian is, incidentally, a convert. Nothing could have been more inspiring to another literary convert, Robert Hugh Benson, who enjoyed all the social advantages that Rolfe lacked: his father had been archbishop of Canterbury. The earnestness of Benson's apocalyptic novel *Lord of the World* (1907) is no match for Rolfe's razor-sharp wit, but it does feature another English pope, Silvester III, who leads the faithful remnant into eternity.

With more than a nod to the apocalypse, in the final weeks of Pius X's life Europe entered the 'war to end all wars'. A chapter had certainly closed in the Anglo-papal relationship: no more was heard about contentious vetoes and rescripts, government ministers could no longer deplore the temporal power of the papacy, for it had been lost, and there was no repeat of the diplomatic incident caused by a hereditary monarch's desire to meet an elected papal one.

CHAPTER 7

FROM HARD CHOICES TO SOFT POWER

Conclaves are never lacking in dramatic intensity, but when fifty-seven cardinals were locked into the enclosure on 31 August 1914 it occurred only a month after Austria's declaration of war against Serbia. This triggered a pan-European war between their respective alliances, the Central Powers of Austria–Hungary and Germany and the Entente (Allied) Powers, Russia, France and Britain. Germany's violation of Belgian neutrality brought Britain into the conflict on 4 August, thereby unleashing pent-up economic and military rivalry between those two states. The conclave presented an opportunity to play out the international conflict in miniature, because four of the red-robed electors were from Austria–Hungary, two were German, six French, and five were of British or Irish birth.[1] In the event, they exercised restraint and did not allow secular rivalries to determine the fate of the Church. Rather, the voting figures noted by Cardinal Piffl of Vienna after each of the ten scrutinies suggest that the cardinals were divided between perpetuating or breaking with the policies of Pius X. Merry del Val was the continuity candidate and received votes in the first five ballots. The candidate who personified change was Giacomo della Chiesa, a former curial insider who had been regarded with such suspicion by Pius's inner circle that he was sent to Bologna in 1907 without the red hat traditionally associated with that archbishopric.[2] His misfortune was to be a protégé of Rampolla, but in 1914 a diplomat of that stamp was precisely what the international situation required. He was elected and became Benedict XV (1914–22).

During the conclave and its immediate aftermath, the British cardinal Francis Aidan Gasquet – Pius X's fiftieth and final choice for the hat – was acutely conscious that the German-speaking states were so well served by their ambassadors to the Holy See that clerical Rome was decidedly pro-German. He sought to counter this. In conversation with Rennell Rodd, who was Britain's ambassador to Italy throughout the war, and in correspondence with the foreign secretary, Sir Edward Grey, Gasquet proposed the creation of a

British diplomatic mission to the Holy See, the first since that of Sir Edward Carne in the 1550s. The career diplomat Sir Henry Howard, who had been a contemporary of Gasquet in the school at Downside, resided in Rome, so was able to fill the new role of envoy extraordinary and minister plenipotentiary within weeks of the cardinal making the suggestion. Howard's appointment facilitated the first papal audience for a serving British prime minister, the opportunity for which arose when H.H. Asquith visited France and Italy in the spring of 1916 to discuss that summer's military campaigns. A Congregationalist by upbringing, Asquith confessed to nerves before his meeting with Benedict on 1 April. Later that year Howard was succeeded by a man of similar social credentials, Count John de Salis, whose title was imperial and whose estates were Irish. The count's sister-in-law was a Borghese by marriage, which gave him instant access to Roman society at the highest level: any card was worth playing as part of the Great Game.

In 1914 what the Vatican feared most was Russian domination of Eastern Europe, which it suspected would lead to the reunification of Russian and Greek Orthodoxy in Constantinople and, consequently, to its own eclipse. According to this line of thinking, the Central Powers represented Western Christendom's principal line of defence, an assumption that was soon complicated by their alliance with the Ottoman Empire, where Christians enjoyed freedom of worship but were otherwise treated as second-class citizens. The pope could not publicly take sides. Ably assisted by his secretary of state, Cardinal Pietro Gasparri, Benedict maintained a policy of studied impartiality throughout the conflict, praying for peace and repeatedly petitioning the warring parties to reach a negotiated settlement. He sought to dissuade additional states from declaring war, only to be thwarted by Italy in 1915 and the United States in 1917. His most prominent diplomatic intervention, the Peace Note issued in August 1917, aimed to restore the *status quo ante bellum*, but was roundly rejected – or ignored – by the various powers (except staunchly Catholic Austria–Hungary), which had no use for a papal mediator and had developed war aims far beyond those which had obtained three years earlier. According to a secret clause in the Treaty of London (April 1915), France, Britain and Russia had already indicated to their new ally, Italy, that they were happy to support Italian opposition to papal involvement in any peace negotiations. In due course the Holy See was firmly excluded from the Paris peace conference in 1919 and could do nothing to ameliorate the terms of the notoriously imbalanced Versailles treaty.

In Britain commentators of all Christian denominations and none heard what they wanted to hear from the pope, if impaired wartime communications allowed them to hear anything at all. In 1915 a polemicist writing as 'Francis Tyrrell' asked whether Benedict's silence on German atrocities in Belgium could be defended, the clear inference being that it could not.[3] That 'silence' contrasted with the example of Cardinal Mercier, archbishop of Mechelen/ Malines, who led resistance to the German occupation of his homeland. Cardinal Bourne and Bishop Keating of Northampton did what they could to explain Benedict's position in print, but could not shift entrenched public opinion.[4] The introduction of conscription in January 1916 brought many more individuals and families into the conflict and prompted two Catholic laymen, Francis Meynell and Stanley Morison, to publicise Benedict's consistent – and consistently ignored – appeals by founding the Guild of the Pope's Peace. With the pontiff's authorisation, this small group published *A Little Book of Prayers for Peace*, compiled by the Catholic convert and lifelong peace campaigner E.I. Watkin. They achieved little else and Watkin maintained that the Guild's efforts were thwarted by the English hierarchy, who had proved to be remarkably selective mediators of the pope's messages to his flock.

When Benedict finally issued his Peace Note it reminded British observers of his earlier 'silence' and triggered renewed public assertions of the pope's pro-German stance. The government sought clarification from their mission to the Holy See and received a candid assessment of the papal character from the junior diplomat J.D. Gregory:

> The present pope is a very decided mediocrity. He has the mentality of a little official, the inexperience of a parochial Italian who has hardly travelled at all and a tortuous method of conducting affairs which arises from years of office work connected with a fifth rate diplomacy [...] He is without any particular charm or personality and he is obstinate and bad-tempered to a marked degree.[5]

Gregory nevertheless concluded that Benedict was 'neither temperamentally nor politically pro-German'. Two months later, and with time on his hands after being ousted as rector of the English College, Archbishop John McIntyre cast himself as a well-informed source by pointing out that Benedict had recently rejoiced when General Allenby entered Jerusalem, a reaction which rankled with the Ottoman Empire's allies in Berlin. Surely, McIntyre argued, this proved that the pope was pro-British after all.[6]

In some senses Benedict and Gasparri had never been anything other than pro-British, for they fully appreciated the convergence of interests between the Church's worldwide mission and Britain's extensive imperial administration. Nor did war prevent Benedict maintaining his pastoral responsibilities towards Britain. Most significantly, the ecclesiastical map was redrawn only five years after the creation of the archbishoprics of Birmingham and Liverpool. Archbishop Ilsley of Birmingham petitioned Rome for the Welsh dioceses to be removed from his jurisdiction and Benedict responded with the apostolic letter *Cambria Celtica* (7 February 1916), creating a separate province headed by an archbishop in Cardiff. The other significant papal intervention in Britain during the war years was the appointment of an apostolic visitor to Scotland in 1917. This was Mgr William Brown, whose interest in education chimed well with the pressing need to provide schools for the rapidly expanding Catholic population of western Scotland, schools that the Church could ill afford. Brown negotiated the relevant terms of the Education (Scotland) Act (1918), whereby Catholic schools were funded by local authorities in exactly the same manner as other schools, along the same lines as had obtained in England and Wales since the Education Act of 1902. To its critics, this amounted to 'Rome on the rates'.

During the final phase of Benedict's pontificate war in Ireland topped the Anglo-papal agenda. Again Gasquet intervened, discussing Ireland with the pope whenever occasion permitted.[7] As in the Great War, Benedict had no intention of openly taking sides, which was not what the predominantly Catholic Irish nationalists wanted as they fought for independence from Britain. The Vatican's lukewarm Irish policy was much resented by Mgr John Hagan, rector of the Irish College from 1919 and the figurehead for Irish nationalism in Rome. Hagan's only consolation was that Gasquet and other English prelates had no influence over the Church in Ireland. At least Benedict was able to offer some consolation this in 1920 with the beatification of Oliver Plunkett, the martyred seventeenth-century archbishop of Armagh. Visitors to Rome for that celebration included Seán O'Kelly, speaker of the republican Dáil Éireann, who presented the pope with a memorandum on Irish independence. After the distinction of reigning through an exceptionally bloody period of European history, at least Benedict was then spared any knowledge of the Irish Civil War, dying as he did seven weeks after the signing of the Anglo-Irish treaty of December 1921.

Logue, Merry del Val, Bourne and Gasquet all voted again in the conclave of 2–6 February 1922. When the Irish cardinal arrived in Rome, a member of his entourage could not resist an anti-English jibe – 'It was an English-speaking pontiff who gave Ireland to England in the twelfth century; therefore, we do not favor any but an Italian for the throne of St. Peter'[8] – though there was little realistic chance of a non-Italian being elected. As in 1914 Merry del Val led the hard-line *zelanti*, who sought a pastoral pope in the image of Pius X. This time he received no more than seventeen votes: thirty-six were required for election. Opposing them were the *politici*, who wanted a diplomat willing to negotiate with the Italian government and settle the long-standing Roman Question about competing papal and secular claims to temporal power. Gasparri was the undisputed leader of this faction and his personal vote peaked at twenty-four. Both sides having played their strongest suits, they sought a compromise candidate and found one in the person of Achille Ratti, who had been both nuncio in Poland and (briefly) archbishop of Milan. As Pius XI (1922–39), Ratti remained imprisoned in the Vatican until 1929, when Gasparri went to the Lateran to sign interrelated pacts with the Mussolini-led government of Italy:

a treaty to establish Vatican City as an independent state and a concordat to regulate the position of the Church throughout the Italian kingdom.

Ratti's earlier career had been devoted to librarianship. Taking a break from his duties at the Biblioteca Ambrosiana in Milan, he toured Europe in 1906, stopping in London, Oxford, Cambridge and Manchester. In 1914, after transferring to the Vatican library and becoming its prefect, he represented Pius X at the Oxford commemoration of the Franciscan philosopher Roger Bacon's seventh centenary and was in still Britain when war broke out. From 1919 the office of cardinal librarian – the prefect's superior – was held by Gasquet, who was clearly delighted by the election of a scholar-pope, especially one he could claim to know quite well. Never a man to miss a literary opportunity, the English cardinal rapidly produced a 'pen portrait' of the new pontiff.[9] Suddenly, the prospects for Anglo-papal relations could hardly have appeared more promising.

Libraries and literature proved to be a recurring theme in Anglo-papal relations during Pius XI's pontificate. Shortly before Christmas 1931 a wing of the Vatican library collapsed, killing four workmen and one scholar. The king, the master of the rolls and the deputy keeper of the public records sent messages of sympathy.[10] It was feared at the time that 15,000 books had been destroyed. British authors such as the Oxford historian T.S.R. Boase helped to make up the loss with timely publications on papal history, and George Ogilvie-Forbes of the British diplomatic mission, a patriotic Scot, played his part by ensuring that publications of the Scottish History Society were routinely presented to the library.[11] The prolific Catholic apologists Hilaire Belloc and G.K. Chesterton were capable of filling entire shelves and received their rewards in 1934 in the form of papal knighthoods. At the frivolous – not to say scandalous – end of the literary spectrum is a work from the same pontificate that no-one has seen fit to add to the Vatican's collection: Ronald Firbank's novel *Concerning the Eccentricities of Cardinal Pirelli* (1926). It does, however, contain a fictional pope, the Neapolitan Tertius II, who expresses gratification at the increasing number of *inglesi* requesting papal audiences, which was an entirely appropriate reflection of religious developments in contemporary Britain.

Pius repaid British hospitality by receiving George V and Queen Mary during their state visit to Italy in 1923. It was a logical development from Edward VII's entirely private visit to Leo XIII in 1903 and countered any negative impression created by their eldest son in 1918, when he pointedly refused to kiss the fisherman's ring, even though there was no expectation for a non-Catholic to do so.[12] During the morning of 9 May their majesties had meetings with the pope and secretary of state. In the afternoon they returned to the Vatican for private tours of St Peter's, guided by Merry del Val, the museums and galleries with various officials, and the library, where Gasquet was their host.[13] Much to the annoyance of the Foreign Office, Pius continued to deal with his British counterpart as one monarch to another, sending personal messages to the king via the archbishop of Westminster.

In 1935, the year of George V's silver jubilee, the anglophile in the Vatican played his trump card by announcing the canonisation of Thomas More and John Fisher – the first new English saints since Osmund in 1457 – and by letting it be known that he would appreciate attendance by a special representative of the king at the ceremony on 19 May. Any warm words about the loyalty of the king-emperor's millions of Catholic subjects around the globe made not a jot of difference: one man's saint was still another man's traitor, and there was no question of such a representative being sent. Overtures to the universities of Oxford and Cambridge were similarly unsuccessful. Undeterred, during the ceremony itself, the pope used the ewer and basin sent by Queen Victoria to Leo XIII. Even if these gestures were not appreciated, Rome was doing all in its highly distinctive power to convince the British of its friendly intentions, which conveniently doubled up as a way of making the Church appear a little less Italianate in an increasingly anglophone world. The pope's personal regard for his sometime guests was again in evidence at the king's death in 1936, when

> the Holy Father sent to the new monarch a telegram of condolence. All the flags were flown at half-mast in the Papal State and in the extraterritorial possessions of the Holy See. The Cardinal Secretary of State, accompanied by Mgri. Pizzardo and Tardini, called at the British Legation to express the sympathy of the Holy Father.[14]

Within a matter of months the pope had cause to write again, this time consoling Queen Mary on the abdication of her son, the unashamedly antipapal Edward VIII.

However much the pope wished to maintain positive relations with the royal family, the coronation of George VI (1936–52) in May 1937 brought another reminder of the practical difficulties of dealing with Anglican schismatics. Since the previous coronation there had been interesting developments on the ecumenical front. The pontificate had opened with 'conversations' between Catholic and Anglican theologians, approved by Pope Benedict and hosted by Cardinal Mercier at Malines from December 1921. Mercier was on friendly terms with the new pope and secured Pius's permission to develop this initiative. Between March 1923 and May 1925 the group's discussions focused on the theory and practice of papal authority, together with the options for a closer relationship between Rome and Canterbury. However, this was a minority interest and one that was not shared by Cardinal Bourne and the English Catholic community. Rome distanced itself accordingly: Britain's friendship was not worth sacrificing for an Anglo-Catholic elite who were, in any case, perfectly free to submit to Rome whenever they liked. Other ecumenical initiatives emerged in the quest for peace in postwar Europe, initiatives that came from various Protestant denominations and sought to be sufficiently inclusive as to embrace Catholics. Pius responded with the 1928 encyclical *Mortalium animos*, stating unambiguously that 'this Apostolic See has never allowed its subjects to take part in the assemblies of non-Catholics: for the union of Christians can only be promoted by promoting the return to the one true Church of Christ of those who are separated from it.'[15] Thus there was still no question of Catholics attending an Anglican service such as the coronation of a king-emperor, the only exemption being made for the duke of Norfolk in his capacity as earl marshal. The papal envoy, Archbishop Giuseppe Pizzardo, and his suite – Mgr William Godfrey, rector of the English College, and Marchese Guido Pacelli, nephew of secretary of state Cardinal Eugenio Pacelli – led by example and were installed in a tribune constructed outside the west front of Westminster Abbey.

There was every incentive to wait for Anglicans to see the error of their ways because Catholicism in Britain was flourishing. New parishes were created and new churches built, though the most remarkable Catholic building project was surely the reconstruction of the abbey church at Buckfast in Devon. In 1932 its consecration by Cardinal Bourne was the first time since the sixteenth century that an English cardinal had acted as a papal legate in his own country. In the spirit of the times, Catholics organised themselves by means of clubs and societies. Loyalty to the pope was expressed most overtly in the formation of a Society for the Maintenance of the Apostolic See, the objectives of which included prayers for the pope's intentions, making his prerogatives better known, and helping 'in his constant endeavour to establish the Kingship of Christ and his peace among the Nations'.[16] Clubs and societies were similarly active in organising pilgrimages to Rome. 6,300 British and Irish pilgrims visited during the holy year in 1925, and the British were said to have been more numerous than pilgrims of other nations when an extraordinary holy year was celebrated in 1933. A party of distinguished British Catholics travelled to Rome in December 1929 for the beatification of 136 English martyrs of the Reformation era, including Philip Howard, earl of Arundel. They were still there for the beatification of the Scottish Jesuit John Ogilvie (d. 1615) a week later. Reflecting the greater significance of the event, more than 3,000 pilgrims made the journey to Rome for the canonisation of More and Fisher in May 1935.[17]

New parishes required more priests, so the Roman colleges were in expansionist mode in the 1920s. First, Mgr Arthur Hinsley acquired a summer residence at Palazzola for the English College. Then, at the instigation of its rector Mgr William Clapperton, the dilapidated Villa Scozzese at Marino was replaced and a new wing was added to the Scots College. Not to be outdone, Mgr Hagan moved the Irish College from S. Agata dei Goti to a generously proportioned building on Via dei SS. Quattro. All of this preceded Pius XI's own building campaigns, which occurred only after Vatican City came into existence in 1929 and required the apparatus of a state. The Lateran Treaty restored the palace at Castel Gandolfo to papal possession, occasioning further building work; Pius spent his first summer there in 1934, which meant that the villa-dwelling English and Scots seminarians had beaten him to the shores of Lake Albano.

Just as those students went on to link the Rome of Pius XI to parishes throughout Britain, so did the practice of appointing college rectors to Scottish and English bishoprics. Clapperton's predecessor, Donald Macintosh, was a surprise choice for the archbishopric of Glasgow in 1922, but the purpose of such a move became clearer with regard to Westminster. Two future archbishops, Hinsley and Godfrey, were rectors of the English College from 1917 and 1930 respectively; two others, Bernard Griffin and John Carmel Heenan, were among their students in the 1920s. In part this was a conscious Romanising trend that reflected Pius's contribution to the 'age of the dictators' but, in the case of England and Wales, it was also a reaction to Cardinal Bourne's long tenure at Westminster. Echoes of Bourne's Parisian education were found as late as 1931, when he travelled to Rouen as papal legate at the commemoration of St Jeanne d'Arc's execution five centuries earlier. At Bourne's death on 1 January 1935 there was speculation that he might be succeeded by Archbishop Downey of Liverpool or Williams of Birmingham, but Pius was adamant that Hinsley would fill the vacancy, precisely because he was the 'Roman' candidate.

In December 1937 Hinsley was one of the last five cardinals created by Pope Pius. He joined a college that included Joseph MacRory of Armagh and two former envoys to Britain, Lépicier and Pizzardo, but none of these could be regarded as any sort of replacement for Gasquet, the curial cardinal who had all but draped a union flag over his Benedictine habit and died in 1929. Gasquet apart, the most senior British curialists of Pius XI's pontificate were to be found among the canon lawyers of the Rota, of which Mgr John Prior was dean from 1921 and William Heard an auditor after Prior's death in 1926. Heard did indeed become Britain's next curial cardinal, but that was not until 1959. In reality, hats were more likely to be given to pastoral archbishops, and the relatively few posts available in Rome almost invariably went to Italians. Gasquet was effectively irreplaceable as a highly-placed contact in the Vatican, meaning that Britain's socio-political elite had to turn instead to what can be regarded as the cardinal's legacy to his country: the British mission to the Holy See. The Foreign Office appreciated this extraordinary legation as a listening post and saw France re-establish diplomatic relations with the Vatican in 1921, so allowed the wartime expedient to be renewed annually in the postwar period and made it a permanent mission in 1926. Extreme Protestant groups objected to this, though it is telling that the foreign secretary who approved the change, Austen Chamberlain, was struck by the significance of his own action precisely because he was a 'Nonconformist born and bred'.[18]

From Sir Odo Russell – son of the Odo Russell who kept a watching brief on the Vatican in the 1860s – to D'Arcy Osborne there were five British ministers to the Holy See during Pius XI's pontificate. They smoothed political, cultural or religious differences with the *sprezzatura* characteristic of the diplomatic profession. By way of illustration, in 1935 Sir Charles Wingfield did what he could to gloss over the obvious disparity of interest in More and Fisher by delaying the legation's silver jubilee celebration in order to host a reception for the curial and visiting dignitaries as close as possible to the canonisation. The practice developed of appointing a non-Catholic as head of mission, supported by a Catholic as first secretary. The latter role was relished by its holders, as can be glimpsed in the memoir by Sir Alec Randall, which highlights the more picturesque side of the legation's work in the later 1920s, such as finding a cassock for a visiting Anglican bishop whose gaiters were considered a potential source of embarrassment in the Vatican.[19] Another first secretary, Hugh Montgomery, was so deeply affected by his time in Rome that he later resigned from the diplomatic service, entered the Pontifical Beda College for mature students, and enjoyed a second career, as a priest of the Birmingham archdiocese. In the absence of a minister between 1930 and 1933, the secretaries George Ogilvie-Forbes and Ivone Kirkpatrick acted as *chargés d'affaires* and compiled the legation's annual reports. Those submitted by Ogilvie-Forbes were much the liveliest of the entire pontificate.

Reflecting on his time in Rome in the later 1920s, Randall identified five areas of active negotiation between Britain and the Holy See.[20] At that point the Roman Question loomed largest in the mission's work, as debate reached a crescendo during the negotiation of the 1929 Lateran pacts. Thereafter, Ogilvie-Forbes spied opportunities for British trade with the newly created Vatican City state, where he noted that most of the telephone cables were already of British manufacture. Citing the inferiority of Italian cigars and cigarettes, he speculated that the Vatican might be interested in a contract with the British–American Tobacco Company, only to decide that financial services would probably be a better bet.[21] Two of the five active negotiations related to India and other parts of the Empire: Catholic missions in British overseas territories, and the Portuguese *Padroado*, which determined appointments to the bishopric of Bombay. Another matter of shared interest was Britain's postwar mandates in Palestine and Iraq, territories with Christian minorities of whom the Vatican felt particularly protective. Looking back to 1914–16, Randall recalled that 'Cardinal Gasparri practically told [...] Sir Henry Howard that he preferred Protestant England to Catholic France as ruler of Palestine.'[22] Once traditional French claims to protect the Holy Places had been dealt with by treaty, Britain and the Vatican developed a good working relationship in Palestine. Overshadowing this harmony, though, was the threat posed by the Balfour Declaration of 1917 and the British government's determination that the mandate would give way to the creation of two new states, one of them a Jewish homeland. By 1924, when Sir Herbert Samuel, Britain's (Jewish) high commissioner in Palestine, met Gasparri in Rome, there was a strong feeling among Palestinian Catholics that Protestants, Zionists and Orthodox were uniting against them.[23] Indeed, the Vatican was becoming increasingly alarmed at British and French policies across the Middle Eastern mandates, which favoured the interests of Muslims and Jews, while sacrificing those of the Christian minorities.[24]

When relations between Britain and the Holy See reached an obvious crisis it was not over Palestine, but the fifth area of negotiation identified by Randall: Malta. Embedded in wider issues of language, nationalism and Mussolini's imperial dreams in the Mediterranean region was a personal battle of wills between the pope and Gerald Strickland, the island's prime minister from 1927. Strickland led the Constitutional Party, which championed the mutual interests of Britain and Malta. His opponents were the Italian-speaking Nationalist Party, which included a number of clerics, such as traditionally participated in Maltese politics. With Malta located between Mussolini's Italy and Italy's North African colonies, Strickland feared the spread of *italianità* on the island. Once in office, he pursued anti-Italian educational policies and voiced an anticlericalism and antipapalism that British observers might have found odd in a cradle Catholic. In return, Pius showed his support for the Maltese clergy by conferring the title of 'archbishop-bishop' upon the bishop of Malta, whose only suffragan was the bishop of Gozo. Strickland held talks with Gasparri in Rome in November 1928, but was kept at a distance from the short-tempered pontiff. In accordance with the terms agreed during that visit, Mgr Paschal Robinson, previously apostolic visitor in Palestine, was sent to Malta as apostolic delegate. All appeared to have gone well, until the Vatican published an edited version of Robinson's entirely balanced report, limited to criticism of Strickland. This was clearly the pope's work. Confident of papal support, in April 1930 the Maltese bishops issued a pastoral letter declaring it to be a mortal sin to vote for Strickland's party in the forthcoming election. The Foreign Office could not accept such Vatican-backed interference in the electoral process and the permanent under-secretary Sir Robert Vansittart declared the pope to be a 'full-blown idiot'.[25] The Maltese constitution was suspended, leaving Strickland in office. At that point the British minister to the Holy See, Henry Chilton, went on leave, acquired another posting and was not replaced. There matters remained until Strickland admitted defeat in March 1932 and asked both the pope and the archbishop-bishop for their blessings. He lost that year's election. Education remained at the heart of the British mission's extensive Maltese business with the Holy See, though it was 1934 before a new minister was appointed.

One issue that ceased to be of pressing concern in Anglo-papal relations was Ireland. The Irish Free State came into being in December 1922, the new political map bearing no relation to the ecclesiastical one: the diocese and the wider province of Armagh straddled the border between the new republic and British Ulster. The new state acquired a separate relationship with the Holy See, beginning with the apostolic delegation of Mgr Salvatore Luzio in the civil war context of 1923, though it was not until 1929/30 that full diplomatic relations were established. North of the new border, the reigning pontiff was regarded as nothing less than the devil incarnate among Ulster's Protestant majority, but it was a seventeenth-century pope who ignited a very particular outbreak of sectarian violence in 1933. On the strength of a claim that it depicted William III landing at Carrickfergus in 1690, the government of Northern Ireland purchased a painting attributed to the Dutch artist Pieter van der Meulen and hung it in their parliament buildings at Stormont. They bought more than they bargained for, because the enterprise in the lower portion of the canvas is blessed from on high by a distinctly papal figure towards the upper left-hand corner. This would indeed reflect political reality up to 1689, when William shared a common cause with Innocent XI, but not that of 1690. Whatever its subject matter and message, the work had been on display for a matter of weeks when it was attacked by Protestant extremists, who slashed the canvas and hurled paint at the pope. The authorities understood that message and it was not displayed again for some decades.

Britain's Anglicanism, its Presbyterianism, and the more distant reaches of its ecclesiastical spectrum were unfortunate, perhaps, but could be conveniently overlooked when the Church was encountering hostility in other quarters of the globe. Britain's moderation and restraint – expressed in 1926 in another Roman Catholic Relief Act – contrasted with the persecution of Catholics in Mexico and the systematic anticlericalism of Republican Spain. Nazi Germany proved to be a false friend, breaking the terms of its 1933 concordat and adding anti-Catholic initiatives to its racial and neo-pagan ones. Above all, in the Vatican's eyes, bland Britain was not Bolshevik Russia. Even its Socialists were Christian. On the other hand, Britain had no corresponding need of the pope. At the time of the Lateran pacts, the Maltese crisis and the conflict in Abyssinia in the mid 1930s Pius was perceived by the Foreign Office as being too close to Italy's Fascist government. Opinion began to change when his anti-Nazi encyclical *Mit brennender Sorge* was smuggled into Germany in 1937 and again when he pointedly stayed at Castel Gandolfo during Hitler's visit to Rome in 1938.[26] Symbolic gestures were one thing, but what practical steps could be taken to strengthen the Anglo-papal relationship as the European powers lurched towards another war? There was still no papal envoy at the Court of St James, so in 1938 the Vatican tested the water by sending Mgr Godfrey as apostolic visitor to the Catholic seminaries and colleges of England, Scotland and Malta. By the end of the year Godfrey had been raised to the newly created post of apostolic delegate to Great Britain. According to papal convention, Godfrey should not have been sent to his home country, suggesting that this odd appointment was designed to make the papacy appear less foreign and therefore less suspect. As if to emphasise the point, his residence on the edge of Wimbledon Common had a suburban anonymity about it. However much this development potentially improved relations between Britain and the Vatican at a sensitive juncture, it created confusion within the Church, because Cardinal Hinsley was used to being the principal conduit for Anglo-papal communications and suddenly there was doubt over the precise division of responsibilities between himself and Godfrey, who did not enjoy the familiar, if unwelcome, status of a nuncio.

In his last contact with the British elite he had done so much to cultivate, Pius met the prime minister, Neville Chamberlain, and foreign secretary, Lord Halifax, in January 1939. He was decidedly unimpressed: if they were the best that Britain could offer to tame Hitler's aggression then the prospects for peace looked grim. The eighty-one-year-old Pius lacked the strength needed for the looming fight and died on 10 February. He had determined that three weeks would elapse between his death and the opening of the conclave. This meant that all sixty-two electors had ample time to travel to Rome, though it also ensured that the secular powers had a sizeable window of opportunity in which to try to influence the election. The French were at the forefront of attempts to secure victory for the secretary of state, Cardinal Pacelli, in the hope that he would continue the Vatican's anti-Nazi rhetoric. The British took a supporting role, which boiled down to their minister D'Arcy Osborne having lunch with Hinsley and concluding that he was likely to vote for Pacelli.[27] In the event, such was the dearth of eligible talent that it took only three ballots for Pacelli to secure two-thirds of the votes. The new pope, Pius XII (1939–58), was a much-travelled diplomat whose brief visits to Britain up to and including the coronation of 1911 did not loom exceptionally large in his *curriculum vitae* or inspire anything like the profound affection for Germany that he acquired during his nine years as nuncio in Munich and Berlin.

Pius XII's German experience was neatly balanced by that of his secretary of state, Luigi Maglione, a sometime nuncio in Paris. On paper they were ideally placed to facilitate talks between France, Germany and neighbouring states. In practice, Britain rejected the pope's invitation to sit round an inclusively large table, suggesting that he concentrate on getting Germans and Poles, French and Italians to settle their differences in separate negotiations. This came to nothing. Germany invaded Poland on 1 September and various declarations of war were triggered. Inadequately prepared, Italy was a 'non-belligerent'. The pope was scrupulously neutral, because the Lateran treaty prevented him from commenting on Italian government policy, and if that policy was to wage war, then he was obliged to remain silent. Consequently, British opinion picked up where it had left off in the Great War, the Foreign

Office regarding Pius's response to the German invasion of neutral Holland, Belgium and Luxembourg as unhelpfully lukewarm.

Belying his reputation for indecision, in December 1939 Pius produced his Five Peace Points far more swiftly than Benedict XV had issued his Peace Note, but to as little effect. In Britain Hinsley did what he could to publicise the Peace Points as the basis for postwar international cooperation. At the same time, though, he was careful to avoid pacifistic irrelevance by reviving Cardinal Bourne's role of wartime patriot and putting his ideas into concrete form. The result was the Sword of the Spirit, launched on 1 August 1940, presumably with covert government assistance.[28] This movement was not exclusively Catholic, which put Hinsley at odds with his fellow bishops, but tellingly he received no reprimand from Rome. His contribution was evidently appreciated as much in the Vatican as it was in London and his death in March 1943 was felt as acutely in one as in the other.

It was in the winter of 1939–40 that the relationship between Britain and the Holy See took the earliest of its peculiar wartime twists. A necessarily shadowy group of German army officers sought to communicate with Britain by means of Germans in the Vatican, possibly Fr Robert Leiber, the pope's private secretary, or Mgr Ludwig Kaas, the negotiator of the 1933 Reichskonkordat between Nazi Germany and the Holy See. Either way, the line led to D'Arcy Osborne. Their offer was to remove Hitler in exchange for certain territorial conditions. Osborne played things cautiously, wary of falling into a Nazi trap, and events moved on.

By May 1940 Italy was poised to enter the war. Finding themselves in what was about to become enemy territory, the students of the English and Scots colleges were evacuated, with their rectors – Macmillan and Clapperton – following at the end of the month. The Beda and its rector, Mgr Duchemin, had already found refuge at Upholland, Lancashire, in 1939. On 10, June Italy declared war on France and Britain; the British ambassador to the Quirinale, Sir Percy Loraine, left Rome the following day. As Britain was not at war with the Holy See there was no need to withdraw D'Arcy Osborne. Indeed, there was every reason to retain him in the heart of an enemy capital. In theory Osborne should have been safe in Rome, but on 13 June he moved into the Vatican, accompanied by his secretary, butler and pet dog. The French, Polish and Belgian ambassadors to the Holy See made the same move. Initially, their accommodation was extremely spartan, though they were later settled into an annexe to the convent of S. Marta, just inside the Vatican's boundary wall. When the Belgians left, the British occupied the entire top floor of the building. Other ambassadors came and went, but Osborne remained in the Vatican throughout the war, apart from two months in 1943, when he went to London for instructions and returned with a knighthood. He was therefore just as much a prisoner as the pope, who also chose to retreat from the wider city. To claustrophobia was added paranoia, for the Vatican was known to be a 'nest of spies' and the incarcerated diplomats were sitting targets whose servants could be bribed and whose visitors were strictly monitored. Osborne's diplomatic bag went to London via Lisbon or Berne, but was opened by the enemy as a matter of course, making it extremely difficult for him to frame genuinely useful dispatches. Not until August 1943 was he able to use a secure cipher.

One of the British minister's daily responsibilities was to provide the pope with a digest of news broadcast by the BBC. Osborne listened disconsolately as France fell, as Buckingham Palace was bombed, and as Coventry burned, and longed to hear words of condemnation from the pope, but none were uttered. On the other hand, Pius pleaded with him to use his supposed influence in London to dissuade the Allies from bombing Rome. It made no difference. Strategic targets in and around the city were bombed on a number of occasions and, on 5 November 1943, British bombs fell within the walls of Vatican itself. This exceptional incident was probably an accidental violation of the Holy See's neutrality, though it was not beyond the realms of possibility that someone wanted to make a deliberately antipapal gesture on the anniversary of the Gunpowder Plot. By that stage Italy was out of the war and the Germans had assumed control of Rome. This was the period in which Allied prisoners of war, most of them British, were released from Italian camps and left to fend for themselves. Thousands made for Rome, where they were assisted by a necessarily secretive network headed by the Irish curialist Mgr Hugh O'Flaherty. Osborne's butler, the resourceful John May, was a key member of this group, while the minister himself discreetly arranged financial support for his compatriots.

Allied forces entered Rome in June 1944; three months later Britain's prime minister and foreign secretary visited the city. Following the recent death of Cardinal Maglione, Pius was acting as his own secretary of state, so while Winston Churchill had his papal audience Anthony Eden passed the time at a cinema. This may have been dictated by protocol, but it inadvertently shed light on the emerging global order: as in the 1910s, the major powers had no intention of allowing the pope any role in shaping the postwar world. The new international 'listening post' was the United Nations, to which the Holy See did not gain 'permanent observer' status until 1964, let alone membership. Rome and the Vatican could be safely relegated to the realm of the ornamental: Britain's Princesses Margaret and Elizabeth paid private visits to the pope in 1949 and 1951 respectively.[29] In 1952 King George VI's death was marked in Rome in the same manner as his father's had been: Mgr William Heard celebrated a requiem mass for him at the church of S. Silvestro, two cardinals attending discreetly behind a screen.[30] Similarly, a seasoned diplomat and future cardinal, Archbishop Fernando Cento, was sent as the extraordinary papal envoy to Elizabeth's coronation in 1953. Still there was still no question of him being robed and in the sanctuary.

The Vatican had never been among the Foreign Office's top priorities, and steadily became a diplomatic backwater during the remainder of Pius XII's pontificate. D'Arcy Osborne found it difficult to adapt to postwar conditions, retired from the diplomatic service in 1947, and spent the remainder of his life in Rome, the final months of it as the twelfth duke of Leeds. The legation was retained and another four ministers presented their credentials to Papa Pacelli: Sir Victor Perowne (1947–51), Sir Walter Roberts (1951–4), Sir Douglas Howard (1954–7) and Sir Marcus Cheke (1957–60). According to their successor Mark Pellew, the only reason they remained ministers, instead of being upgraded to ambassadors, was inertia in London.[31] Then again, there was precious little business for them to undertake, whatever their status. Britain's rapid withdrawal from its global responsibilities seriously diminished its utility in the pope's eyes and nowhere more so than in Palestine, where Pius regretted the end of the British mandate and the creation of the state of Israel. At the same time, the Vatican's new preoccupation was with the 'Iron Curtain countries', where Britain could do nothing for Catholics living under communist rule. In his annual report for 1948, therefore, Perowne could only conclude that Anglo-Vatican relations were 'friendly but uneventful'.[32] By 1955–6 Howard had even less to report, so provided a list of the heads of foreign missions with comments about the pastimes of the ambassadors and the social attributes of their wives.[33] The pontificate ended quietly, with Marcus Cheke and the pope sharing a mutual interest in beekeeping.[34] On the other side of the diplomatic coin, Godfrey remained as apostolic delegate until 1954, at which point an American, Gerald O'Hara, moved from the nunciature in Dublin to succeed him. Still the Vatican was playing it cautiously, O'Hara representing a compromise between the native-born Godfrey and the more obviously 'foreign' majority of Vatican diplomats, who were still predominantly Italian.

One means by which Pius maintained his wartime impartiality was to create no cardinals until 1946. When he did so, it was with the clear intention of internationalising the Sacred College. Among the beneficiaries were Bernard Griffin and John Francis D'Alton, archbishops of Westminster and Armagh respectively.[35] It fell to Cardinal Griffin to act as papal legate at celebrations to mark the centenary of the restoration of the hierarchy in England and Wales in 1950, and to lead British representation at the canonisation of Pius X in 1954. Most insular dioceses, particularly those in England, carved out new parishes to serve the steadily expanding suburbs, and Pius X was an obvious dedication for their relatively modest, quickly constructed churches. From Dundee to Bristol, Barrow to Grimsby, St Pius X became a feature of the suburban landscape. Paradoxically, Pius XII was a more remote figure, plagued by the consequences of medical quackery, which only added to his mystique among the faithful. For new Elizabethans of a less pious stamp there was an alternative and somewhat improbable papal icon. From 1949 onwards the British painter Francis Bacon exhibited a sequence of screaming popes, inspired by the Velázquez portrait of Innocent X in the Palazzo Doria Pamphilj. It was an example of *aggiornamento*, of bringing a pope 'up to date', and in that sense it effectively set an example for the next pontificate.

The conclave of October 1958 was the first in which cardinals from Australia, Chile, China, Colombia, Cuba, Ecuador, India, Mozambique and the Soviet Union cast ballots in a papal election. It was the Cold War conclave, two cardinals being unable to travel to Rome from beyond the Iron Curtain. One feature it lacked was a British dimension, because Cardinal Griffin died in 1956 and his archiepiscopal successor, the former apostolic delegate Godfrey, remained hatless because Pius XII made no more cardinals after 1953. The patriarch of Venice, Angelo Roncalli, was elected in the eleventh ballot and became Pope John XXIII (1958–63), the second pope of that name and regnal number to be recognised in England, after Baldassare Cossa in the fifteenth century. Pope John came with diplomatic experience in Bulgaria, Greece, Turkey and France, a sequence of postings that lay behind his policy of seeking constructive engagement with the powers of Eastern Europe, rather than the papacy's previous uncompromising confrontation with communism. Britain was peripheral to such a policy and its steady withdrawal from both colonial and mandated territories seriously diminished its significance to the Vatican in other spheres.

In the absence of empire a new agenda was required to sustain the Anglo-papal relationship. Ironically enough, it began to be shaped by an agreement to which neither party was a signatory. The Treaty of Rome (1957) brought the six-member European Economic Community into being from 1 January 1958. The Holy See could never qualify to join such a trading bloc, but successive popes nevertheless recognised its potential to unite the previously warring states of Europe and to do so by means of a shared Christian culture. Catholicism by the back door was precisely what Protestants in Britain and Denmark feared when their governments applied to join a group whose citizens happened to be predominantly Catholic. Prime Minister Harold Macmillan had no such scruple, likening the EEC to the Carolingian Empire, and devoted his premiership (1957–63) to negotiating Britain's admission. That entailed high-level visits to Rome, Italy being one of the six, which in turn obliged British dignitaries to pay their respects to the pope. Between 1959 and 1961 the guest list was particularly impressive: Princess Margaret returned to the Vatican, this time with her mother; Macmillan visited with his foreign secretary Alec Douglas-Home; Queen Elizabeth and the duke of Edinburgh also paid a return visit, this time of the state variety. The closest that 'good Pope John' came to reciprocating this level of interest and respect was his hospital visit to Marcus Cheke, before the British minister died of a heart condition in 1960.[36]

In the spirit of closer European cooperation, Macmillan's cabinet repeatedly discussed the possibility that the apostolic delegate in London might be upgraded to an internuncio, to match their minister to the Holy See. Some government ministers responded by proudly displaying their knowledge of the Congress of Vienna (1815), which stipulated that the nuncio to a particular state should enjoy precedence as doyen of the diplomatic corps, and managed to shelve the matter, though it also helped that the Catholic bishops did not want a nuncio of any rank breathing down their necks. Thus the diplomatic relationship remained imbalanced, however much both sides enthused about the new European order. In January 1963 Macmillan was again at the Vatican, this time accompanied by his EEC negotiator Edward Heath. He was, however, a broken man in need of whatever consolation the pope could offer, for French president Charles de Gaulle had just delivered his first veto of Britain's membership of the Community.

For a pope with little obvious interest in the British Isles, it is all the more remarkable that three of John's fifty-two new cardinals were from that region, a higher proportion than in any other twentieth-century pontificate. This trio – Archbishop Godfrey, Mgr Heard, who was dean of the Rota from 1958, and Michael Browne, the Irish master general of the Dominican Order – reflected the spirit of their respective hierarchies and that of the curia, for they were theologically conservative and intensely loyal to the Holy See, and were determined to retain anything and everything that distinguished Catholics from Protestants. It did not follow that they acted as some sort of faction: such was the personal antipathy between Godfrey and Heard that they insisted on taking separate cars to the same event. When, in January 1959, John announced a new ecumenical council, men of such a stamp could only understand it as a continuation of the centralising agenda of 1869–70, but what this visionary pope sought was nothing short of the complete renewal of the Church and entirely new ways of presenting eternal truths. The British bishops were conditioned to receive orders from Rome without expressing their own opinions, so were tardy in sending their proposals for the council's deliberations and made exceedingly modest suggestions when they finally got round to doing so.

Alongside the council's preparatory commissions, John established the Secretariat for Promoting Christian Unity as a response to the ecumenical initiatives from which Rome had hitherto held aloof on the grounds that Christian unity meant only one thing: submission to the Holy See. Geoffrey Fisher, the archbishop of Canterbury, regarded this as too good an opportunity to miss, so quickly tacked a visit to Rome onto his imminent tour of Jerusalem and Istanbul. With no cameras present to record their ground-breaking encounter, pope and primate spent sixty-seven minutes together on 2 December 1960. John's knowledge of non-Catholics was informed by his experience of living in Orthodox and Muslim societies, so Fisher gave him a quick lesson in the essentials of Anglicanism. The redoubtable archbishop retired a few months later, though one can sense his abiding impact on John in comments he made to Canon Bernard Pawley in June 1961: 'I'm very fond of Anglicans; you're friendly, you're sincere. I like the English character, its robustness.'[37] As preparations for the council advanced, more British non-Catholic churchmen followed in Fisher's wake: Archibald Craig, moderator of the Church of Scotland, Mervyn Stockwood, bishop of Southwark, and Arthur Morris, bishop of St Edmundsbury and Ipswich, all received papal audiences between March and May 1962.

When the much-anticipated council finally opened in October that year the British and Irish hierarchies were present in force, supported by secretaries and *periti* (theological experts), while non-Catholic 'observers' of various denominations watched proceedings from their tribune in St Peter's Basilica. Even had the pope's health not been weakening by that stage, the purpose of this vast exercise was to let the Church as a whole find its own way in the modern world, rather than allow itself to be dictated to by a papal monarch. That freedom involved debates between what began as a conservative majority, including the British and Irish bishops, and a progressive minority, who were inspired by Newman's *Essay on the Development of Christian Doctrine* (1845), which argued that human understanding of divine truth becomes fuller and clearer over time. Even by November the tide of conciliar opinion was beginning to turn against the conservatives. Cardinal Godfrey died two months later, so was not required to embrace the 'spirit of the council' or put its reforms in practice. His colleagues enjoyed no such escape and, with their accustomed loyalty to the Holy See, made the necessary transition with neither fuss nor enthusiasm.

Electors in the conclave that convened after John's death in June 1963 had two options: to vote for the late pope's preferred successor, Giovanni Battista Montini... or against him. Cardinal Heard had already identified Montini as 'the next pope' and, with only fractionally less conviction, D'Arcy Osborne had predicted that the archbishop of Milan would be the 'next Pope but one, or possibly next'.[38] Much was at stake. A vote for Montini was a vote for the council and a reforming agenda, with whatever consequences that might bring. A vote against him was designed to limit the perceived damage that had already been done to the Church. For the most part it is not known how individual cardinals voted, but neither Heard nor Browne were enthusiasts for the council, which suggests that, regardless of what seemed likely to happen, they could have favoured a conservative such as Giuseppe Siri of Genoa.[39] Montini's election was secured in the sixth ballot and a future British cardinal, Thomas Winning, was among the crowds in the piazza watching for the white smoke.

After Pius II in the fifteenth century, Paul VI (1963–78) was only the second pope to have visited Winning's native Scotland. Indeed, his personal experience of the British Isles was easily more extensive than that of any other Italian prelate of his generation. Taking time off from his official duties as a junior papal diplomat, Montini made an extensive tour of England, Scotland and Ireland in 1934, staying at monasteries such as Quarr, Downside and Fort Augustus. He listened to a debate in the House of Commons and felt conscious of the 'real absence' of Christ in museum-like Anglican cathedrals.[40] Throughout World War II he was the senior official in the Secretariat of State with whom the incarcerated diplomats had their most regular dealings, so much so that he was criticised for over-friendliness with the 'Anglo-Saxons'. Indeed, such was his friendship with D'Arcy Osborne that he would gladly have received the British minister into the Church. Among his fellow curialists Montini's reputation was that of a 'dangerous' radical, whose interests include the worker-priest movement in France and the un-Catholic ecumenical impulses that led to the creation of the World Council of Churches in 1948. Attempting to secure a piece by the novelist Graham Greene for the Vatican daily *L'Osservatore romano* did nothing to improve his reputation. As long as Pius XII remained in control Montini was safe, but when that pope's health faltered Montini's enemies – led by another anglophile, Cardinal Pizzardo – seized their chance. In the second half of 1954 the archbishopric of Milan was vacant and Montini was appointed to it. Like Giacomo della Chiesa in Bologna nearly half a century earlier, he was denied the red hat traditionally bestowed on the holder of this historically important see. Undeterred, ecumenically-minded Anglicans made their way to Milan, sensing that Montini could be the man to change official Roman attitudes towards 'separated brethren'. Through such contacts Montini acquired an understanding of Anglicanism without parallel in the Italian hierarchy. At the earliest opportunity Pope John reversed the injustice done to Montini, naming him first among his new cardinals in December 1958. A naturally shy man, he kept a low profile during the first session of the Second Vatican Council, though Cardinal Godfrey's secretary Derek Worlock identified him as an arch-reformer, the covert leader of the anti-curial progressives.[41]

The council's deliberations continued each autumn until 1965. Its very catholicity meant that little occurred which could be identified as unique to the history of Anglo-papal relations. Even when Paul urged the departing bishops of England, Ireland, Scotland and Wales to send priests to the African portion of the 'Third World', it did not represent a departure from the missionary past. Similarly, although some of the official Anglican, Presbyterian, Methodist and Congrega-tional observers at the council happened to be British, they represented their denominations, not their home states, just as Archbishop Michael Ramsey represented the entire Anglican Communion, rather than the Church of England, when he visited Pope Paul in March 1966.[42] On that occasion the emerging Ulster Unionist Ian Paisley nevertheless denounced Ramsey as a 'traitor to Protestant Britain'.[43] The emotional intensity of the archbishop's visit, symbolised in Paul's gift to Ramsey of his Milanese episcopal ring, was not rekindled when the next archbishop of Canterbury, the evangelical Donald Coggan, paid his visit to the ailing pontiff in April 1977. There was no personal chemistry between them. In the meantime, though, an Anglican Centre had been established in Rome and the Anglican–Roman Catholic International Commission (ARCIC) was founded to discuss how ecumenical understanding might be furthered between the two traditions. The nature of authority – not least papal authority – in the Church came within the remit of ARCIC's deliberations. Three agreed statements on this subject were issued between 1976 and 1998.[44] Again, though, there was nothing exclusively British about these developments.

In spite of Paul's genuine commitment to ecumenism, British Catholics were conditioned to pray for the conversion of their fellow countrymen, rather than to pray with them on parallel spiritual paths. They were natural ultramontanes who wanted what Rome alone could provide: a pilgrimage destination, papal leadership, instead of episcopal collegiality, and saints who had suffered martyrdom rather than to compromise their faith or their loyalty to the pope. In comparison with Catholics in other nations, they did not ask for much, and Paul was able to oblige. Early in the pontificate he opened the new edge-of-town Scots College on the Via Cassia. In 1969 hundreds of Scots celebrated in Rome when Gordon Gray, archbishop of St Andrews and Edinburgh, became the first Scottish cardinal since the sixteenth century. These developments met the desire for papal leadership. As for saints, Oliver Plunkett, John Ogilvie and the various English and Welsh martyrs of the Reformation era had all been recognised as 'blessed' but, apart from More and Fisher, had yet to be elevated to sainthood. The forty English and Welsh martyrs – including Philip Howard – were canonised first, on 25 October 1970, with an estimated 10,000 pilgrims in attendance. The official British position on the martyrs was unchanged from what it had been with regard to More and Fisher in 1935, and Archbishop Ramsey assumed his patriotic duty as head of the religious arm of the State arguing that the canonisation risked opening up old wounds. It would be better, he suggested, for the pope to seek reconciliation by rescinding Pius V's 400-year-old excommunication of Elizabeth I.[45] Paul responded to this as best he could in the circumstances, referring to the Anglican Church as an 'ever-beloved sister' in his homily to the pilgrims. The canonisations of Plunkett and Ogilvie followed in 1975 and 1976 respectively, making these forty-two British and Irish saints a clear majority among the total of seventy-two created in the course of Paul's pontificate. Thus did the pope who had toured the island nations four decades earlier make his clearest contribution to the dedications and corporate lives of Catholic churches and schools. In the final months of his life, Paul obliged the Scottish faithful one last time, by declaring 'venerable' the Edinburgh-born Poor Clare Margaret Sinclair (d. 1925).

In the 1930s those same actions would have signalled the strength and vitality of the Catholic Church in potentially hostile territory. By the 1970s they were traditional measures taken to reassure a community that had not requested the liturgical, administrative and pastoral changes ushered in by Vatican II, but had been required to absorb them all the same. To the cultural confusion created by the council was added widespread surprise and disappointment in 1968, when Paul broke with his 'radical' past by rejecting expert advice on responsible family planning in order to uphold the Church's traditional teaching on birth control in the encyclical *Humanae vitae*. British Catholics responded in two ways that were already familiar in continental Europe. Starting with Charles Davis, clerical intellectuals denounced Rome and, in the case of Davis on the subject of birth control, accused the pope of lying. The Church lost some of its most talented priests. At the same time, the laity took to voting with their feet: mass attendance and Catholic baptisms both began a steady decline. Was this really the dialogue with the modern world that the reformers had intended?

Although the trials of being a Catholic in the era of Paul VI have become intimately associated with David Lodge's novel *How far can you go?* (1980), it was specifically papal fiction that loomed large during the 1970s, and that after a lean period for anything other than Borgia-related novels. Easiest to dismiss are the comic fantasies of Bruce Marshall and Robert Rankin. At the opposite extreme, Kingsley Amis and Anthony Burgess both opted to rewrite papal history, four centuries of it in the case of Amis's *The Alteration* (1976), which concludes with the pontificate of John XXIV, a plain-speaking Yorkshireman inspired by Harold Wilson. Burgess's epic *Earthly Powers* (1980) substitutes the conclave that elected John XXIII in 1958 with one that elects the entirely fictional Gregory XVII. Less ambitious but nonetheless delightful is Robert Player's historically-sensitive *Let's Talk of Graves, of Worms, and Epitaphs* (1975), which sees a Manning-inspired Anglican archdeacon enthusiastically welcomed to Rome by Pius IX, but consigned to a career in Catholic education once the pope learns that he is a married man. With suspicious convenience, his wife dies just days later, freeing the less-than-heartbroken widower for the Roman priesthood, the cardinalate and election to the papacy, as Pope Paschal IV.

Papal fiction was at least a reasonably familiar genre, but popes in films were more experimental and in keeping with the spirit of the age. Pius XII pioneered film as a means of communicating with the faithful. *Pastor Angelicus* (1942) combined archive footage of his travels before 1939 with new material recording the strict formalities of his papal routine. His lean frame and air of superiority suited the medium perfectly, though Britain's wartime prisoner in the Vatican, D'Arcy Osborne, was irritated to find that filming in the gardens disrupted one of his much-needed walks. In the international film productions of Paul VI's pontificate British actors were cast as popes in historical dramas.

In *The Agony and the Ecstasy* (1965), Rex Harrison's Julius II wields a sword for the glory of the faith, and Alec Guinness's Innocent III, enthroned in the cathedral of Monreale, exudes gravitas in the otherwise lightweight *Brother Sun, Sister Moon* (1972). Guinness could draw on the experience of a real papal audience, at Castel Gandolfo in 1958, though what he encountered there was the all-too-human reality of Pius XII afflicted by hiccups. By the 1960s film and television made it easy to distinguish fat popes from thin popes and anything in between. Popes could also be distinguished by their actions or inactions, and what came to set the late Pius XII apart was his record of 'silence' on the fate of the Jews under Nazi rule. German playwright Rolf Hochhuth's controversial work on the subject, translated as *The Representative* and produced by the Royal Shakespeare Company in January 1963, remains the most intensely critical treatment of any pope seen on a British stage. On balance, British audiences preferred their popes to be mildly entertaining, whether it was Alec McCowen chain-smoking his way through Peter Luke's 1968 dramatisation of Rolfe's *Hadrian VII*, or Irish comedian Dave Allen doing a papal striptease on BBC television in 1975.

Books and films filled something of a void for, with the exception of mounting concern over sectarian violence in Northern Ireland, this was a relatively quiet period in terms of Anglo-Vatican diplomacy. Nothing was as dramatic as changes to the cast of leading characters in 1963–4: after a lengthy interregnum John Carmel Heenan became the eighth archbishop of Westminster, Igino Eugenio Cardinale arrived in Wimbledon as the first non-anglophone apostolic delegate, and Harold Wilson moved into Downing Street. As preparations advanced for Wilson's visit to the Vatican in April 1965, the question of Britain's imbalanced diplomatic relationship with the Holy See reappeared on the cabinet table. The familiar arguments about the delegate's status were rehearsed, accompanied by new ones about the British minister as the only surviving head of mission who was not styled 'ambassador'. No action was taken and the diplomatic relationship remained unchanged when Edward Heath paid his second visit to the Vatican, in October 1972, this time as prime minister. Wilson had kept Britain's EEC application on the table after de Gaulle's second veto and, with Heath at the helm, Britain finally joined the Community in 1973. Protestant suspicions about 'Europe' and Catholicism could at least by allayed by the timely replacement of an Italian apostolic delegate with one from non-EEC Switzerland. This was Archbishop Bruno Heim, who remained in post for the next twelve years. The intervention that Heim regarded as his greatest achievement came early in his posting. During the winter of 1975–6 Cardinal Heenan died and Archbishop Beck of Liverpool resigned. On paper – and in his own mind – the Londoner Worlock was the obvious choice for Westminster, with Liverpool appropriate for a northerner. Heim engineered the very opposite: Dom Basil Hume, the well-connected abbot of Ampleforth in Yorkshire, went to Westminster, while Worlock was translated from Portsmouth to Liverpool.

Pope Paul's reforms meant that Gray and Hume had an austere conclave experience in August 1978, but what it lacked in conclavists, octogenarian cardinals and colour-coded canopies over the electors' chairs it made up for in a battle for the reforming legacy of the previous two pontiffs. In a maximum of four ballots a compromise candidate was found in Albino Luciani, the genial patriarch of Venice. During the thirty-three days of his brief pontificate, John Paul I proved himself to be a true heir of the last two popes, dispensing with a coronation in favour of a simpler inauguration. What remained unclear was how he intended to appease the conservatives who still looked to Cardinal Siri for leadership. Seven weeks after the August conclave Gray, Hume and more than 100 other electors went through the same process once more.[46] In Karol Wojtyła they chose a pope who paid lip service to the reforming tradition of his predecessors but who proved to be one of the most authoritarian, centralising popes of the twentieth century. Paul VI's vacillation gave way to John Paul II's decisiveness, the sociology of Vatican II to Christocentric personalism, and cautious Ostpolitik to an overt determination to break the power of communism in Soviet-dominated Eastern Europe, all of it underpinned by the greatest personality cult in papal history. However much 'liberal' clerics quietly resented his policies, the Polish pope was an inspiration for conservative politicians such as Britain's Margaret Thatcher and Ronald Reagan of the United States, who came to power in 1979 and 1980 respectively. A pope who opposed communism in Europe and liberation theology in Latin America, a pope who could attract crowds such as that estimated at more than a million in Dublin's Phoenix Park in September 1979, was the pope for them. In Thatcher's case there was a curious longer-term attraction to the papacy: her visit to John Paul II in 1980 followed one to Paul VI in 1977, when she was leader of the opposition, and was succeeded by a less formal encounter with Benedict XVI in 2009. For a Methodist who had turned Anglican and for the leader of a political party that traced its origins to the anti-Catholic exclusion crisis and Williamite revolution of the 1680s, she was suspiciously keen to be granted a papal audience and cover her head in black lace. The combination of conservative religious principles and elective monarchy was evidently irresistible.

Within the Church, British responses to the new pontificate were suitably restrained but none the less earnest. In 1980 the Friends of the Holy Father was founded as a fund-raising body in indirect succession to the Society for the Maintenance of the Apostolic See. The same year saw 2,000 English and Welsh Catholics meet in Liverpool for a National Pastoral Congress co-ordinated by Archbishop Worlock. Just as Worlock was a relatively late convert to the reforms of Vatican II, so the congress confirmed that, fifteen years after the council closed, at least a portion of the British laity had finally been infused with its spirit. Among other things, they requested full corporate membership of the British Council of Churches and criticised Rome's policy regarding divorced and remarried Catholics. In Heim's absence, the *chargé d'affaires* Mgr Mario Oliveri confirmed Rome's disquiet about the entire exercise by sending a critical report on its proceedings. Those who participated in the congress were certainly out of step with the new culture in the Vatican, so Hume and Worlock deftly countered the critics by presenting their report on the congress alongside an invitation to the pope to visit England and Wales. They gambled that a successful visit would prove the Catholic population's underlying loyalty to Rome. In their haste, they omitted to mention the scheme to their counterparts in Scotland. Once Scotland was safely included in the programme, plans for the first visit to Britain by a reigning pope then proceeded quietly throughout 1981. Widespread interest did not develop until March 1982, when antipapal protestors in Liverpool disrupted an address by the archbishop of Canterbury, Robert Runcie, and Pastor Jack Glass stood in the Glasgow Hillhead by-election as a candidate for the Protestant Crusade Against the Papal Visit.

Away from the glare of publicity, preparations included the normalisation of diplomatic relations. Sir Mark Heath's status was raised to that of British ambassador to the Holy See, and Heim became the first pro-nuncio to the Court of St James, where there was no amendment to the tradition that the longest-serving ambassador served as doyen of the diplomatic corps. In neither case did it make any practical difference to the work they undertook. Heath presented his credentials to Pope John Paul on 1 April. The following day Argentine forces invaded the South Atlantic islands known as the Falklands or Malvinas and plans for the impending papal visit were suddenly complicated by Britain's military campaign to regain control over them. As the two world wars had amply demonstrated, popes had to be extremely careful not to favour one belligerent over another. In this case, favouring largely Protestant Britain over Catholic Argentina would have added insult to injury.

Easter Sunday fell on 11 April and Archbishop Runcie's representative, Terry Waite, paid a brief visit to Rome to co-ordinate the Easter messages to be delivered by the pope and the archbishop. On the diplomatic level, papal mediation was considered from the outset and Heath's office on Rome's Via Condotti was suddenly a hive of activity.[47] With Heim once again on leave, Oliveri certainly regarded Vatican mediation as a viable option.[48] In mid April attention turned to proposals issued by the American secretary of state, which the pope supported by means of a communication to President Reagan.[49] However, nothing came of this. Prayers for peace were equally unproductive, with naval engagements beginning in early May. On 11 May Hume returned from Rome and speculated that the papal visit might have to be cancelled unless there was a ceasefire, though the Foreign and Commonwealth Office (FCO) considered that he had 'over-dramatised' the situation.[50] Asserting themselves as Hume could not, the archbishops of Glasgow and Liverpool, Winning and Worlock, took matters into their own hands by launching a two-man rescue mission to Rome on 17 May. Francis Pym, the foreign secretary, was aware of their travel arrangements and insisted that Heath beat them to the Vatican and propose that the political dimension of the papal visit, including a meeting between the pope and the prime minister, be abandoned as the price of salvaging the greater whole, which was due to begin only eleven days later.[51] Both initiatives bore fruit. That of Winning and Worlock led to their cardinals, Gray and Hume, returning to Rome at short notice for a mass with the pope and the Argentine cardinals on 21 May and to equally hasty arrangements for a balance-redressing papal visit to Argentina. Pope and premier exchanged written communications, so the lack of a face-to-face meeting made no practical difference.

On 28 May John Paul II finally landed at Gatwick airport and began a six-day 'pastoral' visit designed to avoid anything that could be construed as political favouritism towards a warring state. The English and Welsh portion of the programme was based around the seven sacraments: baptism at Westminster Cathedral and renewal of baptismal promises at Wembley Stadium, confirmation at Coventry airport, first communion in Cardiff, penance and reconciliation in Liverpool, anointing of the sick at Southwark Cathedral, ordination in Manchester, and marriage at York. Not to be outdone, Scottish Catholics – presumably joined by others from Northern Ireland – turned out in vast numbers for the papal mass in Glasgow's Bellahouston Park on 1 June. There was extensive television coverage of all the set-piece events, though the wider public was probably most struck by the ecumenical highlights, particularly the pontiff's reception at Canterbury Cathedral, where he and Runcie prayed at the site of Becket's martyrdom, and his meeting with the moderator of the Church of Scotland, beneath the General Assembly's statue of John Knox. In spite of the pastoral emphasis, a visit to Buckingham Palace was retained. It was therefore the secretary of state, Cardinal Agostino Casaroli, who called on the prime minister. While British and Argentine forces battled for control of Goose Green, he received the full Thatcherite exposition of Britain's need to defend the 'God-fearing people' of the Falklands.[52] Elsewhere in London, for anyone seeking an even more complete papal experience, there was a production of Papa Wojtyła's dramatic 'meditation', *The Jeweller's Shop*. With some financial exceptions, the visit was an all-round success and, from an anglocentric perspective, has been described as the 'most significant diplomatic event of the 1980s'.[53] The hierarchies proved to their illustrious guest that they had forged a distinctively insular brand of Catholicism, implicitly loyal to Rome but shorn of previous ultramontane excesses.

Little more than a fortnight after the pope's return to Rome and less than a week after his hastily arranged visit to Argentina, the Milan-based Banco Ambrosiano collapsed and the body of its chairman, Roberto Calvi, was discovered hanging beneath Blackfriars Bridge in central London. The Institute for Religious Works – popularly known as the Vatican Bank – had been the bank's principal investor. As if that were not enough, Calvi was also a member of the darkly influential P2 Masonic lodge. From that point onwards the Vatican came to be regarded as a byword for corruption and this sinister shift was seen nowhere more starkly than in David Yallop's theory that John Paul I was murdered.[54] This notion was dismissed by another British author, John Cornwell, who had his own axe to grind, arguing that Pius XII's silence about the Holocaust was enough to prevent his proposed canonisation.[55] With the reality of recent papal history making such headlines, it is perhaps little wonder that papal fiction appeared to have lost its previous sparkle, for in Graham Greene's short story 'The Last Word' (1988) the very survival of Christianity hinges on the figure of the frail, deposed John XXIX. Only on screen did British 'popes' continue to entertain, perhaps unintentionally in the case of John Gielgud's portrayal of Pius XII in *The Scarlet and the Black* (1983), a film in which D'Arcy Osborne is even more lightly sketched. The satirical television puppet show *Spitting Image* (1984–96) played it safe by emphasising John Paul II as a global icon, but in 1988 the press got wind of plans for a comedy drama called *Pope Dave*. Britain was still enough of a Christian country for these to be scrapped on grounds of poor taste, though they nevertheless mutated into a feature film, *The Pope must Die* (1991), with a plot dependent on popular notions of corruption in the curia.

Back in the real world, Anglo-papal diplomatic relations had settled down nicely: Heim retired in 1985, returning occasionally with chocolates for the queen mother from his native Switzerland, and was succeeded by Archbishop Luigi Barbarito, while David Lane became Britain's new ambassador to the Holy See. After the excitement of the Falklands episode, the business with which they dealt could only seem straightforward. Attention shifted from politics to religion, for British Christianity in the 1980s was remarkably vibrant and Catholicism was positively fashionable, even if a string of high-profile conversions owed more to the quiet charisma of Basil Hume than they did to the megastar in the Vatican. Those Anglicans who did not convert tested the boundaries of what was possible: how far could they proceed along the path to Rome without going through the required formalities? Buckingham Palace vetoed plans for the prince and princess of Wales to attend the pope's private mass during their visit to the Vatican in 1985, but when eighty-five more English and Welsh martyrs of the Reformation period were beatified in 1987 at least one Anglican church hosted a celebration of the event. In 1989 it was a *festa* for Anglicans and Catholics alike when Archbishop Runcie visited Rome in his capacity as head of the Anglican Communion: Ian Paisley's antipapal protests merely added to the general excitement of the occasion. For its part, Rome regarded the Church of England as the heart and soul of the Anglican

Communion and as long as Runcie resisted calls for women to be ordained as priests – as had already happened in some Anglican provinces – members of ARCIC II dared to hope that Roman recognition of Anglican orders might be just around the corner.

Collective fervour is difficult to maintain and the 1990s proved to be a relatively quiet decade for the Anglo-papal relationship. In 1991 Newman was declared venerable – the stepping stone to beatification – and in 1992 seventeen Irish martyrs of the sixteenth and seventeenth centuries were beatified, as was the Scottish-born philosopher Duns Scotus the following year. The ordination of women priests in the Church of England from 1994 onwards and the election of women bishops in other Anglican provinces dashed any dreams of Rome recognising Anglican orders, let alone fantasies of corporate reunion. Archbishop Barbarito, a full nuncio for the last four years of his posting, remained at Wimbledon until 1997, when he was succeeded by Pablo Puente Buces, while a succession of British diplomats completed their careers with a relatively undemanding and thoroughly enjoyable Vatican posting.[56] The British government's complete lack of interest in the Holy See can be measured by the fact that John Major did not pay a single visit to the Vatican during the six-and-a-half years of his premiership. Once again it fell to a fictional pope to fill the void: *Hadrian VII* was revived at Chichester in 1995, with Derek Jacobi in the title role.

Pope John Paul was clearly ailing well before the diagnosis of Parkinson's disease was announced in 2001. There was leaderless drift in the curia. Canonisations and beatifications continued apace, but any British connections were decidedly tenuous: Bl. Columba Marmion was born in Ireland in 1858 and Bl. Cyprian Iwene Tansi died in Leicester in 1964.[57] Pilgrims turned out in healthy numbers for the holy year in 2000, during which Queen Elizabeth paid her fourth visit to the Vatican and the duke of Edinburgh his fifth. Even the Anglican–Roman Catholic courtship trundled wearily on, in the form of an exhibition about Anglicanism held in the Vatican's Sala Sistina in 2002.[58]

While the pontiff grew weaker, in 1997 a dynamic new element entered the Anglo-papal relationship: a British government dominated by committed Christians who sought to put faith into action both nationally and globally. That was what the Church did anyway, in the fields of education, conflict prevention and resolution, and international development. Indeed, the Vatican had been exercising such 'soft power' long before any secular politician employed the term in a sound bite. It took a while for the orbits of the Vatican and Britain's Labour government to become aligned, but it helped that prime minister Tony Blair was only nominally Anglican by that stage. In 2003 he paid his first official visit to the Vatican, during which he attended John Paul's early morning mass and was said to have received communion from the pope. Next, in July 2004, Hume's successor at Westminster, Cormac Murphy-O'Connor, took the initiative by inviting the chancellor of the exchequer, Gordon Brown, to address a Vatican seminar on the funding of Third World development in a globalised economy. This provided a platform for Brown to introduce the International Finance Facility, a scheme designed to support development projects by raising money in the financial markets. Without such an intervention states appeared unlikely to meet the Millennium Development Goals set by the United Nations. Towards the end of that year Brown returned to the theme of ending global poverty when he delivered the Catholic Agency for Overseas Development (CAFOD) annual lecture in memory of Pope Paul VI.[59] Thereafter Britain used its presidencies of the European Union and the G8 group of leading industrialised powers to 'make poverty history' by means of fair trade, financing development and cancelling Third World debt. At last post-imperial Britain had discovered an agenda that it could share unreservedly with the Holy See, one which enjoyed widespread support among Catholics and non-Catholics alike.

When 'John Paul the Great' died in April 2005 the Establishment of a previously antipapal nation could hardly have turned out in greater force. While flags flew at half mast across what had been a denominational divide, the prince of Wales and the British political elite attended vespers at Westminster Cathedral. Between 1939 and 1978 the sixteenth and seventeenth dukes of Norfolk had invariably represented British monarchs at papal funerals, coronations and inaugurations. This time the prince, the archbishop of Canterbury, the prime minister and the leaders of other political parties all flew to Rome for the funeral. Most remarkably, the prince's marriage ceremonies were postponed by twenty-four hours: the pope took priority over everyone and everything else. Sixteen days later this level of interest was maintained when the duke of Edinburgh represented the queen at the next pope's inaugural mass.

Three of the six British and Irish cardinals created by John Paul II – Tomás Ó Fiaich and Cahal Daly of Armagh and Thomas Winning of Glasgow – never had the opportunity to vote in a conclave. The survivors were Murphy-O'Connor, Desmond Connell of Dublin, and Keith O'Brien, who succeeded Cardinal Gray as archbishop of St Andrews and Edinburgh, none of whom was *papabile* in the conclave of 18–19 April 2005. All but two of the electors on that occasion had been promoted by John Paul and, rather than create a break with the recent past, they rapidly elected Joseph Ratzinger, the man who for twenty-four years had 'enforced' doctrinal orthodoxy and clerical discipline through the Congregation for the Doctrine of the Faith (CDF). This work tended to overshadow his earlier career as an academic theologian and his contribution to the Second Vatican Council, at which he served as *peritus* to Cardinal Josef Frings, one of the leading reformers. Like other 'northerners' at the council, Ratzinger was profoundly influenced by John Henry Newman's works. For Ratzinger, therefore, Britain was the home of Newman. British media commentators did not operate on the same rarefied level and, in the early years of Benedict XVI's pontificate (2005–13), attention was frequently drawn to his membership of the Hitler Youth. As if to reinforce the point, Hochhuth's *The Representative* was revived in London in 2006. In spite of the example set by leading political figures, early twenty-first-century Britain was proving to be as post-Christian as it was post-industrial; popes belonged firmly in the realm of entertainment. Thus Piers Paul Read's novel *The Death of a Pope* (2009) was inspired by the conclave of 2005, and the casting of the actor Brian Blessed as Pius II in a feature film, *The Conclave* (2006), was imaginative, to say the least.

In the most recent conclave the cardinals had voted for continuity and got precisely that: ever-increasing inertia and decay in a dysfunctional curia. Benedict the shy scholar was not strong enough to impose his authority on those around him. He had a strategic sense of the Church's global mission, but his Italian officials busied themselves with local preoccupations. He appreciated the suffering experienced by the victims of sexually abusive priests, behaviour that was age-old and had traditionally been covered up, but was powerless to prevent a reaction such as Ireland's withdrawal of its ambassador to the Holy See. Ironically, if there was light in the darkness of Benedict's experience of the world beyond the oratory and the study, it came from Britain and the Anglicanism in which he took a scholarly interest. In Rowan Williams, archbishop of Canterbury from 2002 to 2012, he dealt with an Anglican primate who could match him intellectually; Benedict's appreciation went so far as to invite Williams to celebrate an Anglican eucharist at his private altar. What Williams did not know was how Rome intended to respond to requests for corporate reunion made by Anglicans from various branches of the Communion who remained distressed by the ordination of women to the priesthood and the episcopate. Even the British Catholic hierarchies were kept in the dark. Consequently, it came as a complete surprise to a number of the interested parties when, in November 2009 Cardinal William Levada, prefect of the CDF, announced the creation of the Personal Ordinariate of Our Lady of Walsingham for groups of Anglicans who desired corporate union with Rome. Its status was set out in the apostolic constitution *Anglicanorum coetibus*.[60] In one sense the Ordinariate can be interpreted as Benedict's belated apology for Rome's initial suspicion of Newman, offering special concessions to his latter-day successors. In another, it was a case of the right hand not knowing what the left was doing.

The convergence of interests achieved by the Vatican and the Blair government towards the end of John Paul II's pontificate might suggest that greater clarity and openness was to be found in that particular Anglo-papal relationship, but that would be to reckon without a cost-cutting drive in the FCO around the time of Benedict's election. The impending retirement of Ambassador Kathryn Colvin in October 2005 prompted plans to rationalise Britain's diplomatic presence in Rome, where there had been two embassies for as long as anyone could remember, only one of which undertook consular work, and where financial savings could surely be found. An all-party parliamentary group was founded by Catholic MP David Amess to lobby for the retention of the embassy to the Holy See, but what sort of mission should it become in order to justify its continued existence? If it dealt with the micro-state that is Vatican City and acted as a glorified tourist agency, its position was indeed difficult to justify. If, on the other hand, it were to become Britain's gateway to the Church as a global entity, then it offered great potential to develop the contacts created in 2003–04. Extraordinarily, the vacancy was advertised publicly, prompting much contemporary comment.[61] This proved to be a superfluous exercise, because the job went to the ultimate insider. Francis Campbell was one of the FCO's brightest stars, who knew Rome from his two years as first secretary at the other embassy and had been seconded to 10 Downing Street to act as Blair's private secretary. It was in the latter capacity that he had arranged the prime minister's visit to the Vatican. What he offered was a vision of the embassy's potential to facilitate contact and co-operation between Britain and the Holy See across a range of policy areas. With his new posting Campbell broke the mould twice over, as the first Catholic head of Britain's mission to the Holy See for more than eight decades and as the first ambassador sent there at a relatively early stage in his career.

Campbell did not take up the post until December 2005. In the meantime, arrangements were made to move the chancery from busy Via Condotti to a more secure location in the grounds of the embassy to Italy on Via XX Settembre. The Vatican assented to that. Where it drew the line was at moving the ambassador's residence from a thoroughly agreeable villa at Porta S. Sebastiano to a house in the grounds of the Villa Wolkonsky, residence of the ambassador to Italy, which would have suggested that there was no separation whatsoever between the two British missions. It fell to Campbell to find his own accommodation. Another move followed in 2006, once the new arrangements had been made in Rome: relations with the Holy See ceased to be part of the FCO's European department and were classed instead alongside the United Nations, the Organisation for Economic Co-operation and Development, and other supranational bodies. The embassy facilitated contacts in policy areas such as climate change, community cohesion, disarmament, education, international development, and inter-religious dialogue, with Benedict supporting a British initiative when he purchased the first Immunisation Bond to finance vaccination programmes in poor countries. Blair and Brown each paid two further visits to the Vatican, and five other ministers visited relevant curial departments. At no stage of their long history had Britain and the papacy been bound together quite so closely by so many and varied mutual interests.

High-level contacts were complemented by invitations to the pope to make a state visit to Britain. Benedict's acceptance was formally announced in March 2010 and set in motion plans for a four-day visit to Edinburgh, Glasgow,

London and Birmingham the following September, by which time – ironically enough – there had been a change of government. In contrast to the pastoral visit of 1982, this state visit benefited from the authorities' vast experience of putting on ceremonial events, complete with lines of alternating union flags and yellow and white papal ones along the Mall. In all four cities crowds turned out in consistently impressive numbers, but they lived in a celebrity-obsessed culture and may well have been more attracted by a sighting of the man than a keenness to hear his message. The secular dimension of the visit consisted of a meeting between the two heads of state at the Palace of Holyroodhouse on 16 September and an address to politicians, diplomats, academics, business leaders and other representatives of 'civil society' in Westminster Hall the following day. Benedict surely spoke for many of his more recent predecessors when he praised Britain's political stability and 'natural instinct for moderation'. Westminster itself was now so tolerant that, from 2009, a Catholic priest ministered to MPs – some of whom happened to be as papal knights – their families and staff. However, toleration could easily be another term for indifference and, before his audience could congratulate themselves too heartily, Benedict cautioned against the marginalisation of Christianity in (unspecified) tolerant nations.[62] Indeed, the politicians in that audience well understood that Catholics now formed Britain's largest church-going denomination, but they also showed no sign of wishing to halt the secularising agenda dictated by an even greater proportion of the electorate or the increasing demands of other faiths.

From Westminster Hall the pope was driven the shortest of distances to Westminster Abbey. Here was another opportunity for reconciliation, this time organised by much more receptive hosts. Aware of the pope's liturgical and musical tastes, the dean and his colleagues ensured that Benedict saw and heard the best that the Anglican tradition could offer. With the wounds of so many centuries at least superficially healed, the final leg of the papal visit was to Birmingham, for the beatification of the former Anglican John Henry Newman on 19 September.[63] As a rule popes do not travel out of Rome to conduct such ceremonies, so Benedict's journey to Cofton Park demonstrated the intensity of his intellectual debt to Newman. Fittingly, it is in the academic sphere that a lasting memorial to the visit may be found, for 2015 saw the foundation of the Benedict XVI Centre for Religion and Society at St Mary's University, Twickenham, where the pope had addressed an inter-religious gathering on the second day of his visit.

So much of what was achieved in terms of repairing the long-fractured Anglo-papal relationship depended on the Blair–Brown regime in London and on Francis Campbell in Rome. It also depended on the status accorded to the Holy See within the FCO. All that changed in 2010–11, first with the change of government, then with Campbell's departure from Rome and, no less significantly, with Vatican relations being put back into the FCO's European department. Ministerial contacts with the curia became relatively few and far between and prime minister David Cameron expressed neither a clear understanding of religious matters nor any interest in visiting the Vatican, thereby disproving his claim to be the 'heir to Blair'. Campbell's successors in Rome, Nigel Baker and, from 2016, Sally Axworthy, continued to emphasise the embassy's global connections and significance, even if these were at odds with the European Union-centred framework within which they were obliged to operate.

On 28 February 2013 Pope Benedict captured the world's imagination by announcing the first voluntary resignation in papal history. He had created ninety cardinals, only one of whom, Seán Brady of Armagh, was from the British Isles. Murphy-O'Connor had recently turned eighty and lost his right to vote, leaving Cardinal O'Brien as the sole elector from Britain. No sooner had media attention fixed on O'Brien than accusations appeared in the press of sexual impropriety on his part towards serving and former priests.[64] In the glare of publicity, he chose not to participate in the conclave. Thus, while the youthful octogenarian Murphy-O'Connor cheerfully embraced the opportunities presented by a culture of 24-hour rolling news, no British cardinal voted for the archbishop of Buenos Aires, Jorge Mario Bergoglio, when he became the first non-European pope in nearly thirteen centuries. The British government's priorities were indicated by the dispatch of a lower-profile royal, the duke of Gloucester, to represent the queen at the inauguration of Pope Francis. The Church had long engaged in global mission, but here was a pope for a truly globalised world. Whereas Benedict had stressed the need for re-evangelisation in post-Christian Europe, Francis made no effort to conceal his Latin American and Asian priorities, thereby reflecting the relative strength of Christianity in the so-called Global South. When Queen Elizabeth and Archbishop Justin Welby of Canterbury paid their visits to the Vatican in 2014 they were one head of state and one religious leader among so many others from all continents, keen to ingratiate themselves with the enigmatic pontiff.

In the light of these developments, a more satisfying conclusion to this narrative may be sought by looking back to September 2010 and the state visit of Benedict XVI, which represented the culmination of a centuries-old relationship between the bishops of Rome and the relatively distant island of Britain. It resulted from a new-found – and all-too-fleeting – unity of purpose between the Church and a secular power, a shared dynamic vision of Christianity in action far removed from the thoroughly worldly accommodation facilitated by the likes of John Shirwood and Andrew Forman in the pre-Reformation period. It vindicated the relative moderation of a figure such as Cardinal Philip Thomas Howard, who sought to advance the Catholic cause in post-Reformation Britain without resorting to the more incautious means advocated by some of his contemporaries. That it happened at all was a tribute to the diplomats who maintained lines of communications in often unpromising circumstances, even if few of them were inconvenienced quite as obviously as the voluntary prisoner D'Arcy Osborne. Above all it was a pilgrimage, the reverse of St Wilfrid's travels to Rome. It may not have incorporated visits to shrines past and present, but the 'outstanding saints' Edward the Confessor and Margaret of Scotland were recalled by the pope as models of royal piety in his address to Queen Elizabeth in Edinburgh, and he noted that Westminster Hall was the site of Thomas More's trial for treason, the point at which the former lord chancellor's loyalty to the Holy See became certain to end in his martyrdom.[65] However, Westminster was but a halt on the journey, for the ultimate – if relatively unglamorous – destination was Birmingham, the place where John Henry Newman settled after making his submission to Rome. Away from the crowds and the trappings of a state visit, perhaps the most telling illustration of the Anglo-papal relationship in the early twenty-first century is an image of Pope Benedict pausing for reflection in front Newman's private altar at the Birmingham Oratory: a pope's heart speaks to that of his British guide in the mysteries of the Christian faith. Consequently, a story that began at a church dedicated to St Peter on the marginal Essex coast ends with Peter's successor in the heart of England. Benedict XVI came not as a papal overlord, but as a humble pilgrim, and his presence confirmed that the early modern breach with Rome had been healed: the process of reconciliation was apparently complete.

NOTES

Introduction

1. *Daily Telegraph*, 20 January 2016.
2. Louis Duchesne and Cyrille Vogel (eds), *Le liber pontificalis*, 3 vols (Paris, 1955–7). Portions of the whole are available in English translation, all by Raymond Davis: *The Book of Pontiffs (Liber pontificalis)* (rev. edn, Liverpool, 2010), *The Lives of the Eighth-Century Popes* (2nd edn, Liverpool, 2007) and *The Lives of the Ninth-Century Popes (Liber pontificalis)* (Liverpool, 1995), cover the years to 715, 715–817 and 817–91 respectively.
3. His *Liber pontificalis* is examined in Rodney M. Thomson, *William of Malmesbury* (Woodbridge, 1987), pp. 119–38.
4. *The* Historia Pontificalis *of John of Salisbury*, ed. and tr. M. Chibnall (Oxford, 1986); John of Salisbury, *Policraticus*, ed. and tr. C.J. Nederman (Cambridge, 1990).
5. William Thomas, *The Historie of Italie* (London, 1549).
6. John Bale, *Acta Romanorum pontificum* (Basel, 1558), translated and expanded by John Studley as *The Pageant of Popes* (London, 1574).
7. Gregorio Leti, *The Life of Donna Olimpia Maldachini, who Governed the Church, During the Time of Innocent the X* (London, 1667), pp. 96–7. Leti's *oeuvre* included *Il nepotismo di Roma, or, The History of the Popes Nephews*, tr. William Aglionby (London, 1669).
8. Richard Wilfrid Selby, *Bonifacius viii. e familia Caietanorum principum Romanus pontifex, Iohannis Rubei opus* (Rome, 1651).
9. Alexander Bower, *History of the Popes*, 7 vols (London, 1748–66).
10. Alexander Gordon, *Lives of Pope Alexander VI and his son Caesar Borgia*, 2 vols (London, 1729).
11. William Roscoe, *Life and Pontificate of Leo the Tenth*, 6 vols (London, 1806).
12. Leopold von Ranke, *The Ecclesiastical and Political History of the Popes of Rome during the Sixteenth and Seventeenth Centuries*, tr. Sarah Austin, 3 vols (London, 1840).
13. Mary Allies, *Pius VII* (London, 1875), p. ix.
14. Such as G.A.F. Wilks, *The Popes: a Historical Summary* (London, 1851) or William Taylor, *Popes of Rome: from the Earliest Times to Pius IX* (London, 1870).
15. T.W. Allies, *The Formation of Christianity*, 8 vols (London, 1865–96).

16. *Papal Jubilee Library* (London, 1887).

17. James Paton, *British History and Papal Claims from the Norman Conquest to the Present Day* (London, 1893).

18. *Apostolicae curae* (18 September 1896): http://www.papalencyclicals.net/Leo13/ l13curae.htm [accessed 30 June 2016].

19. *Calendar of Entries in the Papal Registers relating to Great Britain and Ireland*, ed. W.H. Bliss et al. (London, 1893–).

20. Mandell Creighton, *A History of the Papacy from the Great Schism to the Sack of Rome*, 6 vols (London, 1882–97).

21. Ludwig von Pastor, *The History of the Popes from the Close of the Middle Ages*, tr. F.I. Antrobus, F.R. Kerr, E. Graf and E.F Peeler, 40 vols (London, 1899–1953).

22. Horace K. Mann, *The Lives of the Popes in the Middle Ages*, 18 vols (London, 1902–32).

23. W.F. Barry, *The Papal Monarchy from St Gregory the Great to Boniface VIII, 590–1303* (London, 1902); *The Papacy and Modern Times: a Political Sketch, 1303–1870* (London, 1911).

24. Frederick William Rolfe, *Chronicles of the House of Borgia* (London, 1901).

25. Herbert M. Vaughan, *The Medici Popes* (London, 1908); Cecilia M. Ady, *Pius II: the Humanist Pope* (London, 1913).

26. Eric John, Douglas Woodruff and J.M.W. Bean, *The Popes: A Concise Biographical History* (London, 1964); Geoffrey Barraclough, *The Medieval Papacy* (London, 1968); Michael E. Mallett, *The Borgias: The Rise and Fall of a Renaissance Dynasty* (London, 1969).

27. J.N.D. Kelly, *Oxford Dictionary of the Popes* (Oxford, 1986); Eamon Duffy, *Saints and Sinners: A history of the Popes* (New Haven and London, 1997).

28. Examples of Chadwick's *oeuvre*: *Catholicism and History: the Opening of the Vatican Archives* (Cambridge, 1978); *The Popes and European Revolution* (Oxford, 1981); *A History of the Popes 1830–1914* (Oxford, 1998). The Rhodes' trilogy in chronological order of subject matter: *The Power of Rome in the Twentieth Century: The Vatican in the Age of the Liberal Democracies, 1870–1922* (London, 1983), *The Vatican in the Age of the Dictators, 1922–1945* (London, 1973), *The Vatican in the Age of the Cold War, 1945–1980* (Norwich, 1992).

29. Pollard's publications include: *The Vatican and Italian Fascism, 1929–1932: A Study in Conflict* (Cambridge, 1985), *The Unknown Pope: Benedict XV (1914–1922) and the Pursuit of Peace* (London, 1999), *Money and the Rise of the Modern Papacy: Financing the Vatican, 1850–1950* (Cambridge, 2005), *The Papacy in the Age of Totalitarianism, 1914–1958* (Oxford, 2014). Cornwell's papal books are: *A Thief in the Night: The Mysterious Death of Pope John Paul I* (London, 1989), *Hitler's Pope: The Secret History of Pius XII* (London, 1999), *Breaking Faith: The Pope, the People and the Fate of Catholicism* (London, 2001), *A Pontiff in Winter: The Dark Face of John Paul II's Papacy* (London, 2004).

30. Z.N. Brooke, *The English Church and the Papacy from the Conquest to the Reign of John* (new edn., Cambridge, 1989); William E. Lunt, *Financial Relations of the Papacy with England to 1327* (Cambridge, MA, 1939) and *Financial Relations of the Papacy with England, 1327–1534* (Cambridge, MA, 1962).

31. C.H. Lawrence (ed.), *The English Church and the Papacy in the Middle Ages* (rev. edn, Stroud, 1999).

32. C.R. Cheney, *Innocent III and England* (Stuttgart, 1976); Jane E. Sayers, *Papal Government and England during the Pontificate of Honorius III (1216–1227)* (Cambridge, 1984).

33. Jane E. Sayers, *Papal Judges Delegate in the Province of Canterbury, 1198–1254: A Study in Ecclesiastical Jurisdiction and Administration* (Oxford, 1971); Paul C. Ferguson, *Medieval Papal Representatives in Scotland: Legates, Nuncios, and Judges-Delegate, 1125–1286* (Edinburgh, 1997).

34. Katherine Harvey, *Episcopal Appointments in England, c. 1214–1344: From Episcopal Election to Papal Provision* (Farnham, 2014).

35. A.D.M. Barrell, *The Papacy, Scotland and Northern England, 1342–1378* (Cambridge, 1995).

36. Karsten Plöger, *England and the Avignon Popes: The Practice of Diplomacy in Late Medieval Europe* (London, 2005); Margaret Harvey, *England, Rome and the Papacy 1417–1464: The Study of a Relationship* (Manchester, 1993); William E. Wilkie, *The Cardinal Protectors of England: Rome and the Tudors before the Reformation* (Cambridge, 1974); Catherine Fletcher, *Our Man in Rome: Henry VIII and his Italian Ambassador* (London, 2012).

37. A.O. Meyer, *England and the Catholic Church under Queen Elizabeth*, tr. J.R. McKee (London, 1967); Gordon Albion, *Charles I and the Court of Rome: A Study in 17th Century Diplomacy* (Louvain, 1935).

38. Matthias Buschkühl, *Great Britain and the Holy See 1746–1870* (Dublin, 1982); James P. Flint, *Great Britain and the Holy See: The Diplomatic Relations Question, 1846–1852* (Washington, DC, 2003); C.T. McIntire, *England against the Papacy 1858–1861: Tories, Liberals, and the Overthrow of Papal Temporal Power during the Italian Risorgimento* (Cambridge, 1983); Saho Matsumoto-Best, *Britain and the Papacy in the Age of Revolution, 1846–1851* (Woodbridge, 2003); Ambrose Macaulay, *The Holy See, British Policy and the Plan of Campaign, 1885–93* (Dublin, 2002).

39. Thomas E. Hachey, *Anglo-Vatican Relations, 1914–1939: Confidential Annual Reports of the British Ministers to the Holy See* (Boston, 1972); Thomas Moloney, *Westminster, Whitehall and the Vatican: The Role of Cardinal Hinsley, 1935–43* (Tunbridge Wells, 1985); Owen Chadwick, *Britain and the Vatican during the Second World War* (Cambridge, 1986).

40. *Britain and the Holy See: A Celebration of 1982 and the Wider Relationship Proceedings of the 2012 Rome Colloquium* (Rome, 2013).

41. *The Complete Works of John Gower*, ed. G.C. Macaulay (Grosse Pointe, MI, 1968), II, pp. 206–25.

42. *The Complete Plays of John Bale*, ed. Peter Happé, 2 vols (Cambridge, 1985–6); Barnabe Barnes, *The Devil's Charter*, ed. Jim C. Pogue (New York and London, 1980).

43. John Cooney, *Scotland and the Papacy: Pope John Paul II's Visit in Perspective* (Edinburgh, 1982); Leslie J. Macfarlane and J. McIntyre (eds), *Scotland and the Holy See: The Story of Scotland's links with the Papacy down the Centuries* (Edinburgh, 1982).

Chapter 1   I Follow Peter

1. *Bede's Ecclesiastical History of the English People* [hereafter *Ecclesiastical History*] ed. Bertram Colgrave and R.A.B. Mynors (Oxford, 1992), iii.22.

2. Davis, *The Book of Pontiffs*, p. 6.

3. Adolf von Harnack, 'Der Brief des britischen Königs Lucius an den Papst Eleutherus', *Sitzungsberichte der Königlich Preussischen Akademie der Wissenschaften zu Berlin* (1904), pp. 909–16.

4. Arthur W. Haddan and William Stubbs, *Councils and Ecclesiastical Documents relating to Great Britain and Ireland* I (Oxford, 1869), pp. 7–10.

5. Both sources are examined by E.A. Thompson, *Saint Germanus of Auxerre and the end of Roman Britain* (Woodbridge, 1984).

6. *Ecclesiastical History*, iii.4.

7. Bede's dating is somewhat confused and does not correspond to Gregory's extant letters: *The Letters of Gregory the Great*, ed. John R.C. Martyn, 3 vols (Toronto, 2004).

8. *Letters of Gregory the Great*, 3, pp. 778–95.

9. *Ecclesiastical History*, i.27.

10. Ibid., i.29. Gregory's letter to Mellitus, 18 July 601, contains revised instructions for the missionaries: *Letters of Gregory the Great*, 3, pp. 802–03.

11. *Ecclesiastical History*, ii.6.

12. Ibid., ii.19.

13. Ibid., iv.18.

14. Quoted in Michael Lapidge (ed.), *Archbishop Theodore: Commemorative Studies on his Life and Influence* (Cambridge, 1995), p. 23.

15. *The Life of Bishop Wilfrid by Eddius Stephanus*, ed. Bertram Colgrave (Cambridge, 1927).

16. Ibid., ch. 34.

17. Ibid., ch. 45.

18. Ibid., ch. 46.

19. Ibid., ch. 47.

20. Ibid., ch. 63.

21. Ibid., ch. 39, ch. 37.

22. *Ecclesiastical History*, iii.25.

23. *Life of Bishop Wilfrid*, ch. 56.

24. Ibid., ch. 54.

25. *The Earliest Life of Gregory the Great by an Anonymous Monk of Whitby*, ed. Bertram Colgrave (Lawrence, KS, 1968), p. 91. There is, however, an allusion to the purchase of English slave-boys in Gaul in *Letters of Gregory the Great*, 2, pp. 408–09.

26. *Ecclesiastical History*, v.21.

27. *Life of Bishop Wilfrid*, ch. 42.

28. Davis, *The Book of Pontiffs*, p. 94.

29. Davis, *The Lives of the Ninth-Century Popes*, pp. 8–9.

30. *Aldhelm: The Prose Works*, tr. Michael Lapidge and Michael W. Herren (Ipswich, 1979), p. 164, letter vi.

31. Haddan and Stubbs, *Councils* I, pp. 440–3.

32. *English Historical Documents* [hereafter *EHD*] I, ed. Dorothy Whitelock (London, 1955), 191.

33. *EHD* I, 204: this letter of Pope Leo III to Cenwulf of Mercia confirms that the tribute was still being paid in 798.

34. *Alfred the Great: Asser's* Life of King Alfred *and other contemporary sources*, tr. Simon Keynes and Michael Lapidge (Harmondsworth, 1983), p. 69.

35. Ibid., p. 70.

36. *The Anglo-Saxon Chronicle*, ed. and tr. Dorothy Whitelock, David C. Douglas and Susie I. Tucker (London, 1961), 874.
37. Ibid., 889.
38. Ibid., 883; *Alfred the Great*, p. 88.
39. Dorothy Whitelock, M. Brett and C.N.L. Brooke (eds), *Councils and Synods with other Documents relating to the English Church I: AD 871–1204, i: 871–1066* (Oxford, 1981), pp. 12–13.
40. *Alfred the Great*, p. 126.
41. Ibid., pp. 94–6.
42. N. Brooks, *The Early History of the Church of Canterbury: Christ Church from 597 to 1066* (Leicester, 1984), pp. 210–13.

Chapter 2   Papal Monarchs and their Subjects

1. H.E.J. Cowdrey, *The Register of Pope Gregory VII 1073–1085* (Oxford, 2002), 2.55a.
2. D. Whitelock, M. Brett and C.N.L. Brooke (eds), *Councils and Synods with other Documents relating to the English Church I: AD 871–1204, i: 871–1066* (Oxford, 1981), pp. 109–13.
3. William of Malmesbury, *The Deeds of the Bishops of England* (*Gesta pontificum anglorum*), ed. D. Preest (Woodbridge, 2002), p. 118.
4. P. McGurk, D.N. Dumville, M.R. Godden and A. Knock (eds), *An Eleventh-Century Anglo-Saxon Illustrated Miscellany (British Library Cotton Tiberius B.V. part I)* (Copenhagen, 1983), esp. pp. 74–5.
5. *Anglo-Saxon Chronicle*, 997.
6. A.W. Haddan and W. Stubbs, *Councils and Ecclesiastical Documents relating to Great Britain and Ireland* III (Oxford, 1871), p. 559.
7. A.O. Anderson (ed. and tr.), *Early Sources of Scottish History, AD 500 to 1286*, 2 vols (Edinburgh and London, 1922), 1, p. 480.
8. *EHD* I, 230.
9. *Anglo-Saxon Chronicle*, 1022.
10. *EHD* I, 53.
11. *The Life of King Edward who Rests at Westminster*, ed. F. Barlow (2nd edn., Oxford, 1992), pp. 28–37.
12. Ibid., pp. 54–7.
13. Also told by William of Malmesbury, *Gesta regum Anglorum/The History of the English Kings*, ed. and tr. R.A.B. Mynors, R.M. Thomson and M. Winterbottom, I (Oxford, 1998), 238.7.
14. *The Letters of Lanfranc Archbishop of Canterbury*, ed. H. Clover and M. Gibson (Oxford, 1979), 4.
15. Ibid., 3.
16. Cowdrey, *Register of Pope Gregory VII*, 1.70.
17. *EHD* II, 99–101; *Letters of Lanfranc*, 38–9.
18. *EHD* II, 106; *Letters of Lanfranc*, 52.
19. Eadmer, *The Life of St Anselm, Archbishop of Canterbury*, ed. and tr. R.W. Southern (Oxford, 1962), p. 105.
20. This and subsequent Anglo–papal contacts during the period 1100–35 are listed in M. Brett, *The English Church under Henry I* (Oxford, 1975), pp. 234–46.
21. William of Malmesbury, *Gesta regum Anglorum*, I, 421.2.

22. Ibid., 435.2.
23. Henry, archdeacon of Huntingdon, *Historia Anglorum: The History of the English People*, ed. Diana Greenway (Oxford, 1996), pp. 758–9.
24. *EHD* II, 159.
25. The name Nicholas Breakspear and an account of his Hertfordshire origins first appear in Matthew Paris's contribution to the thirteenth-century history of the abbots of St Albans: *Gesta abbatum monasterii sancti Albani*, ed. H.T. Riley, 3 vols (London, 1867), I, pp. 112–13.
26. *The Correspondence of Thomas Becket, Archbishop of Canterbury, 1162–1170*, ed. and tr. A.J. Duggan (Oxford, 2000), I, 10.
27. *EHD* II, 157.
28. *Correspondence of Thomas Becket*, I, 12.
29. *EHD* II, 126.
30. *Correspondence of Thomas Becket*, I, 37.
31. *EHD* II, 155.
32. Ibid., 156.
33. A.W. Haddan and W. Stubbs (eds), *Councils and Ecclesiastical Documents relating to Great Britain and Ireland* II (Oxford, 1873), pp. 245–6.
34. The marriage, which was later annulled, is discussed by D.L. d'Avray, *Dissolving Royal Marriages 860–1600* (Cambridge, 2014), pp. 53–7.
35. Honorius III renewed the Bull in 1218. For this later text see E.L.G. Stones (ed. and tr.), *Anglo-Scottish Relations 1174–1328: Some Selected Documents* (London, 1965), pp. 28–33.
36. *Selected Letters of Pope Innocent III concerning England (1198–1216)*, ed. C.R. Cheney and W.H. Semple (London, 1953), 30.
37. Ibid., 45.
38. F.M. Powicke and C.R. Cheney (eds), *Councils and Synods with other Documents relating to the English Church* II, i (Oxford, 1964), p. 18; Sayers, *Papal Government*, p. 162; *EHD* III, 17.
39. *Selected Letters of Pope Innocent III*, 53.
40. Ibid., 67.
41. *EHD* III, ed. H. Rothwell (London, 1975), 20.
42. *EHD* III, 21; *Selected Letters of Pope Innocent III*, 80.
43. *Selected Letters of Pope Innocent III*, 81 and 84.
44. As related in *The Book of St Gilbert*, ed. R Foreville and G. Keir (Oxford, 1987). The first canonisation of an Irish saint, that of Malachy O'More in 1190, pre-dated this level of scrutiny.
45. R.W. Southern, *Robert Grosseteste: The Growth of an English mind in Medieval Europe* (Oxford, 1986), pp. 276–81.
46. R.E. Treharne and I.J. Sanders, *Documents of the Baronial Movement of Reform and Rebellion 1258–1267* (Oxford, 1973), 5 and 32; *EHD* V, 37.
47. Powicke and Cheney, *Councils and Synods* II, ii, pp. 725–92.

Chapter 3   Rome, Capital of the World?

1. In order of wealth, the fifteen were Rouen, Winchester, Aquileia, Auch, Canterbury, Cologne, Mainz, Salzburg, Trier, York, Durham, Langres, Narbonne, Toledo and Ely: Konrad Eubel, *Hierarchia Catholica medii et recentioris aevi* II (revised edn., Münster, 1914).

2. Henry Gee and William J. Hardy, *Documents Illustrative of English Church History* (London, 1896), XXXI.
3. E.L.G. Stones (ed. and tr.), *Anglo-Scottish Relations 1174–1328: Some Selected Documents* (Oxford, 1965), pp. 162–75.
4. Declaration of Arbroath (6 April 1320): http://www.constitution.org/scot/arbroath.txt [accessed 30 June 2016].
5. *Inter singula* (11 July 1317) http://www.inrebus.com/cambridgebull.php [accessed 30 June 2016].
6. For a full list of English royal embassies to Avignon during the pontificates of Clement VI and Innocent VI (1342–62) see Karsten Plöger, *England and the Avignon Popes*, pp. 233–46.
7. Gee and Hardy, *Documents*, 35.
8. *EHD* IV, ed. A.R. Myers (London, 1969), 376.
9. Ibid., 377.
10. Gee and Hardy, *Documents*, XXXVI.
11. Biblioteca Apostolica Vaticana, MS Vat. lat. 4116. Other manuscript copies survive in Madrid and Seville.
12. Published in L. Macfarlane, 'An English account of the election of Urban VI, 1378', *Bulletin of the Institute of Historical Research* 26 (1953), pp. 75–85.
13. *EHD* IV, 382–3.
14. Ibid., 384.
15. *Chronicle of Adam Usk, 1377–1421*, ed. and tr. C. Given-Wilson (Oxford, 1997), pp. 204–05.
16. The university's coat of arms includes a crescent moon in recollection of Benedict's original name, Pedro de Luna. His bulls of foundation were dated at Peníscola on 28 August 1413.
17. *EHD* IV, 395.
18. British Library, Cotton MS Cleopatra C.iv; Bodleian Library, Oxford, Arch. Selden MS B.23.
19. *EHD* IV, 397.
20. Ibid., 398.
21. Kemp's promotion was another snub to Chichele of Canterbury, who did not die until 1443.
22. The text of the bull (7 January 1451) is available at http://www.universitystory.gla.ac.uk/papal-bull/ [accessed 30 June 2016].
23. The process is traced in A.R. Malden (ed.), *The Canonization of Saint Osmund: from the Manuscript Records in the Muniment Room at Salisbury Cathedral* (Salisbury, 1901).
24. Pius II, *Commentaries*, 1, I–II, ed. and tr. M. Meserve and M. Simonetta (Cambridge, MA, and London, 2003), p. 19.
25. Ibid., pp. 20–9.
26. The names of cardinals acting as 'relators' are found in Archivio Secreto Vaticano [hereafter ASV], Cam. Apost., Oblig. et Solut. 83, which details promotions to major benefices between 1466 and 1488.
27. ASV, Reg. Suppl. 670.
28. Shirwood's text is analysed by A.E. Moyer, *The Philosophers' Game: Rithmomachia in Medieval and Renaissance Europe* (Ann Arbor, MI, 2001).
29. For sources, see D.L. d'Avray, *Dissolving Royal Marriages 860–1600* (Cambridge, 2014), pp. 190–219.

30. Pio Paschini (ed.), *Il Carteggio fra il Card. Marco Barbo e Giovanni Lorenzi (1481–1490)* (Vatican City, 1948), p. 143.
31. His role as relator to major benefices can be traced in ASV, Arch. Concist., Acta Camerarii I, which covers the years 1489–99.

Chapter 4   Of Swords and Roses

1. ASV, Arch. Concist., Acta Camerarii I.
2. *The Julius Exclusus of Erasmus*, tr. Paul Pascal, ed. J. Kelley Sowards (Bloomington, Ind., 1968).
3. *Henry VIII Fid. Def.: His Defence of the Faith and its Seven Sacraments*, intro. Richard Rex (Sevenoaks, 2008).
4. For analysis and sources, see D.L. d'Avray, *Dissolving Royal Marriages 86–1600* (Cambridge, 2014), pp. 220–6.
5. Ibid., pp. 227–9.
6. *EHD* V (1485–1558), ed. C.H. Williams (London, 1967), 92.
7. Ibid., 96.
8. Ibid., 98.
9. Ibid., 100.
10. Ibid., 103.
11. Reginald Pole, *Pro ecclesiasticae unitatis defensione* (Rome, 1539): completed by May 1536.
12. *Complete Plays of John Bale*, vol. 1.
13. His legation became the subject of a poem, extracts from which can be found in Charles Burns, 'Marco Grimani in Scotland, 1543–1544: a versified account of his legation', *Renaissance Studies* 2, 2 (1988), pp. 299–311.
14. Thomas, *Historie of Italie*, p. 72^v.
15. Matthias Flacius Illyricus and Pietro Paolo Vergerio, *Wonderfull Newes of the Death of Paule the. iii. last Byshop of Rome*, tr. William Baldwin (London, 1552).
16. Reginald Pole, *De summo pontifice Christi in terris vicario eiusque officio potestate liber vere singularis eruditionis* (Farnborough, 1969).
17. Reginald Pole to Marcellus II, 28 April 1555, *The Correspondence of Reginald Pole*, 3, ed. Thomas F. Mayer (Aldershot, 2004), p. 91.
18. *EHD* V(A) (1558–1603), ed. Ian W. Archer and F. Douglas Price (London and New York, 2011), 9.
19. John Jewel, *Apologia* (London, 1562).
20. *Regnans in excelsis* (25 February 1570): http://www.papalencyclicals.net/Pius05/p5regnans.htm [accessed 30 June 2016]; *EHD* V(A), 72.
21. For an English translation of its bull of foundation, *Quoniam divinae bonitati* (1 May 1579), see Michael E. Williams, *The Venerable English College Rome: a History* (2nd edn., Leominster, 2008), pp. 272–80.
22. John Leslie, *De origine, moribus et rebus gestis Scotorum* (Rome, 1578).
23. William Cecil, Baron Burghley, *The Execution of Justice in England* (Ithaca, NY, 1965).
24. Anthony Munday, *The English Roman Life*, ed. Philip J. Ayres (Oxford, 1980). It was originally published in 1582.

25. *Inter gravissimas* (24 February 1582): http://www.bluewaterarts.com/calendar/NewInterGravissimas.htm [accessed 30 June 2016].

26. *Calendar of State Papers and Manuscripts, relating to English Affairs, existing in the Archives and Collections of Venice, and in other Libraries of Northern Italy* [hereafter *CSP Ven*] 8, ed. Horatio F. Brown (London, 1894), 920.

27. Pellevé had been on a French mission to Scotland in 1582, which was the closest he got to Ireland.

28. Robert Tofte, *'Discourse' to the Bishop of London*, ed. Robert C. Melzi (Geneva, 1989); Henry Wotton, *The State of Christendom* (London, 1657), p. 4; Edwin Sandys, *A Relation of the State of Religion* (London, 1605).

29. Fynes Moryson, *An Itinerary* (London, 1617).

30. *The Troublesome Reign of King John* I, v. The play is attributed to George Peele.

31. Christopher Marlowe, *Edward the Second* I, iv, 97–104.

32. Quoted by Bernard and Margaret Pawley, *Rome and Canterbury through Four Centuries* (Oxford, 1974), p. 25.

33. By John Fraser and George Crichton respectively.

34. The English Benedictine congregation was revived by the papal brief *Ex incumbenti* (1619).

35. *CSP Ven* 10, ed. Horatio F. Brown (London, 1900), 431.

36. Paolo Sarpi's account of this episode was translated into English by Christopher Potter: *The History of the Quarrels of Pope Paul V. with the State of Venice* (London, 1626).

37. For the text of the oath see http://faculty.history.wisc.edu/sommerville/361/oath%20allegiance.htm, [accessed 30 June 2016].

38. *CSP Ven* 10, 532.

39. *CSP Ven* 11, ed. Horatio F. Brown (London, 1904), 117.

40. Ibid., 566.

41. *CSP Ven* 16, ed Allen B. Hinds (London, 1910), 742.

42. Barnes, *The Devil's Charter*.

43. John Webster, *The White Devil*, IV, iii.

44. *The Historie of Eurialus and Lucretia* (London, 1639).

45. For Gregory's letter to Charles, dated 20 April, and the prince's reply to the pope, dated 20 June, together with related material, see http://www.british-history.ac.uk/rushworth-papers/vol1/pp78-140 [accessed 30 June 2016].

46. *Vita Mariae Stuartae Scotiae reginae* (Rome, 1624); *De duplici statu religionis apud Scotos* (Rome, 1628).

47. *CSP Ven* 18, ed. Allen B. Hinds (London, 1912), 611.

48. Ibid. 21, ed. Allen B. Hinds (London, 1916), 466.

49. Ibid. 23, ed. Allen B. Hinds (London, 1921), 585.

50. Ibid. 24, ed. Allen B. Hinds (London, 1923), 329.

51. His papers from this period eventually appeared in English as *The Memiors of Gregorio Panzani*, ed. Joseph Berington (Birmingham, 1793).

52. *SCP Ven* 24, 70.

53. Withiam Lithgow, *Rare Adventures and Painful Peregrinations* (Glasgow, 1906), p. 18.

54. *CSP Ven* 11, 536.

55. William Prynne, *Hidden Workes of Darkenes brought to Publike Light* (London, 1645).

Chapter 5   Converging Interests

1. James Shirley, *The Cardinal, a Tragedie* (London, 1652).
2. *The Scarlet Gown*, tr. Henry Cogan (London, 1653), p. 22.
3. Girolamo Lunadoro, *The Court of Rome*, tr. Henry Cogan (London, 1654).
4. Giovanni Battista Rinuccini, *Il cappuccino scozzese* (Macerata, 1644).
5. *Commentarius Rinuccinianus de sedis apostolicae legatione ad foederatos Hiberniae catholicos per annos 1645–1649*, ed. Joannes Kavanagh, 6 vols (Dublin, 1932–49).
6. *CSP Ven* 33, ed. Allen B. Hinds (London, 1932), 62.
7. Ibid. 34, ed. Allen B. Hinds (London, 1933), 365.
8. Stefano Cavelli, *A Short Account of the Life and Death of Pope Alexander the vii*, tr. Philip Ayres (London, 1667).
9. *CSP Ven* 36, ed. Allen B. Hinds (London, 1937), 67.
10. Theophilus Garencières, *The Famous Conclave, wherein Clement VIII was Elected Pope*, tr. Samuel Lowndes (London, 1670).
11. *CSP Ven* 36, 333.
12. *EHD* VIII, ed. Andrew Browning (London, 1953), 140.
13. Thomas Traherne, *Roman Forgeries* (London, 1673).
14. *A Letter from the Pope to his Distressed Sons the Catholicks in England* (London, 1674).
15. *CSP Ven* 38, ed Allen B. Hinds (London, 1947), 239.
16. Gregorio Leti, *The Ceremonies of the Vacant See*, tr. John Davies (London, 1671); Leti, *The New Pope*, tr. John Davies (London, 1677).
17. *Room for News, or, News from Rome* (London, 1673); Benjamin Harris, *The Plot Discover'd* (London, 1678).
18. John Oldham, *Tom Tell-Troth* (London, 1679); *The Tears of Rome* (London, 1680).
19. *The Works of Nathaniel Lee*, ed. Thomas B. Stroup and Arthur L. Cooke, vol. 2 (New Brunswick, NJ, 1955).
20. *Domestick Intelligence* 39 (London, 1679).
21. *The Solemn Mock Procession of the Pope, Cardinals, Iesuits, Fryers, Nuns &c* (London, 1680).
22. Christopher Ness, *The Devils Patriarck* (London, 1683), pp. 108–13.
23. John Michael Wright, *An Account of his Excellence Roger Earl of Castlemaine's Embassy, from his Sacred Majesty James the IId … to His Holiness Innocent XI* (London, 1688).
24. Wright, *An Account*, pp. 22, 50, 70, 71–2.
25. *The Pope in a Passion; or, Bad News for England* (London, 1689); *The Pope, the Devil and the Chancellor* (London, 1689).
26. T.D.'s elegy is contained within T.L., *The Life and Reign of Innocent XI, Late Pope of Rome* (London, 1690), at pp. 75–6.
27. For example, Cooney, *Scotland and the Papacy*, p. 11, states that the pope sent troops to Ireland.
28. *EHD* VIII, 153.
29. Quoted by John Ingamells, *A Dictionary of British and Irish Travellers in Italy 1701–1800* (New Haven and London, 1997), p. 856.
30. Reproduced in Edward Corp, *The Stuarts in Italy 1719–1766: A Royal Court in Permanent Exile* (Cambridge, 2011), p. 57. Gualterio protected England from 1717.

31. Dr Richard Rawlinson, diaries 1720–6, Oxford, Bodleian Library, MSS. Rawl. 1180–7.

32. *Unigenitus* (8 September 1713): http://www.papalencyclicals.net/Clem11/c11unige.htm [accessed 30 June 2016].

33. *In eminenti* (28 April 1738): http://www.papalencyclicals.net/Clem12/c12inem engl.htm [accessed 30 June 2016].

34. Edward Gregg, 'The financial vicissitudes of James III in Rome', in Edward Corp (ed.), *The Stuart Court in Rome: the Legacy of Exile* (Aldershot and Burlington, VT, 2003), pp. 77–8.

35. Adrien Charpentiers's portrait of Dashwood is at West Wycombe House, Buckinghamshire.

36. Attrib. John Thorpe and Charles Plowden, *A Candid and Impartial Sketch of the Life and Government of Pope Clement XIV* 3 vols ('Dublin', i.e. London). To this Cordell responded with a *Letter* (1785); Louis-Antoine Caraccioli, *The Life of Pope Clement XIV*, tr. Charles Cordell (London, 1776) and Louis-Antoine Caraccioli, *Interesting Letters of Pope Clement XIV*, tr. Charles Cordell, 2 vols (London, 1777).

37. Quoted by Ingamells, *Dictionary*, p. 127.

38. Cardinal Pierre de Bernis, quoted by Ingamells, *Dictionary*, p. 403.

39. Quoted by Bernard Ward, *The Dawn of the Catholic Revival in England 1781–1803*, II (London, 1909), pp. 195–6.

Chapter 6   'God Bless our Pope, the Great, the Good'

1. From the refrain of Cardinal Nicholas Wiseman's hymn 'Full in the panting heart of Rome'.

2. Bernard Ward, *The Eve of Catholic Emancipation*, vol. 3 (London, 1912), p. 202.

3. Ibid., pp. 203–204.

4. *EHD* XI (1783–1832), ed. A. Aspinall and E.A. Smith (London, 1959), 459.

5. George Eliot, *Middlemarch: a Study of Provincial Life* (London and Edinburgh, 1871–2), chaps. 19–22.

6. Nicholas Wiseman, *Recollections of the Four Last Popes and of Rome in their Times* (London, 1858), p. 335.

7. Charles Michael Baggs, *A Discourse on the Supremacy of the Roman Pontiffs* (Rome, 1836), *The Papal Chapel* (Rome, 1836), *The Ceremonies of Holy-Week* at the Vatican and S. John Lateran's (Rome, 1839), and *The Pontifical Mass sung at S. Peter's on Easter Sunday, the Festival of SS. Peter and Paul, and Christmas Day* (Rome, 1840).

8. *The Letters and Diaries of John Henry Newman* III, ed. Ian Ker and Thomas Gornall (Oxford, 1979), p. 266.

9. William Ewart Gladstone, *The State in its Relations with the Church* (London, 1838).

10. For example Henry T. Worley, *Borgia: a Tragedy* (London, 1843) or Emma Robinson, *Caesar Borgia* (London, 1846).

11. *Praedecessores nostros* (25 March 1847): http://www.papalencyclicals.net/Pius 09/p9praede.htm [accessed 30 June 2016].

12. George Townsend, *Journal of a Tour in Italy, in 1850, with an Account of an Interview with the Pope, at the Vatican* (Cambridge, 2014), p. 165.

13. Ibid., pp. 162–3.

14. Westminster; Beverley, Birmingham, Clifton, Hexham, Liverpool, Plymouth, Newport, Northampton, Nottingham, Salford, Shrewsbury and Southwark. Subsequent divisions created the dioceses of Southwark (1851), Leeds (1878), Middlesbrough (1878), Portsmouth (1882), Menevia (1898), Brentwood (1917), Lancaster (1924), Arundel and Brighton (1965), East Anglia (1976), Hallam (1980) and Wrexham (1987).

15. *EHD* XII (1833–74) ed. G.M. Young (London, 1956), 120.

16. *The Times*, 7 November 1850; *EHD* XII, 121.

17. Nicholas Wiseman, *An Appeal to the Reason and Good Feeling of the English People: on the Subject of the Catholic Hierarchy* (London, 1850).

18. George Bowyer, *The Cardinal Archbishop of Westminster and the new Hierarchy* (London, 1850); Samuel Warren, *The Queen or the Pope?* (Edinburgh and London, 1850); Travers Twiss, *The Letters Apostolic of Pope Pius IX, Considered with Reference to the Law of England and the Law of Europe* (London, 1851).

19. *EHD* XII, 122.

20. Luigi Carlo Farini, *The Roman State: from 1815 to 1850*, tr. William Ewart Gladstone, 4 vols (London, 1851–4).

21. Quoted by McIntire, *England against the Papacy*, p. 220.

22. *The Tablet*, 11 June 1898.

23. *Attempted Assassination of Pope Pius the IX: Sudden Death of the Assassin, who had Daggers and Revolvers on his Person to Perpetrate the Bloody Deed!* (Dublin, 1865).

24. *The Tablet*, 11 June 1898.

25. https://archive.org/stream/whatisangloconti00angl#page/6/mode/2up [accessed 30 June 2016].

26. William Ewart Gladstone, *The Vatican Decrees in their Bearing on Civil Allegiance* (London, 1874), p. 6. The pamphlet was republished with 'Vaticanism' and 'Speeches of the pope' in *Rome and the Newest Fashions in Religion* (London, 1875).

27. Ibid., pp. 6 and 61.

28. [Lord Acton], *The Times*, 9 November 1874; John Henry Newman, *A Letter Addressed to His Grace the Duke of Norfolk on Occasion of Mr Gladstone's Recent Expostulation* (1875); [William Clifford] *The Tablet*, 5 December 1874; William Bernard Ullathorne, *Mr Gladstone's Expostulation Unravelled* (London, 1875); Henry Edward Manning, *The Vatican Decrees in their Bearing on Civil Allegiance* (London, 1875).

29. *The Tablet*, 9 February 1878.

30. Obituary of Sir George Errington, *The Tablet*, 27 March 1920.

31. *The Tablet*, 25 June 1887.

32. Quoted by V.A. McClelland, *Cardinal Manning: his Public Life and Influence 1865–1892* (London, 1962) p. 195.

33. *Saepe nos* (24 June 1888): http://www.vatican.va/holy_father/leo_xiii/encyclicals/documents/hf_l-xiii_enc_24061888_saepe-nos_en.html [accessed 30 June 2016].

34. *Etsi cunctas* (21 December 1888): http://www.vatican.va/holy_father/leo_xiii/encyclicals/documents/hf_l-xiii_enc_21121888_etsi-cunctas_en.html [accessed 30 June 2016].

35. *The Tablet*, 19 and 26 June 1897; *Catholic Times*, 25 June 1897.

36. Rennell Rodd, *Social and Diplomatic Memories, 1902–1919* (London, 1922–3), pp. 26–8; John XXIII, *Journal of a Soul*, tr. Dorothy M. White (London, 1965),

p. 181. Another account appears in B.J.C. McKercher, *Esme Howard: A Diplomatic Biography* (Cambridge, 1989), pp. 34–6.

37. Herbert Vaughan, *The Sufferings of Leo XIII and a Way of Conciliation* (London, 1888), pp. 20–1.

38. Like Manning, Vaughan was cardinal priest of SS. Andrea e Gregorio al Monte Celio.

39. The letter appeared in *The Tablet*, 12 January 1901.

40. Shane Leslie, *Cardinal Gasquet: a Memoir* (London, 1953), p. 80.

41. *Amantissima voluntatis* (14 April 1895): http://www.papalencyclicals.net/Leo13/l13amantissima.htm [accessed 30 June 2016].

42. Étienne Fernand Portal, *Les ordinations anglicanes* (Arras, 1894).

43. *Satis cognitum* (29 June 1895): http://w2.vatican.va/content/leo-xiii/en/encyclicals/documents/hf_l-xiii_enc_29061896_satis-cognitum.html [accessed 30 June 2016].

44. *Apostolicae curae* (18 September 1896): http://www.papalencyclicals.net/Leo13/l13curae.htm [accessed 30 June 2016].

45. *Caritatis studium* (25 July 1898): http://www.vatican.va/holy_father/leo_xiii/encyclicals/documents/hf_l-xiii_enc_25071898_caritatis-studium_en.html (accessed 29 September 2015).

46. *Immortale Dei* (1 November 1885): http://www.vatican.va/holy_father/leo_xiii/encyclicals/documents/hf_l-xiii_enc_01111885_immortale-dei_en.html [accessed 30 June 2016].

47. *Rerum novarum* (15 May 1891): http://www.vatican.va/holy_father/leo_xiii/encyclicals/documents/hf_l-xiii_enc_15051891_rerum-novarum_en.html (accessed 30 June 2016).

48. Quoted by McClelland, *Cardinal Manning*, p. 159.

49. Hartwell de la Garde Grissell, *Sede vacante* (Oxford, 1903).

50. Rodd, *Social and Diplomatic Memories*, pp. 30–6.

51. *The Tablet*, 13 August 1904.

52. *Sapienti consilio* (29 June 1908): http://w2.vatican.va/content/pius-x/la/apost_constitutions/documents/hf_p-x_apc_19080629_sapienti-consilio-index.html [accessed 30 June 2016].

53. The Scots College remained under the protection of the prefect of Propaganda who, from 1902 to 1916, was the Genoese Carmelite Girolamo Maria Gotti.

54. *Pascendi Dominici gregis* (8 September 1907): http://w2.vatican.va/content/pius-x/en/encyclicals/documents/hf_p-x_enc_19070908_pascendi-dominici-gregis.html [accessed 29 September 2015].

55. Arnold Harris Matthew, *The Life and Times of Rodrigo Borgia, Pope Alexander VI* (London, 1912).

56. Michael Field, *Borgia, a Period Play* (London, 1905); Algernon Charles Swinburne, *The Duke of Gandia* (London, 1908).

Chapter 7   From Hard Choices to Soft Power

1. The five being Logue of Armagh, Merry del Val, Farley of New York, Bourne of Westminster and the Rome-based Benedictine Gasquet.

2. He was finally raised to the cardinalate on 25 May 1914, on the same occasion as Gasquet.

3. Francis Tyrrell, *The Pope and the Great War. The Silence of Benedict XV. Can it be Defended?* (London, 1915).
4. Francis Bourne, 'The pope and the war', *The Tablet*, 5 June 1915; Frederick William Keating, 'The neutrality of the Holy See', *The Dublin Review*, July 1915, pp. 134–45; both articles were also published as Catholic Truth Society pamphlets.
5. 'The Vatican, the British Mission to the Vatican and the attitude of Roman Catholics towards the war', 30 November 1917, The National Archives [TNA], WO106/1516. For context see John Duncan Gregory, *On the Edge of Diplomacy: Rambles and Reflections, 1902–1928* (London, 1929).
6. *The Universe*, 18 January 1918.
7. Shane Leslie, *Cardinal Gasquet, a Memoir* (London, 1953), pp. 247–51.
8. *New York Times*, 31 January 1922.
9. Francis Aidan Gasquet, *His Holiness Pope Pius XI: A Pen Portrait* (London 1922).
10. Thomas E. Hachey, *Anglo-Vatican Relations, 1914–1939: Confidential Annual Reports of the British Ministers to the Holy See* (Boston, 1972), p. 219.
11. T.S.R. Boase, *Boniface VIII* (London, 1933).
12. Philip Ziegler, *King Edward VIII* (London, 1990), pp. 82–3.
13. Hachey, *Anglo-Vatican Relations*, pp. 43–4.
14. *The Tablet*, 1 February 1936.
15. *Mortalium animos* (6 January 1928): http://w2.vatican.va/content/pius-xi/en/encyclicals/documents/hf_p-xi_enc_19280106_mortalium-animos.html [accessed 30 June 2016].
16. Quoted by Michael J. Walsh, 'Catholics, society and popular culture' in V. A. McClelland and Michael Hodgetts, *From without the Flaminian Gate: 150 Years of Roman Catholicism in England and Wales 1850–2000* (London, 1999), p. 360.
17. *The Tablet*, 1 June 1935.
18. Alec Randall, *Vatican Assignment* (London, 1956), p. 8.
19. Ibid., p. 47.
20. Ibid., p. 26.
21. Hachey, *Anglo-Vatican Relations*, pp. 201–02.
22. Ibid., p. 49.
23. Ibid., p. 61.
24. Ibid., pp. 186–7.
25. Quoted by Anthony Rhodes, *The Vatican in the Age of the Dictators* (London, 1973), p. 61.
26. *Mit brennender Sorge* (14 March 1937): http://w2.vatican.va/content/pius-xi/en/encyclicals/documents/hf_p-xi_enc_14031937_mit-brennender-sorge.html [accessed 30 June 2016].
27. MacRory was the only other elector from the British Isles.
28. My thanks to Michael Walsh for this speculative insight.
29. The pope's gift to Princess Margaret, a travelling icon, was auctioned at Christie's in 2006: http://www.christies.com/Lotfinder/lot_details.aspx?intObjectID=4702880#top [accessed 30 June 2016].
30. Information from Cormac Murphy-O'Connor, who was present.
31. M. Pellew, 'The diplomatic and political relationship: the 20th century', in *Britain and the Holy See*, p. 60.
32. TNA, FO 371/79874.
33. TNA, FO 371/118005.
34. *Catholic Herald*, 1 July 1960.

35. After Manning and Vaughan, Griffin was the third English cardinal-priest of SS. Andrea e Gregorio al Monte Celio.
36. *Catholic Herald*, 1 July 1960.
37. Andrew Chandler and Charlotte Hansen (eds), *Observing Vatican II: The Confidential Reports of the Archbishop Canterbury's Representative, Bernard Pawley, 1961–1964* (Cambridge, 2013), p. 69.
38. Cormac Murphy-O'Connor, *An English Spring: Memoirs* (London and New York, 2015), p. 35; Chadwick, *Britain and the Vatican*, p. 97.
39. Cardinal D'Alton died on 1 February 1963, so Browne was the only Irish elector.
40. Peter Hebblethwaite, *Paul VI: the First Modern Pope* (London, 1993), pp. 125–7.
41. Longley, *The Worlock Archive*, p. 128.
42. The observers are listed in Alberic Stacpoole (ed.), *Vatican II by Those who were There* (London, 1986), pp. 361–4.
43. Owen Chadwick, *Michael Ramsey: A Life* (Oxford, 1990), p. 318.
44. *Authority in the Church I*: http://www.prounione.urbe.it/dia-int/arcic/doc/e_arcic_authority1.html; *Authority in the Church II*: http://www.prounione.urbe.it/dia-int/arcic/doc/e_arcic_authority2.html; *The Gift of Authority (Authority in the Church III)*: http://www.prounione.urbe.it/dia-int/arcic/doc/e_arcicII_05.html [accessed 30 June 2016].
45. Chadwick, *Michael Ramsey*, p. 325.
46. They included Timothy Manning, archbishop of Los Angeles, the last cardinal of the Irish diaspora to have been born in British-ruled Ireland.
47. TNA, FCO 7/4572, 'Vatican reactions to the Falkland islands crisis', covers 2 April to 21 June 1982.
48. Ibid., D.A.S. Gladstone, Western European Department, to Mr Fearn, South America Department, 16 April 1982.
49. Ibid., John Paul II to Ronald Reagan, 17 April 1982.
50. Ibid., D.A.S. Gladstone to Mr Goodison, 12 May 1982.
51. Ibid., Francis Pym to Embassy to the Holy See, 17 May 1982.
52. Ibid., Clive Whitmore, prime minister's principal private secretary, to Brian Fall, Foreign and Commonwealth Office, 28 May 1982.
53. Eliza Filby, *God and Mrs Thatcher: The Battle for Britain's Soul* (London, 2015), p. 280.
54. David Yallop, *In God's Name: An Investigation into the Murder of Pope John Paul I* (London, 1984).
55. *A Thief in the Night; Hitler's Pope*.
56. John Broadley (1988–91), Andrew Palmer (1991–5) and Maureen MacGlashan (1995–8).
57. Beatified in 2000 and 1998 respectively.
58. 'Anglicanism and the Western church: continuity and change' was organised jointly by the Vatican Museums, Norwich Cathedral and the British Embassy to the Holy See. The ambassador from 1998 to 2002 was Mark Pellew, a keen Anglican.
59. Gordon Brown, *Speeches,1997–2006* (London, 2006), pp. 226–35.
60. http://w2.vatican.va/content/benedict-xvi/en/apost_constitutions/documents/hf_ben-xvi_apc_20091104_anglicanorum-coetibus.html [accessed 30 June 2016]. For the background to this document see *The Anglo-Catholic*, 15 July 2011, http://www.theanglocatholic.com/2011/07/the-genesis-of-anglicanorum-coetibus/ [accessed 30 June 2016].

61. For example *The Tablet*, 23 July 2005.
62. Peter Jennings (ed.), *Benedict XVI and Blessed John Henry Newman* (London, 2010), pp. 102–06.
63. Dominic Barberi, best known for receiving Newman into the Church in 1845, had been beatified by Paul VI in 1963.
64. *The Observer*, 23 February 2013.
65. Jennings, *Benedict XVI*, pp. 51, 102–03.

BIBLIOGRAPHY

Archives, newspapers, periodicals and websites are as cited.

Ady, Cecilia M., *Pius II: The Humanist Pope* (London, 1913).

Albion, Gordon, *Charles I and the Court of Rome: A Study in 17th Century Diplomacy* (Louvain, 1935).

Alcuin, *The Bishops, Kings, and Saints of York*, tr. Peter Godman (Oxford, 1982).

Aldhelm: The Prose Works, tr. Michael Lapidge and Michael W. Herren (Ipswich, 1979).

Alfred the Great: Asser's Life of King Alfred *and other Contemporary Sources*, tr. Simon Keynes and Michael Lapidge (Harmondsworth, 1983).

Allies, Mary, *The Life of Pius VII* (London, 1875).

Allies, T.W., *The Formation of Christendom* (8 vols, London, 1865–96).

Allison, A.F., and D.M. Rogers (eds), *The Contemporary Printed Literature of the English Counter-Reformation between 1558 and 1640*, 2 vols (Aldershot, 1989–94).

Allmand, Christopher, *Henry V* (New Haven and London, 2011).

Amis, Kingsley, *The Alteration* (London, 1976).

Anderson, A.O. (ed. and tr.), *Early Sources of Scottish History, AD 500 to 1286*, 2 vols (Edinburgh and London, 1922).

Anderson, W.J. (ed.), 'Abbé Paul MacPherson: History of the Scots College Rome', *Innes Review* 12 (1961).

The Anglo-Saxon Chronicle, ed. and tr. Dorothy Whitelock, David C. Douglas and Susie I. Tucker (London, 1961).

Anon., *The Scarlet Gown*, tr. Henry Cogan (London, 1653).

——— *The Solemn mock procession of the Pope, Cardinals, Jesuits, fryers, nuns &c;: exactly taken as they marcht through the citty of London, November ye 17th, 1680* (London, 1680).

——— *The Tears of Rome: or the despair of the Pope for the ill success of the Plot* (London, 1680).

——— *The Popes evidence to a Cardinal, one of his Privados, about the Deliverance of the Earl of Shaftsbury out of the Tower* (London, 1681).

——— *A Dialogue between the Pope, the Devil and the Chancellor* (London, 1689).

——— *The Pope in a Passion; or, Bad News for England* (London, 1689).

——— *Attempted Assassination of Pope Pius the IX* (Dublin, 1865).

——— *Papal Jubilee Library* (London, 1887).

——— *The Earliest Life of Gregory the Great by an Anonymous Monk of Whitby*, ed. Bertram Colgrave (Lawrence, KS, 1968).

The Letters of Saint Anselm of Canterbury, ed. and tr. Walter Fröhlich, 3 vols (1990–4).

Atherstone, Andrew, 'The canonisation of the forty English martyrs: an ecumenical dilemma', *Recusant History* 30 (2011), pp. 573–87.

Baggs, Charles Michael, *A Discourse on the Supremacy of the Roman Pontiffs* (Rome, 1836).

—— *The Papal Chapel* (Rome, 1836).

—— *The Ceremonies of Holy-Week at the Vatican and S. John Lateran's* (Rome, 1839).

—— *The Pontifical Mass sung at S. Peter's on Easter-Sunday, the Festival of SS. Peter and Paul, and Christmas day* (Rome, 1840).

Bale, John, *Acta Romanorum pontificum* (Basel, 1558).

—— and John Studley, *The Pageant of Popes* (London, 1574).

The Complete Plays of John Bale, ed. Peter Happé, 2 vols (Cambridge, 1985–6).

Barlow, Frank, *The English Church, 1000–1066: A History of the later Anglo-Saxon Church* (London, 1979).

—— *The English Church, 1066–1154: A History of the Anglo-Norman Church* (London, 1979).

—— *Thomas Becket* (London, 1986).

—— (ed.), *The Life of King Edward who rests at Westminster* (2nd edn., Oxford, 1992).

—— *Edward the Confessor* (New Haven and London, 1997).

—— *William Rufus* (New Haven and London, 2000).

Barnes, Barnabe, *The Devil's Charter*, ed. Jim C. Pogue (New York and London, 1980).

Barnes, Patricia M. and W.R. Powell (eds), *Interdict Documents* (London, 1960).

Barraclough, Geoffrey, *The Medieval Papacy* (London 1968).

Barrell, A.D.M., *The Papacy, Scotland and Northern England, 1342–1378* (Cambridge, 1995).

Barry, W.F., *The Papal Monarchy from St Gregory the Great to Boniface VIII, 590–1303* (London, 1902).

—— *The Papacy and Modern Times: A Political Sketch, 1303–1870 (London, 1911).*

Baumgartner, Frederic J., *Behind Locked Doors: A History of the Papal Elections* (New York and Basingstoke, 2003).

Bayne, C.G., *Anglo-Roman Relations, 1558–1565* (Oxford, 1913).

Bebbington, David, *The Mind of Gladstone: Religion, Homer, and Politics* (Oxford, 2004).

The Correspondence of Thomas Becket, Archbishop of Canterbury, 1162–1170, ed. and tr. Anne J. Duggan, 2 vols (Oxford, 2000).

Bede's Ecclesiastical History of the English People, ed. Bertram Colgrave and R.A.B. Mynors (Oxford, 1992).

Bellenger, Dominic Aidan, and Stella Fletcher, *Princes of the Church: A History of the English Cardinals* (Stroud, 2001).

Benson, Robert Hugh, *Lord of the World* (London, 1907).

Berkeley, Joan, *Lulworth and the Welds* (Gillingham, 1971).

Bethel, Slingsby, *The Present Interest of England Stated* (London, 1671).

The Letters and Charters of Cardinal Guala Bicchieri, Papal Legate in England, 1216–1218, ed. Nicholas Vincent (Woodbridge, 1996).

Black, Jeremy, *The British and the Grand Tour* (London, 1985).

Boardman, Stephen I., *The Early Stewart Kings: Robert II and Robert III, 1371–1406* (Edinburgh, 2007).

Boase, T.S.R., *Boniface VIII* (London, 1933).

Bolton, Brenda, *Innocent III: Studies on Papal Authority and Pastoral Care* (Aldershot, 1995).

—— and Anne J. Duggan (eds), *Adrian IV, the English Pope (1154–1159): Studies and Texts* (Aldershot, 2003).

Bombi, Barbara, 'Papal legates and their preaching of the crusades in England between the twelfth and the thirteenth centuries', in Maria Pia Alberzoni and Pascal Montaubin (eds), *Legati, delegate e l'impresa d'Oltremare (secoli XII-XIII) / Papal Legates, Delegates and the Crusades (12th–13th Century)* (Turnhout, 2015), pp. 211–61.

Bossy, John, *The English Catholic Community, 1570–1850* (London, 1975).

Botrugno, Lorenzo, 'United Kingdom and Holy See: the diplomatic relations question', in *Britain and the Holy See: A Celebration of 1982 and the Wider Relationship* (Rome, 2013), pp. 70–92.

Boureau, Alain, *The Myth of Pope Joan*, tr. Lydia G. Cochrane (Chicago and London, 2001).

Bourne, Francis, 'The pope and the war', *The Tablet*, 5 June 1915.

Bower, Alexander, *History of the Popes*, 7 vols (London, 1748–66).

Bowyer, George, *The Cardinal Archbishop of Westminster and the new Hierarchy* (London, 1850).

Breeze, Andrew, 'Did a woman write the Whitby Life of St Gregory?', *Northern History* 49 (2012), pp. 345–50.

Brentano, Robert, *Rome before Avignon: A Social History of Thirteenth-Century Rome* (London, 1974).

Brett, Martin, *The English Church under Henry I* (London, 1975).

Britain and the Holy See: A Celebration of 1982 and the Wider Relationship: Proceedings of the 2012 Rome Colloquium (Rome, 2013).

Broderick, John F., *The Holy See and the Irish Movement for the repeal of the Union with England, 1829–1849* (Rome, 1951).

Brooke, Z.N., *The English Church and the Papacy from the Conquest to the Reign of John* (new edn., Cambridge, 1989).

Brooks, Nicholas, *The Early History of the Church of Canterbury: Christ Church from 597 to 1066* (Leicester, 1984).

Brown, Gordon, *Speeches, 1997–2006* (London, 2006).

Brown, Michael, *James I* (revised edn., East Linton, 2000).

Brown, Peter, *The Rise of Western Christendom: Triumph and Diversity AD 200–1000* (Oxford, 1996).

Bruce, Steve, *No Pope of Rome: Anti-Catholicism in Modern Scotland* (Edinburgh, 1985).
—— *Paisley: Religion and Politics in Northern Ireland* (Oxford, 2007).

Burgess, Anthony, *Earthly Powers* (Harmondsworth, 1980).

Burns, Charles, 'Papal gifts to Scottish monarchs: the Golden Rose and the Blessed Sword', *Innes Review* 20 (1969), pp. 150–94.
—— (ed.), *Calendar of Papal Letters to Scotland of Clement VII of Avignon, 1378–1394* (Edinburgh, 1976).
—— 'Marco Grimani in Scotland, 1543–1544: a versified account of his legation', *Renaissance Studies* 2 (1988), pp. 299–311.

Burns, J.H., *Scottish Churchmen and the Council of Basle* (London, 1962).
—— and Thomas M. Izbicki (eds), *Conciliarism and Papalism* (Cambridge, 1997).

Buschkühl, Matthias, *Great Britain and the Holy See 1746–1870* (Dublin, 1982).

Caine, Hall, *The Eternal City* (London, 1902).

Cairns, F., 'The *Lucubratiunculae Tiburtinae* of Robert Flemming (1477)', *Humanistica Lovaniensia* 39 (1990), pp. 54–66.

Calendar of Entries in the Papal Registers relating to Great Britain and Ireland, ed. W.H. Bliss (vols 1–5, with C. Johnson, vol. 3, with J.A. Twemlow, vols 4 –5), J.A. Twemlow (vols 6–14), Michael J. Haren (vols 15, 18–19), Anne P. Fuller (vols 16–17, 20) (London, 1893–).

Calendar of Scottish Supplications to Rome, ed. E.R. Lindsay and A.I. Cameron (vol. 1), Annie I. Dunlop (vol. 2), Annie I. Dunlop and Ian B. Cowan (vol. 3), Annie I. Dunlop and David MacLauchlan (vol. 4) (Edinburgh, 1934–70, Glasgow, 1983).

Calendar of State Papers relating to English Affairs in the Vatican Archives, ed. J.M. Rigg, 2 vols (London, 1916–26).

Calendar of State Papers and Manuscripts, relating to English Affairs, existing in the Archives and Collections of Venice, and in other Libraries of Northern Italy, ed. Horatio F Brown (vols 8–12) and Allen B. Hinds (vols 13–38) (London, 1894–1947).

Camm, Bede (ed.), *Lives of the English Martyrs declared Blessed by Pope Leo XIII in 1886 and 1895*, 2 vols (London, 1904–05).

Caraccioli, Louis-Antoine, *The Life of Pope Clement XIV*, tr. Charles Cordell (London, 1776).

—— *Interesting Letters of Pope Clement XIV*, tr. Charles Cordell, 2 vols (London, 1777).

Carpenter, David A., *The Minority of Henry III* (London, 1990).

Carpenter, Humphrey, *Robert Runcie: The Reluctant Archbishop* (London, 1996).

Cavelli, Stefano, *A Short Account of the Life and Death of Pope Alexander the vii*, tr. Philip Ayres (London, 1667).

Cecil, William, Baron Burghley, *The Execution of Justice in England* (Ithaca, NY, 1965).

Chadwick, Owen, *Catholicism and History: The Opening of the Vatican Archives* (Cambridge, 1978).

—— The *Popes and European Revolution* (Oxford, 1981).

—— *Britain and the Vatican during the Second World War* (Cambridge, 1986).

—— *Michael Ramsey: A Life* (Oxford, 1990).

—— *A History of the Popes 1830–1914* (Oxford, 1998).

Chambers, David, *Cardinal Bainbridge in the Court of Rome, 1509 to 1514* (London, 1965).

Champ, Judith, *The English Pilgrimage to Rome: A Dwelling for the Soul* (Leominster, 2000).

Chandler, Andrew and Charlotte Hansen, eds, *Observing Vatican II: The Confidential Reports of the Archbishop Canterbury's Representative, Bernard Pawley, 1961–1964* (Cambridge, 2013)

Chaney, Edward and Timothy Wilks, *The Jacobean Grand Tour: Early Stuart Travellers in Europe* (London and New York, 2013).

Chapman, Mark D., *The Fantasy of Reunion: Anglicans, Catholics, and Ecumenism, 1833–1882* (Oxford, 2014).

Charles-Edwards, T.M., *Early Christian Ireland* (Cambridge, 2000).

Cheney, C.R., *Innocent III and England* (Stuttgart, 1976).

Chrimes, S.B., *Henry VII* (New Haven and London, 1999).

Clarke, Peter D. and Anne J. Duggan (eds), *Pope Alexander III (1159–81): The Art of Survival* (Farnham, 2012).

Clarke, Peter and Michael Questier (eds), *Papal Authority and the Limits of the Law in Tudor England* (Cambridge, 2015).

Clarke, Peter D. and Patrick N.R. Zutshi, *Supplications from England and Wales in the Registers of the Apostolic Penitentiary, 1410–1503*, 3 vols (2013–15).

[Clement X], *A Letter from the Pope to his Distressed Sons the Catholicks in England* (London, 1674).

A Homily of Pope Clement XI … upon Occasion of the Pretender's being there Present (London, 1717).

Clonmore, Lord (William Howard), *Pope Pius XI and World Peace* (London, 1937).

Collins, Jeffrey, 'The gods' abode: Pius VI and the invention of the Vatican Museum', in Clare Hornsby (ed.), *The Impact of Italy: The Grand Tour and Beyond* (London, 2000), pp. 175–94.

Cooney, John, *Scotland and the Papacy: Pope John Paul II's Visit in Perspective* (Edinburgh, 1982).

—— *John Charles McQuaid: Ruler of Catholic Ireland* (Dublin, 1999).

Conn, George, *Vita Mariae Stuartae Scotiae reginae* (Rome, 1624).

—— *De duplici statu religionis apud Scotos* (Rome, 1628).

Corkery, James, 'John Paul II: universal pastor in a global age', in James Corkery and Thomas Worcester (eds), *The Papacy since 1500: From Italian Prince to Universal Pastor* (Cambridge, 2010), pp. 223–42.

Cornwell, John, *A Thief in the Night: The Death of Pope John Paul I* (London, 1989).

—— *Hitler's Pope: The Secret History of Pius XII* (London, 1999).

—— *Breaking Faith: The Pope, the People, and the Fate of Catholicism* (London, 2001).

—— *A Pontiff in Winter: The Dark Face of John Paul II's Papacy* (London, 2004).

Corp, Edward (ed.), *The Stuart Court in Rome: The Legacy of Exile* (Aldershot and Burlington, VT, 2003).

—— *The Stuarts in Italy 1719–1766: A Royal Court in Permanent Exile* (Cambridge, 2011).

Cowdrey, H.E.J., *Pope Gregory VII 1073–1085* (Oxford, 1998).

—— *The Register of Pope Gregory VII 1073–1085* (Oxford, 2002).

Creighton, Mandell, *A History of the Papacy from the Great Schism to the Sack of Rome*, 6 vols (London, 1882–97).

Cubitt, Catherine, *Anglo-Saxon Church Councils, c. 650–c.850* (London, 1995).

Dahmus, Joseph H., *William Courtenay, Archbishop of Canterbury, 1381–1396* (University Park, PA, 1966).

Dandelet, Thomas James, *Spanish Rome 1500–1700* (New Haven and London, 2001).

Darragh, James, 'The apostolic visitations of Scotland, 1912 and 1917', *Innes Review* 41 (1990), pp. 7–118.

Davie, Grace, 'A papal funeral and a royal wedding: reconfiguring religion in the twenty-first century', in Jane Garnett, Matthew Grimley *et al.* (eds), *Redefining Christian Britain: Post 1945 Perspectives* (London, 2006), pp. 106–12.

Davies, C.S.L., 'Bishop John Morton, the Holy See, and the accession of Henry VII', *English Historical Review* 102 (1987), pp. 2–30.

Davies, John, 'A cult from above: the cause for canonisation of John Fisher and Thomas More, *Recusant History* 28 (2007) pp. 458–74.

Davies, R.G., 'Richard II and the Church in the years of the "tyranny"', *Journal of Medieval History* 1 (1974), pp. 329–62.

—— 'After the execution of Archbishop Scrope: Henry IV, the papacy, and the English episcopate, 1405–8', *Bulletin of the John Rylands University Library* 59 (1976–7), pp. 40–74.

—— 'Martin V and the English episcopate', *English Historical Review* 92 (1977), pp. 309–44.

—— 'The Anglo-papal concordat of Bruges, 1375: a reconsideration', *Archivum Historiae Pontificiae* 19 (1981), pp. 97–146.

Davies, R.R., *The Revolt of Owain Glyn Dŵr* (Oxford, 1995).

Davies, Wendy, *Wales in the Early Middle Ages* (Leicester, 1982).

Davis, Raymond (tr.), *The Lives of the Ninth-Century Popes (Liber pontificalis)* (Liverpool, 1995).

—— (tr.), *The Lives of the Eighth-Century Popes* (2nd edn., Liverpool, 2007).

—— (tr.), *The Book of Pontiffs (Liber pontificalis)* (revised edn., Liverpool, 2010).

D'Avray, D.L., *Dissolving Royal Marriages 860–1600* (Cambridge, 2014).

—— *Papacy, Monarchy and Marriage 860–1600* (Cambridge, 2015).

Deanesly, Margaret, *Augustine of Canterbury* (London, 1964).

De la Bedoyere, Michael, *Cardinal Bernard Griffin, Archbishop of Westminster* (London, 1955).

De Mattei, Roberto, *Pius IX*, tr. John Laughland (Leominster, 2004).

Denton, J.H., *Robert Winchelsey and the Crown 1294–1313: A Study in the Defence of Ecclesiastical Liberty* (Cambridge, 1980).

Dizionario biografico degli italiani, 81 vols (Rome, 1960–).

Douglas, David C., *William the Conqueror* (New Haven and London, 1999).

Douie, Decima L., *Archbishop Pecham* (Oxford, 1952).

Doyle, Peter, 'To whom shall we turn? Aspects of the relationship between the English and Welsh hierarchy and Rome, 1880s–1920s', *Recusant History* 29 (2009) pp. 523–39.

Duchesne, L. and Cyrille Vogel (eds), *Le liber pontificalis*, 3 vols (Paris, 1955–7).

Duffy, Eamon (ed.), *Challoner and his Church: A Catholic Bishop in Georgian England* (London, 1981).

The Correspondence of Thomas Becket, Archbishop of Canterbury, 1162–1170, ed. and tr. Anne J. Duggan, 2 vols (Oxford, 2000).

Duncan, A.A.M., *Scotland: The Making of a Kingdom* (Edinburgh, 1975).

Dunn, Geoffrey D. (ed.), *The Bishop of Rome in Late Antiquity* (Farnham, 2015).

Eadmer, *The Life of St Anselm, Archbishop of Canterbury*, ed. and tr. R.W. Southern (Oxford, 1962).

Earle, John Charles, *A Manual of the Lives of the Popes, from St Peter to Pius IX, for the use of students* (London, 1866).

The Life of Bishop Wilfrid by Eddius Stephanus, ed. Bertram Colgrave (Cambridge, 1927).

Edwards, Francis, *Robert Persons: The Biography of an Elizabethan Jesuit, 1546–1610* (St Louis, MO, 1995).

Edwards, John, *Mary I: England's Catholic Queen* (New Haven and London, 2013).

Eliot, George, *Middlemarch: A Study of Provincial Life* (Edinburgh and London, 1871–2).

English Historical Documents I (c. 500–1042), ed. Dorothy Whitelock (London, 1955); II (c. 1042–1189), ed. David C. Douglas and G.W. Greenaway (London, 1953); III (c. 1189 – 1327), ed. Harry Rothwell (London, 1975); IV (1327–1485), ed. A.R. Myers (London, 1969); V (1485–1558), ed. C.H. Williams (London, 1967); V(A) (1558–1603), ed. Ian W. Archer and F. Douglas Price (London and New York, 2011); VIII (1660–1714), ed. Andrew Browning (London, 1953); XI (1783–1832), ed. A. Aspinall and E.A. Smith (London, 1959); XII (1833–74) ed. G.M. Young (London, 1956).

The English Hospice in Rome, The Venerabile sexcentenary issue, 21 (1962).

Eubel, Konrad *et al.*, *Hierarchia catholica medii et recentioris aevi*, 8 vols (Münster, 1898–).

—— *The Julius Exclusus of Erasmus*, tr. Paul Pascal, ed. J. Kelley Soward (Bloomington, Ind., 1968).

Faber, Frederick William, *Devotion to the Pope* (London, 1860).

Farini, Luigi Carlo, *The Roman State: From 1815 to 1850*, tr. William Ewart Gladstone, 4 vols (London, 1851–4).

Ferguson, Paul C., *Medieval Papal Representatives in Scotland: Legates, Nuncios, and Judges-Delegate, 1125–1286* (Edinburgh, 1997).

Field, Michael, *Borgia, a Period Play* (London, 1905).

Filby, Eliza, *God and Mrs Thatcher: The Battle for Britain's Soul* (London, 2013).

Firbank, Ronald, *Concerning the Eccentricities of Cardinal Pirelli* (London, 1926).

Flacius Illyricus, Matthias, and Pietro Paolo Vergerio, *Wonderfull Newes of the Death of Paule the. iii. last Byshop of Rome*, tr. William Baldwin (London, 1552).

Fletcher, Catherine, *Our Man in Rome: Henry VIII and his Italian Ambassador* (London, 2012).

Flint, James P., *Great Britain and the Holy See: The Diplomatic Relations Question, 1846–1852* (Washington, DC, 2003).

Foot, Sarah, *Monastic Life in Anglo-Saxon England, c. 600–900* (Cambridge, 2006).

—— *Æthelstan: The First King of England* (New Haven and London, 2011).

Foreville, Raymonde and Gillian Keir (eds), *The Book of St Gilbert* (Oxford, 1987).

Fothergill, Brian, *The Cardinal King* (London, 1958).

—— *Nicholas Wiseman* (London, 1963).

Gallagher, Charles R., 'The perils of perception: British Catholics and papal neutrality, 1914–1923', in James Corkery and Thomas Worcester (eds), *The Papacy since 1500: From Italian Prince to Universal Pastor* (Cambridge, 2010), pp. 162–81.

Gameson, Richard (ed.), *St Augustine and the Conversion of England* (Stroud, 1999).

Garencières, Theophilus, *The Famous Conclave, wherein Clement VIII was Elected Pope: with the intrigues and cunning devices of that ecclesiastical assembly*, tr. Samuel Lowndes (London, 1670).

Gash, Norman, *Lord Liverpool: The Life and Political Career of Robert Banks Jenkinson, second earl of Liverpool, 1770–1828* (London, 1984).

Gasquet, Francis Aidan, *His Holiness Pope Pius XI: A Pen Portrait* (London 1922).

—— *Monastic life in the Middle Ages: With a note on Great Britain and the Holy See, 1792–1806* (London, 1922).

Gee, Henry, and William J. Hardy, *Documents Illustrative of English Church History* (London, 1896).

Gibbs, M., 'The decrees of Agatho and the Gregorian plan for York', *Speculum* 48 (1973), pp. 213–46.

Gibson, Margaret, *Lanfranc of Bec* (Oxford, 1978).

Gildas: The Ruin of Britain and Other Works, ed. and tr. Michael Winterbottom (Chichester, 1978).

Gill, Joseph, *Eugenius IV: Pope of Christian Union* (London, 1961).

Gilley, Sheridan, 'The years of equipoise, 1892–1943', in V.A. McClelland and Michael Hodgetts (eds), *From Without the Flaminian Gate: 150 Years of Roman Catholicism in England and Wales 1850–2000* (London, 1999), pp. 21–61.

Gillingham, John, *Richard I* (New Haven and London, 1999).

Gladstone, William Ewart, *The State in its Relations with the Church* (London, 1838).

—— *The Vatican Decrees in their bearing on Civil Allegiance* (London, 1874), republished with 'Vaticanism' and 'Speeches of the pope' in *Rome and the Newest Fashions in Religion* (London, 1875).

Glasfurd, Alec, *The Antipope (Peter de Luna, 1342–1423): A Study in Obstinacy* (London, 1965).

Gordon, Alexander, *Lives of Pope Alexander VI and his son Caesar Borgia*, 2 vols (London, 1729).

Gouwens, Kenneth and Sheryl E. Reiss (eds), *The Pontificate of Clement VII: History, Politics, Culture* (Aldershot, 2005).

The Complete Works of John Gower, ed. G.C. Macaulay, 3 vols (Grosse Pointe, MI, 1968).

Graham, Robert A., *Vatican Diplomacy: A Study of Church and State on the International Plane* (Princeton, NJ, 1959).

Greene, Graham, *The Last Word and Other Stories* (London, 1990).

Gregg, Edward, 'The financial vicissitudes of James III in Rome', in Edward Corp (ed.), *The Stuart Court in Rome: The Legacy of Exile* (Aldershot and Burlington, VT, 2003), pp. 65–83.

The Letters of Gregory the Great, ed. John R.C. Martyn, 3 vols (Toronto, 2004).

Gregory, John Duncan, *On the Edge of Diplomacy: Rambles and Reflections, 1902–1928* (London, 1929).

Griffi, Pietro, *Il 'De officio collectoris in regno Angliae'*, ed. Michele Monaco (Rome, 1973).

Grissell, Hartwell de la Garde, *Sede vacante, being a Diary Written during the Conclave* (Oxford, 1903).

Guinness, Alec, *Blessings in Disguise* (London, 1985).

Hachey, Thomas E., *Anglo-Vatican Relations, 1914–1939: Confidential Annual Reports of the British Ministers to the Holy See* (Boston, 1972).

Haddan, Arthur W. and William Stubbs (eds), *Councils and Ecclesiastical Documents relating to Great Britain and Ireland*, 3 vols (Oxford, 1869–73).

Hagerty, James, *Cardinal Hinsley: Priest and Patriot* (Oxford, 2008).

—— *Cardinal John Carmel Heenan: Priest of the People, Prince of the Church* (Leominster, 2012).

Haines, Roy M., *Archbishop John Stratford: Political Revolutionary and Champion of the Liberties of the English Church* (Toronto, 1986).

Halifax, Charles Lindley Wood, Viscount, *Leo XIII and Anglican Orders* (London, 1912).

Hall, Joseph, *An Answer to Pope Urban his Inurbanity* (London, 1629).

Haller, William, *Foxe's Book of Martyrs and the Elect Nation* (London, 1963).

Hamilton, Donna B., *Anthony Munday and the Catholics, 1560–1633* (Aldershot, 2005).

Harnack, Adolf von, 'Der Brief des britischen Königs Lucius an den Papst Eleutherus', *Sitzungsberichte der Königlich Preussischen Akademie der Wissenschaften zu Berlin* (1904), pp. 909–16.

[Harris, Benjamin], *Room for News, or, News from Rome* (London, 1673).

—— *The Plot Discover'd* (London, 1678).

Harris, Robert, *Conclave* (London, 2016).

Harriss, G.L., *Cardinal Beaufort: A Study of Lancastrian Ascendancy and Decline* (Oxford, 1988).

Harvey, Katherine, *Episcopal Appointments in England, c. 1214–1344: From Episcopal Election to Papal Provision* (Farnham, 2014).

Harvey, Margaret, 'Martin V and Henry V', *Archivum historiae pontificiae* 24 (1986), pp. 49–70.

—— 'An Englishman at the Roman curia during the Council of Basle: Andrew Holes, his sermon of 1433 and his books', *Journal of Ecclesiastical History* 42 (1991), pp. 19–38.

—— *England, Rome and the Papacy 1417–1464: The Study of a Relationship* (Manchester, 1993).

—— *The English in Rome 1362–1420: Portrait of an Expatriate Community* (Cambridge, 1999).

Hastings, Adrian, *A History of English Christianity 1920–2000* (4th edn., London, 2001).

Haynes, Renée, *Philosopher King: The Humanist Pope Benedict XIV* (London, 1970).

Head, Constance, 'Pope Pius II and the Wars of the Roses', *Archivum historiae pontificiae* 8 (1970), pp. 139–78.

Hebblethwaite, Peter, *John XXIII: Pope of the Council* (London, 1984).

—— *In the Vatican* (Oxford, 1986).

—— *Paul VI: The First Modern Pope* (London, 1993).

Heenan, John Carmel, *Cardinal Hinsley: A Memoir* (London, 1944).

Henry VIII Fid. Def.: His Defence of the Faith and its Seven Sacraments, intro. Richard Rex (Sevenoaks, 2008).

Henry, archdeacon of Huntingdon, *Historia Anglorum: The History of the English People*, ed. Diana Greenway (Oxford, 1996).

Higham, N.J., *The Convert Kings: Power and Religious Affiliation in early Anglo-Saxon England* (Manchester, 1997).

—— (ed.), *Wilfrid: Abbot, Bishop, Saint* (Donington, 2013).

Hochhuth, Rolf, *The Representative*, tr. Robert D. MacDonald (London, 1963).

Hogan, Linda, 'Mixed reception: Paul VI and John Paul II on sex and war', in James Corkery and Thomas Worcester (eds), *The Papacy since 1500: From Italian Prince to Universal Pastor* (Cambridge, 2010), pp. 204–22.

Hollister, C. Warren, *Henry I* (New Haven and London, 2001).

Holmes, George, *The Good Parliament* (Oxford, 1975).

Holmes, J. Derek, *More Roman than Rome: English Catholicism in the Nineteenth Century* (London, 1978).

Holt, J.C., *Magna Carta* (Cambridge, 1965).

Hornsby-Smith, Michael P., (ed.), *Catholics in England 1950–2000: Historical and Sociological Perspectives* (London, 1999).

Howard, Anthony, *Basil Hume: The Monk Cardinal* (London, 2005).

Hughes, John Jay, *Absolutely Null and Utterly Void: The Papal Condemnation of Anglican Orders, 1896* (London, 1968).

Hughes, Philip, *Saint John Fisher: The Earliest English Life* (London, 1935).

—— *Pope Pius the Eleventh* (London, 1937).

—— (ed.), *The Popes' New Order: A Systematic Summary of the Social Encyclicals and Addresses, from Leo XIII to Pius XII* (London, 1943).

Ingamells, John, *A Dictionary of British and Irish Travellers in Italy 1701–1800* (New Haven and London, 1997).

Selected Letters of Pope Innocent III concerning England (1198–1216), ed. C.R. Cheney and W.H. Semple (London, 1953).

The Letters of Pope Innocent III (1198–1216) concerning England and Wales: A Calendar with an Appendix of Texts, ed. C.R. Cheney and M.G. Cheney (Oxford, 1967).

Jacob, E.F., *Archbishop Henry Chichele* (London, 1967).

—— 'To and from the court of Rome in the early fifteenth century', *Essays in Later Medieval History* (Manchester, 1968), pp. 58–78.

James I, *Triplici nodo, triplex cuneus, or, An Apologie for the Oath of Allegiance* (London, 1607).

Jedin, Hubert, *A History of the Council of Trent*, tr. Ernest Graf, 2 vols (London, 1957–61).

Jennings, Peter (ed.), *Benedict XVI and Blessed John Henry Newman* (London, 2010).

Jewel, John, *Apologia* (London, 1562).

'The *Eulogium ad Alexandrum papam tertium* of John of Cornwall', *Mediaeval Studies* 13 (1951), pp. 253–300.

John XXIII, *Journal of a Soul*, tr. Dorothy M. White (London, 1965).

John of Salisbury, *Historia pontificalis*, ed. and tr. Marjorie Chibnall (Oxford, 1986).

—— *Policraticus*, ed. and tr. Cary J. Nederman (Cambridge, 1990).

The Chronicle of John of Worcester III, ed. and tr. P. McGurk (Oxford, 1998).

John, Eric, Douglas Woodruff and J.M.W. Bean, *The Popes: A Concise Biographical History* (London, 1964).

Keating, Frederick William, 'The neutrality of the Holy See', *The Dublin Review*, July 1915, pp. 134–45.

Kenny, Anthony, *A Path from Rome* (Oxford, 1985).

Kent, Peter C., *The Pope and the Duce: The International Impact of the Lateran Agreements* (London, 1981).

—— and John F. Pollard (eds), *Papal Diplomacy in the Modern Age* (New York, 1994).

Keogh, Dáire, *Ireland and the Vatican: The Politics and Diplomacy of Church-State Relations 1922–1960* (Cork, 1995).

—— and Albert McDonnell (eds), *The Irish College, Rome and its World* (Dublin, 2008).

—— and Albert McDonnell (eds), *Cardinal Paul Cullen and his World* (Dublin, 2011).

Ker, Ian, *John Henry Newman: A Biography* (Oxford, 1988).

King, Edmund, *King Stephen* (New Haven and London, 2010).

Kirby, D.P., 'Bede, Eddius Stephanus and the "Life of Wilfrid"', *English Historical Review* 98 (1983), pp. 101–14.

Krautheimer, Richard, *The Rome of Alexander VII 1655–1667* (Princeton, NJ, 1985).

Kuttner, Stephan, 'Cardinalis: the history of a canonical concept', *Traditio* 3 (1945), pp. 129–214.

The Letters of Lanfranc, Archbishop of Canterbury, ed. V. Helen Clover and Margaret T. Gibson (Oxford, 1979).

Lapidge, Michael (ed.), *Archbishop Theodore: Commemorative Studies on his Life and Influence* (Cambridge, 1995).

Lawrence, C.H. (ed.), *The English Church and the Papacy in the Middle Ages* (revised edn., Stroud, 1999).

Lawson, M.K., *Cnut: The Danes in England in the Early Eleventh Century* (London, 1993).

Lee, Frederick George, *The Validity of the Holy Orders of the Church of England Maintained and Vindicated* (London, 1869).

The Works of Nathaniel Lee, ed. Thomas B. Stroup and Arthur L. Cooke, 2 vols (New Brunswick, NJ, 1955).

Leslie, John, *De origine moribus, et rebus gestis Scotorum* (Rome, 1578).

Leslie, Shane, *Cardinal Gasquet, a Memoir* (London, 1953).

Leti, Gregorio, *The Life of Donna Olimpia Maldachini, who Governed the Church, During the Time of Innocent the X* (London, 1667).

—— *Il nepotismo di Roma, or, The History of the Popes Nephews*, tr. William Aglionby (London, 1669).

—— *The Ceremonies of the Vacant See*, tr. John Davies (London, 1671).

—— *The New Pope*, tr. John Davies (London, 1677).

Lingard, John, The *Antiquities of the Anglo-Saxon Church* (London, 1806).

Lithgow, William, *Rare Adventures and Painful Peregrinations* (Glasgow, 1906).

Llewellyn, Peter, *Rome in the Dark Ages* (new edn., London, 1993).

Longley, Clifford, *The Worlock Archive* (London, 2000).

L., T., *The Life and Reign of Innocent XI, Late Pope of Rome* (London, 1690).

Luke, Peter, *Hadrian VII* (London, 1968).

Lunadoro, Girolamo, *The Court of Rome*, tr. Henry Cogan (London, 1654).

Lunt, William E., *Financial Relations of the Papacy with England to 1327* (Cambridge, MA, 1939).

—— *Financial Relations of the Papacy with England, 1327–1534* (Cambridge, MA, 1962).

McCabe, M.P., 'Vatican Involvement in the Irish Civil War: Monsignor Salvatore Luzio's Apostolic Delegation, March–May 1923', *Journal of Ecclesiastical History* 62 (2011), pp. 89–106.

Macaulay, Ambrose, *The Holy See, British Policy and the Plan of Campaign, 1885–93* (Dublin, 2002).

McClelland, V.A., *Cardinal Manning: His Public Life and Influence, 1865–1892* (London, 1962).

—— and Michael Hodgetts (eds), *From without the Flaminian Gate: 150 Years of Roman Catholicism in England and Wales 1850–2000* (London, 1999).

McCluskey, Raymond (ed.), *The Scots College Rome 1600–2000* (Edinburgh 2000).

McCoog, Thomas M., *The Society of Jesus in Ireland, Scotland, and England, 1589–97: Building the Faith of Saint Peter upon the King of Spain's Monarchy* (Farnham, 2012).

Macdougall, Norman, *James III* (revised edn., Edinburgh, 2009).

—— *James IV* (Edinburgh, 2006).

Macfarlane, L. 'An English account of the election of Urban VI, 1378', *Bulletin of the Institute of Historical Research* 26 (1953), pp. 75–85.

Macfarlane, Leslie J., and J. McIntyre (eds), *Scotland and the Holy See: The Story of Scotland's links with the Papacy down the Centuries* (Edinburgh, 1982).

McGinty, Stephen, *This Turbulent Priest: A Life of Cardinal Winning* (London, 2003).

McGurk, P. (ed.), *An Eleventh-Century Anglo-Saxon Illustrated Miscellany (British Library Cotton Tiberius B.V. part I): together with leaves from British Library Cotton Nero D. II* (Copenhagen, 1983).

Machin, G.I.T., 'The Liberal government and the eucharistic procession of 1908', *The Journal of Ecclesiastical History* 34 (1983), pp. 559–83.

McIntire, C.T., *England against the Papacy 1858–1861: Tories, Liberals, and the Overthrow of Papal Temporal Power during the Italian Risorgimento* (Cambridge, 1983).

McIntyre, John, 'The pope and the war', *The Universe*, 18 January 1918.

McKercher, B.J.C., *Esme Howard: A Diplomatic Biography* (Cambridge, 1989).

McKitterick, Rosamond, John Osborne, Carol M. Richardson and Joanna Story (eds), *Old St Peter's, Rome* (Cambridge, 2013).

McLeod, Hugh (ed.), *World Christianities c. 1914–c. 2000* (Cambridge, 2006).

Maddicott, J.R., *Simon de Montfort* (Cambridge, 1994).

Maguire, John Francis, *Rome, its Ruler and its Institutions* (London, 1857).

—— *Pontificate of Pius the Ninth* (London, 1870).

Malden, A.R. (ed.), *The Canonization of Saint Osmund: From the Manuscript Records in the Muniment Room at Salisbury Cathedral* (Salisbury, 1901).

Mallett, Michael E., *The Borgias: The Rise and Fall of a Renaissance Dynasty* (London, 1969).

Mann, Horace K., *The Lives of the Popes in the Middle Ages*, 18 vols (1st edn., London, 1902–32).

Manning, Henry Edward, *The Vatican Decrees and their Bearing on Civil Allegiance* (London, 1875).

—— *The True Story of the Vatican Council* (London, 1877).

Markus, R.A., 'The chronology of the Gregorian mission to England: Bede's narrative and Gregory's correspondence', *Journal of Ecclesiastical History* 14 (1963), pp. 16–30.

—— 'Pelagianism: Britain and the continent', *Journal of Ecclesiastical History* 37 (1986), pp. 191–204.

—— *Gregory the Great and his World* (Cambridge, 1997).

Marshall, David R., Susan Russell, and Karin Wolfe (eds), *Roma Britannica: Art Patronage and Cultural Exchange in Eighteenth-Century Rome* (London, 2011).

Massaro, Thomas, 'The social question in the papacy of Leo XIII', in James Corkery and Thomas Worcester (eds), *The Papacy since 1500: From Italian Prince to Universal Pastor* (Cambridge, 2010), pp. 143–161.

Marshall, Bruce, *Urban the Ninth* (London, 1973).

—— *Marx the First* (London, 1975).

—— *Peter the Second* (London, 1976).

Mathew, Arnold Harris, *The Life and Times of Rodrigo Borgia, Pope Alexander VI* (London, 1912).

Matsumoto-Best, Saho, *Britain and the Papacy in the Age of Revolution, 1846–1851* (Woodbridge, 2003).

Mayr-Harting, Henry, *The Coming of Christianity to Anglo-Saxon England* (3rd edn., London, 1991).

Menache, Sophia, *Clement V* (Cambridge, 1998).

Merry del Val, Rafael, *The Truth of Papal Claims* (London, 1902).

—— *Memories of Pope Pius X* (London, 1939).

Meyer, A.O., *England and the Catholic Church under Queen Elizabeth*, tr. J.R. McKee (London, 1967).

Meynell, Wilfrid, *Life of Leo XIII, by John Oldcastle, with chapters by the Cardinal Archbishop of Westminster* (London, 1887).

Meyrick, Thomas, *Lives of the Early Popes, St Peter to St Silvester* (London, 1878).

Miller, John, *James II* (New Haven and London, 2000).

Milman, Henry Hart, *The History of Latin Christianity, including that of the Popes to the Pontificate of Nicolas V*, 6 vols (London, 1854–5).

Minerbi, Sergio I., *The Vatican, the Holy Land and Zionism 1895–1925* (Oxford, 1986).

Minnich, Nelson H., *The Fifth Lateran Council (1512–1517): Studies on its Membership, Diplomacy and Proposals for Reform* (Aldershot, 1993).

Mollat, G., *The Popes at Avignon 1305–1378*, tr. Janet Love (Edinburgh, 1963).

Moloney, Thomas, *Westminster, Whitehall and the Vatican: The Role of Cardinal Hinsley, 1935–43* (Tunbridge Wells, 1985).

Mooney, Gary, 'British diplomatic relations with the Holy See, 1793–1830', *Recusant History* 14 (1978), pp. 193–210.

Moore, John C. (ed.), *Pope Innocent III and his World* (Aldershot, 1999).

Morris, Colin, *The Papal Monarchy: The Western Church from 1050 to 1250* (Oxford, 1989).

Moryson, Fynes, *An Itinerary* (London, 1617).

Moyer, Ann E., *The Philosophers' Game: Rithmomachia in Medieval and Renaissance Europe* (Ann Arbor, MI, 2001).

Munday, Anthony, *The English Roman Life*, ed. Philip J. Ayres (Oxford, 1980).

Murphy-O'Connor, Cormac, *An English Spring: Memoirs* (London and New York, 2015).

Myres, J.N.L., 'Pelagius and the end of Roman rule in Britain', *Journal of Roman Studies* 50 (1960), pp. 21–36.

Ness, Christopher, *The Devils Patriarck* (London, 1683).

Newman, John Henry, *An Essay on the Development of Christian Doctrine* (London, 1845).

——— *A Letter Addressed to His Grace the Duke of Norfolk on Occasion of Mr Gladstone's Recent Expostulation* (London, 1875).

The Letters and Diaries of John Henry Newman III, ed. Ian Ker and Thomas Gornall (Oxford, 1979).

Newsome, David, *The Convert Cardinals: John Henry Newman and Henry Edward Manning* (London, 1993).

Norman, Edward, *Anti-Catholicism in Victorian England* (London, 1968).

Norwich, John Julius, *The Popes: A History* (London, 2011).

Oakley, Francis, *The Conciliarist Tradition: Constitutionalism in the Catholic Church 1300–1870* (Oxford, 2003).

O'Carroll, Ciarán, 'Pius IX: pastor and prince', in James Corkery and Thomas Worcester (eds), *The Papacy since 1500: From Italian Prince to Universal Pastor* (Cambridge, 2010), pp. 125–42.

ÓhAnnracháin, Tadhg, *Catholic Reformation in Ireland: The Mission of Rinuccini, 1645–1649* (Oxford, 2002).

Oldham, John, *Tom Tell-Troth* (London, 1679).

Olleson, Philip, *Samuel Wesley: The Man and his Music* (Woodbridge, 2003).

O'Neil, Robert J., *Cardinal Herbert Vaughan: Archbishop of Westminster, Bishop of Salford, Founder of the Mill Hill Missionaries* (Tunbridge Wells, 1995).

The Ecclesiastical History of Orderic Vitalis, ed. and tr. Marjorie Chibnall, 6 vols (Oxford, 1968–80).

Ormrod, W. Mark, *Edward III* (New Haven and London, 2013).

Ortenberg, Veronica, 'Archbishop Sigeric's journey to Rome in 990', *Anglo-Saxon England* 19 (1990), pp. 197–246.

Oxenham, Frank Nutcombe, *Dr. Pusey's Eirenicon Considered in Relation to Catholic Unity: A Letter to the Rev. Father Lockhart* (London, 1866).

——— *The Validity of the Papal Claims* (London, 1897).

Oxford Dictionary of National Biography, 60 vols (Oxford, 2004).

Pantin, W.A., 'The *Defensorium* of Adam Easton', *English Historical Review* 51 (1936), pp. 675–80.

The Memoirs of Gregorio Panzani, ed. Joseph Berington (Birmingham, 1793).

Paravicini Bagliani, Agostino, *Cardinali di curia e 'familiae' cardinalizie dal 1227 al 1254* (Padua, 1972).

The Parliament Rolls of Medieval England, 1275–1504, 4: Edward III, 1327–1348, ed. Seymour Phillips and Mark Ormrod, 5: Edward III, 1351–77, ed. Mark Ormrod (Woodbridge, 2005).

Parmiter, Geoffrey de C., *The King's Great Matter: A Study of Anglo-Papal Relations 1527–1534* (London, 1967).

Partner, Peter, *Renaissance Rome 1500–1559: A Portrait of a Society* (Berkeley, CA, 1976).

Paschini, Pio (ed.), *Il carteggio fra il Card. Marco Barbo e Giovanni Lorenzi (1481–1490)* (Vatican City, 1948).

Pastor, Ludwig von, *The History of the Popes from the Close of the Middle Ages*, ed. and tr. Frederick Ignatius Antrobus, Ralph Francis Kerr, Ernest Graf and E.F. Peeler, 40 vols (London, 1891–1953).

Paton, James, *British History and Papal Claims from the Norman Conquest to the Present Day* (London, 1893).

Pattenden, Miles, *Pius IV and the Fall of the Carafa: Nepotism and Papal Authority in Counter-Reformation Rome* (Oxford, 2013).

Patterson, W.B., *King James VI and I and the Reunion of Christendom* (Cambridge, 1997).

Pawley, Bernard (ed.), *The Second Vatican Council: Studies by Eight Anglican Observers* (London, 1967).

—— and Margaret Pawley, *Rome and Canterbury through Four Centuries: A Study of the Relations between the Church of Rome and the Anglican Churches, 1530 to 1973* (London, 1974).

Paz, D.G., *Popular anti-Catholicism in mid-Victorian England* (Stanford, CA, 1992).

Peele, George, *The Troublesome Reign of John, King of England*, ed. Charles R. Forker (Manchester, 2011).

Pereiro, James, *Cardinal Manning: An Intellectual Biography* (Oxford, 1998).

Pellew, Mark, 'The diplomatic and political relationship: the 20th century', in *Britain and the Holy See: A Celebration of 1982 and the Wider Relationship* (Rome, 2013), pp. 59–69.

Phillips, Seymour, *Edward II* (New Haven and London, 2011).

Pincus, Steve, *1688: The First Modern Revolution* (New Haven and London, 2009).

Pius II, *The Historie of Eurialus and Lucretia*, tr. Charles Aleyn (London, 1639).

—— *Commentaries*, 1, I–II, ed. and tr. M. Meserve and M. Simonetta (Cambridge, MA, and London, 2003).

Platina, Bartolomeo, *Lives of the Popes*, 1: Antiquity, ed. and tr. Anthony F. D'Elia (Cambridge, MA, and London, 2008).

Player, Robert, *Let's Talk of Graves, of Worms, and Epitaphs* (London, 1975).

Plöger, Karsten, *England and the Avignon Popes: The Practice of Diplomacy in Late Medieval Europe* (London, 2005).

Pole, Reginald, *Pro ecclesiasticae unitatis defensione* (Rome, 1539).

—— *De summo pontifice Christi in terris vicario eiusque officio potestate liber vere singularis eruditionis* (Farnborough, 1969).

The Correspondence of Reginald Pole, 3, ed. Thomas F. Mayer (Aldershot, 2004).

Pollard, John F., *The Unknown Pope: Benedict XV (1914–1922) and the Pursuit of Peace* (London and New York, 1999).

—— *The Vatican and Italian Fascism, 1929–1932: A Study in Conflict* (Cambridge, 1985).

—— *Money and the Rise of the Modern Papacy: Financing the Vatican, 1850–1950* (Cambridge, 2005).

—— *The Papacy in the Age of Totalitarianism, 1914–1958* (Oxford, 2014).

The Pope in Britain: Collected Homilies and Speeches (Slough, 1982).

Portal, Étienne Fernand, *Les ordinations anglicanes* (Arras, 1894).

Powicke, F.M., and C.R. Cheney (eds), *Councils and Synods with other Documents relating to the English Church, II: 1205–1313*, 2 vols (Oxford, 1964).

Prestwich, Michael, *Edward I* (New Haven and London, 1997).

Prynne, William, *Romes Master-peece* (London, 1643).

—— *Hidden Workes of Darkenes brought to Publike Light* (London, 1645).

Questier, Michael C. (ed.), *Stuart Dynastic Policy and Religious Politics, 1621–1625* (Cambridge, 2009).

Randall, Alec, *Vatican Assignment* (London, 1956).

Ranke, Leopold von, *The Ecclesiastical and Political History of the Popes of Rome during the Sixteenth and Seventeenth Centuries*, tr. Sarah Austin, 3 vols (London, 1840).

Rankin, Robert, *The Antipope* (London, 1981).

Read, Piers Paul, *The Death of a Pope* (London, 2009).

Renzi, William A., 'The Entente and the Vatican during the period of Italian neutrality, August 1914–May 1915', *The Historical Journal* 13/3 (1970), pp. 491–508.

Rhodes, Anthony, *The Vatican in the Age of the Dictators, 1922–1945* (London, 1973).

—— *The Power of Rome in the Twentieth Century: The Vatican in the Age of the Liberal Democracies* (London, 1983).

—— *The Vatican in the Age of the Cold War, 1945–1980* (Norwich, 1992).

Rhodes, M.J., *His Holiness Pope Pius IX and the Temporal Rights of the Holy See: An address* (London, 1859).

Riley, Henry T. (ed.), *Gesta abbatum monasterii sancti Albani*, 3 vols (London, 1867).

Rinuccini, Giovanni Battista, *Il cappuccino scozzese* (Macerata, 1644).

—— *Commentarius Rinuccinianus de sedis apostolicae legatione ad foederatos Hiberniae catholicos per annos 1645–1649*, ed. J. Kavanagh, 6 vols (Dublin, 1932–49).

Robbins, Keith, *England, Ireland, Scotland Wales: The Christian Church 1900–2000* (Oxford, 2008).

Robinson, Emma, *Caesar Borgia* (London, 1846).

Robinson, I.S., *The Papacy, 1073–1198: Continuity and Innovation* (Cambridge, 1990).

—— tr. and annot., *The Papal Reform of the Eleventh Century: Lives of Pope Leo IX and Pope Gregory VII* (Manchester, 2004).

Robinson, John Martin, *Cardinal Consalvi 1757–1824* (London, 1987).

Rodd, Rennell, *Social and Diplomatic Memories 1902–1919* (London, 1925).

Rolfe, Frederick William, *Chronicles of the House of Borgia* (London, 1901).

—— *Hadrian the Seventh: A Romance* (London, 1904).

—— *Don Tarquinio: A Kataleptic Phantasmatic Romance* (London, 1905).

Roscoe, William, *Life and Pontificate of Leo the Tenth*, 6 vols (London, 1806).

Ross, Charles, *Edward IV* (New Haven and London, 1998).

—— *Richard III* (New Haven and London, 2011).

Sack, James J., *From Jacobite to Conservative: Reaction and Orthodoxy in Britain, c. 1760–1832* (Cambridge, 1993).

Sagovsky, Nicholas, *On God's Side: A Life of George Tyrrell* (Oxford, 1990).

Sanderson, Margaret H.B., *Cardinal of Scotland: David Beaton, c .1494–1546* (revised edn., Edinburgh, 2001).

Sandys, Edwin, *A Relation of the State of Religion* (London, 1605).

Sarpi, Paolo, *The History of the Quarrels of Pope Paul V. with the State of Venice*, tr. Christopher Potter (London, 1626).

Saul, N., *Richard II* (New Haven and London, 1999).

Sayers, Jane E., *Papal Government and England during the Pontificate of Honorius III (1216–1227)* (Cambridge, 1984).

—— *Innocent III: Leader of Europe 1198–1216* (Harlow, 1994).

—— *Original Papal Documents in England and Wales from the Accession of Pope Innocent III to the Death of Pope Benedict XI (1198–1304)* (Oxford, 1999).

Scarisbrick, J.J., *Henry VIII* (New Haven and London, 2009).

Schiefen, Richard J., *Nicholas Wiseman and the Transformation of English Catholicism* (Shepherdstown, WV, 1984).

Schlott, René, 'Papal requiems as political events since the end of the Papal State', *European Review of History/Revue européenne d'histoire* 15/6 (2008), pp. 603–14.

Schofield, A.N.E.D., 'England and the Council of Basel', *Annuarium historiae conciliorum* 5 (1973), pp. 1–117.

Schofield, Nicholas and Gerard Skinner, *The English Vicars Apostolic 1688–1850* (Oxford, 2009).

Scott, Geoffrey, 'The English Benedictine procurators in Curia Romana (1607–1808)', *Downside Review* 133 (2015), pp. 42–64.

Selby, Richard Wilfrid, *Bonifacius viii. e familia Caietanorum principum Romanus pontifex, Iohannis Rubei opus* (Rome, 1651).

Seldon, Anthony, with Peter Snowdon and Daniel Collings, *Blair Unbound* (London, 2007).

Shaw, Christine, *Julius II: The Warrior Pope* (Oxford, 1993).

Shirley, James, *The Cardinal, a Tragedie* (London, 1652).

Signorotto, Gianvittorio and Maria Antonietta Visceglia (eds), *Court and Politics in Papal Rome 1492–1700* (Cambridge, 2002).

Simmonds, Gemma, 'Jansenism versus papal absolutism', in James Corkery and Thomas Worcester (eds), *The Papacy since 1500: From Italian Prince to Universal Pastor* (Cambridge, 2010), pp. 90–106.

Sims-Williams, Patrick, *Britain and Early Christian Europe: Studies in Early Medieval History and Culture* (Aldershot, 1995).

Smyth, Alfred P., *Warlords and Holy Men: Scotland AD 800–1000* (London, 1984).

Somerville, Robert (ed.), *Scotia pontificia: Papal Letters to Scotland before the Pontificate of Innocent III* (Oxford, 1982).

Southern, R.W., *Robert Grosseteste: The Growth of an English mind in Medieval Europe* (Oxford, 1986).

—— *Saint Anselm: A Portrait in a Landscape* (Cambridge, 1990).

Stacpoole, Alberic (ed.), *Vatican II by those who were there* (London, 1986).

Stewart, Ian, 'Gordon Gray, Scottish cardinal', *Innes Review* 44 (1993) pp. 168–80.

Stones, E.L.G. (ed. and tr.), *Anglo-Scottish Relations 1174–1328: Some Selected Documents* (London, 1965).

Storey, R.L., 'Papal provisions to English monasteries', *Nottingham Medieval Studies* 35 (1991), pp. 77–91.

Swinburne, Algernon Charles, *The Duke of Gandia* (London, 1908).

Taouk, Youssef, 'The Guild of the Pope's Peace: a British peace movement in the First World War', *Recusant History* 29 (2008), pp. 252–71.

Taylor, William, *The Popes of Rome: From the Earliest Times to Pius IX* (London, 1870).

Thomas, William, *The Historie of Italie* (London, 1549).

Thompson, E.A., *Saint Germanus of Auxerre and the end of Roman Britain* (Woodbridge 1984).

Thomson, J.A.F., 'Innocent VIII and the Scottish Church', *Innes Review*, 19 (1968), pp. 23–31.

Thomson, Rodney M., *William of Malmesbury* (Woodbridge, 1987).

Thorpe, John and Charles Plowden (attrib.), *A Candid and Impartial Sketch of the Life and Government of Pope Clement XIV*, 3 vols ('Dublin', i.e. London, 1785–6).

Tofte, Robert, *'Discourse' to the Bishop of London*, ed. Robert C. Melzi (Geneva, 1989).

Townsend, George, *Journal of a Tour in Italy, in 1850, with an Account of an Interview with the Pope at the Vatican* (Cambridge, 2014).

Traherne, Thomas, *Roman Forgeries* (London, 1673).

Treharne, R.E., and I.J. Sanders (eds), *Documents of the Baronial Movement of Reform and Rebellion 1258–1267* (Oxford, 1973).

Twiss, Travers, *The Letters Apostolic of Pope Pius IX, Considered with Reference to the Law of England and the Law of Europe* (London, 1851).

Tyerman, Christopher, *England and the Crusades, 1095–1588* (Chicago, 1988).

Tyrrell, Francis, *The Pope and the Great War. The Silence of Benedict XV. Can it be Defended?* (London, 1915).

Ullathorne, William Bernard, *Mr Gladstone's Expostulation Unravelled* (London, 1875).

Ullmann, Walter, *The Growth of Papal Government in the Middle Ages: A Study in the Ideological relation of Clerical to Lay Power* (3rd edn., London, 1970).

—— *A Short History of the Papacy in the Middle Ages* (London, 1972).

The Chronicle of Adam Usk, 1377–1421, ed. and tr. Chris Given-Wilson (Oxford, 1997).

Vauchez, André, *Sainthood in the Later Middle Ages*, tr. Jean Birrell (Cambridge, 1997).

Vaughan, Herbert, *The Sufferings of Leo XIII and a Way of Conciliation* (London, 1888).

Vaughan, Herbert M., *The Last of the Royal Stuarts: Henry Stuart, Cardinal Duke of York* (London, 1906).

—— *The Medici Popes* (London, 1908).

Vespasiano da Bisticci, *The Vespasiano Memoirs: Lives of Illustrious Men of the XVth Century* (Toronto, 1997).

Vickers, Mark, *By the Thames Divided: Cardinal Bourne in Southwark and Westminster* (Leominster, 2013).

Wall, Bernard, *Report on the Vatican* (London, 1956).

Wallace, Lillian P., *The Papacy and European Diplomacy 1869–1878* (Chapel Hill, NC, 1948).

Wallace-Hadrill, J.M., *Bede's Ecclesiastical History of the English People: A Historical Commentary* (Oxford, 1988).

Walsh, Katherine, *A Fourteenth Century Scholar and Primate: Richard FitzRalph in Oxford, Avignon, and Armagh* (Oxford, 1981).

Walsh, Michael J., 'Catholics, society and popular culture', in V.A. McClelland and Michael Hodgetts (eds), *From without the Flaminian Gate: 150 Years of Roman Catholicism in England and Wales 1850–2000* (London, 1999) pp. 346–70.

—— *The Westminster Cardinals: The Past and the Future* (London and New York, 2008).

—— 'John Paul II and his canonizations', *Studies in Church History* 47: Saints and Sanctity, ed. Peter Clarke and Tony Claydon (Woodbridge, 2011), pp. 415–37.

Ward, Bernard, *The Dawn of the Catholic Revival in England, 1781–1803*, 2 vols (London, 1909).

—— *The Eve of Catholic Emancipation: Being the History of the English Catholics during the First Thirty Years of the Nineteenth Century*, 3 vols (London, 1911–12).

Warren, Samuel, *The Queen or the Pope? The question considered in its political, legal, and religious aspects in a letter to Spencer H. Walpole* (Edinburgh and London, 1850).

Warren, W.L., *King John* (New Haven and London, 1998).

—— *Henry II* (New Haven and London, 2000).

Watt, John A., *The Theory of Papal Monarchy in the Thirteenth Century: The Contibution of the Canonists* (London, 1965).

Waugh, Evelyn, *The Life of the Right Reverend Ronald Knox Fellow of Trinity College, Oxford, and Protonotary Apostolic to His Holiness Pope Pius XII* (London, 1959).

Weigel, George, *Witness to Hope: The Biography of Pope John Paul II* (New York, 1999).

Wheeler, Michael, *The Old Enemies: Catholic and Protestant in Nineteenth-century English Culture* (Cambridge, 2006).

White, George, *His Holiness Pope Pius IX* (London, 1867).

Whitelock, Dorothy, M. Brett and C.N.L. Brooke (eds), *Councils and Synods with other Documents relating to the English Church AD 871–1204*, 2 vols (Oxford, 1981).

Wickham, Chris, *Medieval Rome: Stability and Crisis of a City 900–1150* (Oxford, 2015).

Wilkie, William E., *The Cardinal Protectors of England: Rome and the Tudors before the Reformation* (Cambridge, 1974).

Wilkinson, Alan, *Christian Socialism: Scott Holland to Tony Blair* (London, 1998).

Wilks, G.A.F., *The Popes: A Historical Summary* (London, 1851).

William of Malmesbury, *Gesta regum Anglorum/The History of the English Kings*, ed. and tr. R.A.B. Mynors, Rodney M. Thomson and Michael Winterbottom, 2 vols (Oxford, 1998–9).

——, *The Deeds of the Bishops of England (Gesta pontificum Anglorum)*, ed. D. Preest (Woodbridge, 2002).

Williams, Glanmor, *The Welsh Church from Conquest to Reformation* (revised edn., Cardiff, 1976).

Williams, Michael E., *The Venerable English College Rome: A History* (2nd edn., Leominster, 2008).

Wiseman, Nicholas, *An Appeal to the Reason and Good Feeling of the English People: on the Subject of the Catholic Hierarchy* (London, 1850).

—— *Recollections of the Last Four Popes and of Rome in their Times* (London, 1858).

Wojtyla, Karol, *The Jeweller's Shop: A Meditation on the Sacrament of Matrimony Passing on Occasion into a Drama*, tr. Boleslaw Taborski (London, 1980).

Worley, Henry T., *Borgia: A Tragedy* (London, 1843).

Wotton, Henry, *The State of Christendom* (London, 1657).

Wolffe, Bertram, *Henry VI* (New Haven and London, 2001).

Wood, Diana, *Clement VI: The Pontificate and Ideas of an Avignon Pope* (Cambridge, 1989).

Worcester, Thomas, 'Pius VII: modernism in an age of revolution and reaction', in James Corkery and Thomas Worcester (eds), *The Papacy since 1500: From Italian Prince to Universal Pastor* (Cambridge, 2010), pp. 107–24.

Wordsworth, Christopher, *An Anglican Answer to the 'Apostolic Letter of Pope Pius IX to all Protestants'* (London, 1869).

Wright, John Michael, *An Account of his Excellence Roger Earl of Castlemaine's Embassy, from his Sacred Majesty James the IId ... to His Holiness Innocent XI* (London, 1688).

Yallop, David, *In God's Name: An Investigation into the Murder of Pope John Paul I* (London, 1984).

Yorke, Barbara, *Kings and Kingdoms of Early Anglo-Saxon England* (London, 1990).

—— *The Conversion of Britain: Religion, Politics and Society in Britain c. 600–800* (Harlow, 2006).

Ziegler, Philip, *King Edward VIII* (London, 1990).

Zizola, Giancarlo, *Il conclave: storia e segreti* (Rome, 1993).

INDEX OF NAMES